Inequalities in Sub-Saharan Africa

Scan to see all titles in this series.

Inequalities in Sub-Saharan Africa

Multidimensional Perspectives and Future Challenges

Anda David, Murray Leibbrandt, Vimal Ranchhod, and Rawane Yasser, Editors

A copublication of the Agence française de développement and the World Bank

Africa Development Forum Series

The **Africa Development Forum Series** was created in 2009 to focus on issues of significant relevance to Sub-Saharan Africa's social and economic development. Its aim is both to record the state of the art on a specific topic and to contribute to ongoing local, regional, and global policy debates. It is designed specifically to provide practitioners, scholars, and students with the most up-to-date research results while highlighting the promise, challenges, and opportunities that exist on the continent.

The series is sponsored by Agence française de développement and the World Bank. The manuscripts chosen for publication represent the highest quality in each institution and have been selected for their relevance to the development agenda. Working together with a shared sense of mission and interdisciplinary purpose, the two institutions are committed to a common search for new insights and new ways of analyzing the development realities of the Sub-Saharan Africa region.

Advisory Committee Members

Agence française de développement
Thomas Melonio, Executive Director, Innovation, Research and Knowledge Directorate
Carl Bernadac, Director, Head of Economic Assessment and Public Policy Department

World Bank
Andrew Dabalen, Chief Economist, Africa Region
Cesar Calderon, Lead Economist, Africa Region
Chorching Goh, Lead Economist, Program Leader, Africa Region
Aparajita Goyal, Lead Economist, Africa Region

Sub-Saharan Africa

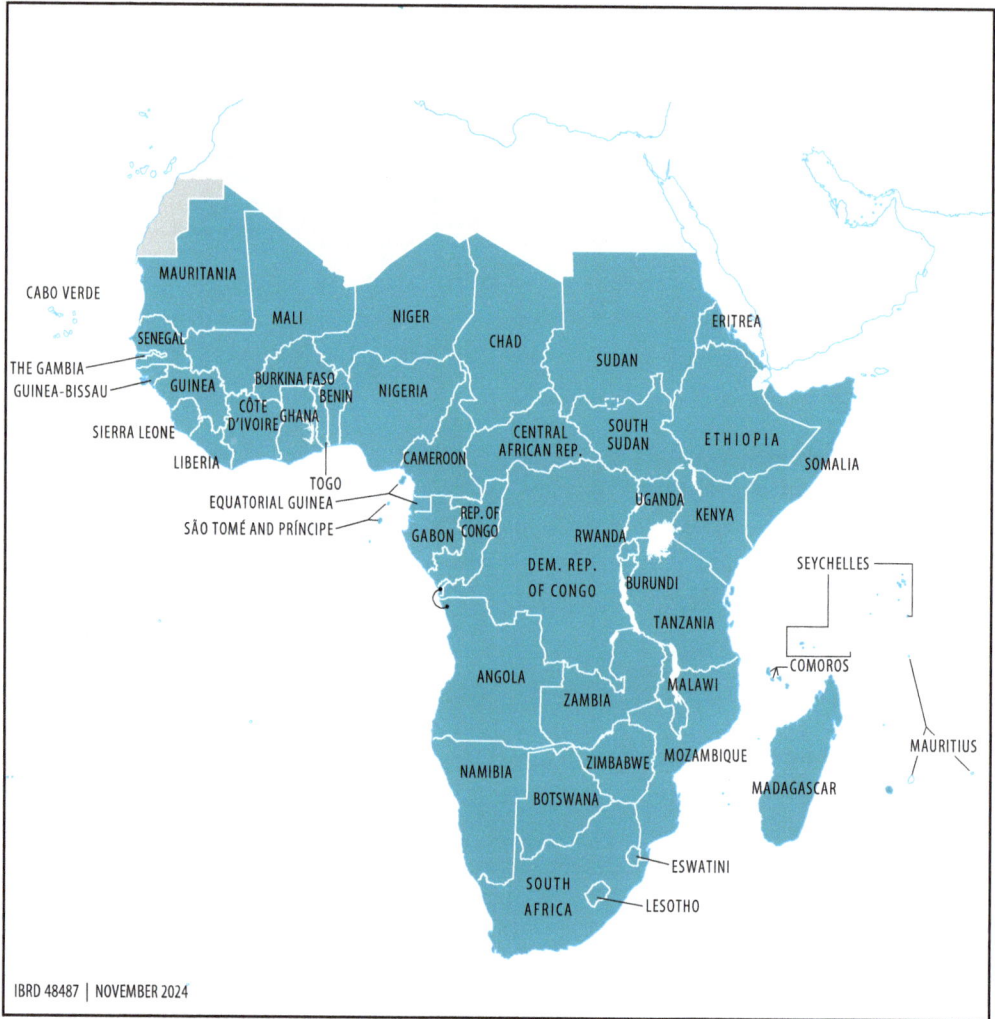

IBRD 48487 | NOVEMBER 2024

Source: World Bank.

Titles in the Africa Development Forum Series

2025

Inequalities in Sub-Saharan Africa: Multidimensional Perspectives and Future Challenges (2025), Anda David, Murray Leibbrandt, Vimal Ranchhod, Rawane Yasser (eds.)

Migration: Africa's Untapped Potential (2025), Mohamed Abdel Jelil, Samik Adhikari, Quy-Toan Do, Heidi Kaila, Federica Marzo, Olive Nsababera, Ganesh Seshan, Maheshwor Shrestha

2024

*Migrants, Markets, and Mayors: Rising above the Employment Challenge in Africa's Secondary Cities (2024), *Migrants, marchés et maires : Relever le défi de l'emploi dans les villes secondaires d'Afrique* (2024), Luc Christiaensen, Nancy Lozano-Gracia (eds.)

2023

*Africa's Resource Future: Harnessing Natural Resources for Economic Transformation during the Low Carbon Transition (2023), *Les ressources naturelles, un enjeu clé pour l'avenir de l'Afrique : ressources naturelles et transformation économique dans un contexte de transition vers des économies décarbonées* (2023), James Cust, Albert Zeufack (eds.)

*L'Afrique en commun: tensions, mutations, perspectives (2023), *The Commons: Drivers of Change and Opportunities for Africa* (2023), Stéphanie Leyronas, Benjamin Coriat, Kako Nubukpo (eds.)

2021

Social Contracts for Development: Bargaining, Contention, and Social Inclusion in Sub-Saharan Africa (2021), Mathieu Clouthier, Bernard Harborne, Deborah Isser, Indhira Santos, Michael Watts

Industrialization in Sub-Saharan Africa: Seizing Opportunities in Global Value Chains (2021), Kaleb G. Abreha, Woubet Kassa, Emmanuel K. K. Lartey, Taye A. Mengistae, Solomon Owusu, Albert G. Zeufack

2020

*Les systèmes agroalimentaires en Afrique. Repenser le rôle des marches (2020), *Food Systems in Africa: Rethinking the Role of Markets* (2021), Gaelle Balineau, Arthur Bauer, Martin Kessler, Nicole Madariaga

*The Future of Work in Africa: Harnessing the Potential of Digital Technologies for All (2020), *L'avenir du travail en Afrique : exploiter le potentiel des technologies numériques pour un monde du travail plus inclusif* (2021), Jieun Choi, Mark A. Dutz, Zainab Usman (eds.)

2019

All Hands on Deck: Reducing Stunting through Multisectoral Efforts in Sub-Saharan Africa (2019), Emmanuel Skoufias, Katja Vinha, Ryoko Sato

*The Skills Balancing Act in Sub-Saharan Africa: Investing in Skills for Productivity, Inclusivity, and Adaptability (2019), *Le développement des compétences en Afrique subsaharienne, un exercice d'équilibre : Investir dans les compétences pour la productivité, l'inclusion et l'adaptabilité* (2020), Omar Arias, David K. Evans, Indhira Santos

*Electricity Access in Sub-Saharan Africa: Uptake, Reliability, and Complementary Factors for Economic Impact (2019), *Accès à l'électricité en Afrique subsaharienne : adoption, fiabilité et facteurs complémentaires d'impact économique* (2020), Moussa P. Blimpo, Malcolm Cosgrove-Davies

2018

*Facing Forward: Schooling for Learning in Africa (2018), *Perspectives : l'école au service de l'apprentissage en Afrique* (2019), Sajitha Bashir, Marlaine Lockheed, Elizabeth Ninan, Jee-Peng Tan

Realizing the Full Potential of Social Safety Nets in Africa (2018), Kathleen Beegle, Aline Coudouel, Emma Monsalve (eds.)

2017

*Mining in Africa: Are Local Communities Better Off? (2017), *L'exploitation minière en Afrique : les communautés locales en tirent-elles parti?* (2020), Punam Chuhan-Pole, Andrew L. Dabalen, Bryan Christopher Land

*Reaping Richer Returns: Public Spending Priorities for African Agriculture Productivity Growth (2017), *Obtenir de meilleurs résultats : priorités en matière de dépenses publiques pour les gains de productivité de l'agriculture africaine* (2020), Aparajita Goyal, John Nash

2016

Confronting Drought in Africa's Drylands: Opportunities for Enhancing Resilience (2016), Raffaello Cervigni, Michael Morris (eds.)

2015

*Africa's Demographic Transition: Dividend or Disaster? (2015), *La transition démographique de l'Afrique : dividende ou catastrophe ?* (2016), David Canning, Sangeeta Raja, Abdo Yazbeck

Highways to Success or Byways to Waste: Estimating the Economic Benefits of Roads in Africa (2015), Ali A. Rubaba, Federico Barra, Claudia Berg, Richard Damania, John Nash, Jason Russ

Enhancing the Climate Resilience of Africa's Infrastructure: The Power and Water Sectors (2015), Raffaello Cervigni, Rikard Liden, James E. Neumann, Kenneth M. Strzepek (eds.)

The Challenge of Stability and Security in West Africa (2015), Alexandre Marc, Neelam Verjee, Stephen Mogaka

Land Delivery Systems in West African Cities: The Example of Bamako, Mali (2015), *Le système d'approvisionnement en terres dans les villes d'Afrique de l'Ouest : L'exemple de Bamako* (2015), Alain Durand-Lasserve, Maÿlis Durand-Lasserve, Harris Selod

Safety Nets in Africa: Effective Mechanisms to Reach the Poor and Most Vulnerable (2015), *Les filets sociaux en Afrique : méthodes efficaces pour cibler les populations pauvres et vulnérables en Afrique subsaharienne* (2015), Carlo del Ninno, Bradford Mills (eds.)

2014

Tourism in Africa: Harnessing Tourism for Growth and Improved Livelihoods (2014), Iain Christie, Eneida Fernandes, Hannah Messerli, Louise Twining-Ward

Youth Employment in Sub-Saharan Africa (2014), *L'emploi des jeunes en Afrique subsaharienne* (2014), Deon Filmer, Louise Fox

2013

Les marchés urbains du travail en Afrique subsaharienne (2013), *Urban Labor Markets in Sub-Saharan Africa* (2013), Philippe De Vreyer, François Roubaud (eds.)

Enterprising Women: Expanding Economic Opportunities in Africa (2013), Mary Hallward-Driemeier

Securing Africa's Land for Shared Prosperity: A Program to Scale Up Reforms and Investments (2013), Frank F. K. Byamugisha

The Political Economy of Decentralization in Sub-Saharan Africa: A New Implementation Model (2013), Bernard Dafflon, Thierry Madiès (eds.)

2012

Empowering Women: Legal Rights and Economic Opportunities in Africa (2012), Mary Hallward-Driemeier, Tazeen Hasan

Financing Africa's Cities: The Imperative of Local Investment (2012), *Financer les villes d'Afrique : l'enjeu de l'investissement local* (2012), Thierry Paulais

Structural Transformation and Rural Change Revisited: Challenges for Late Developing Countries in a Globalizing World (2012), *Transformations rurales et développement : les défis du changement structurel dans un monde globalisé* (2013), Bruno Losch, Sandrine Fréguin-Gresh, Eric Thomas White

Light Manufacturing in Africa: Targeted Policies to Enhance Private Investment and Create Jobs (2012), *L'Industrie légère en Afrique : politiques ciblées pour susciter l'investissement privé et créer des emplois* (2012), Hinh T. Dinh, Vincent Palmade, Vandana Chandra, Frances Cossar

Informal Sector in Francophone Africa: Firm Size, Productivity, and Institutions (2012), *Les entreprises informelles de l'Afrique de l'ouest francophone : taille, productivité et institutions* (2012), Nancy Benjamin, Ahmadou Aly Mbaye

2011

Contemporary Migration to South Africa: A Regional Development Issue (2011), Aurelia Segatti, Loren Landau (eds.)

Challenges for African Agriculture (2011), Jean-Claude Deveze (ed.)

*L'Économie politique de la décentralisation dans quatre pays d'Afrique subsaharienne : Burkina Faso, Sénégal, Ghana et Kenya (2011), *The Political Economy of Decentralization in Sub-Saharan Africa: A New Implementation Model in Burkina Faso, Ghana, Kenya, and Senegal* (2011), Bernard Dafflon, Thierry Madiès (eds.)

2010

Gender Disparities in Africa's Labor Market (2010), Jorge Saba Arbache, Alexandre Kolev, Ewa Filipiak (eds.)

*Africa's Infrastructure: A Time for Transformation (2010), *Infrastructures africaines, une transformation impérative* (2010), Vivien Foster, Cecilia Briceño-Garmendia (eds.)

*Available in French

All books in the Africa Development Forum series that were copublished by Agence française de développement and the World Bank are available for free at http://hdl.handle.net/10986/2150.

Contents

Maps

Tables

Foreword: Lost in Inequality?

Is there such a thing as a Kuznets curve?

The growing disparity between the rich and poor remains one of the critical challenges of recent decades, affecting countries across all continents, irrespective of their gross domestic product per capita. This widening gap not only impedes efforts to eradicate extreme poverty but also hinders progress toward social justice and resilience-building. Rising inequalities pose substantial barriers to sustainable development, and it is within this context that this book, *Inequalities in Sub-Saharan Africa: Multidimensional Perspectives and Future Challenges*, contributes to ongoing debates, offering a comprehensive analysis of the current challenges and future perspectives of inequality on the African continent.

With the 2030 Agenda for Sustainable Development fast approaching, the lack of significant progress on Sustainable Development Goal 10, which aims to reduce inequality within and among countries, is alarming. This failure, as noted by Melonio and Tremel (2021),[1] contrasts sharply with the proliferation of international initiatives aimed at addressing inequality. The United Nations recently underscored the urgency of the matter by launching the "Pact for the Future," which explicitly highlights the central role that reducing inequalities must play in building peaceful, just, and inclusive societies. Similarly, the G-20 has reiterated its historical commitment to promoting social, economic, and political inclusion, with a focus on tools such

---

[1] Melonio, Thomas, and Laëtitia Tremel. 2021. "Climate, Biodiversity, Inequalities … How to Steer the SDGs Back on Track." AFD Policy Paper No. 7. Agence française de développement, Paris. https://www.afd.fr/sites /afd/files/2021-07-05-39-38/PP007_Climate_biodiversity_inequalities_SDGs.pdf.

as wealth taxation and minimum corporate tax rates, championed by scholars like Gabriel Zucman[2] and Lucas Chancel[3] as critical mechanisms to combat wealth concentration.

These initiatives have gained further relevance in the context of post-COVID recovery and the ongoing geopolitical crisis resulting from the Russian Federation's invasion of Ukraine. The resulting spikes in food and energy prices have disproportionately impacted both low- and high-income countries, further exacerbating global inequalities. In addition, rising sovereign debt levels, compounded by the fiscal pressures of transitioning to a low-carbon economy, have intensified the need to expand the fiscal base. Brazil has placed the fight against inequality at the forefront of its G-20 presidency, and we expect South Africa, the next G-20 presidency, to maintain that priority. In Europe, efforts to tax large technology companies reflect not only a desire for tax fairness but also the need to protect local economies and address the inequality gap these corporations have widened.

Despite the intensification of calls for wealth taxation and inequality reduction, progress has been slow. A key challenge lies in creating a viable political path for implementing progressive taxation policies. Resistance from those benefiting from the current system often stalls efforts, making progress difficult. Moreover, reducing inequality requires not only ex-post redistribution but also pre-distribution mechanisms that address inequality at its roots. Policies targeting education, competition, financial markets regulation, and industrial development all hold the potential to create more-equitable economic opportunities, ensuring access to credit, job creation, and more-balanced economic growth.

Africa, despite facing unique and profound challenges, is often overlooked in these global discussions. This book seeks to place the continent's specific issues—such as income inequality, unequal access to education and health care, climate vulnerability, and inclusive growth—at the center of the conversation.

This book goes further by advocating for innovative "outside the box" policies, including competition reforms and bargaining frameworks that shift the balance between capital and labor. Given that inequality in Africa is deeply rooted in historical, economic, and institutional factors, a stronger focus on pre-distribution policies is necessary. These systemic changes can help reshape the conditions under which inequality emerges and persists.

In addition to policy reforms, it is vital to strengthen the research and academic infrastructure that underpin our understanding of inequality. Equity concerns must be addressed within the scientific field, and African research capabilities must be bolstered. This volume, written in

---

[2] Zucman, Gabriel. 2024. "For a Coordinated Minimum Taxation Standard for Ultra-High-Net-Worth Individuals." https://gabriel-zucman.eu/files/report-g20.pdf.
[3] World Inequality Lab. 2022. "World Inequality Report 2022." https://wir2022.wid.world/www-site /uploads/2021/12/WorldInequalityReport2022_Full_Report.pdf.

collaboration with the African Center of Excellence for Inequality Research, calls for a greater focus on empowering African researchers as part of a broader development strategy. By doing so, it aligns with the Agence française de développement's commitment to supporting research as a critical tool for sustainable development.

Thomas Melonio
Chief Economist
Executive Director of Innovation, Strategy and Research
Agence française de développement (French Development Agency)

Acknowledgments

The Agence française de développement and the editors of this book express their deepest gratitude to the many individuals and institutions that have contributed to the completion of this book on multidimensional inequalities in Africa.

This work would not have been possible without the invaluable research and insights contributed by the diverse group of scholars and institutions that have partnered with the African Centre of Excellence for Inequality Research (ACEIR). The work represents a contribution from this remarkable partnership over ACEIR's first 5 years as a center of excellence within the African Research Universities Alliance. Their rigorous analyses and dedication have been instrumental in shaping the breadth and depth of the research presented in this volume.

Many of the analyses presented in the book draw on work that has been undertaken within the framework of the EU-AFD Research Facility on Inequalities, funded by the European Commission. We would like to thank Mathilde Cournut and Antonio Teixeira for their continued support of the research projects funded through the EU-AFD Research Facility on Inequalities.

We are grateful for Etienne Charrière's valuable support throughout the editorial process. We would also like to thank Hélène Djoufelkit, Sophie Salomon, Isabelle Ensarguet, Haajirah Esau, and Felipe Korreales, whose support has made this book possible. We are also grateful for Harald Winkler's valuable feedback and suggestions.

This collective effort reflects our shared vision of advancing knowledge to foster a more-equitable future for Africa. Heartfelt thanks are also extended to the reviewers whose valuable feedback and insights considerably improved this book.

About the Editors and Contributors

Editors

Anda David is a senior researcher at the Agence française de développement (French Development Agency [AFD]) and the lead economist on inequality. Her current research centers on inequality and sustainability. Between 2004 and 2015, Anda collaborated with various international organizations on these issues, including the International Labour Organization, the Organisation for Economic Co-operation and Development, and the World Bank. She joined AFD's Research Division in December 2015 and leads the research program on inequalities. Anda is currently scientific coordinator of the European Union–AFD Research Facility on Inequality and, since January 2021, has been based at the AFD's regional bureau for Southern Africa in Johannesburg, South Africa. She holds a PhD from Paris Dauphine University in development economics, with a focus on migration and labor markets.

Murray Leibbrandt is the chair of poverty and inequality research at the University of Cape Town and director of the African Centre of Excellence for Inequality Research (ACEIR) within the African Universities Alliance. He served as director of the Southern Africa Labour and Development Research Unit at the University of Cape Town from 2002 until July 2023. Leibbrandt is a member of the Academy of Sciences of South Africa (ASSAf) and a nonresident senior research fellow at the United Nations University–World Institute for Development Economics Research (UNU–WIDER), as well as has recently served on the Executive Committee of the International Economics Association. From 2007 to 2019, he was founding principal investigator on the National Income Dynamics Study, South Africa's national longitudinal study. Currently, he is principal investigator for the national panel study in the Health and Aging in Africa: Longitudinal Studies in South Africa project. Throughout his career, Leibbrandt has worked closely with policy communities in Africa, especially in South Africa. He holds a BSocSc (Hons) in economics from Rhodes University in South Africa and a master's degree and PhD in economics from the University of Notre Dame in Indiana.

Vimal Ranchhod is a professor in the School of Economics at the University of Cape Town, deputy director of the Southern Africa Labour and Development Research Unit, and head of ACEIR's South African Node. His research focuses on labor markets, education, poverty and inequality, and discrimination. Ranchhod has published articles in several journals, including the *British Journal of Sociology, Economics of Education Review, Journal of Development Economics, World Bank Economic Review*, and *World Development*. His research was awarded a Best Paper Prize at the African Econometrics Society conference, as well as the Francis Wilson Memorial Prize for Best Published Paper. Ranchhold is a member of the ASSAf and is currently an elected member of the council of the Economics Society of South Africa. He has taught courses on labor economics, applied econometrics, microeconomic theory, development economics, and the economics of inequality. He holds an MA and PhD in economics from the University of Michigan, as well as a bachelor's of commerce with honors in economics from the University of the Witwatersrand, Johannesburg.

Rawane Yasser is a researcher at the AFD working on inequalities, poverty, labor markets, and international migration. She has worked at the Interdisciplinary Laboratory for the Evaluation of Public Policies at Sciences Po Paris on gender inequalities in the labor market as the Women in Business Chair. Yasser has coordinated and implemented impact evaluations at the International Food Policy Research Institute, evaluating the impact of agricultural development projects in Djibouti, Ghana, Kenya, and Tanzania. She joined the AFD Research Division in November 2021. Yasser holds a master's degree in development economics from Paris 1 Panthéon Sorbonne at the Institute of Economic and Social Development Studies, with a focus on the economic evaluation of development policies and projects.

Contributors

Richmond Atta-Ankomah is a development economist and senior research fellow at the Institute of Statistical, Social and Economic Research (ISSER), University of Ghana. Before joining ISSER in early 2017, he was research associate at the Development Policy and Practice Unit, School of Social Sciences and Global Studies, The Open University, United Kingdom. He has worked as a research associate at the ACEIR since 2018 and was visiting research fellow at The Open University between 2017 and 2019. His research interests broadly converge around development issues concerning households and firms in Sub-Saharan Africa (SSA). He has extensive experience in designing and implementing various research protocols, including those used for impact evaluations. He holds a PhD in development economics from The Open University.

Fabio Andrés Díaz Pabón is a research fellow on Sustainable Development Goals (SDGs) and the African Agenda 2063, hosted by ACEIR at the University of Cape Town in South Africa. He is honorary research associate in the Department of Political and International Studies at Rhodes University in South Africa and a member of the Comunicación y Democracia research group of the Universidad del Tolima in Colombia. He is a transdisciplinary researcher who critically engages global challenges by integrating insights from multiple fields, including economics, development studies, sociology, politics, and systems thinking. His current areas of research explore challenges to achieving the SDGs and the African Agenda 2063 in Africa; the role of international treaties, such as the Maputo Protocol, in reducing gender inequities in Africa; the impact of technological innovation on development outcomes; and the interaction of labor earnings and capital income in conditioning income and wealth inequalities. He holds both an MA and PhD in development studies from Erasmus University, Rotterdam, and an MSc in industrial engineering from Universidad de los Andes.

Hélène Djoufelkit is deputy executive director of sustainable solutions at AFD. She began her career with AFD in 2004 in the Research Department, working mainly on the link between economic rents and development in resource-rich countries; franc zone macroeconomics; and innovative financing instruments, such as a debt service suspension mechanism for AFD loans. In 2008, she was appointed senior advisor to the executive director for France at the International Monetary Fund and the World Bank, in charge of African issues. Starting in 2012, she spent 4 years as deputy country director of the AFD Office in the Arab Republic of Egypt. In 2016, she returned to Paris as head of the Corporate Strategy and Accountability Unit. She holds a PhD and MA in development economics from the Centre d'études et de recherches sur le développement international.

Samuel Kipruto is a senior analyst and advisor to the National Information Platform for Food and Nutrition project, an initiative of the European Commission supported by the United Kingdom Department for International Development and the Bill & Melinda Gates Foundation. Prior to the current appointment, he was senior economist and statistician at the Kenya National Bureau of Statistics, with more than 25 years of experience working in survey design, data collection, processing, and analysis, with a strong focus on nutrition, poverty, and inequality. Kipruto has a wealth of experience handling large data sets, including censuses and large surveys. He is currently a member of the ACEIR's East Africa Node, working on inequality trends and diagnostics, as well as the impact of fiscal policy on inequality and poverty, among other projects in Kenya. He holds a master's degree in economic policy management from the University of Ghana, Legon.

Damiano Kulundu Manda is an associate professor of economics in the Department of Economics and Development Studies, University of Nairobi, Kenya. He has 34 years of experience teaching at the university level, with more than 25 years of teaching and supervising postgraduate research papers and theses. He has vast experience in managing research at national-level institutions and international research networks. His research focus covers applied research in labor markets, inequality, poverty, gender, climate change, and other cross-cutting issues. Previously, he was associate director, School of Economics, University of Nairobi (2017–19); head, Social Sector Division, Kenya Institute for Public Policy Research and Analysis; and manager of research, African Economic Research Consortium (AERC). He is currently coordinator of the ACEIR's Kenya Node at the University of Nairobi. He is a researcher and member of the AERC, ACEIR, and the Economists Society of Kenya. He has done consultancy work for the United Nations Children's Fund (UNICEF), the UNU–WIDER, and the World Bank, among others. He holds a PhD in economics from Gothenburg University, Sweden, and master's and undergraduate degrees in economics from the University of Nairobi.

Monica Lambon-Quayefio is an applied microeconomist whose broad research focuses on gender and labor markets, social protection, education, and digital innovations in agriculture. Her research uses a mix of experimental approaches and quantitative methods to explore the impact of interventions and policies. Lambon-Quayefio is an affiliate of the Abdul Latif Jameel Poverty Action Lab and senior lecturer in the Department of Economics at the University of Ghana. She holds a PhD and MA in economics from Clark University in Massachusetts.

Jacqueline Mosomi is an economist with more than 10 years of experience specializing in microeconomics, labor economics, and household survey data analysis and management. Her research is dedicated to understanding and addressing gender disparities in economic outcomes, particularly in developing country contexts. Her current research continues to explore the intersection of gender, labor markets, and economic development, aiming to inform evidence-based policy making and promote inclusive economic growth and equitable societal outcomes. Mosomi holds a PhD in economics from the University of Cape Town, focusing on trends in the gender wage gap in the labor market.

Moses Kinyanjui Muriithi is an associate professor of economics and head of the Economics Unit in the Department of Economics and Development Studies at the University of Nairobi, Kenya. In addition to teaching, Muriithi is engaged in research and consultancies, especially with the Kenyan Ministries of Health, Planning and Finance, and with international organizations, such as the AERC, the International Development Research Centre in Canada, the Joint United Nations Programme on HIV/AIDS, the Regional Consortium for Generational Economics Research (CREG), UNICEF, the United Nations Foundation, the United States Agency for International Development, the World Bank, the World Health Organization, and the World Resources Institute. He has more than 18 years of experience in leadership and applied research, with research affiliations with the ACEIR, based at the University of Cape Town, South Africa; the AERC, in Nairobi; CREG, in Dakar, Senegal; Global NTA, based at the Universities of Hawaii and California at Berkeley; and the Rural Access and Agricultural Marketing Project in Washington, DC. He holds a PhD in health economics from the University of Nairobi.

Reuben Mutegi is a lecturer on educational planning and the economics of education at the School of Education, University of Nairobi, Kenya. His research areas are related to education and health policies, impact evaluation, monitoring and evaluation, labor dynamics, inequality, intergenerational accounting, and demographic dividends. He is a team member of the National Transfer Accounts and Counting Women's Work global research projects. He previously worked at the United States International University–Africa. He received an African Research Universities Alliance–Carnegie Early Career Research Fellowship in 2022. He holds a doctoral degree in educational planning and a master's degree in educational planning and the economics of education from the University of Nairobi.

Germano Mwabu is professor emeritus of economics at the University of Nairobi, Kenya. His research interests are in poverty and inequality analysis, health economics, national transfer accounts, and development economics. He codirected (jointly with Professor Erik Thorbecke) an AERC collaborative research project on poverty, income distribution, and labor markets in SSA from 1998 to 2005. He has held short-term research appointments at the Brookings Institution, Cornell University, Kobe University, Leuven University, the University of Gothenburg, and the World Bank. He holds a PhD in economics from Boston University.

Abena D. Oduro is an associate professor in the Department of Economics at the University of Ghana, Legon. Her current research is in women's economic empowerment; gender and trade policy; gender and employment security; and poverty, inequality, and vulnerability analysis. Oduro has published on gender-responsive budgeting, intimate partner violence, and gender and asset ownership. She is associate editor of *Feminist Economics* and coeditor of the journal's planned special issue on "Gendering the Debt Crisis: Feminist Political Economy Perspectives on Debt and the Global South." She is a member of the ACEIR and the International Association for Feminist Economics. Recent publications include the chapters "Gender and Development" (with Vera Acheampong, in *Handbook of African Economic Development*, 2024) and "Individualizing Wealth and Asset Measures in the Global South: Challenges and New Directions for Research" (with Hema Swaminathan, in *A Research Agenda for Financial Resources within the Household*, 2024). Obduro holds an MLitt in economics from the University of Glasgow, United Kingdom.

Annalena Oppel is a research fellow in the Atlantic Fellows for Social and Economic Equity program, where she contributes to fellowship curriculum development, teaching, and mentoring. Her work involves interdisciplinary approaches to inequality research, particularly those focused on inequality perceptions, political preferences, and economic uncertainty. Oppel also works on social protection and taxation in contexts in the Global South. Prior to joining the London School of Economics, she was a research associate at the UNU–WIDER; a visiting fellow at Harvard University; and a consultant with partners such as the German Agency for International Cooperation, the Global Development Network, and the Overseas Development Institute. She holds a PhD in development studies from the Institute of Development Studies at the University of Sussex, United Kingdom.

Robert Darko Osei is an associate professor at the ISSER, University of Ghana, Legon, as well as vice dean for the School of Graduate Studies. His main areas of research include evaluative poverty and rural research, the macro and micro implications of fiscal policies, aid effectiveness, and other economic development policy concerns. He holds a PhD in economics from the University of Nottingham in the United Kingdom, examining aid, trade, and growth in rural Ghana.

Nkechi S. Owoo is an associate professor of economics at the University of Ghana, Legon. Her research focuses on spatial econometrics, health and demographic economics, poverty and inequality, gender economics, and climate change and environmental sustainability. She currently represents the Africa region on the Governing Board of the International Union for the Scientific Study of Population, based in France, and is an invited researcher with the Abdul Latif Jameel Poverty Action Lab. Owoo has been a visiting scholar in the World Bank's Development Economics Research Group in Washington, DC; a nonresident research fellow at the Center for Global Development in Washington, DC; and research fellow at the IZA Institute of Labour Economics in Bonn, Germany. She is associated with the Partnership for Economic Policy in Nairobi, Kenya, and the ACEIR and the Environment for Development Initiative, both in Accra, Ghana. Owoo was nonresident senior research fellow at the Population Institute in Washington, DC, and visiting research fellow at Cornell University and the University of Michigan, as well as the University of Pretoria in South Africa and the University of Bristol in the United Kingdom. She holds a PhD in economics from Clark University in Massachusetts.

Cecilia Poggi is an economist and social protection research officer at the AFD. Her projects explore the evolution of social protection systems and program extension, the study of households' and workers' vulnerabilities, and the reinforcement of regulations to promote decent employment. She has extensively researched the role of informal work, digital labor platforms for workers in emerging and developing countries, and gender inequality. She trained as a development economist with specialization in labor economics and quantitative analysis. Before joining AFD in 2018, she worked as a consultant for research institutes, the United Nations Food and Agriculture Organization, and the World Bank on issues related to employment, migration, poverty, and data collection tools for households and enterprises. She holds a PhD in economics and an MSc in development economics from the University of Sussex, United Kingdom.

Serge Rabier is a sociodemographer at the AFD, where he initiates and coordinates research programs on population issues and themes related to gender equality. After a career in the banking sector, consulting, and working as an educational engineer in France and Southeast Asia, Rabier focused on the consideration and integration of gender in public policies, particularly in sexual and reproductive health and rights and population policies, as the executive director of a development organization (2001–15). He has carried out various missions as a gender expert on population policies, in particular for the African Development Bank (2018–19). Between 2012 and 2018, he worked as an associate lecturer in development policies at the Universities of Paris Descartes and Paris 1 Panthéon Sorbonne in the master's programs. From 2013 to 2019, he was a member of the High Council for Equality between Women and Men, an advisory body reporting to the Prime Minister of France. In September 2019, he joined AFD as a research fellow in the Economic Diagnostics and Public Policies Department. Rabier holds a PhD in demography from the Sorbonne Paris Cité University and a master's degree in political science from the Institut d'Etudes Politiques Paris.

Mike Savage is a professor of sociology at the London School of Economics, where he was founding codirector of the International Inequalities Institute, one of the world's leading centers for teaching and research on multidimensional inequality issues. He works on class and stratification, and his research with the BBC on the Great British Class Survey attracted huge public interest on its launch in 2013. Savage is a fellow of the British Academy and was awarded the Seigfried Landshut Prize by the Hamburg Institute for Social Research in 2023. His recent publications include the coauthored *Social Class in the 21st Century* (2015) and *The Return of Inequality: Social Change and the Weight of the Past* (2021). Savage holds an MA in modern social history and a PhD in sociology from the University of Lancaster, United Kingdom.

Muna Shifa is a senior research officer at the Southern Africa Labour and Development Research Unit at the University of Cape Town, South Africa. She is also a member of the research team at the ACEIR. Her research interests include measuring multidimensional poverty and inequality, socioeconomic-related inequalities in health outcomes, climate change–related social vulnerability, climate change impacts and welfare outcomes, inequality and conflict, social cohesion and inequality, gender and intersectional inequality, and land tenure systems and rural livelihoods. She holds a PhD and a master's degree in economics from the University of Cape Town, as well as a BSc in statistics from Addis Ababa University, Ethiopia.

Linda Zanfini is a development economist responsible for research on education, training, and vocational integration at the AFD. Her research also focuses on the research institutions and systems of the Global South. Before joining AFD's Research Department, she worked as an evaluator of cooperation policies; as a policy advisor in France's Ministry for Europe and Foreign Affairs; and AFD's Strategy Department, where she was responsible for corporate social responsibility. She also lectured at the University of Paris–Sud. She holds a PhD in development economics from the University of Paris Ouest-Nanterre La Défense.

Claire Zanuso is head of the Impact Evaluation Team at the AFD. She joined the AFD in 2016 and has since led the development of impact evaluations, including geospatial impact evaluations, within the agency's evaluation portfolio. Her current research focuses on labor market issues, youth aspirations, and impact evaluation of sustainable infrastructure in developing countries. Zanuso holds a PhD in development economics from Paris-Dauphine University.

Mary Zhang is a research fellow and departmental lecturer on global and area studies at the University of Oxford, United Kingdom. She is a social policy researcher. Her research aims to enhance an equitable, inclusive, and sustainable future for marginalized and vulnerable groups. Zhang's work is organized around investigating the intersectionality among poverty, marginality, social justice, and other significant challenges, such as food insecurity and climate change; enhancing gender equality, linking the empowerment of women and sexual and gender minority groups in global value chains with the quality of governance; and advancing sustainable development, addressing environmental and climate challenges and adaptation strategies for a just transition to a greener future. She holds an MPhil and PhD in psychology from the University of Cambridge, United Kingdom.

Rocco Zizzamia is a postdoctoral researcher at the Center for the Study of African Economies in the Department of Economics and at the Oxford Martin School, University of Oxford, United Kingdom. He is affiliated with Somerville College in Oxford as a Fulford Junior Research Fellow (2023–25). His research focuses on social protection and labor markets. In his current work, Zizzamia is studying the potential to leverage innovations in the design and delivery of social protection systems to increase household resilience to poverty and extreme climate events, such as floods and droughts. He has researched labor markets, inequality, poverty alleviation, poverty dynamics, and social stratification. He is a research affiliate with the Southern Africa Labour and Development Research Unit, University of Cape Town, South Africa, and currently editor of the Centre for the Study of African Economies, University of Oxford's Working Paper Series. Zizzamia holds a PhD in international development and a master's degree in development studies from the University of Oxford, United Kingdom.

Executive Summary

Background and Context

The adoption of the United Nations' 2030 Agenda for Sustainable Development in 2015 signaled the commitment of world leaders to reduce inequalities. Sustainable Development Goal 10 has been devoted to this challenge, having the aim of "reducing inequalities within and across countries." This goal stems from two recognitions.

First, by addressing inequalities, the goal of eradicating extreme poverty can be reached more quickly. Second, the current levels of inequalities in many countries are high, with significant consequences for their development trajectories, such as impeding growth, macroeconomic stability, and poverty reduction. Socioeconomic inequalities can cause political, social, and economic instability and undermine the resilience required to adjust to shocks. Therefore, reducing inequalities is crucial not only to eradicate poverty but also to achieve social justice, cohesion, and development.

In *Development as Freedom,* Sen (2000) approached inequalities through the lens of capabilities. He noted that inequality of incomes can differ substantially from inequality in several other "spaces," such as well-being, freedom, and aspects of quality of life. These aspects can include health, labor, education, and social protection, thus highlighting inequality as a multidimensional phenomenon. As such, a holistic approach is needed to address the various drivers and consequences of inequalities.

This has been the approach of the European Union–Agence française de développement (EU–AFD) Research Facility on Inequalities, under which more than 100 papers have been published since 2017. One of the program's leading partners is the African Centre of Excellence for Inequality Research (ACEIR), whose goal is to contribute to deep, multidimensional, and interdisciplinary understanding of inequalities in African country contexts and to continental and global understanding of how inequalities can be overcome. The content of this book draws from the extensive research led in the framework of the EU–AFD Research Facility on Inequalities and by the network of ACEIR researchers.

Thus, this book focuses on economic and social inequalities in Africa, with the former relating primarily to disparities in income or wealth and the latter referring mainly to differences in opportunities, including disparities in access to services, health care, education, and decent employment. The book examines vertical inequalities among individuals or households, as well as horizontal inequalities between groups (that is, gender, ethnicity, religion, race, or space).

Among the striking global trends of the past decades, the decrease in extreme poverty is one of the most important. The African dynamics within this global picture are interesting. Over the past 30 years, Africa has experienced an important rise in economic growth. However, the progress in reducing poverty has been slow. The incidence of poverty on the continent is higher than elsewhere and, while Africa has been part of the growth miracle, this has not translated into massive reductions in poverty as in other regions. This phenomenon implies that many individuals are locked outside the growth process, reflecting the noninclusiveness of growth in Africa. Perhaps the high and increasing inequalities and the texture of these are the principal culprits involved in failing to translate growth into poverty reduction (Clementi et al. 2022).

Africa hosts 7 of the world's 10 most unequal countries and stands out as a region of extreme inequality by international standards (Chancel et al. 2019; Odusola et al. 2017). The continent also has the highest gap between the average incomes of the top 10 percent and the bottom 50 percent, which is larger than the gaps in other regions with extreme inequality (Chancel et al. 2019). On average, in Africa, the richest 10 percent received 54 percent of total income in 2019, while the bottom 50 percent received only 9 percent (Chancel et al. 2023). Beyond income inequalities, the long-run impact of colonialism in Africa has resulted in the intergenerational transmission of wealth, land, education, and health, which drives the persistent characteristic of inequalities on the continent.

Because of the specific nature of its inequalities and its growing role in global inequality, Africa is integral to the global discussion about inequality. The African context raises important research and policy gaps in the global discussion. Moreover, the continent is increasingly important, because the major driver of global population growth is population growth in Sub-Saharan Africa.

Today's African population is, on average, a very poor population, located mostly within the bottom end of the global income distribution. As such, the people of Africa are crucial to the discussion about global inequalities. Drawing on recent research, this book illuminates African inequality dynamics, including the distribution of outcomes and opportunities.

The study of inequalities has gained significant importance, with the publication of several acclaimed books showing that reducing inequality, as a reflection of the texture of society, can translate economic growth into poverty reduction and development more generally (Bourguignon 2004). This work includes important research on African inequality, with major reports published in recent years (Chancel et al. 2023; Odusola et al. 2017; World Bank 2022). This body of work highlights, among other things, that Southern Africa is the most unequal subregion in the world. Yet, given the currently available data and its limitations in availability and quality, the ability to conduct research and provide results on African inequality is severely limited.

This book adds to these analyses by offering a holistic and in-depth discussion on African inequality. A range of case studies, including for countries such as Burkina Faso, Ghana, Kenya, Malawi, South Africa, and Zambia, are included, thus capturing the heterogeneities and commonalities of African inequalities from a wide range of perspectives. By understanding the major challenges and identifying where the biggest knowledge gaps are, the book provides an important review of and new contributions to the research on inequality on Africa.

Key Messages

The book highlights the main levels and trends of inequalities across regions and countries within Africa before providing a detailed analysis of the multidimensional aspects of inequalities in the continent and the new policy actions. The key messages from the book follow.

Part 1: State of Play

1. *The overview of inequalities in Africa illustrates a multilayered heterogeneity, with different levels and trends across regions and countries within Africa's aggregate level of inequality, as well as obstacles and limits to measuring, understanding, and conceptualizing these inequalities (chapter 1).*

A common thread emerges around the high and increasing inequalities in many African countries. Detailed and context-sensitive analysis is crucial to account for sociocultural and institutional specificities and the historical factors that have shaped the continent's trajectory.

2. *To capture the multilayered and multidimensional aspects of inequalities in Africa, better-quality data are needed that go beyond income and consumption (chapter 2).*

Given that multidimensional inequalities work together to produce aggregate levels of inequality, each dimension and aspect of inequality must be quantified. However, regular and good-quality long-term data are scarce in Africa. Recent methodological advances that combine tax, national accounts, and survey data can solve some of the challenges in estimating wealth and income inequality based on survey data only.

Part 2: Analyzing and Tackling Multidimensional Inequalities

3. *Education and health are key aspects of people's well-being, and inequalities in these areas fundamentally skew opportunities to participate in the labor market, which undergirds consequent income inequality (chapter 3).*

For the most part, disparities in access to health care, health outcomes, and educational attainment are driven by similar factors, such as household socioeconomic circumstances and poverty, geographical location, and gender. Social norms are also key determinants of households' and women's access to quality health care and education. Collectively, these inequalities can shape opportunities for individuals to escape from poverty and move up in income distribution through favorable labor market outcomes.

4. *With its large share of informal and casual employment, a relatively small formal sector, and the precariousness of the youth population, labor market dynamics are key to understanding inequality dynamics in Africa (chapter 4).*

Wage inequality is relatively high in many African countries. In addition to wage dispersion, unemployment rates are very high, particularly in Southern Africa. Countries with low unemployment rates tend to have large informal sectors, raising concerns about the underemployment, precariousness, and vulnerability of the people employed in those sectors. In terms of horizontal inequalities, women are more likely to find employment in informal jobs or be self-employed, and they are disproportionately likely to be engaged in unpaid family work. These employment and wage differentials also apply to certain racial and ethnic groups in some countries. Finally, Africa has the highest levels of youth who are not in employment, education, or training.

5. *With their intersectional characteristic, gender inequalities are deep-seated in African countries and have persisted in three dimensions: (1) economic (participation in income-generating activities and access to and ownership of resources), (2) social (access to health and education), and (3) political (participation in decision-making at the household, community, and national levels) (chapter 5).*

The influence of gender norms and stereotypes is considerable in all African contexts. Gender inequalities are particularly manifested in the household, with women often having limited voice and decision-making power, being burdened by unpaid care work, and being subjected to domestic violence. Through formal rules and informal norms, these inequalities extend to communities and societies, and discrimination against women severely constrains African societies. A gender lens must be applied to the policy-making process to limit discrimination against women in the social, economic, and political spheres.

6. *Within-country spatial inequality in access to basic services (electricity, safe sanitation, and clean water) is a key component of national inequality in most African countries, with significant implications for health, education, and labor market employment opportunities (chapter 6).*

The emergence and persistence of contemporary spatial inequalities in Africa originate in the long-run, colonial legacies that have impacted the nature of each country's postindependence political settlements. The importance of spatial inequalities is made clear by large differences across areas in specific demographic characteristics of households, such as gender of the household head, levels of educational attainment within the household, and racial or ethnic composition of the area.

7. *In Africa, substantial rural-to-urban migration in many countries and substantial international migratory movements are occurring, most of which are happening within the region, with inequality being both a driver and an outcome (chapter 7).*

The financial and social constraints of migration correlate with inequalities in sending areas. Those who are poor, vulnerable, and are subject to discrimination are often unable to migrate. Migration can have direct and indirect effects on inequality. Direct effects occur through remittances sent back to migrant households, which then can change the patterns of household expenditures. Indirect effects occur predominantly through labor market shifts within the sending and receiving communities and because of the new patterns of expenditure and investment. Beyond economic inequalities, norms, institutions, and climate change are major contemporary forces shaping the interlinkages between migration and inequality.

8. *The evidence on intergenerational (between generations) and intragenerational (over a person's lifetime) mobility suggests that high levels of immobility exist in Africa (chapter 8).*

The evidence highlights an imperative to focus policy attention on the structural factors underlying inequalities of opportunity and consequent inequalities in earnings, income, and wealth. These factors include both formal policies and rules and informal norms that can affect equitable access to quality health care and education, as well as the distribution of labor market opportunities, assets, and wealth across and within generations. Across generations, the future of children is still strongly linked to the socioeconomic status of their parents. Within generations, the persistence of poverty, risk of falling into poverty, and low rates of upward mobility into a stable middle class and elite indicate the persistence of inequality over a person's lifetime.

9. *Policies to tackle inequality range from conventional instruments that change incomes directly ("inside the box"), such as labor market policies, tax policies, and social expenditure policies, to policies that change the social relations that condition incomes ("outside the box"), such as competition policy and bargaining frameworks that alter the relative rewards to capital and labor (chapter 9).*

Traditional policies for inequality reduction, such as social safety nets, taxation, and labor market policies, have been used extensively in Africa, with varying levels of success across countries. Although traditional policies remain important, they face constraints in many African countries, including high informality, low industrialization with high foreign ownership, and high poverty rates. These limiting factors and the climate emergency make the case for rethinking policy options to include regulatory frameworks for the adoption and development of new technologies and asset- and capital-sharing schemes.

Part 3: Pushing Knowledge Frontiers and Policy Actions

10. *Climate change has been responsible for increasing inequalities both between and within countries, with Africa disproportionately affected by temperature change and extreme weather events, even though the continent contributes less than 5 percent of global carbon emissions (chapter 10).*

The climate crisis is marked by significant inequalities between Africa and the rest of the world, as well as between and within African countries, with vulnerability to climate impacts strongly linked to income and wealth. Thus, it is vital to develop a better understanding of climate change inequalities, both between and within countries, when designing adaptation and mitigation actions.

11. *Inequality has played a central role in impeding sustainable and inclusive economic growth in Africa, making it imperative to think beyond economic growth and explicitly consider environmental boundaries (chapter 11).*

Patterns of economic growth in Africa have not been inclusive due to several key factors, including high levels of initial inequalities, high dependence on mining and extractive industries, and low responsiveness of employment to economic growth. Global economic growth patterns have been unsustainable from an environmental perspective. These issues require explicit attention to forge growth processes that provide an enabling environment for the whole population in African economies and ensure that transitions to inclusive and sustainable growth in developed countries do not hamper development in low-income countries.

References

Bourguignon, François. 2004. "The Poverty-Growth-Inequality Triangle." Working Paper 125. Indian Council for Research on International Economic Relations, New Delhi.

Chancel, Lucas, Denis Cogneau, Amory Gethin, and Alix Myczkowski. 2019. "Income Inequality in Africa, 1990–2017." WID.world Issue Brief 2019/6. World Inequality Lab. Paris School of Economics and University of California, Berkeley.

Chancel, Lucas, Denis Cogneau, Amory Gethin, Alix Myczkowski, and Anne-Sophie Robilliard. 2023. "Income Inequality in Africa, 1990–2019: Measurement, Patterns, Determinants." *World Development* 163: 106162. https://doi.org/10.1016/j.worlddev.2022.106162.

Clementi, Fabio, Michele Fabiani, Vasco Molini, and Rocco Zizzamia. 2022. "Are We Really Painting the Devil on the Walls? Polarization and Its Drivers in Sub-Saharan Africa in the Past Two Decades." *Journal of African Economies* 31 (2): 124–46. https://doi.org/10.1093/jae/ejab006.

Odusola, Ayodele F., Giovanni Andrea Cornia, Haroon Bhorat, and Pedro Conceição, eds. 2017. *Income Inequality Trends in Sub-Saharan Africa: Divergence, Determinants and Consequences: Overview.* New York: United Nations Development Programme, Regional Bureau for Africa.

Sen, Amartya. 2000. *Development as Freedom.* New York: Anchor Books. https://search.library.wisc.edu/catalog/999977297202121.

World Bank. 2022. *Inequality in Southern Africa: An Assessment of the Southern African Customs Union.* Washington, DC: World Bank. https://doi.org/10.1596/37283.

Abbreviations

ACEIR	African Centre of Excellence for Inequality Research
AERC	African Economic Research Consortium
AFD	Agence française de développement (France)
AFDB	African Development Bank
ALMP	active labor market policy
ASSAf	Academy of Sciences of South Africa
CO$_2$	carbon dioxide
DFID	Department for International Development (United Kingdom)
DHS	Demographic and Health Surveys
EU–AFD	European Union–Agence française de développement
FAO	Food and Agriculture Organization
FGM	female genital mutilation
GBV	gender-based violence
GDP	gross domestic product
GEP	growth elasticity of poverty
GLSS	Ghana Living Standards Survey
GSPS	Ghana Socioeconomic Panel Survey
GSS	Ghana Statistical Service
HIV/AIDS	human immunodeficiency virus/acquired immunodeficiency syndrome
ILO	International Labour Organization
IMF	International Monetary Fund
IPCC	Intergovernmental Panel on Climate Change
IPV	intimate partner violence

ISSER	Institute of Statistical, Social and Economic Research (Ghana)
KNBS	Kenya National Bureau of Statistics
LFP	labor force participation
LSE	London School of Economics and Political Science
MICS	Multiple Indicator Cluster Surveys
MIF	Multidimensional Inequality Framework
MPI	Multidimensional Poverty Index
NEET	not in employment, education, or training
NIDS	National Income Dynamics Study
OECD	Organisation for Economic Co-operation and Development
OHCHR	Office of the High Commissioner for Human Rights (United Nations)
PGI	poverty-growth-inequality
PPP	purchasing power parity
PSNP	Productive Safety Net Program
SACU	Southern African Customs Union
SALDRU	Southern Africa Labour and Development Research Unit
SDG	Sustainable Development Goal
SES	socioeconomic status
SEZ	special economic zone
SIGI	Social Institutions and Gender Index
SSA	Sub-Saharan Africa
Stats SA	Statistics South Africa
STEM	science, technology, engineering, and mathematics
UIS	United Nations Educational, Scientific and Cultural Organization Institute for Statistics
UN	United Nations
UNAIDS	Joint United Nations Programme on HIV/AIDS
UNDP	United Nations Development Programme
UNFCCC	United Nations Framework Convention on Climate Change
UNICEF	United Nations Children's Fund
UNU–WIDER	United Nations University–World Institute for Development Economics Research
WASH	water, sanitation, and hygiene
WEF	World Economic Forum
WHO	World Health Organization
WID	World Inequality Database
WMO	World Meteorological Organization

PART 1
State of Play

Chapter **1**

Overview of Inequalities in Africa

Anda David, Rocco Zizzamia, Murray Leibbrandt, Rawane Yasser, and Vimal Ranchhod

Introduction

While development agendas have focused primarily on poverty reduction in Africa, discussions of global inequality have paid little attention to inequalities in the region. Yet, the world's 10 most unequal countries are in Africa, which stands out as having extreme inequality by international standards (Chancel et al. 2019; Odusola et al. 2017).

Recently, Africa has witnessed distributional issues that have become more central in policy and public debates because of how inequality shapes inclusive growth (or the lack thereof). Over the past few years, the continent has experienced an important rise in economic growth; however, progress in reducing poverty has been slow, implying that much of the population is locked out of the growth process. High and increasing inequality could be the principal reason for the failure to translate growth into poverty reduction (Clementi et al. 2022).

Africa has the highest gap between the average incomes of the top 10 percent and the bottom 50 percent, which is even larger than the gaps in other regions with extreme inequality (the gap in Africa is around 20 times that in the Brazil, India, and the Middle East) (Chancel et al. 2019). This striking characteristic of inequality on the continent deserves both analytical and political attention.

However, several challenges may hamper this analysis. First, given the current data and their limitations in availability and quality, the ability to conduct research and provide results on inequalities in Africa is limited. Data quality in Africa has lagged behind other regions. The World Income Inequality Database (WIID)[1] indicates only 5 high-quality, country-year observations of distributional indicators for Sub-Saharan Africa (SSA) from 1900 to 2006, compared to 65 for Central and South America and 719 for Western Europe (Zizzamia, David, and Leibbrandt 2021). Second, unlike poverty, inequality lacks a normative and commonly acknowledged approach, because inequality is a relative concept with changing boundaries and no universal norm.

Moreover, inequality reduction is more difficult than poverty reduction, especially in Africa. Due to the strong intergenerational transmission of status engendered by the colonial past, asset distribution is persistent, rendering inequality more assiduous than poverty and growth. Another reason is that the structures that shape policies, and thus inequalities, such as institutions, social norms, and political regimes, do not change easily.

This chapter provides an overview of inequality in Africa and highlights some specificities and heterogeneities among countries in the region. The chapter also examines the evolution of inequality in Africa compared to other countries, by looking at income and wealth distributions over the years, and explains the distinct features of this inequality.

Inequality in Africa: Levels and Trends

Despite the difficulties of measuring and reducing inequalities, several reports and databases provide an idea of the levels and trends of inequality in Africa. Among world regions, Africa has the highest level of income inequality. This section explores the levels and trends of inequalities in Africa as a whole, as well as at the regional and country levels.

Inequality in Africa as a Whole

Before exploring the evolution of inequality over the recent decades in Africa, this chapter examines the current inequality levels of the continent as a whole.

Levels

The most recent update of the World Inequality Database (WID) estimates that, on average in Africa, the richest 10 percent of the population received 54 percent of the total income in 2019, while the bottom 50 percent received only 9 percent (Chancel et al. 2023). These figures place Africa as a continent with one of the highest levels of income inequality. The income share of the top 10 percent is 34 percent in Europe, 47 percent in the United States, 55 percent in Latin America, and 61 percent in the Middle East.

What distinguishes Africa's income distribution is the large gap between the income shares of the top 10 percent and the bottom 50 percent. In Africa, the average income of the top 10 percent is about 30 times higher than that of the bottom 50 percent. This ratio is lower in other regions and countries with extreme inequality, such as Brazil, India, and the Middle East, where the ratio is around 20. These findings point to the heavily polarized nature of income inequality in Africa.

According to the WIID, the average Gini coefficient in Africa in 2020 was 0.53, compared to the other low-income and lower-middle-income countries, at 0.41 (UNU-WIDER 2023). The upper bound of Africa's range of Gini indexes exceeds that of the other developing countries, highlighting a distinct feature of Africa, which is extreme inequality. A total of 76 percent of African countries (41 of 54) have Gini indexes above the median Gini for all low-income and lower-middle-income countries.

Trends

This overview on the recent level of inequality is complemented by examining the evolution of inequality in Africa in recent decades. A replication of Lakner and Milanovic's (2016) elephant curve of global income growth between 1990 and 2016 illustrates that, in Africa, a majority of individuals make up the lowest part of the income distribution (the poorest individuals, who are locked out of growth) (refer to figure 1.1). Based on data from the WID, figure 1.1 shows the shares of Sub-Saharan Africans in each income group in 1990 and 2016, replicating the curve of global inequality and economic growth. The figure indicates that the Sub-Saharan African population became more concentrated in the bottom quarter of the distribution, with 33 percent of the population of the world's 10th percentile of the income distribution residing in SSA in 2016, compared to 21 percent in 1990, and almost no representation of Sub-Saharan Africans in the top 0.1 percent. From this figure, it is evident that, compared to the rest of the world, the condition of the Sub-Saharan African population has worsened as Africa's share in the lowest 30 percent of the income distribution has increased.

Figure 1.1 **SSA's Share of the Global Income Distribution and Income Growth, 1990 and 2016**

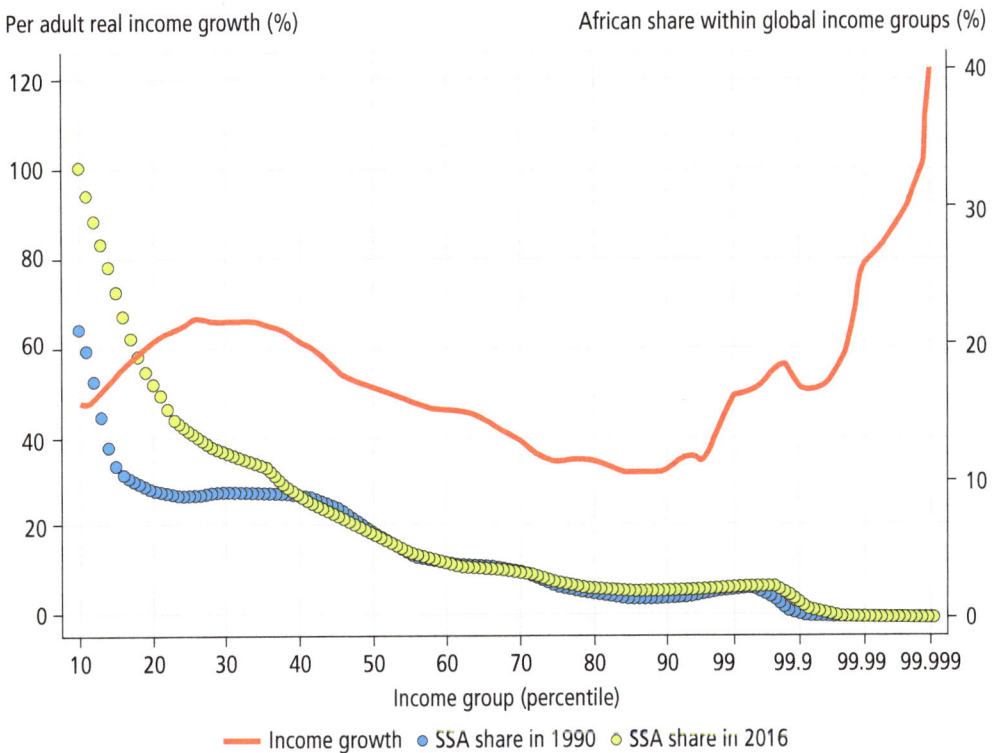

Per adult real income growth (%)

African share within global income groups (%)

— Income growth   ● SSA share in 1990   ○ SSA share in 2016

Source: Authors' calculations based on replication files from the World Inequality Database.
Note: The left y-axis is the cumulative growth rate between 1990 and 2016 of pre-tax national income measured in 2016 purchasing power parity euros. In 2016, 33 percent of the population in the world's 10th percentile of the income distribution were residents of SSA. The figure includes the following countries and the available surveys used for each country: Benin (2003, 2011, 2015), Burkina Faso (1994, 1998, 2003, 2014), Burundi (1998, 2006, 2013), Cameroon (1996, 2001, 2007, 2014), Côte d'Ivoire (1985–88, 1993, 1998, 2002, 2008, 2015), Ethiopia (1995, 1999, 2004, 2010), Ghana (1991, 1998, 2005, 2012), Guinea (1994, 2002, 2007, 2012), Guinea-Bissau (1991, 1993, 2002, 2010), Kenya (1994, 1997, 2005), Lesotho (1994, 2002, 2010), Madagascar (1997, 1999, 2001, 2005, 2010, 2012), Malawi (1997, 2004, 2010), Mali (1994, 2001, 2006, 2009), Mauritania (1995, 2000, 2004, 2008, 2014), Mozambique (1996, 2002, 2008), Niger (1994, 2005, 2007, 2011, 2014), Nigeria (1992, 2003, 2009), Rwanda (2000, 2005, 2010, 2013), Senegal (2001, 2005, 2011), South Africa (1996, 2002, 2006, 2008, 2011), Tanzania (1991, 2000, 2007, 2011), Togo (2006, 2011, 2015), Uganda (1992, 1996, 1999, 2002, 2005, 2009, 2012), and Zambia (1991, 1996, 1998, 2002, 2004, 2006, 2015). SSA = Sub-Saharan Africa.

Figure 1.2 Total Income Growth in Africa, by Percentile of the Income Distribution, 1980–2016

Per adult real income growth (%)

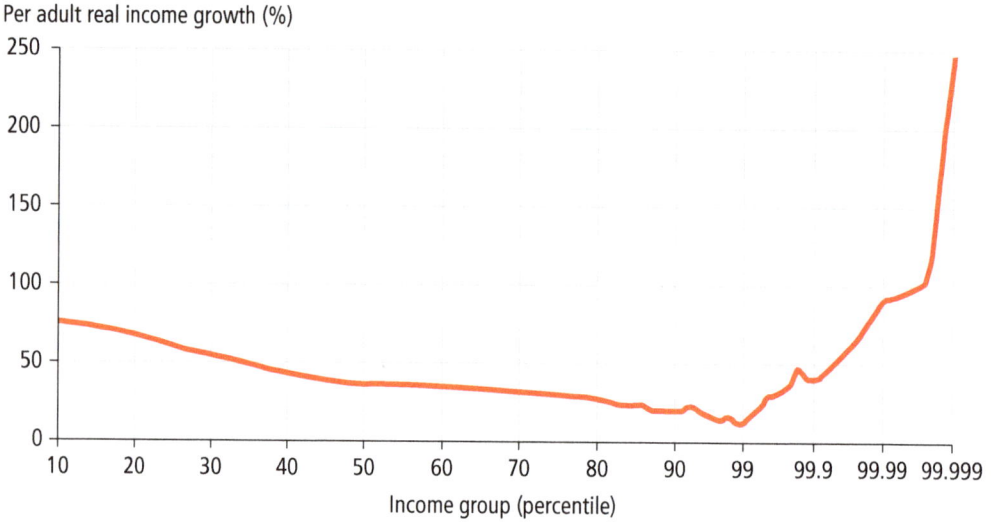

Income group (percentile)

Source: Authors' calculations based on replication files from the World Inequality Database.
Note: Real income growth is the cumulative growth rate between 1980 and 2016 of pre-tax national income measured in 2016 purchasing power parity euros. Income in the bottom 10 percent of the top 1 percent of global earners grew at 13 percent between 1980 and 2016. The top 1 percent captured 27 percent of total growth.

Figure 1.2 presents the growth incidence curve for Africa between 1980 and 2016. The figure shows that inequality has increased, benefiting wealthy and super-wealthy individuals. The well-being of other segments of the population has barely improved, with the top 1 percent of earners capturing 27 percent of total growth. A decomposition analysis shows that 75 percent of African inequality can be attributed to within-country inequality (Chancel et al. 2023).

A recent update from the WID shows that the share of the top 10 percent in Africa decreased from 55 percent to 54 percent, while the share of the bottom 50 percent increased from 8 percent to 9 percent (refer to figure 1.3).

The overall high level of inequality in Africa hides important regional variations, which are explored in the next subsection.

Levels and Trends at the Regional and Country Levels

The consensus from the research is that Africa is characterized as having had heterogeneous inequality levels and trends in recent years, prompting studies to look beyond the continental averages and examine inequalities at the country level.

Figure 1.3 Evolution of Income Distribution in Africa

Share of regional income (%)

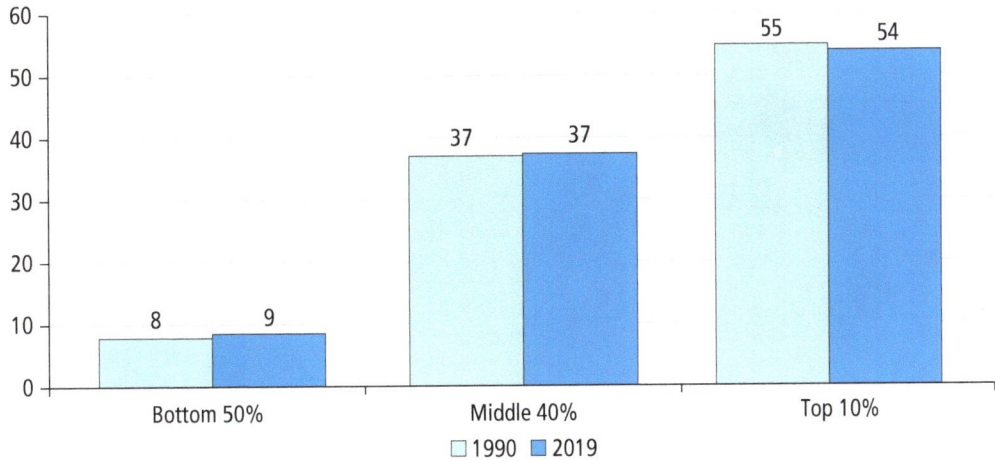

Source: Based on Chancel et al. 2023.

Levels

There is great regional variation in the level of inequality across the continent, with a concentration of high inequality in Southern Africa and less inequality in the Sahara and the northern part of the continent (Chancel et al. 2019; Odusola et al. 2017; Zizzamia et al. 2021), with 7 of the world's 10 most unequal countries in SSA. This pattern is confirmed across inequality measures, such as the top 10 percent of shares versus the bottom 40 percent, or the Gini indexes of the countries (refer to maps 1.1–1.3).

Southern Africa is considered the most unequal region, with countries such as South Africa and Botswana having the top 10 percent of shares exceeding 65 percent (Chancel et al. 2023). Central Africa has lower inequality levels, but they are high from an international perspective (refer to maps 1.1 and 1.2). In the Republic of Congo in 2022, 56 percent of national income was held by the top 10 percent of the distribution, while the bottom 40 percent income share was 6 percent. Countries in East Africa have lower levels of income inequality. For example, in Kenya, the bottom 40 percent of income share in 2022 was around 8 percent, while the top 10 percent received 49 percent of national income.

Inequality is lower in the North and West regions of Africa. The lowest levels of inequality are in Northern Africa. Algeria is the least unequal country on the continent: In 2022, the top 10 percent of the distribution received 38 percent of national income, while the bottom 40 percent received 13 percent. However, these numbers should be read with caution given concerns about the reliability and availability of data in many African countries.

Map 1.1 Top 10 Percent of Income Shares in Africa, 2022

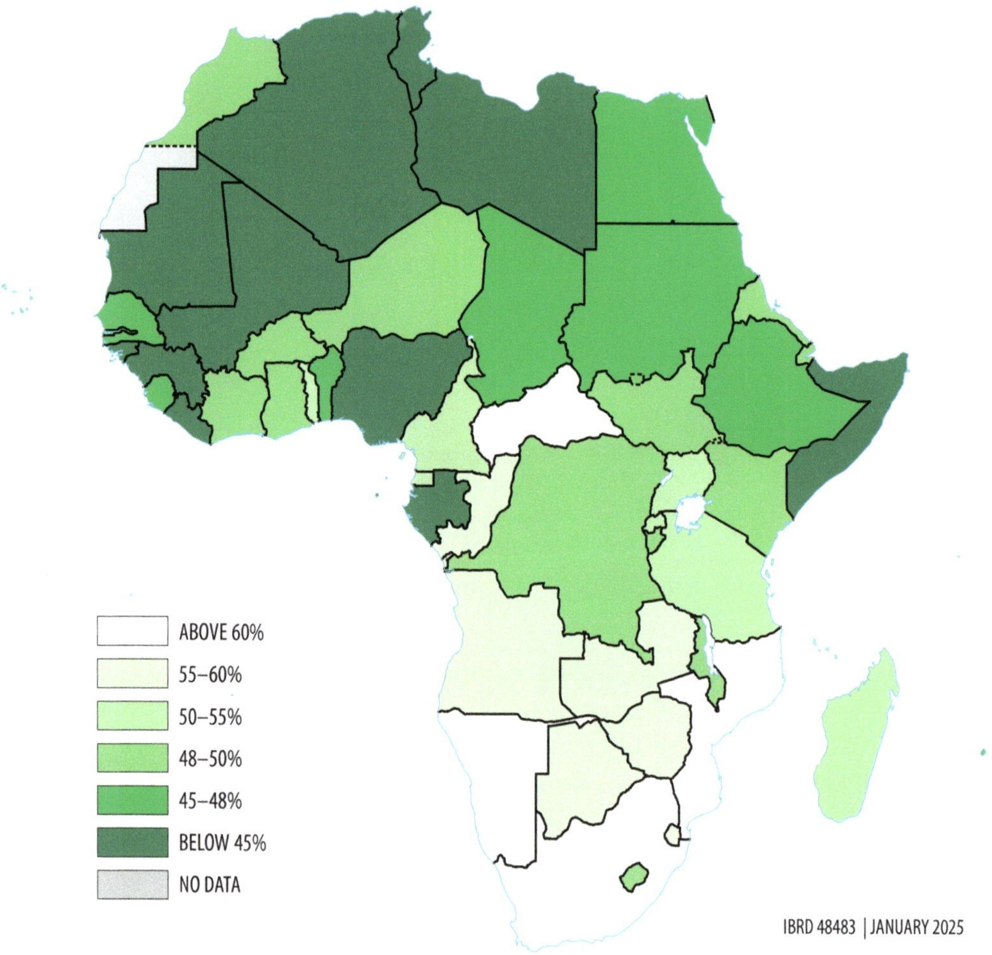

ABOVE 60%
55–60%
50–55%
48–50%
45–48%
BELOW 45%
NO DATA

IBRD 48483 | JANUARY 2025

Source: Authors' elaboration based on data from the World Inequality Database from 2022.
Note: The estimates combine survey, fiscal, and national accounts data.

Map 1.2 Bottom 40 Percent of Income Shares in Africa, 2022

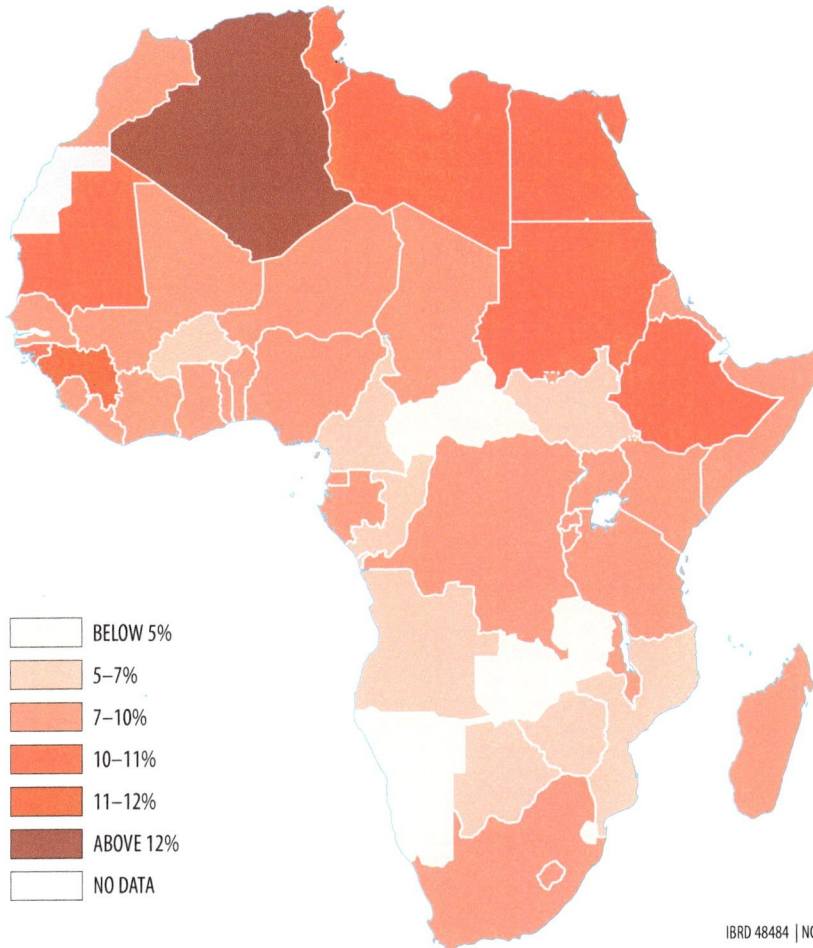

	BELOW 5%
	5–7%
	7–10%
	10–11%
	11–12%
	ABOVE 12%
	NO DATA

IBRD 48484 | NOVEMBER 2024

Source: Authors' elaboration based on data from the World Inequality Database from 2022.
Note: The estimates combine survey, fiscal, and national accounts data.

A distinctive feature of African inequality is the prevalence of extreme inequality in some countries, which is not observed in other developing regions. In Africa, eight countries have Gini coefficients that are higher than 0.60: Angola, Burkina Faso, the Central African Republic, the Republic of Congo, Eswatini, Namibia, South Africa, and Zambia (UNU-WIDER 2023) (refer to map 1.3).

Map 1.3 Gini Coefficients of African Countries, 2020

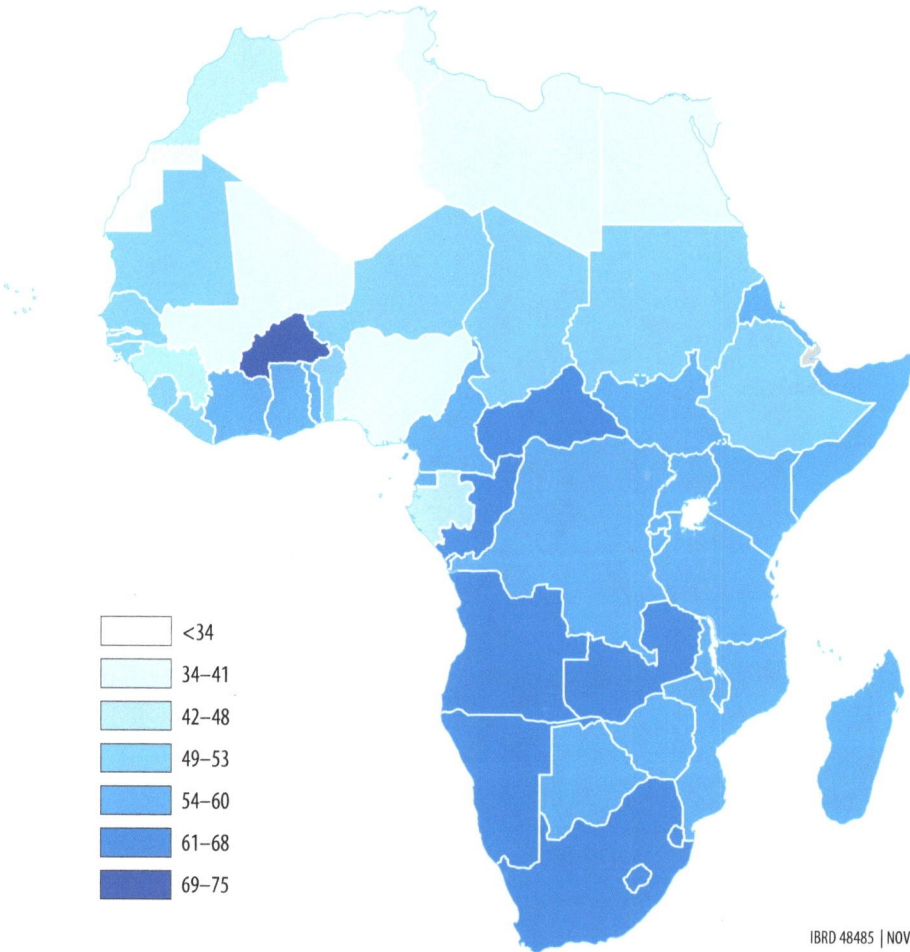

Legend:
- <34
- 34–41
- 42–48
- 49–53
- 54–60
- 61–68
- 69–75

IBRD 48485 | NOVEMBER 2024

Source: Authors' elaboration using data from UNU-WIDER 2023.

Trends

The heterogeneity across countries also appears in the evolution of inequality. In Africa from 1991 to 2011, the level of inequality declined in 17 countries, but it increased in 12 countries (Cornia 2017).

Most of the continent-level income inequality comes from the within-country component rather than from average income differences between countries (Chancel et al. 2023). Inequality remained stable from 1990 to 2019, with the exception of Southern Africa, where it increased significantly. Studying the income distribution in South Africa since 1913, Alvaredo and Atkinson (2022) found that the share of the top 1 percent was over 25 percent in 1913; for the top 0.5 percent, the share was around 18 percent; and for the top 0.1 percent, it was around 8 percent. There was a downward trend until the 1980s, when the share of the top 1 percent was halved, although it increased again after 2002.

Wealth Inequality

A distinguishing feature of African inequality is the level and persistence of wealth inequality (World Bank 2022; Zizzamia et al. 2021). In this context, understanding the role of wealth in replicating inequality or breaking the cycle of intergenerational poverty is important. However, wealth inequality in Africa remains under-researched, mainly because of a lack of access to data on wealth. Because wealth is not taxed directly in most countries, there are insufficient fiscal data on wealth; therefore, obtaining reliable data requires compiling data from several sources. The recent expansion of household and panel surveys across Africa provides new possibilities to study the relationship between income and wealth inequality.

De Magalhães and Santaeulàlia-Llopis (2018) used panel data from Malawi, Tanzania, and Uganda to study the channels of transmission between income and wealth distribution. They found a low correlation between income and wealth inequality in these countries, which points to an inability to accumulate wealth based on income. Rural households also exhibited a lower transmission of income to wealth inequality compared to urban households. The top 1 percentile of the income distribution of rural households holds a smaller share of wealth compared to the top urban households. The findings point to high levels of income mobility for all households, whereby income volatility constitutes a constraint on the accumulation of wealth. Therefore, those who are rich in income do not remain rich long enough to accumulate wealth, which points to the persistent characteristic of wealth inequality in Africa.

A recent report by the World Bank (2022) focused on the countries in the Southern African Customs Union, which are characterized by significant inequalities in all dimensions of wealth. The top 10 percent of the population holds 56.9 percent of total household assets in Botswana (2018), 68.4 percent in Namibia (2018), and 68.6 percent in South Africa (2019). The distribution of total household wealth is also highly concentrated in the top 10 percent of the income distribution, led by South Africa at 71.7 percent and Namibia at 71.3 percent (World Bank 2022).

In South Africa, wealth inequality may even be higher than consumption or income inequality (Shifa et al. 2023). Focusing on the distribution of wealth between 1993 and 2017 shows the extreme level of wealth concentration in South Africa, with the top 10 percent owning 86 percent of aggregate wealth, and the top 0.1 percent owning close to one-third of aggregate wealth (Chatterjee, Czajka, and Gethin 2022). Such high levels of inequality are observed in all forms of assets—housing, pension funds, and financial assets—and have shown no sign of decreasing since the end of apartheid.

An important dimension of wealth inequality in Africa is gender inequality in access to and ownership of assets and land (refer to chapter 5). Large differences exist between men and women in the ownership of assets, as well as in who controls assets and wealth (Gaddis, Lahoti, and Swaminathan 2022; Gaddis, Lahoti, and Wenjie 2018).

Beyond Income and Wealth Inequalities

Although measures of income and wealth inequalities provide an overarching view of inequality in Africa, focusing on inequalities beyond monetary measures is crucial for understanding the dynamics of how inequalities are created and perpetuated. This work entails understanding how inequalities evolve in other dimensions and how these dimensions interact. Inequalities in education, health, labor markets, and climate are critical forces that drive and are interlinked with the observed income and wealth inequalities.

Access to quality education plays a central role in reducing inequalities. SSA has the highest rates of educational exclusion of any region (refer to chapter 3). Although access to primary education has increased in most African countries, inequalities persist in secondary and higher education, and gender disparities remain. The unequal distribution of educational opportunities results in the transmission of unequal opportunities across generations, as inequalities in education also impact labor market outcomes. The labor market is one of the strongest drivers of inequalities in Africa (refer to chapter 4), with a large share of informal labor, precariousness among youth, and a relatively small formal sector. Africa also experiences persistent inequalities in access to health care services, particularly maternal, newborn, and child health services, and has the highest maternal mortality rates in the world. Another deep-seated aspect of inequalities in most African countries is the significant level of gender inequality, which has persisted in access to health and education, employment, income-generating activities, and assets and wealth (chapter 5).

Climate change–related inequality is the most-challenging development issue in Africa, as it is the continent most vulnerable to its consequences. The impacts of climate change are not equally distributed across the world. Africa, in particular, is disproportionately affected by temperature change, extreme weather events, and the spread of disease, even though the continent contributes less than 5 percent of global carbon emissions (refer to chapter 10). Within countries, vulnerability to climate impacts is strongly linked to inequalities in income and wealth.

Finally, Africa is characterized by a deep urban-rural divide and unequal access to basic services and infrastructure (Clementi et al. 2022). Understanding both rural and urban contexts and the interaction between them is crucial for analyzing African inequalities (refer to chapter 6).

Particularities of Inequality Analysis in Africa

The diversity of income and wealth inequalities in Africa reflects specific characteristics that have shaped inequality dynamics on the continent. Historical and institutional features have led to the region's extreme income and wealth inequalities.

The current levels of inequality in Africa and their evolution over recent decades reveal their persistence. The region's history has been marked by its colonial legacy. Many studies have pointed to the type of colonization experienced by most African countries as the main driver behind the continent's high levels of inequalities (Alvaredo, Cogneau, and Piketty 2021; Chancel et al. 2023; Cornia 2017). European settler colonialism has resulted in a high concentration of productive assets (land and capital) and limited Indigenous people's access to education and employment. Further, in the countries with the highest income shares of the richest 10 percent, such as Botswana, Eswatini, Namibia, and South Africa, a significant number of people of European descent remains.

The consequences of colonialism have continued after independence and still shape inequalities in Africa. The colonial past has had long-term impacts on institutions, societies, the nature of growth, and therefore, on the persistence of inequality. The concentration of assets and wealth in the hands of a minority of settlers has created a dualistic structure of colonial administrations and companies specializing in exporting natural resources, which has persisted after independence through the expansion of extractive industries (Alvaredo et al. 2021; Chancel et al. 2023). Characterized by high capital intensity and limited employment creation, extractive industries can perpetuate income inequality.

The long-term impact of this type of colonialism has shaped African inequalities through the intergenerational transmission of wealth, land, education, and health that drives the persistence of inequalities on the continent. Access to and ownership of land are specific sources of wealth and assets important in the African context. The unequal distribution of land that took place during the colonial period has continued well after independence (Chancel et al. 2023). The legal and normative rules for land and other assets are key for understanding livelihood trajectories and socioeconomic mobility in Africa. In contrast with many developing countries in Asia, land reforms in Africa have been limited, hampering a more-equal distribution of land.

Another important dimension of inequality in Africa is the nature of the continent's pattern of growth, which has been characterized by low poverty alleviation elasticity compared to other regions, implying that noninclusive growth is driven by high levels of inequality (Odusola et al. 2017). An important strand of literature has explored the role of structural transformation in the evolution of inequality. Unlike other regions, where value-added shares shifted from agriculture to manufacturing, research points to a shift in the percentage structure of value-added shares from low-inequality to high-inequality sectors in Africa (Cornia 2017; Odusola et al. 2017). As agricultural employment decreased, labor was absorbed in services or urban unemployment rather than manufacturing.

The patterns of inequality in Africa are also a reflection of the region's fiscal space, which is small compared to that of other developing regions, and the distributional effectiveness of policies remains disputed (Chancel et al. 2023). Research has shown the positive impact of social protection on inequality reduction, suggesting that social protection should be a priority (Odusola et al. 2017). Yet, the coverage and quality of social protection in Africa remain below global averages. In Africa, redistribution through taxation is limited, and most tax systems tend to be regressive (Odusola et al. 2017). Government expenditure on public services also falls below global averages, especially in education and health.

Intrahousehold inequality is important, as the social relations inside the household are crucial for inclusive growth for women and youth. However, income statistics are typically collected at the household level, which assumes that all income and consumption are equally divided among household members. Ignoring inequality within households leads to underestimating overall inequality. De Vreyer and Lambert (2021) have attempted to account for the weight of intrahousehold inequalities, finding that intrahousehold consumption inequalities account for 14 percent of inequality in Senegal. Often, intrahousehold inequalities follow gender lines. The high frequency of polygamous households and large sizes of households in some African countries are important specificities that shape inequalities (Zizzamia et al. 2021). Accurate assessment of inequalities in the African context entails accounting for such particularities.

In many African countries, household assets are held jointly by men and women; however, this does not imply that there is equal access to or control of assets. Thus, understanding the decision-making processes within households is necessary. Gender disparities in ownership and asset use are significant in Africa, especially in SSA. As chapter 5 further elaborates, a more-egalitarian pattern can be achieved through structural change in the growth process, by moving away from the existing patterns of wealth distribution. Closing the gender gap in land ownership could promote a more-egalitarian gender distribution of asset ownership (Oduro and Doss 2018).

Inequality of opportunity and slow social mobility can affect people's livelihoods, as well as the distribution of wealth and assets. It is important to understand the role of wealth in replicating inequality to be able to make more-equitable policy decisions. Inequality of opportunity implies that inherited circumstances, such as gender, race, location of birth, and family background, can affect an individual's life outcomes, such as earnings, educational attainment, and occupation. Inequality of opportunity can manifest in disparities in access to health care, health care outcomes, access to quality education, and educational outcomes (refer to chapter 3). These disparities can contribute to the persistence of inequalities and thus hamper social mobility.

Intergenerational mobility is the extent to which people's life outcomes are correlated with those of their parents, and inertia in the transmission of assets between generations makes inequality more persistent than poverty. This issue is especially concerning in Africa, where children's futures are still strongly linked to their parents' socioeconomic status (SES; refer to chapter 8). Brunori, Palmisano, and Peragine (2016) have estimated that exogenous and group-based circumstances account for 30 percent to 40 percent of total inequality in 11 SSA countries. Malawi, Tanzania, and Uganda have the highest shares of inequality of opportunity in total inequality measured at the national level, and the Comoros, Madagascar, and Rwanda have the lowest shares. In South Africa, evidence has shown that the opportunities available to children are closely related to their parents' SES, pointing to a high degree of persistence of intergenerational earnings (Finn, Leibbrandt, and Ranchhod 2017; Piraino 2015).

Conclusion

This chapter's overview of inequalities in Africa shows a picture of multilayered heterogeneity, with different levels and trends across regions and countries but also different obstacles and limits to measuring, understanding, and conceptualizing inequalities. Nonetheless, a common thread emerges, showing high and increasing inequalities in many African countries. Better data are needed that go beyond income and consumption and beyond the accessibility and affordability of basic services. In addition, contextualized, detailed analyses that account for not only sociocultural specificities but also the institutional and historical factors that have shaped countries' trajectories are needed. To tackle inequalities, these must be understood in terms of their determinants and current manifestations in society. Over the past decades, development interventions across the continent have focused on poverty reduction. A shift toward inequalities and the roles they play in reducing poverty and creating more-resilient economies must involve a variety of stakeholders, including governments, development agencies, financial institutions, and academia.

Note

1. WIID is developed by UNU-WIDER and presents a comprehensive set of information on income inequality statistics. The database provides information on income inequality through different sources of income inequality measures for each country. The World Inequality Database (WID), developed by the World Inequality Lab, provides information on the historical evolution of the distribution of income and wealth based on a methodology combining different data sources (national accounts, survey data, fiscal data, and wealth rankings) to provide accurate series.

References

Alvaredo, Facundo, and A. B. Atkinson. 2022. "Top Incomes in South Africa in the Twentieth Century." *Cliometrica* 16 (3): 477–546. https://doi.org/10.1007/s11698-021-00235-4.

Alvaredo, Facundo, Denis Cogneau, and Thomas Piketty. 2021. "Income Inequality under Colonial Rule. Evidence from French Algeria, Cameroon, Tunisia, and Vietnam and Comparisons with British Colonies 1920–1960." *Journal of Development Economics* 152: 102680. https://doi.org/10.1016/j.jdeveco.2021.102680.

Brunori, Paolo, Flaviana Palmisano, and Vito Peragine. 2016. "Inequality of Opportunity in Sub-Saharan Africa." Policy Research Working Paper No. 7782, World Bank, Washington, DC.

Chancel, Lucas, Denis Cogneau, Amory Gethin, and Alix Myczkowski. 2019. "Income Inequality in Africa, 1990–2017." WID.world Issue Brief 2019/6, World Inequality Lab, Paris School of Economics and University of California, Berkeley.

Chancel, Lucas, Denis Cogneau, Amory Gethin, Alix Myczkowski, and Anne-Sophie Robilliard. 2023. "Income Inequality in Africa, 1990–2019: Measurement, Patterns, Determinants." *World Development* 163: 106162. https://doi.org/10.1016/j.worlddev.2022.106162.

Chatterjee, Aroop, Léo Czajka, and Amory Gethin. 2022. "Wealth Inequality in South Africa, 1993–2017." *World Bank Economic Review* 36 (1): 19–36. https://doi.org/10.1093/wber/lhab012.

Clementi, Fabio, Michele Fabiani, Vasco Molini, and Rocco Zizzamia. 2022. "Are We Really Painting the Devil on the Walls? Polarization and Its Drivers in Sub-Saharan Africa in the Past Two Decades." *Journal of African Economies* 31 (2): 124–46. https://doi.org/10.1093/jae/ejab006.

Cornia, Giovanni. 2017. "Inequality Levels, Trends and Determinants in Sub-Saharan Africa: An Overview of Main Changes since the Early 1990s." In *Income Inequality Trends in Sub-Saharan Africa: Divergence, Determinants and Consequences*, edited by Ayodele F. Odusola, Giovanni Cornia, Haroon Bhorat, and Pedro Conceição, 23–51. New York: United Nations Development Programme, Regional Bureau for Africa.

De Magalhães, Leandro, and Raül Santaeulàlia-Llopis. 2018. "The Consumption, Income, and Wealth of the Poorest: An Empirical Analysis of Economic Inequality in Rural and Urban Sub-Saharan Africa for Macroeconomists." *Journal of Development Economics* 134: 350–71. https://doi.org/10.1016/j.jdeveco.2018.05.014.

De Vreyer, Philippe, and Sylvie Lambert. 2021. "Inequality, Poverty, and the Intra-Household Allocation of Consumption in Senegal." *World Bank Economic Review* 35 (2): 414–35. https://doi.org/10.1093/wber /lhz052.

Finn, Arden, Murray Leibbrandt, and Vimal Ranchhod. 2017. "Patterns of Persistence: Intergenerational Mobility and Education in South Africa." SALDRU Working Paper No. 175, Southern Africa Labour and Development Research Unit, University of Cape Town, South Africa.

Gaddis, Isis, Rahul Lahoti, and Hema Swaminathan. 2022. "Women's Legal Rights and Gender Gaps in Property Ownership in Developing Countries." *Population and Development Review* 48 (2): 331–77. https://doi.org/10.1111/padr.12493.

Gaddis, Isis, Rahul Lahoti, and Li Wenjie. 2018. "Gender Gaps in Property Ownership in Sub-Saharan Africa." Policy Research Working Paper No. 8573, World Bank, Washington, DC.

Lakner, Christoph, and Branko Milanovic. 2016. "Global Income Distribution: From the Fall of the Berlin Wall to the Great Recession." *World Bank Economic Review* 30(2), 203–32.

Oduro, Abena D., and Cheryl R. Doss. 2018. "Changing Patterns of Wealth Distribution: Evidence from Ghana." *Journal of Development Studies* 54 (5): 933–48. https://doi.org/10.1080/00220388.2018.1430769.

Odusola, Ayodele F., Giovanni Andrea Cornia, Haroon Bhorat, and Pedro Conceição, eds. 2017. *Income Inequality Trends in Sub-Saharan Africa: Divergence, Determinants and Consequences: Overview.* New York: United Nations Development Programme, Regional Bureau for Africa.

Piraino, Patrizio. 2015. "Intergenerational Earnings Mobility and Equality of Opportunity in South Africa." *World Development* 67: 396–405. https://doi.org/10.1016/j.worlddev.2014.10.027.

Shifa, Muna, Rejoice Mabhena, Vimal Ranchhod, and Murray Leibbrandt. 2023. "An Assessment of Inequality Estimates for the Case of South Africa." WIDER Working Paper No. 2023/90, United Nations University, World Institute for Development Economics Research, Helsinki, Finland. https://doi .org/10.35188/UNU-WIDER/2023/398-7.

UNU-WIDER (United Nations University, World Institute for Development Economics Research). 2023. *World Income Inequality Database (WIID) Companion—Version 28* (November 2023). UNU-WIDER, Helsinki, Finland. https://doi.org/10.35188/UNU-WIDER/WIIDcomp-281123.

World Bank. 2022. *Inequality in Southern Africa: An Assessment of the Southern African Customs Union.* Washington, DC: World Bank. https://doi.org/10.1596/37283.

Zizzamia, Rocco, Anda David, and Murray Leibbrandt. 2021. "Inequality in Sub-Saharan Africa: A Review Paper." AFD Research Paper 207, Agence française de développement, Paris.

Chapter **2**

Measurement of Inequality

Muna Shifa, Richmond Atta-Ankomah, and Samuel Kipruto

Introduction

Although the role of inequality in economic and social well-being outcomes has been recognized in recent years, a unified and simple approach to conceptualizing and measuring inequality is lacking. Inequality is a multidimensional phenomenon including both *economic* (for example, income and other labor market outcomes) and *noneconomic* (for example, life satisfaction and health status) dimensions of well-being. Therefore, before analyzing inequality, it is important to determine the relevant evaluative space,[1] which can often be linked to the purpose of the inequality analysis (Sen 1992).

Even if the focus is confined to measures of economic inequality, there is still a need to distinguish among its different aspects. The analysis must respond to the questions of inequality of what and among whom. For example, *vertical inequality* measures inequalities among individuals or households, and *horizontal inequality* measures inequalities among social groups (for example, ethnicity or gender) or spatial units. Another contrast is between *intragenerational mobility,* which compares an individual's economic status across their lifetime, and *intergenerational mobility,* which compares a person's economic status to that of their parents. Furthermore, analysis of *inequality of outcomes* measures inequalities in the distribution of economic outcomes such as income or earnings, and analysis of *inequality of opportunities* measures inequalities in the distribution of opportunities to acquire those outcomes. Knowing these differences is critical for understanding the impacts of various forms of inequality on other social outcomes and policy discussions. For example, work on the relationship between inequality and negative social outcomes has found that horizontal inequality, rather than vertical inequality, matters in explaining conflict outcomes (Hillesund et al. 2018).

Although Sustainable Development Goal (SDG) 10 emphasizes assessing progress on multiple dimensions of inequality, income data have traditionally been used as the welfare basis for measuring inequality. The fundamental premise in using income to evaluate welfare is that income is a critical means for obtaining other well-being outcomes. Moreover, income and wealth inequality are often associated with other dimensions of inequalities, such as inequality in access to basic services. In addition, using prices is the best way to aggregate the values of the goods and services that are important for well-being.

Yet, the limitations of using income or other resources to measure individual well-being have been widely acknowledged (Sen 1992; Stiglitz, Sen, and Fitoussi 2009). Neither income nor consumption data capture free or subsidized social transfers. In addition, people have different levels of ability to convert income or other resources into valuable achievements, because many factors, like social and institutional structures (such as the role of women in society), power structures, personal conditions (such as physical and mental health), environmental characteristics, and other factors, can affect the extent to which people can convert income and other resources into valuable achievements (Sen 1992, 1999).

According to Sen's capability approach (Sen 2004), individuals' living conditions should be assessed for functionings, capabilities, and achievements.[2] Thus, capabilities, which represent individuals' actual opportunities for well-being, should be regarded as a relevant evaluative space for analyzing well-being inequalities. The capability approach has been used as a conceptual framework for calculating the Human Development Index and the global Multidimensional Poverty Index (MPI),[3] as well as for developing the Multidimensional Inequality Framework (MIF).

Measuring trends in inequality in practice is challenging in many developing nations, regardless of whether the analysis considers resources or functioning and capabilities as the relevant evaluative space. In Sub-Saharan Africa (SSA), only a few countries gather high-quality, timely data on income or other well-being indicators (refer to figure 2.1). This chapter provides an overview of some of the main challenges for assessing inequality in SSA, as well as the approaches utilized to address them.

Overview of Data Availability in SSA

The availability of high-quality, timely household survey data is critical for monitoring progress toward poverty and inequality reduction and achievement of the SDGs. Despite the increase in the number of surveys since the 1980s, most SSA countries have a gap in the frequency and quality of survey data available. Since the 1980s, only 20 of the 46 SSA countries that completed income or consumption surveys have collected at least five surveys (refer to figure 2.1). Between 1900 and 2006, the World Income Inequality Database contained only 5 country-year observations of high-quality income or consumption data for SSA, compared to 65 for Central and South America and 719 for Western Europe (Zizzamia, David, and Leibbrandt 2021). Similarly, according to the 2022 Poverty and Shared Prosperity report (World Bank 2022), only 9 of the 91 countries that completed 2 comparable household surveys between 2014 and 2019 are in SSA. Such data gaps make it impossible to carry out timely assessments of the impacts of policies or shocks.

There has been a significant increase in the number of surveys used to measure nonmonetary welfare indicators, such as education, nutrition, and living standards (refer to Alkire and Robson 2022). In particular, Demographic and Health Surveys (DHSs) and Multiple Indicator Cluster Surveys are widely used to measure multidimensional poverty and key SDG indicators.[4] Although the DHS data provide relatively comparable indicators for measuring the nonmonetary dimensions of well-being across time and countries, comparing progress on reducing inequality across countries is difficult due to differences in survey timing and frequency (refer to Shifa and Leibbrandt 2022).

Figure 2.1 Survey Data Availability in Sub-Saharan Africa, 1980–2019

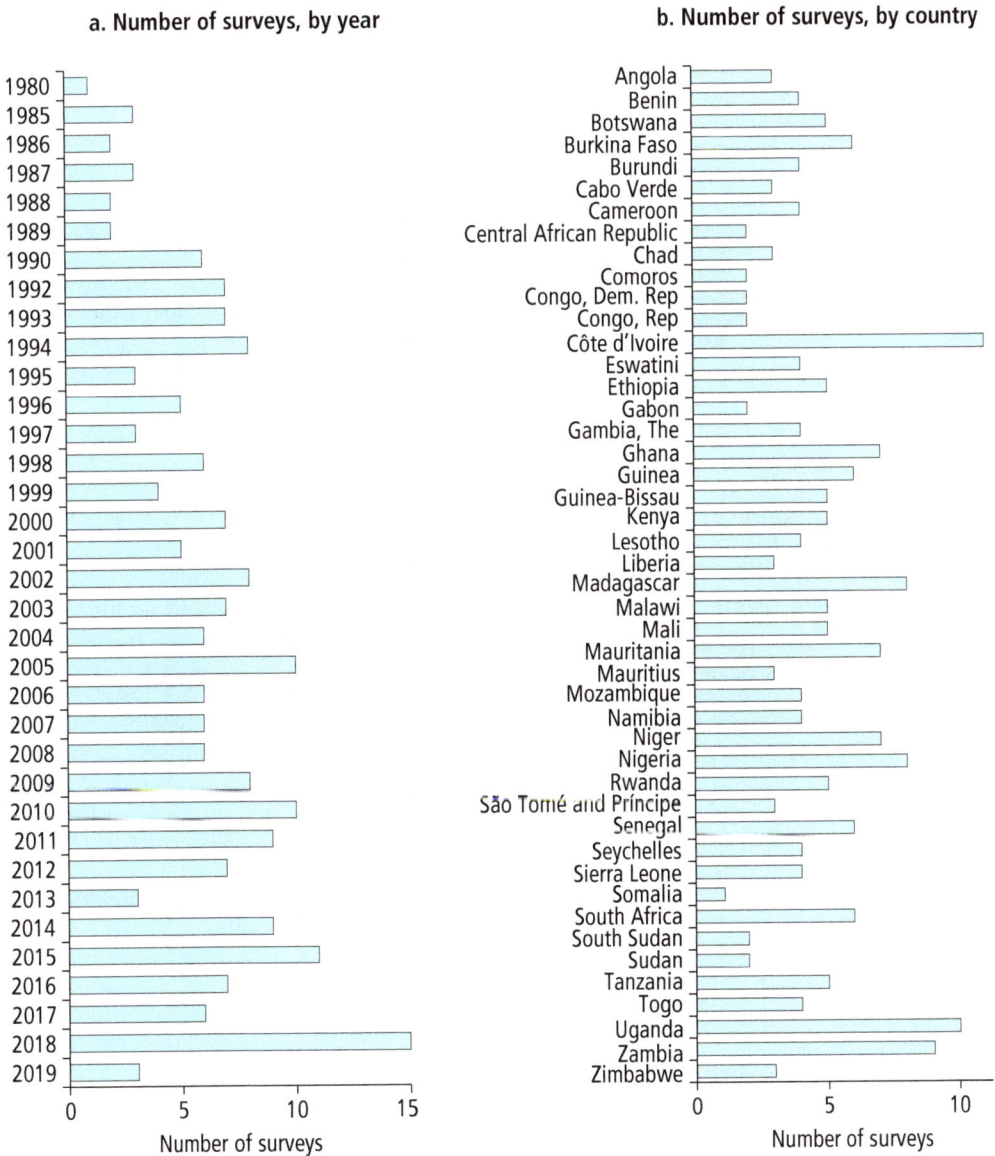

a. Number of surveys, by year

b. Number of surveys, by country

Source: Authors' calculations using data from PovcalNet (https://pip.worldbank.org/).
Note: No surveys were conducted in 1981–1984 and 1991.

Main Challenges for Inequality Measurement in SSA

This section highlights the key problems in analyzing the various dimensions and elements of inequality in SSA. It then considers recent methodological advancements that have helped overcome some of these obstacles, focusing on Ghana, Kenya, and South Africa.

Measuring Income Inequality

The Gini coefficient is the most widely used measure for estimating income inequality. Other commonly used measures include percentile ratios, such as the shares of income that go to the top 10 percent and the top 1 percent, and the Palma ratio (the top 10 percent income share divided by the bottom 40 percent income share). The Gini coefficient (G) can be calculated using the following formula:

$$G = \sum_{i=1}^{N} \sum_{j=1}^{N} \frac{\left| y_i - y_j \right|}{2N^2 \mu} \qquad (2.1)$$

where, y_i and y_j denote the income levels of individuals i and j, respectively; N is population size; and μ is the mean income of the society. The Gini coefficient ranges in value from 0 to 1, where a value of 0 represents perfect equality such that income is distributed equally across all members of a society, and a value of 1 represents perfect inequality such that one person receives all the income in that society.

The Gini coefficient is a measure of relative inequality. Relative inequality measures satisfy the scale-invariant property: increasing everyone's income by the same proportion will not change relative inequality measures.[5]

In contrast, a proportionate change in everyone's income will increase measured inequality if an absolute inequality measure is used, like the absolute Gini coefficient or standard deviation. Although there is no right or wrong approach to choosing an inequality measure, using relative and absolute inequality measures can reveal contradicting trends in inequality (Niño-Zarazúa, Roope, and Tarp 2017; Ravallion 2020). For instance, Niño-Zarazúa et al. (2017) demonstrated that, whereas measures of absolute inequality reveal an increasing trend in global income inequality, measures of relative inequality indicate a declining trend.

Given the prevalence of informality and self-employment in the agriculture and other sectors in many SSA countries, measuring income is difficult. As a result, inequality analyses in SSA rely heavily on consumption data. Using consumption data rather than income can lead to an underestimation of the level of income inequality (Clementi et al. 2020), because traditional consumption surveys do not adequately represent the goods and services used by the top income deciles. Another reason for underestimation arises because rich individuals and households tend to save more, while poor individuals and households tend to smooth consumption more. In addition, high-income individuals and households are underrepresented in both income and consumption surveys (Ravallion 2022).

Various approaches have been used to correct the underestimation of income inequality due to the use of consumption data and missing high-income earners. These approaches include reweighting the data, using a micro-behavioral model to address selective survey response, and using external data like income tax records and national accounts (Chancel et al. 2023; Ravallion 2022). Clementi et al. (2020) have shown that, after adjusting for underreporting of consumption data in six SSA countries,[6] the Gini coefficient estimates increased by about 20 percent.

An alternative approach is to transform consumption data into income data, by using modeling and data from similar countries that have both income and consumption data (Chancel et al. 2023; Gradín 2021). Chancel et al. (2023) have estimated income inequality in African countries between 1990 and 2019 by combining surveys, tax data, and national accounts. However, these approaches make strong assumptions and have limitations. In addition, few countries in SSA conduct surveys that collect both types of data.

South Africa has relatively better data from tax records and other surveys that collect income and consumption data. Recent research combining tax and survey data in South Africa suggests that income and wealth inequality in the country has continued to increase after 2008 (Alvaredo and Atkinson 2022; Assouad, Chancel, and Morgan 2018; Bassier and Woolard 2021; Chatterjee, Czajka, and Gethin 2022). However, based only on survey data, the evidence suggests that income inequality has remained stable or even decreased since 2008 (Checchi, Cupak, and Munzi 2021; Hundenborn, Leibbrandt, and Woolard 2018; Stats SA, SALDRU, and AFD 2019).

In Ghana, the primary source of data for measuring both consumption and income inequality is the Ghana Living Standards Survey (GLSS). There have been seven rounds of the GLSS, beginning with the first round in 1998/99, with an average time interval of about 4–5 years between rounds. However, the methods and content of the questionnaires used for measuring consumption and income have changed significantly, raising concerns about the comparability of the inequality measures over time (Atta-Ankomah, Lambon-Quayefio, and Osei 2023). In addition, public payroll data on wages have been used to measure inequality in Ghana, but these data cover only a small proportion of the population. Information from Ghana's Ministry of Finance indicates that just more than 2 million people, or 8.2 percent of the working population, pay income taxes in Ghana.

Because of the unavailability of reliable income data in most SSA countries, including Ghana and Kenya, Gradín (2021) used a Gini series on consumption to estimate income inequality based on parameter estimates from the relationship between income inequality and consumption, using countries that have data on both measures.

Measuring Wealth Inequality

Using income does not adequately reflect the disparities in access to economic resources. Wealth is a key economic resource used to smooth consumption and assist individuals in mitigating the negative effects of shocks. Measuring wealth at the household or individual level requires information on the value of the stock of assets (financial and nonfinancial assets) at a given point in time, as well as the total value of outstanding liabilities. *Wealth* is defined as the net worth of the stock of total assets less the value of all liabilities. Because many families have negative or zero net wealth (that is, the total value of liabilities for these families is greater than or equal to the value of total assets), standard inequality indexes such as the Gini coefficient are inappropriate. Other measurements, such as the top 10 percent and the bottom 50 percent wealth shares, as well as the mean or median net wealth ratio, are used.

Data for assessing wealth are scarce in developing countries, including those in SSA. The National Income Dynamics Study (NIDS) is one of the few recent household surveys that have gathered data on wealth (assets and liabilities) in South Africa. The evidence from using wealth data demonstrates that wealth is far more unequally distributed in South Africa than income (Daniels and Augustine 2016; Mbewe and Woolard 2016). Efforts have been made to collect similar data in Ghana. However, the information on the value of assets is based on a subjective valuation by the respondents, or the method assumes that the respondents have perfect information concerning the market value of assets, which may not be true, especially in a developing country. Consequently, most studies on wealth inequality have often used asset indexes created from a household's ownership of durable assets as a proxy measure of wealth. The results from such studies show no consistent trend (upward or downward) in asset inequality (refer to, for example, Atta-Ankomah et al. 2020). A study by Oduro and Doss (2018) has shown changes in the portfolio of household wealth over time in Ghana.

When evaluating wealth inequality using household surveys, it is difficult to capture the top owners of wealth. To account for the missing information, some studies have combined survey data with tax data to estimate wealth inequality in South Africa (Chatterjee et al. 2022; Orthofer 2016). Chatterjee et al. (2022) have assessed the distribution of personal wealth in South Africa between 1993 and 2017 by combining microdata from income tax returns, household surveys, and macroeconomic balance sheet statistics. Nevertheless, replicating such an analysis in other SSA countries would be difficult due to a lack of survey data on wealth and of sufficient fiscal statistics given that income and wealth are not effectively taxed in most countries. Furthermore, because of tax evasion, even administrative tax figures are likely to underestimate the amount of wealth disparity in SSA (Zizzamia et al. 2021).

Considering Intrahousehold Income and Wealth Inequality

Income, consumption, and wealth statistics are typically collected at the household level. In addition, to account for household size and composition, per capita or adult equivalent techniques are used. These approaches assume that all income and consumption are pooled within families and divided evenly among household members. Ignoring inequality within households leads to underestimating both overall inequality and poverty levels. For example, using a survey with disaggregated consumption data, De Vreyer and Lambert (2021) showed that intrahousehold consumption inequality accounts for 14 percent of inequality in Senegal. Collecting nationally representative, complex surveys in a similar manner would be difficult, and such surveys are rare.

Analysis of income or wealth inequality by gender is challenging due to a lack of disaggregated income or wealth data. Well-being indicators such as education are often used to measure individual-level outcomes and gender inequalities. Likewise, earnings data have been used to examine gender inequality, but the quality and availability of such data are relatively limited in most SSA countries. For example, whereas South Africa has reasonably good quality and high-frequency labor force surveys (refer to Kerr 2021), such data are not gathered as frequently in Ghana and Kenya.

The most recent independent labor force survey in Kenya was done in 1998/99. However, most of the country's national surveys, such as the Welfare Monitoring Surveys (1992, 1994, and 1997), the Kenya Integrated Household Surveys (2005/06 and 2015/16), and the Kenya Continuous Household Survey Programme (2019, 2020, 2021, and 2022), have included labor modules.

In the case of Ghana, only one labor force survey has been collected to date, and these data are helpful only for studying inequalities in wage income across individuals, which is similar to the GLSS data sets (refer to Atta-Ankomah et al. 2020). A recent analysis of public sector payroll data is also helpful, but this encounters similar challenges, as it does not capture the private and informal sectors (GSS 2022). For studies of wealth and assets, some researchers have collected new data with relatively smaller sample sizes to examine gender gaps and inequalities in wealth and assets at the individual level in Ghana (Deere et al. 2013; Doss, Meinzen-Dick, and Bomuhangi 2014; Oduro, Deere, and Catanzarite 2015).

Analyzing Horizontal and Spatial Inequality

Horizontal inequality assesses inequality in well-being outcomes across well-defined social groups (Stewart 2008). In general, ethnic characteristics (such as tribe, religion, or language) are used to describe social groups in the examination of horizontal inequality in SSA countries. Furthermore, because ethnic groups tend to cluster in spatial units (Alesina, Michalopoulos, and Papaioannou 2016), assessing ethnic inequality frequently corresponds to measuring spatial inequality (inequality between regions in a given country).

Horizontal inequality can be measured using inequality measures such as the population-weighted Gini coefficient and population weighted coefficient of variation. While the Gini coefficient for measuring ethnic inequality is calculated by comparing the average income of every ethnic group with that of every other ethnic group, the coefficient of variation compares the average income of a given group with the overall average income.

The population-weighted coefficient of variation (GCOV) is the most commonly used index for measuring spatial inequalities (Gluschenko 2018). It is calculated using the following formula:

$$GCOV = \frac{\sqrt{\sum_g^m \left(Y_g - \overline{Y}_w\right)^2 * p_g}}{\overline{Y}_w} \qquad (2.2)$$

where m is the number of groups (racial, ethnic, or spatial units), p_g is the population share of group g, $\overline{Y}_w$ is the population share weighted average income of the groups (the overall mean of the income variable), and Y_g is the average income for group g. The higher the value of GCOV, the larger the inequality between the groups (there is greater horizontal inequality).

In addition to the data availability and other measurement issues that come with assessing vertical inequality, quantifying and comparing horizontal inequalities across countries and over time present a set of challenges (Canelas and Gisselquist 2019; Leipziger 2023). Information on ethnicity is not generally captured in standard household surveys that measure welfare outcomes such as income or consumption. In household surveys that do collect information on ethnicity, such as the DHS, minority groups tend to be underrepresented because they are generally found in distant or conflict-prone locations. In countries with many ethnic groups, the sample size often is not representative enough to estimate horizontal inequality among all ethnic groups. Thus, when analyzing horizontal inequality, many minority ethnic groups are grouped together as "other," which ignores the extent of inequality between the "other" groups. Ghana is a good example of a country with many ethnic groups—it has more than 90 ethnic groups.[7] Interestingly, the available studies of horizontal inequality in Ghana tend to focus on analyzing inequalities between spatial units (regions and districts) rather than ethnic groups (Atta-Ankomah et al. 2020; Cooke, Hague, and McKay 2016; GSS 2015). This issue is due to the above-mentioned challenges associated with using household surveys for measuring horizontal inequalities.

Assessing spatial inequality in SSA presents similar challenges (refer to Shifa and Leibbrandt 2022). Standard income and consumption surveys do not provide a representative sample beyond the first geographic administrative regions. For example, Ghana's GLSS data provide a representative sample at the regional level but not for the districts, which are smaller geographic administrative units within the regions.

Census data provide information on ethnicity and representative subsamples in most countries; however, censuses provide limited information on welfare indicators. Due to a lack of income or consumption data, spatial inequality analysis frequently relies on measuring inequalities in access to basic services. South Africa is an exception, with income data collected using the national census and large surveys, such as community surveys. This information enables the estimation of spatial income disparities at lower levels of spatial units.

However, due to a lack of spatially disaggregated price data, spatial income inequality analysis frequently fails to account for price disparities within a given country. Furthermore, frequent changes in administrative units make long-term comparisons of spatial disparities within a country difficult. In Ghana, for example, administrative regions have gone through a series of reorganizations, with the number of regions increasing from 5 in the early 1960s to the current 16. Similarly, the number of administrative districts has increased from 110 in the late 1980s to 216 at present.

Recent studies have used nighttime luminosity data as a proxy indicator (or predictor) of economic activity to overcome the challenge of measuring ethnic and spatial inequalities over time and across countries (Alesina et al. 2016; Lessmann and Seidel 2017). Alesina et al. (2016), for example, combined satellite image data on light density with ethnographic maps that locate ethnolinguistic group homelands to analyze ethnic inequality globally. One challenge is that using nighttime luminosity data to estimate spatial inequality is likely to underestimate spatial inequality in areas where primary activities such as agriculture are the main economic activity, as is the case in many SSA countries (Gibson et al. 2021). Furthermore, ethnographic maps may be less precise in areas where ethnic groups are not spatially clustered, as is common in urban areas due to migration.

Including Social Mobility and Inequality of Opportunity

There are two types of mobility analysis: *intragenerational mobility,* which examines an individual's economic status over time, and *intergenerational mobility,* which compares an individual's economic status to that of their parents. Researchers have used various methods to measure social mobility (Chetty et al. 2014; Fields and Ok 1996; Iversen, Krishna, and Sen 2021). Absolute and relative mobility metrics can be used to measure both types of mobility. *Absolute intergenerational mobility,* for example, assesses the magnitude of a person's positive or negative change in well-being outcomes compared to their parents (or to their own starting position for intragenerational mobility). *Relative intergenerational mobility* measures the degree to which an individual's well-being status is independent of their parents' well-being status. One widely used relative intergenerational mobility measure is the rank-rank slope measure, which can be calculated using the following formula:

$$Rank_{it} = \alpha_0 + \alpha_1\ Rank_{pt\text{-}1} + X\beta + \varepsilon_{it} \qquad\qquad (2.3)$$

where $Rank_{it}$ measures the rank of a child in the income distribution, $Rank_{pt\text{-}1}$ is the rank of the child's parents in the income distribution, and α_1 denotes the extent to which the child's rank in the income distribution (as an adult) is related to their parents' rank in the income distribution. A larger α_1 implies less mobility across generations.

Income transition matrixes can also be used to measure relative mobility, with the proportion of children moving into the top quintile and whose parents were in the bottom quintile being of particular interest. The main limitation of such measures of relative mobility is that the change could be driven by the worse outcomes of children from high-income families rather than the better outcomes of children from low-income families. One option is to use absolute upward mobility measures, such as calculating the probability that a child with parents in the 25th percentile of the income distribution will have an income level above the national poverty line (Chetty et al. 2014).

The concept of inequality of opportunity is strongly linked to social mobility. Inequality in a particular outcome (for example, income or education) is caused by circumstances (factors over which individuals have limited control), effort levels (factors over which individuals have influence), and policy (Brunori, Ferreira, and Peragine 2013; Roemer 2002). Analysis of inequality of opportunity focuses on measuring the extent to which factors other than effort levels influence an individual's well-being outcomes. However, there are various conceptualizations and frameworks for measuring inequality of opportunity (refer to Bosmans and Öztürk 2021; Brunori et al. 2013).

Empirical analysis of inequality of opportunity often involves estimating the extent to which individuals' well-being outcomes may differ due to disparities in ascribed traits (such as parental socioeconomic situations). For example, one study in Ghana has conceptualized and measured inequality of opportunity using differences in personal circumstances such as place of birth, locality of residence, parental education, and presence of parents in the household (Lambon-Quayefio et al. 2020). Using mediation analysis with data from two waves of the Ghana Socioeconomic Panel Survey (GSPS), Lambon-Quayefio et al. (2020) found that inequality of opportunity accounts for 8.1 percent of total consumption inequality in Ghana.

Social mobility and cross-sectional inequality are also strongly linked. Higher inequality is associated with lower levels of social mobility (Corak 2013; DiPrete 2020), primarily because opportunities for achieving better well-being outcomes are more unequally distributed in countries with high levels of cross-sectional inequalities (Brunori et al. 2013; Corak 2013). In this sense, all three concepts—inequality, social mobility, and inequality of opportunity—are interrelated. To explain these relationships, several underlying mechanisms have been proposed (Durlauf, Kourtellos, and Tan 2022).

Measuring mobility or inequality of opportunity requires data that follow individuals over time as well as information about parental characteristics. In general, data on income (or earnings), education, or occupation status are used as common metrics in mobility analyses. However, unlike in developed countries, where data on income, administrative data, or occupation are readily available, such data are not readily available in developing countries (refer to Iversen et al. 2021).

Analyzing welfare dynamics in SSA is challenging, because few countries collect nationally representative panel data (Dang and Dabalen 2019). To address these issues, Dang and Dabalen (2019) have created synthetic panels for 21 SSA countries (Botswana, Burkina Faso, Cameroon, Chad, Democratic Republic of Congo, Côte d'Ivoire, Ethiopia, Ghana, Madagascar, Malawi, Mauritania, Mozambique, Nigeria, Rwanda, Senegal, Sierra Leone, Swaziland, Tanzania, Togo, Uganda, and Zambia), using at least two comparable cross-sectional surveys.[8] In most cases, the available panel data sets are household panels rather than individual panels, and they span short time periods. For example, the GSPS, has only three available waves of the panel data (2009/10, 2013/14, and 2018).

Researchers face similar challenges with using panel data to estimate welfare mobility at the individual level. For example, the relevant welfare concept (that is, consumption) can be measured only at the household level and not at the individual level, and individual income mobility analysis is restricted to wage income and available only for those in paid employment from one period to the other (refer to Atta-Ankomah et al. [2020] and Atta-Ankomah and Osei [2021] for welfare mobility analysis using Ghanaian panel data).

The NIDS in South Africa provides panel data that follow individuals over time, allowing for the measurement of income mobility between 2008 and 2017. Although household and individual panel data sets can be useful for intragenerational mobility analysis, they are not suitable for measuring intergenerational mobility because information on the income levels of partners and adult children is not available. Due to a lack of such data, the analysis of intergenerational mobility in SSA focuses primarily on educational mobility using cross-sectional data, such as census data (Alesina et al. 2021; Ouedraogo and Syrichas 2021; Razzu and Wambile 2022; Van der Weide et al. 2024). For example, Ouedraogo and Syrichas (2021) analyzed intergenerational mobility using education and occupation data from 28 African countries. The Global Database on Intergenerational Mobility provides estimates of absolute and relative intergenerational mobility (Van der Weide et al. 2024).

One advantage of using education is that, unlike income, education can be quantified with more precision and does not change for adult individuals once acquired. However, unlike income and wealth, education and other nonincome indicators have an upper bound, and estimates from social mobility studies point in opposing directions depending on whether income or nonincome indicators are used (Iversen et al. 2021).

In addition, mobility studies are frequently based on a sample of children who live with their parents, which may introduce a cohabitation selection bias. To reduce cohabitation bias, Piraino (2015) and Finn, Leibbrandt, and Ranchhod (2017) have estimated intergenerational earnings mobility in South Africa using NIDS data, after imputing parental earnings. Such an approach is feasible because the NIDS study asked respondents a series of questions about their nonresident or deceased parents' characteristics (such as age, education, and occupation). The GSPS has similar questions; hence, using the approach used by Piraino (2015) and Finn et al. (2017) to estimate intergenerational wage income mobility in Ghana is feasible.

Multidimensional Inequality

Well-being is a multidimensional concept, and its various components can reinforce or complement one another. Making choices on which dimensions to consider and how to calculate a multidimensional inequality index is necessary for measuring multidimensional inequality using a single index. A straightforward approach for producing a multidimensional inequality index is not as developed as is one for calculating inequality indexes based on a single well-being indicator (such as income). Once the relevant dimensions have been chosen, some methods can calculate a multidimensional inequality index (Aaberge and Brandolini 2014).

Sen's capability approach (Sen 2004) has been widely used as a theoretical framework for computing measures of multidimensional well-being. However, Sen does not provide the list of capabilities deemed important for evaluating individual well-being, because this should be determined based on public participation and context (Sen 2004). Studies that use the capability approach as a framework for analyzing multidimensional poverty and inequality measure only functioning and achievements, due to the difficulty of measuring capabilities as defined by Sen. For instance, using micro-level data, the MPI measures multiple deprivations in education, health, and living standards indicators (Alkire and Foster 2011). To analyze well-being inequalities, however, measures like the MPI are not appropriate because they measure only disadvantages.

By suggesting additional domains and indicators for evaluating multidimensional inequality, the MIF attempts to operationalize Sen's capabilities approach (LSE 2018). The MIF includes seven domains and a variety of subdomains. The domains are (1) life and health; (2) physical and legal security; (3) education and learning; (4) financial security and dignified work; (5) comfortable, independent, and secure living conditions; (6) participation, influence, and voice; and (7) individual, family, and social life. The MIF was used to map multidimensional inequalities in five West African countries (Burkina Faso, Ghana, Mali, Niger, and Senegal) in a recent study (Cavero 2020), revealing significant multidimensional inequality by gender, location, income, and ethnic or religious groups.

Using the MIF with SSA countries is difficult, mostly because it requires so much data, and the existing surveys do not provide information on most of the domains for a given year and over time. Furthermore, the technique does not allow assessment of the multiple advantages and disadvantages experienced at the individual level.

Given the practical difficulties, multidimensional inequality measures frequently rely on a few variables of well-being (such as education, health, access to basic services, and household assets). For instance, in studies (Atta-Ankomah et al. 2020; KNBS 2020; Stats SA et al. 2019) of multidimensional inequality in Ghana, Kenya, and South Africa, dimensions of inequality were examined using various analytical techniques and analyzed mostly independently of one another.

Asset indexes have been widely used to measure multidimensional well-being outcomes. For example, in South Africa (Stats SA et al. 2019), 18 indicators were used as a proxy measure for nonincome dimensions of economic well-being, including access to basic services and household assets (such as ownership of a TV, washing machine, car, and computer). However, this approach does not account for variations in the quality or market value of assets owned by the households, because these are not often measured using monetary values. Furthermore, due to survey comparability problems and because different assets might be valued differently depending on the context, it is challenging to develop comparable inequality indicators and measures across countries.

Conclusion

Given that well-being is a multidimensional notion, it is necessary to quantify the various dimensions and aspects of inequality to track trends in individual or social well-being outcomes. However, most SSA inequality analyses have focused on assessing economic inequality, such as income inequality measured using consumption data. Yet, the availability of good quality and high-frequency, long-term consumption surveys (or related surveys) remains scarce in SSA, making it difficult to evaluate the effects of policies or shocks on a timely basis. Similarly, no nationally representative surveys gather information on assets and liabilities to assess wealth disparities, except for those in South Africa. In addition, both income and wealth surveys significantly underestimate inequality in SSA because of missing data on the top income earners and high-wealth individuals.

This chapter highlights recent methodological advances combining tax, national accounts, and survey data to solve some of the problems with estimating wealth and income inequality based on survey data only. Using such an approach in the context of SSA is still challenging due to the lack of tax data and other relevant data sets. Hence, improving the quality and availability of administrative and survey data in SSA nations is critical.

Notes

1. *Evaluative space* in this context indicates all the information required for evaluating well-being.
2. Sen defined *functionings* as the "various things a person may value doing or being" and *capabilities* as "the alternative combinations of functionings that are feasible for her to achieve" (Sen 1999, 75).
3. Other frameworks, such as the Human Rights Framework, have also been used to measure multidimensional poverty and inequality (refer to Gordon et al. 2003).
4. Refer to Alkire and Robson (2022) for a list of data portals that can be used to locate national multitopic household survey data. Refer also to Zizzamia et al. (2021).
5. For an overview of the main inequality axioms, refer to Shifa and Ranchhod (2019).
6. They adjusted the top part of the consumption distribution using information from the income distribution obtained from the same sample using data from Ghana, Kenya, Malawi, Niger, Nigeria, and Uganda.
7. Refer to https://minorityrights.org/country/ghana/.
8. This includes Ethiopia, Ghana, Malawi, Nigeria, South Africa, Tanzania, and Uganda.

References

Aaberge, Rolf, and Andrea Brandolini. 2014. "Multidimensional Poverty and Inequality." Economic Research and International Relations Area, Bank of Italy, Rome. https://EconPapers.repec.org/RePEc :bdi:wptemi:td_976_14.

Alesina, Alberto, Sebastian Hohmann, Stelios Michalopoulos, and Elias Papaioannou. 2021. "Intergenerational Mobility in Africa." *Econometrica* 89 (1): 1–35. https://doi.org/10.3982/ECTA17018.

Alesina, Alberto, Stelios Michalopoulos, and Elias Papaioannou. 2016. "Ethnic Inequality." *Journal of Political Economy* 124 (2): 428–88. https://doi.org/10.1086/685300.

Alkire, Sabina, and James Foster. 2011. "Counting and Multidimensional Poverty Measurement." *Journal of Public Economics* 95 (7): 476–87. https://doi.org/10.1016/j.jpubeco.2010.11.006.

Alkire, Sabina, and Matthew Robson. 2022. "On International Household Survey Data Availability for Assessing Pre-Pandemic Monetary and Multidimensional Poverty in Developing Countries." *Development Studies Research* 9 (1): 277–95. https://doi.org/10.1080/21665095.2022.2141286.

Alvaredo, Facundo, and A. B. Atkinson. 2022. "Top Incomes in South Africa in the Twentieth Century." *Cliometrica* 16 (3): 477–546. https://doi.org/10.1007/s11698-021-00235-4.

Assouad, Lydia, Lucas Chancel, and Marc Morgan. 2018. "Extreme Inequality: Evidence from Brazil, India, the Middle East, and South Africa." *AEA Papers and Proceedings* 108: 119–23. https://doi.org/10.1257 /pandp.20181076.

Atta-Ankomah, Richmond, Monica P. Lambon-Quayefio, and Robert Darko Osei. 2023. "Differences in Inequality Measurement: Ghana Case Study." WIDER Working Paper No. 2023/91, United Nations University, World Institute for Development Economics Research, Helsinki, Finland. https://ideas.repec .org/p/unu/wpaper/wp-2023-91.html.

Atta-Ankomah, Richmond, and Robert Darko Osei. 2021. "Structural Change and Welfare: A Micro Panel Data Evidence from Ghana." *Journal of Development Studies* 57 (11): 1927–44. https://doi.org/10.1080/00220388.2021.1939864.

Atta-Ankomah, Richmond, Robert Darko Osei, Isaac Osei-Akoto, Felix Ankomah Asante, Abena D. Oduro, Nkechi Owoo, Monica Lambon-Quayefio, and Stephen Afranie. 2020. "Inequality Diagnostics for Ghana." African Center of Excellence for Inequalities Research, University of Cape Town, South Africa.

Bassier, Ihsaan, and Ingrid Woolard. 2021. "Exclusive Growth? Rapidly Increasing Top Incomes Amid Low National Growth in South Africa." *South African Journal of Economics* 89 (2): 246–73. https://doi.org/10.1111/saje.12274.

Bosmans, Kristof, and Z. Emel Öztürk. 2021. "Measurement of Inequality of Opportunity: A Normative Approach." *Journal of Economic Inequality* 19 (2): 213–37. https://doi.org/10.1007/s10888-020-09468-1.

Brunori, Paolo, Francisco H. G. Ferreira, and Vito Peragine. 2013. "Inequality of Opportunity, Income Inequality and Economic Mobility: Some International Comparisons." Policy Research Working Paper No. 6304, World Bank, Washington, DC. https://ideas.repec.org/p/wbk/wbrwps/6304.html.

Canelas, Carla, and Rachel M. Gisselquist. 2019. "Horizontal Inequality and Data Challenges." *Social Indicators Research* 143 (1): 157–72. https://doi.org/10.1007/s11205-018-1932-1.

Cavero, Teresa. 2020. "Analysis of Multidimensional Inequalities in West Africa and a Strategy for Inequality Reduction." DEVCO, AFD, AECID and Oxfam Research Project. Agence Française de Développement, Paris.

Chancel, Lucas, Denis Cogneau, Amory Gethin, Alix Myczkowski, and Anne-Sophie Robilliard. 2023. "Income Inequality in Africa, 1990–2019: Measurement, Patterns, Determinants." *World Development* 163: 106162. https://doi.org/10.1016/j.worlddev.2022.106162.

Chatterjee, Aroop, Léo Czajka, and Amory Gethin. 2022. "Wealth Inequality in South Africa, 1993–2017." *World Bank Economic Review* 36 (1): 19–36. https://doi.org/10.1093/wber/lhab012.

Checchi, Daniele, Andrej Cupak, and Teresa Munzi. 2021. "Empirical Challenges Comparing Inequality across Countries: The Case of Middle-Income Countries from the LIS Database." In *Inequality in the Developing World*, edited by Carlos Gradín, Murray Leibbrandt, and Finn Tarp, 74–106. Oxford, United Kingdom: Oxford University Press. https://doi.org/10.1093/oso/9780198863960.003.0004.

Chetty, Raj, Nathaniel Hendren, Patrick Kline, and Emmanuel Saez. 2014. "Where Is the Land of Opportunity? The Geography of Intergenerational Mobility in the United States." *Quarterly Journal of Economics* 129 (4): 1553–623. https://doi.org/10.1093/qje/qju022.

Clementi, Fabio, Andrew Dabalen, Vasco Molini, and Francesco Schettino. 2020. "We Forgot the Middle Class! Inequality Underestimation in a Changing Sub-Saharan Africa." *Journal of Economic Inequality* 18: 45–70. https://doi.org/10.1007/s10888-019-09432-8.

Cooke, Edgar, Sarah Hague, and Andy McKay. 2016. "The Ghana Poverty and Inequality Report: Using the 6th Ghana Living Standards Survey." University of Sussex, Brighton, UK.

Corak, Miles. 2013. "Income Inequality, Equality of Opportunity, and Intergenerational Mobility." *Journal of Economic Perspectives* 27 (3): 79–102. https://doi.org/10.1257/jep.27.3.79.

Dang, Hai-Anh H., and Andrew L. Dabalen. 2019. "Is Poverty in Africa Mostly Chronic or Transient? Evidence from Synthetic Panel Data." *Journal of Development Studies* 55 (7): 1527–47. https://doi.org/10.1080/00220388.2017.1417585.

Daniels, Reza C., and Taryn Augustine. 2016. "The Measurement and Distribution of Household Wealth in South Africa Using the National Income Dynamics Study (NIDS) Wave 4." SALDRU Working Paper No. 183, Southern Africa Labour and Development Research Unit, University of Cape Town, South Africa. https://ideas.repec.org/p/ldr/wpaper/183.html.

De Vreyer, Philippe, and Sylvie Lambert. 2021. "Inequality, Poverty, and the Intra-Household Allocation of Consumption in Senegal." *World Bank Economic Review* 35 (2): 414–35. https://doi.org/10.1093/wber/lhz052.

Deere, Carmen Diana, Abena D. Oduro, Hema Swaminathan, and Cheryl Doss. 2013. "Property Rights and the Gender Distribution of Wealth in Ecuador, Ghana and India." *Journal of Economic Inequality* 11 (2): 249–65. https://doi.org/10.1007/s10888-013-9241-z.

DiPrete, Thomas A. 2020. "The Impact of Inequality on Intergenerational Mobility." *Annual Review of Sociology* 46 (1): 379–98. https://doi.org/10.1146/annurev-soc-121919-054814.

Doss, Cheryl, Ruth Meinzen-Dick, and Allan Bomuhangi. 2014. "Who Owns the Land? Perspectives from Rural Ugandans and Implications for Large-Scale Land Acquisitions." *Feminist Economics* 20 (1): 76–100. https://doi.org/10.1080/13545701.2013.855320.

Durlauf, Steven N., Andros Kourtellos, and Chih Ming Tan. 2022. "The Great Gatsby Curve." *Annual Review of Economics* 14 (1): 571–605. https://doi.org/10.1146/annurev-economics-082321-122703.

Fields, Gary S., and Efe A. Ok. 1996. "The Meaning and Measurement of Income Mobility." *Journal of Economic Theory* 71 (2): 349–77. https://doi.org/10.1006/jeth.1996.0125.

Finn, Arden, Murray Leibbrandt, and Vimal Ranchhod. 2017. "Patterns of Persistence: Intergenerational Mobility and Education in South Africa." SALDRU Working Paper No. 175, Southern Africa Labour and Development Research Unit, University of Cape Town, South Africa.

Gibson, John, Susan Olivia, Geua Boe-Gibson, and Chao Li. 2021. "Which Night Lights Data Should We Use in Economics, and Where?" *Journal of Development Economics* 149: 102602. https://doi.org/10.1016/j.jdeveco.2020.102602.

Gluschenko, Konstantin. 2018. "Measuring Regional Inequality: To Weight or Not to Weight?" *Spatial Economic Analysis* 13 (1): 36–59. https://doi.org/10.1080/17421772.2017.1343491.

Gordon, David, Shailen Nandy, Christina Pantazis, Simon Pemberton, and Peter Townsend. 2003. *Child Poverty in the Developing World*. Bristol, United Kingdom: The Policy Press.

Gradín, Carlos. 2021. "WIID Companion (March 2021): Data Selection." United Nations University, World Institute for Development Economics Research, Helsinki, Finland. https://doi.org/10.35188/UNU-WIDER/WTN/2021-4.

GSS (Ghana Statistical Service). 2015. *Ghana Poverty Mapping Report*. Accra: GSS.

GSS (Ghana Statistical Service). 2022. *Ghana 2022 Earnings Inequality in the Public Sector*. Accra: GSS.

Hillesund, Solveig, Karim Bahgat, Gray Barrett, Kendra Dupuy, Scott Gates, Håvard Mokleiv Nygård, Siri Aas Rustad, Håvard Strand, Henrik Urdal, and Gudrun Østby. 2018. "Horizontal Inequality and Armed Conflict: A Comprehensive Literature Review." *Canadian Journal of Development Studies/Revue Canadienne d'études Du Développement* 39 (4): 463–80. https://doi.org/10.1080/02255189.2018.1517641.

Hundenborn, Janina, Murray Leibbrandt, and Ingrid Woolard. 2018. "Drivers of Inequality in South Africa." WIDER Working Paper No. 2018/162, United Nations University, World Institute for Development Economics Research, Helsinki, Finland. https://doi.org/10.35188/UNU-WIDER/2018/604-3.

Iversen, Vegard, Anirudh Krishna, and Kunal Sen. 2021. *Social Mobility in Developing Countries*. Oxford, United Kingdom: Oxford University Press. https://global.oup.com/academic/product/social-mobility -in-developing-countries-9780192896858?prevNumResPerPage=20&prevSortField=1&sortField=8&res ultsPerPage=20&start=0&lang=en&cc=gb.

Kerr, Andrew. 2021. "Measuring Earnings Inequality in South Africa Using Household Survey and Administrative Tax Microdata." WIDER Working Paper No. 2021/82, United Nations University, World Institute for Development Economics Research, Helsinki, Finland. https://doi.org/10.35188/UNU -WIDER/2021/020-7.

KNBS (Kenya National Bureau of Statistics). 2020. *Inequality Trends and Diagnostics in Kenya 2020*. Nairobi: KNBS.

Lambon-Quayefio, Monica P., Robert D. Osei, Abena D. Oduro, and Isaac Osei Akoto. 2020. "Understanding the Relationship between Consumption Inequality, Inequality of Opportunity and Education Outcomes in Ghana." AFD Research Paper 159, Agence Française de Développement, Paris.

Leipziger, Lasse Egendal. 2023. "Measuring Ethnic Inequality: An Assessment of Extant Cross-National Indices." *British Journal of Political Science* 53 (2): 652–73. https://doi.org/10.1017/S000712342200014X.

Lessmann, Christian, and André Seidel. 2017. "Regional Inequality, Convergence, and Its Determinants—A View from Outer Space." *European Economic Review* 92: 110–32. https://doi.org /10.1016/j.euroecorev.2016.11.009.

LSE (London School of Economics and Political Science). 2018. *Multidimensional Inequality Framework*. London: LSE.

Mbewe, Samson, and Ingrid Woolard. 2016. "Cross-Sectional Features of Wealth Inequality in South Africa: Evidence from the National Income Dynamics Study." SALDRU Working Paper No. 185, Southern Africa Labour and Development Research Unit, University of Cape Town, South Africa. https://api.semanticscholar.org/CorpusID:157079862.

Niño-Zarazúa, Miguel, Laurence Roope, and Finn Tarp. 2017. "Global Inequality: Relatively Lower, Absolutely Higher." *Review of Income and Wealth* 63 (4): 661–84. https://doi.org/10.1111/roiw.12240.

Oduro, Abena D., Carmen Diana Deere, and Zachary B. Catanzarite. 2015. "Women's Wealth and Intimate Partner Violence: Insights from Ecuador and Ghana." *Feminist Economics* 21 (2): 1–29. https://doi.org /10.1080/13545701.2014.997774.

Oduro, Abena D., and Cheryl R. Doss. 2018. "Changing Patterns of Wealth Distribution: Evidence from Ghana." *Journal of Development Studies* 54 (5): 933–48. https://doi.org/10.1080/00220388.2018.1430769.

Orthofer, Anna. 2016. "Wealth Inequality in South African Evidence from Survey and Tax Data." REDI3x3 Working Paper No. 15, Southern Africa Labour and Development Research Unit, University of Cape Town, South Africa.

Ouedraogo, Rasmane, and Nicolas Syrichas. 2021. "Intergenerational Social Mobility in Africa Since 1920." IMF Working Paper No. 2021/215, International Monetary Fund, Washington, DC. https://doi.org/10.5089 /9781513593807.001.

Piraino, Patrizio. 2015. "Intergenerational Earnings Mobility and Equality of Opportunity in South Africa." *World Development* 67: 396–405. https://doi.org/10.1016/j.worlddev.2014.10.027.

Ravallion, Martin. 2020. "Ethnic Inequality and Poverty in Malaysia since May 1969. Part 1: Inequality." *World Development* 134 (C). https://doi.org/10.1016/j.worlddev.2020.1.

Ravallion, Martin. 2022. "Missing Top Income Recipients." *Journal of Economic Inequality* 20 (1): 205–22. https://doi.org/10.1007/s10888-022-09530-0.

Razzu, Giovanni, and Ayago Wambile. 2022. "Four Decades of Intergenerational Educational Mobility in Sub-Saharan Africa." *Journal of Development Studies* 58 (5): 931–50. https://doi.org/10.1080/00220388.2021.2008366.

Roemer, John E. 2002. "Equality of Opportunity: A Progress Report." *Social Choice and Welfare* 19 (2): 455–71. https://doi.org/10.1007/s003550100123.

Sen, Amartya. 1992. *Inequality Reexamined*. Oxford: Clarendon Press.

Sen, Amartya. 1999. *Development as Freedom*. Oxford: Oxford University Press.

Sen, Amartya. 2004. "Capabilities, Lists, and Public Reason: Continuing the Conversation." *Feminist Economics* 10 (3): 77–80. https://doi.org/10.1080/1354570042000315163.

Shifa, Muna, and Murray Leibbrandt. 2022. "Spatial Inequality in Sub-Saharan Africa." *African Geographical Review* 43 (1): 1–17. https://doi.org/10.1080/19376812.2022.2099916.

Shifa, Muna, and Vimal Ranchhod. 2019. "Handbook on Inequality Measurement for Country Studies." African Center of Excellence for Inequalities Research, University of Cape Town, South Africa.

Stats SA (Statistics South Africa), SALDRU (Southern Africa Labour and Development Research Unit), and AFD (Agence Française de Développement). 2019. *Inequality Trends in South Africa: A Multidimensional Diagnostic of Inequality, 2017*. Pretoria: Stats SA, SALDRU, and AFD.

Stewart, Frances, ed. 2008. *Horizontal Inequalities and Conflict*. London: Palgrave Macmillan UK. https://doi.org/10.1057/9780230582729.

Stiglitz, Joseph, Amartya Sen, and Jean Fitoussi. 2009. "Report of the Commission on the Measurement of Economic Performance and Social Progress." www.stiglitz-sen-fitoussi.fr.

Van der Weide, Roy, Christoph Lakner, Daniel Gerszon Mahler, Ambar Narayan, and Rakesh Gupta. 2024. "Intergenerational Mobility around the World: A New Database." *Journal of Development Economics* 166: 103167. https://doi.org/10.1016/j.jdeveco.2023.103167.

World Bank. 2022. *Poverty and Shared Prosperity 2022: Correcting Course*. Washington, DC: World Bank.

Zizzamia, Rocco, Anda David, and Murray Leibbrandt. 2021. "Inequality in Sub-Saharan Africa: A Review Paper." AFD Research Paper 207, Agence française de développement, Paris.

PART 2

Analyzing and Tackling Multidimensional Inequalities

Chapter 3

Inequalities in Education and Health

Monica Lambon-Quayefio, Vimal Ranchhod, Nkechi Owoo, Moses Muriithi, Linda Zanfini, Reuben Mutegi, and Germano Mwabu

Introduction

Many countries in Sub-Saharan Africa (SSA) have significantly improved access to education and health, which has resulted in improved human capital outcomes in recent years. However, SSA is still characterized by inequalities in both areas, which are closely linked. These inequalities reinforce each other, leading to a situation in which progress in some human capital outcomes is adversely affected by lack of advancement in other dimensions. Access to education and health not only influences people's ability to live better lives but also allows them to participate more effectively in economic and political activities (Sen 2000). Disparities in education and health levels are key determinants of labor market outcomes and, thus, are key drivers of income inequality.

In developing-country contexts, inequalities in education and health are important sources of overall economic inequality, with the two sources primarily engendered by inequality of opportunity (Lambon-Quayefio et al. 2020). *Inequality of opportunity* implies that inherited circumstances, such as gender, race, location of birth, and family background, can affect an individual's life outcomes, such as earnings, educational achievement, and occupation. Inequality of opportunity has been identified as the component of inequality that is most difficult to tackle (Lambon-Quayefio et al. 2020).

For health, inequality of opportunity manifests through disparities in access to health care, health care outcomes, and health knowledge. Similarly, inequality of opportunity in education can manifest through disparities in access to quality education, educational achievements, and command over educational resources. These disparities not only affect individuals' well-being but also contribute to the persistence of inequalities and limit upward mobility, which is why they are treated together in this chapter. Addressing inequality of opportunity in both domains is crucial for reducing fundamental disparities in well-being. Equitable access to education and health is the key lever that policy makers can use to tackle inequality of opportunity to minimize unfair treatment in society.

This chapter highlights the main features of unequal access and outcomes in the domains of education and health by drawing on examples from Burkina Faso, the Democratic Republic of Congo, Côte d'Ivoire, Ghana, Kenya, Malawi, Senegal, South Africa, and Zambia. First, the chapter covers inequalities in primary, secondary, and tertiary education. Second, it focuses on inequalities in access to health care services and maternal and child health outcomes. Finally, the chapter highlights the interlinkages between education and health and how these human capital dimensions can affect labor market outcomes and household welfare in SSA.

Educational Inequalities

Education is one of the most-important contributors to economic development and, recognizing this, African leaders have consistently prioritized education in their development agendas. Since independence, primary school enrollment has increased to more than 80 percent on average, with the African continent experiencing some of the largest increases in elementary school enrollment in the developing regions (UIS 2023). Despite the increase, average enrollment in basic education remains below the 2015 target of universal primary education that was part of the Millennium Development Goals. The data show that SSA has the highest rates of educational exclusion of any region, with one-fifth of children between ages 6 and 11 years not in school, as well as one-third of youth between ages 12 and 14 years. Enrollment rates for education above the primary level are even lower than for primary school. According to the United Nations Educational, Scientific and Cultural Organization's Institute of Statistics, nearly 60 percent of youth between ages 15 and 17 years are not enrolled in school.

Gender disparities remain in enrollment, with girls lagging across the region. At the primary school level, 23 percent of girls drop out, compared to 19 percent of boys. By the time they reach adolescence, girls have a 36-percent exclusion rate, compared to 32 percent for boys (UIS 2023).

Therefore, understanding educational inequality is critical, as the unequal distribution of educational opportunities and outcomes may result in the transmission of unequal opportunities across generations. A more-equitable distribution of educational opportunity is thought to be a catalyst for reducing poverty and income inequality (Földvári and van Leeuwen 2011; Grimm 2005; Park 1996). Social institutions also play an important role in shaping educational equality (Fontanella, Sarra, and Di Zio 2020). The main drivers of inequalities in education include family characteristics, such as wealth status (Lindahl et al. 2015; Nikolai and Helbig 2021), and social and cultural norms that lead to parents investing more in the education of male children versus female children (Erikson and Erikson 2019). The following subsections explore inequality in primary, secondary, and tertiary education in select African countries.

Inequality in Primary and Secondary Education

Over the past decades, enrollment in education in SSA has expanded. From 1971 to 2015, the median proportion of children completing primary school across countries increased from

27 percent to 67 percent, and the median proportion completing lower secondary school increased from 5 percent in 1971 to 40 percent in 2015 (World Bank 2020). However, despite these gains, the quality of education has not improved commensurately, as a high number of students have limited literacy or numeracy skills after years of schooling, in what has been identified as a "learning crisis" (Adeniran, Ishaku, and Akanni 2020; Bold et al. 2018).

The gains in school enrollment have been the result of the implementation of policy reforms targeting primary and secondary education in many African countries. This subsection delves into the inequalities in primary and secondary education, with examples from Burkina Faso, Côte d'Ivoire, Ghana, Kenya, and South Africa. Over the years, these countries have implemented education reforms targeting free primary and secondary education, which has been observed to increase access to education.

In Ghana, the Free and Compulsory Universal Basic Education program was introduced in 1995, and the Free Senior High School and Technical and Vocational program was rolled out in 2017/18. Ghana also introduced the Capitation Grant[1] in 2004 and the School Feeding Program in 2005. Kenya introduced Free Primary and Free Day Secondary Education in 2003 and 2018, respectively (Mutegi, Wanjala, and Muriithi 2017). In Burkina Faso, basic education benefited from the Education Orientation Law (Kouraogo and Dianda 2008), which mandated universal compulsory free basic education in all 45 provinces. These policies aim to improve access to primary and secondary education, particularly for disadvantaged groups, such as girls and poor individuals, with the objective of achieving educational equality. However, the literature (Atta-Ankomah et al. 2020; GSS 2022; KNBS 2020; Ouilili et al. 2020; Stats SA, SALDRU, and AFD 2019) still shows disparities in access, transition rates, and completion rates across the five countries based on gender, area of residence, and geographic location.

The education reform policies have generally been observed to increase access to education. In Burkina Faso, Ghana, Kenya, and South Africa, gross and net enrollment ratios increased significantly following the introduction of the education policies for both primary and secondary education. However, despite these increases, differences exist by gender, area of residence, and geographical area. For enrollment, gender gaps differ across countries, with the gap closing in Kenya, widening in favor of girls in Ghana, and remaining in Côte d'Ivoire, where girls still have less access to school than boys do. In Ghana, for example, the primary net attendance rates of boys and girls were roughly equal in 2005/06 (approximately 68 percent), with the gap widening to about 3.3 percentage points in favor of girls by 2016/17 (Atta-Ankomah et al. 2020). In Kenya, the gap has been closing, with the proportion of boys ages 6–18 years attending school increasing from 77.2 percent in 1994 to 90.9 percent in 2015/16, while the figure for girls increased from 73.3 percent to 90.4 percent (KNBS 2020).

For disparities by income, according to data from the seventh round of the Ghana Living Standards Survey, the junior high school net enrollment rate for those in the highest income quintile is more than three times higher than that of the lowest quintile (51.9 percent versus 16.4 percent), and at the secondary level, the difference is approximately eight times higher (40.3 percent versus 5.5 percent). In Kenya, the proportion of poor children ages 6–18 years attending school increased from

70.9 percent in 1994 to 87.2 percent in 2015/16, while the proportion of nonpoor children attending school increased from 79.4 percent in 1994 to 93.4 percent in 2015/16 (KNBS 2020). These findings highlight the role of income inequality in widening the enrollment gap and ultimately educational attainment and future earnings.

Enrollment data also show disparities across geographical areas within countries. In South Africa, the province of Limpopo has the highest percentage of school-age children attending an educational institution, 98.8 percent in 2017. This high level of attendance reflects the impact of South Africa's progressive education system, which mandates compulsory primary education and provides "no-fee" schools for students from low-income families (Stats SA et al. 2019). In 2017, the Northern and Western Cape had the lowest attendance rates in the country, 92.7 percent and 93.0 percent, respectively.

Kenya also exhibits regional disparities, with some counties, such as Mandera and Wazir, having low rates of access to all levels of basic education, while others have high rates of access. In Burkina Faso and Kenya, large inequalities persist between rural and urban areas, with rural and marginalized populations having lower access to education (KNBS 2020; Ouilili et al. 2020). In Ghana, data from the population and housing census show a sharp north-south divide in educational attainment (GSS 2022).

Disparities also persist for completion rates, with the poorest quintiles having much lower completion rates than the richest quintile in Burkina Faso for both primary and secondary school. In Côte d'Ivoire, nearly 22 percent of students did not complete primary school, 45 percent did not complete lower secondary school, and 70 percent did not complete upper secondary school in the survey period (Sefa-Nyarko, Kyei, and Mwambari 2018). Household income quintile, region of residence, and social norms appear to be the main drivers of educational inequality in most of these countries. These persistent challenges in access to quality primary and secondary education impede access not only to quality higher education but also to decent jobs in the future.

Inequality in Higher Education

Educational attainment is generally positively correlated with household income or consumption levels.[2] In the Southern African Customs Union (SACU) countries (except Lesotho), education is a main driver of wage inequality, and returns to tertiary education range from 80 percent in South Africa to 121 percent in Namibia (World Bank 2020). In South Africa, members of households whose heads have a higher education have an average expenditure that is two, five, and eight times higher than those whose household heads have a secondary school diploma, no secondary school education, and only primary school education, respectively (Stats SA et al. 2019). In Kenya, the differences are smaller, but the average consumption of members of households headed by a person with a higher education is at least three times higher than that of members of households headed by a person with no education (KNBS 2020), and the former also have greater access to mobile phones and the internet.

In Ghana, the incidence of poverty was only 6.4 percent for households whose heads had secondary or higher education, compared to 17.5 percent, 28.8 percent, and 49.7 percent for those whose heads had completed basic education, less than basic education, and no education, respectively (these trends remained nearly unchanged between 2005 and 2017) (Atta-Ankomah et al. 2020). In the Democratic Republic of Congo, poverty does not spare households whose heads have a higher education (26.9 percent of whom are considered poor), but the proportion of poor people is more than twice as high in other households (Poncelet and Kapagama 2020), and the children of fathers with a higher education have greater access to the same level of education, especially in Kinshasa.

The importance of tertiary education in promoting household well-being lies in the fact that it increases the chances of being employed, but the relationship between education and employment is not always linear. For example, in SACU countries (except Lesotho), "people with some form of tertiary education are over 20 percent more likely to have a job than those without formal education" (World Bank 2020, 52). In contrast, in Burkina Faso, the employment rate decreases when the level of education increases, and the employment rate among graduates of higher education is similar to the rate among those with a post-primary education (Kobiane, Ouilili, and Guissou 2020). In Burkina Faso, the supply of tertiary education also does not match the needs of the local economy, thus contributing to unemployment and underemployment.

The same mismatch between skills and jobs can be observed in Côte d'Ivoire (Aka et al. 2020). In this country, a higher education diploma, especially in a technical or professional field, reduces the risk of unemployment, but it increases the risk of underemployment (as graduates are often overeducated). There is also a significant difference between graduates of general and technical or vocational courses, with the latter benefitting from a better "horizontal" match between their qualifications and the needs of the labor market. However, there is also some evidence of overskilling ("vertical mismatch"), as the labor market does not offer enough formal jobs. Greater recognition of private university degrees in the labor market also occurs because the private institutions are better connected to the business world.

Higher education can play a key role in achieving the United Nations Sustainable Development Goals (SDGs) and fighting poverty and inequality, and it is a keystone for the development of education systems. In Africa, policies for universal access to primary and secondary school and the emergence of a middle class has resulted in increased demands for higher education, which—combined with the needs of the labor market—has placed high expectations on the higher education sectors. In most SSA countries, the possibility of higher education remained very low in the first decades after independence and was mainly limited to universities created during the colonial period. The expansion of higher education took place in the late 1980s and early 1990s and continued over the following decades. Initially, higher education was the responsibility of the public sector, as in Burkina Faso, Kenya, and Senegal and, to a lesser extent, in the Democratic Republic of Congo (due to the institutional crisis).

However, private-sector involvement has increased since the 1990s in the Democratic Republic of Congo, Kenya, and Senegal. Today, enrollment rates in higher education have increased significantly throughout the region. However, they remain comparatively low: Fewer than

500,000 students in the Democratic Republic of Congo in 2016 (Poncelet and Kapagama 2020), 15–16 percent in Ghana (Atta-Ankomah et al. 2020), and less than 10 percent in Kenya (KNBS 2020). The share of the private sector varies, from 20 percent of higher education enrollments in Senegal (Dia and Goudiaby 2020) to more than 34 percent in the Democratic Republic of Congo.

Despite the broadening of access to higher education, which can be observed, for example, in Burkina Faso and, to a lesser extent, in South Africa, strong inequalities persist across students, especially according to their starting cultural and economic capital. The fees charged by certain establishments, particularly private ones, represent a real economic barrier to entry, as illustrated by studies on the Democratic Republic of Congo (Poncelet and Kapagama 2020) and Senegal (Dia and Goudiaby 2020). In the Democratic Republic of Congo, the general cost of access to university is relatively low, but most institutions carry out a selection process using academic results or examinations, and the few truly "elitist" universities charge very high fees. In Senegal, the cost of education is also strongly linked to the quality of teaching.

In both countries, scholarships and grants enable a few less-fortunate students to access certain private institutions, thus promoting social diversity but not real integration, which remains hampered by the differential in cultural capital. However, in Senegal, private confessional institutions allow students who have completed their schooling in Arab-Islamic confessional education to access higher education, thus correcting, without completely erasing, a form of inequality.

South Africa—for which information on attainment levels is available—provides further insights and confirms the trends observed in the other SSA countries, namely, strong regional disparities and—above all—inequalities between population groups. The White population has attainment levels that are three times higher than those of the other groups, "reflecting inequalities in access to education during apartheid."

> Furthermore, although all population groups have seen an increase in the post-school qualification share since 1994, the growth has been 10 and 14 percentage points within the White and Indian population groups and only 5 and 7 percentage points within the African and Coloured population groups. This [disparity] has widened the gap in post-school attainment between groups (University of Cape Town, n.d.).

In all these cases, socioeconomic and spatial inequalities overlap and intersect, particularly due to the social geography of higher education, where the urban-rural continuum is correlated with universities with different levels of cost and quality.

Although gender inequality has almost been eliminated in access to primary education and is greatly reduced in secondary education, it persists in higher education. In Kenya, it has even increased over time, as universities were equally attended by male and female students in 1994, and 20 years later, the proportion of male students was 57.6 percent, while that of female students was only 42.4 percent (KNBS 2020). Gender disparities also exist in education sectors, with women often underrepresented in the fields of science, technology, engineering, and mathematics (STEM). The underrepresentation of women in STEM sectors can partly be explained by the social and cultural norms around gender roles in society, which are detailed in chapter 5.

Inequalities also materialize in the unequal value of education, in both quality and recognition by the labor market. In Senegal, there is a double divide between public and private institutions and—within the private sector—between "first-," "second-," and "third-class" educational institutions. Private institutions, especially the elite universities in the central districts of Dakar, offer better quality training and are generally characterized by high costs for attendance. In contrast, in the peripheral regions and the outskirts of large cities, lower-quality and lower-cost institutions attract mainly students from modest backgrounds for short-term studies in vocational fields (Dia and Goudiaby 2020).

In the Democratic Republic of Congo, where places in private higher education institutions are abundant, private higher education has more-favorable staffing levels but fewer qualified teachers than the public sector, which recruits instructors from abroad (Poncelet and Kapagama 2020). Institutions in remote or rural areas are often unaccredited and lack teachers and infrastructure; students from these areas face both poor access and low-quality education. The private sector offers vocational training to meet the needs of the labor market but is not always able to keep pace, as only elite and expensive institutions can guarantee professional integration.

In other words, in these countries, as in other parts of the world, private institutions facilitate access to higher education for populations with limited financial resources or living in remote areas. However, access to quality higher education (private or public) depends largely on students' backgrounds (such as economic, socioprofessional, and parental educational level).

Overall, tertiary education improves access to better jobs and opportunities; thus, it can contribute to a relative reduction in inequalities. However, when the chances of access are very unequal—as in Africa—higher education can also crystallize privileges. This phenomenon is amplified by that of multispeed systems, where students experience different values and live in different contexts, and training for the lower middle classes allows broader access to education and, therefore, a degree of social mobility, but this education has a lower value and fewer returns. This multilayered complexity confronts young people, especially those from lower-middle-class backgrounds, with a glass ceiling and contributes to maintaining and reproducing inequalities, including economic ones, across generations.

Inequality and Inequity in the Use of Health Care Services

The demand for health care is derived from the fundamental demand for good health, which is required for consumption and investment purposes, as argued by Grossman (1972). Thus, demand for health care services provides the necessary insight into how populations access and utilize health care. The use of quality health inputs contributes to better health outcomes. Inequalities in access to health inputs affect the utilization of health services, thus perpetuating inequities in population health outcomes, including those related to mortality, illnesses, and mental health. Health outcomes are the ultimate goals of countries' health programs and policies. Access to health care is central to the performance of health systems, and measurement of access to quality health care has a prominent role in the health policy literature (Levesque, Harris, and Russell 2013). Most studies agree that access to health services is a multidimensional concept that encompasses the financing, organization, and delivery of services and the interactions of groups and individuals that lead to service utilization (for example, refer to Gulliford et al. 2002).

Sustainable access to and improved utilization of health care services are vital for the physical, social (ability to interact with and form meaningful relationships with others), and mental health of the population. This section provides insights into health care utilization through the lens of inequality, citing examples from African countries. The literature (Gulliford et al. 2002; Ilinca et al. 2019; KNBS 2020; Stats SA et al. 2019) has demonstrated that African countries have high levels of inequality in access to health care services.

This assessment concentrates on inequalities in health inputs and how they have affected health care utilization and consequent health outcomes. Health care utilization is often linked to income inequality. The level and distribution of income and poverty levels are often important contributors to health inequalities within populations. People with higher levels of education and incomes tend to be in better health and live longer. Health inequalities can also contribute to increased income inequality, as good health can enhance the opportunity to participate in the labor market. People who are in poor physical or mental health are less likely to work and more likely to be unemployed, compared with people in better health.

Socioeconomic Inequalities in Health Care

Inequality in access to health care has become prominent in SSA as defined by the availability, affordability, accessibility, and acceptability of health services (Gulliford et al. 2002). Access to health care promotes a healthy life and prevents diseases, disabilities, and premature deaths, hence enhancing health equity for all (Munthali et al. 2019). Therefore, addressing health inequality through the provision of health care has become a top priority of both regional and international organizations.

In Kenya, the main socioeconomic factors driving inequality in health care use are total household expenditure, educational achievement, household characteristics, and living standards, all of which are proportionately distributed in favor of richer individuals and better-off households (KNBS 2020). Analysis of access to health care services by area of residence shows that access is higher for rural households than for urban households (KNBS 2020). In 2015, 66 percent of the urban population in Kenya sought health care from a public facility. In South Africa, given the demographic component of poverty, a majority of Black African- and Coloured-headed households, which are the poorest individuals, usually use public facilities, while a majority of households headed by Indians, other Asians, and Whites, which are the richest, use private facilities.

South Africa contrasts with Kenya, where the poor and nonpoor populations seem to utilize both public and private facilities almost equally (KNBS 2020; Stats SA et al. 2019). Malawi contrasts with Kenya; like in South Africa, in Malawi, the poorest individuals are less inclined to use private health facilities. In Zambia, the poor populations use more health services at all levels of care than does the least-poor population (Rudasingwa et al. 2020a).

Inequality analysis shows that, in South Africa, on average, it takes rural households longer to reach a health care facility, compared to their urban counterparts (Stats SA et al. 2019). Inequality trends in South Africa also show substantial differences in health care access by race and across provinces. Using concentration indexes for outpatient, inpatient, and preventive and promotive care, Ilinca et al. (2019) observed that, in Kenya, richer individuals use more health services than their respective population proportion, while groups with a lower socioeconomic status (SES) access a significantly lower share of health care services, irrespective of the type of service. In Burkina Faso, the least-poor segments of the population use more outpatient and inpatient services than do the poor segments, especially for inpatient services. This finding for Burkina Faso is consistent with that for Malawi, where rich groups in the population use more health services than poor groups do (Rudasingwa et al. 2020a).

Atta-Ankomah et al. (2020) have noted that, in seeking health care, Ghanaian households in the upper-income quintiles spend more travel time than those in the lower quintiles, and rural households spend more travel time than urban households. For consultations with doctors, the proportion of women who consult a doctor is higher than that of men on average in Ghana. The rich population consults doctors more than the poor population, as shown by doctor consultations by income quintiles, where the fifth quintile has more doctor consultations than the first quintile.

In Burkina Faso, Rudasingwa et al. (2020b) showed that women from nonpoor households use more institutional delivery services than women from poorer households, and there is a higher level of inequality at public hospitals compared to public health centers. The same paper reported similar findings in Malawi, where there are more institutional deliveries at public hospitals among women from the least-poor households compared with women from poorer households, among whom there are more institutional deliveries at public health centers. In Zambia, persistent inequality in the use of facility-based deliveries is noted across socioeconomic groups. Over 95 percent of the deliveries in the highest quintile are assisted by a health care worker, compared to only 50 percent of those in the lowest quintile (Rudasingwa et al. 2020b).

Inequalities also persist with access to safe drinking water, sanitation, and adequate hygiene (WASH) facilities, which particularly affect the poor and vulnerable populations in rural areas (Acheampong, Opoku, and Tetteh 2024). Unequal access to WASH facilities has severe implications for diseases and poor public health, which are more widespread in rural areas and among the poorest individuals. Using a panel data set of 119 countries between 2004 and 2020, Acheampong et al. (2024) highlighted the roles of income inequality and financial inclusion in accessing improved WASH facilities. Wealth inequalities constitute a major obstacle to accessing basic WASH services, with the richest individuals having better access than poor individuals. Acheampong et al. (2024) also showed that improving financial inclusion reduces the negative effect of income inequality on safe WASH adoption and practices. Social welfare policies could be adopted to tackle income inequality and enhance financial inclusion.

Health Financing

Another issue related to health care services in African countries is health care financing.[3] The means of financing health care in Africa has been identified as a barrier to access to health care and increases the likelihood of the impoverishment of households, especially in developing countries, where direct (out-of-pocket) payments form a greater proportion of the sources of health care financing (WHO 2013). Several African countries are implementing health financing reforms aimed at increasing access to health services and financial risk protection, with the goal of reducing inequities. The reforms are focusing on moving closer to the policy objective of universal health coverage.

The World Health Organization notes that many African countries have put in place mechanisms to protect the poor and vulnerable population groups, including measures that have abolished or reduced user fees at the point of access to health services (WHO 2013). This subsection provides some perspectives on inequalities in health care financing from select African countries.

In South Africa, Black Africans, Coloureds and Indians, and other Asians who reported having a chronic illness had significantly lower levels of access to medical aid relative to Whites.[4] It is also notable that people in rural provinces and Black Africans tend to lag further behind in access to medical aid. Black African women who have chronic illnesses are the least covered by medical aid relative to the rest of the population, especially when compared to Indian, other Asian, and White men. Ataguba (2021) noted that, although private health insurance contributions may reduce income inequality, enrollees are only a small and generally rich minority. Lack of access to medical aid severely constrains access to South Africa's extensive, high-quality private health care system.

In Burkina Faso, the least-poor women disproportionately benefited from total health spending in all public health facilities compared to poor women. However, between 2003 and 2017, there was a continuous reduction of inequality among the poor and least-poor women in the financial benefits offered by public facilities and overall health care spending (Rudasingwa et al. 2020b). This finding is explained in part by health policies, such as the reduction and removal of user fees for delivery services, and performance-based financing schemes that were implemented to improve access to delivery services, especially for poor groups.

Decomposition of public spending into inpatient and outpatient care shows that inpatient care remained largely pro-least-poor. Rudasingwa et al. (2020a) found that, in Burkina Faso, public spending on outpatient care was initially pro-least-poor in 2009 and 2014 but changed to pro-poor in 2017. A benefit incidence analysis of public subsidies for public spending on curative care reveals a pro-least-poor trend in urban settings.

In Malawi, overall spending on maternal care disproportionately benefits the least-poor groups in public hospitals and the poorest groups in public health centers. This finding contrasts with Zambia, where total spending and hospital spending on maternal care were found to be pro-poor (Rudasingwa et al. 2020b). It is also notable that, in Zambia, implementation of universal health coverage policies has led to a reduction in socioeconomic inequality in health spending, particularly at health centers and for curative care (Rudasingwa et al. 2022). In Kenya, the existence of pro-rich, income-related inequalities in health insurance coverage is pronounced, where the wealthiest quintile households are more than 12 times more likely to be covered by any type of health insurance compared to the poorest quintile (Kazungu and Barasa 2017).

In Ghana, being insured significantly reduces catastrophic out-of-pocket medical spending among poor, low-educated, and self-employed households living far from hospitals, compared to their counterparts who live nearby (Fiestas Navarrete et al. 2019). Novignon et al. (2019) noted evidence of significant inequality in the National Health Insurance Scheme membership, which is based on subscription and payment of premiums. Novignon et al. (2019) also found that access to the National Health Insurance Scheme contributes the most to inequality in antenatal care visits in Ghana, especially compared to the contributions of education, area of residence, and wealth status.

Inequality in Maternal and Child Health Outcomes

Maternal health status, child health status, and an equitable distribution of health services provide key indicators of a country's SES (Bintabara, Nakamura, and Seino 2018). In the majority of countries in SSA, large subnational disparities persist in reproductive, maternal, newborn, and child health interventions (Faye et al. 2020). The interior, central, and northwest regions of SSA have the highest levels of child health inequality (Pérez-Mesa, Marrero, and Darias-Curvo 2022).

Ghana has the lowest Gini coefficient for child health (2.6 percent), followed by Kenya (2.9 percent) and South Africa (3.1 percent) (Pérez-Mesa et al. 2022). Family history, home infrastructure, and region of residence have contributed to the observed disparities in child health. Between 1990 and 2015, the maternal mortality rate in Ghana fell from 760 to 319 maternal deaths per 100,000 live births (Apanga and Awoonor-Williams 2018; WHO 2023). However, the country fell short of achieving the 2015 Millennium Development Goal target of no more than 190 maternal deaths per 100,000 live births. In general, there has been progress in reducing maternal mortality in Ghana, with a recent decrease in some relevant indicators,[5] but substantial reduction of the maternal mortality rate is still needed to achieve the SDG objective of no more than 70 maternal deaths per 100,000 live births (Apanga and Awoonor-Williams 2018).

Contrary to Ghana, in Kenya progress in reducing maternal mortality has stalled despite recent global breakthroughs in prenatal and maternal care (Yuen 2022). Obstacles to emergency obstetric care, such as cesarean sections, and insufficient access to high-quality antenatal care have contributed to Kenya's maternal health problems. According to UNICEF (2020), Kenya's maternal mortality rate and infant mortality rate are among the highest in the world, indicating challenges with accessing quality health care for these services. This daunting average picture is made worse by the large disparities in maternal mortality rates between regions, localities, and income groups, with households from lower wealth quintiles and in rural areas being associated with higher health risks.

Interestingly, South Africa, whose income Gini coefficient is higher than the Gini coefficients for Ghana and Kenya, has the lowest maternal and infant mortality rates among the three countries. The World Bank's projection of South Africa's maternal mortality rate was 88 per 100,000 live births in 2020, declining from 105.9 per 100,000 live births in 2019. The Western Cape had the lowest maternal mortality rate, at 43.6 deaths per 100,000 live births (Stats SA 2022).

Although there are large differences in maternal, infant, and child mortality rates among the three countries, inequalities in related services remain a challenge and are similar in each country. Disparities in access to and quality of maternal and child health services and, therefore, disparities in health outcomes, are influenced by locality, income or wealth, and education. For instance, the 2017 Ghana Maternal Health Survey revealed considerable disparities in maternal and child mortality (Adu, Mulay, and Owusu 2021; Bixby et al. 2022). Anarwat, Salifu, and Akuriba (2021) also observed that inequalities in maternal and child health care services in Ghana are a result of differences in location, income level, and education.

Similar narratives have emerged on the nature of inequality in maternal, neonatal, and child health services in Kenya and South Africa. According to Sidze et al. (2022), inequalities in access to and usage of maternal, neonatal, and child health services are considerable in Kenya, and maternal and child health outcomes are mostly influenced by SES and location (urban or rural). In rural Kenya, maternal mortality is still relatively high compared to urban areas, and the quality of maternal health care for women in lower income brackets is much lower in rural versus urban settings. The northeastern regions have the largest disparities in health outcomes, according to Keats et al. (2018), and compared to wealthier women, women residing in Kenya's most-disadvantaged regions have, on average, less access to proper delivery care. Inequalities in the quality of maternal health care can result in disparities in mother and infant health outcomes (Hodin 2017).

To minimize the inequalities in health outcomes, all three countries have implemented interventions that seek to deal with the source of inequalities in access to and quality of maternal and child health care services: the National Health Insurance Scheme in Ghana, universal health care in Kenya, and the Clinton Health Access Initiative in South Africa. Although such interventions are important and have received support from various governments, particularly during periods of favorable macroeconomic performance or uncertainty, such social programs are often the first to experience funding cuts. These cuts in social funding may, therefore, have negative implications for health outcomes. Using data from countries in SSA, Chauvet et al. (2020) have documented the negative effects that fiscal austerity has on infant mortality and health inequalities.

Interlinkages among Education, Health, and Labor Market Outcomes

Education and health are key determinants of employment and, therefore, key channels for the generation and persistence of income inequality. In general, access to education and health care not only influences people's ability to lead better lives but also allows them to participate effectively in economic and political activities.

Link between Educational Inequality and Labor Market Outcomes

Economists have considered the effects of education on the earnings of individuals for a long time, including the seminal works by Becker (1964, 1975) and Mincer (1974). The general idea is that individuals have a choice of how much education to obtain. They choose optimally by comparing the costs associated with obtaining a particular level of education to the corresponding returns (benefits) that accrue from that level, relative to other levels of education. This optimization problem by individuals provides the core motivation for most educational interventions, which aim to make it less costly to attain higher levels of schooling through building local schools, subsidizing tuition fees, or creating mandatory schooling rules, which carry some form of penalty for noncompliance.

Higher levels of education are costly to obtain, due to the actual costs of studying as well as the opportunity costs associated with foregoing wages while studying, and thus the decision to obtain a higher level of education reflects its relatively greater returns. The most-common form of capturing the returns to education is through higher wages. Other returns include stronger employment prospects, job security, better employment conditions, increased occupational safety, and the higher status associated with certain types of employment. By implication, a greater degree of inequality in educational attainment is generally associated with a greater degree of earnings dispersion.

Empirical investigations of the returns to a particular level of schooling have mostly followed the spirit of the work by Mincer (1974), who proposed that a measure of the returns to education could be obtained by examining the earnings across groups with different levels of education. A standard Mincerian equation models wages as a function of age and education, where age is used as a proxy for potential experience in the labor market. This approach and its subsequent variations remain one of the most-common approaches used to identify the returns to education. Nonetheless, there are valid critiques of the approach, as it does not deal with issues of endogeneity arising from self-selection or unobservable factors that may also be correlated with individuals' circumstances, nor does it deal with externalities in the rates of return to education between different groups.

The combination of inequality in educational outcomes and the various rates of return to education provides a key link to understanding labor market inequality. Conceptually, this combination can be thought of as a mixture of endowment effects and price effects and is a widely used decomposition method for understanding changes in observed wage inequality.

Empirical Findings on Returns to Education in Africa

An influential paper by Psacharopoulos (1985) has examined the returns to education across various regions. The paper found that, in Africa, the social returns to primary education were substantially higher than they were for secondary or tertiary levels of education. However, questions remain about the findings, as there were data for only four African countries, and there were additional concerns about the quality of the data that were available.

The evidence from a broader set of countries and more-recent data indicates that the social returns to primary education are generally much lower than they are for secondary or tertiary levels of education. It also indicates that, in some countries, the returns to tertiary education are even greater than those for secondary education. The implications of these findings are that higher levels of educational attainment may not always lead to greater equality in the labor market and, in some cases, educational inequality and labor market inequality may be negatively related, although higher levels of educational attainment would coincide with higher levels of individual income.

For example, in South Africa, Branson et al. (2012) have shown that the increase in returns to post-secondary education has directly counteracted the equalizing gains that have been made by increased educational attainment, resulting in consistent levels of inequality over time. This issue makes the mapping among educational attainment, educational inequality, and labor market inequality even more complex. Thus, there is a need for careful consideration of the context and specificities of the local labor market to understand these nuances. In addition, the analysis should remember that the returns to education are themselves dynamic parameters, reflecting technological, structural, and demographic variables.

Link between Health Inequality and Labor Market Outcomes

Across Africa are striking disparities in health care access and health outcomes between different socioeconomic groups. In a context like that of SSA, early-life health inequality is a precursor to economic inequality in adulthood (Smith-Greenaway 2020). The different forms of inequalities in health have important implications not only for adult health but also for children's health and, therefore, human capital development. Consequently, health inequalities, both in access to and quality of health care, can lead to lower productivity for adults and poor health for children, which can affect current and future labor market outcomes, respectively.

According to Ataguba and Alaba (2012), inequalities in health have implications for multiple deprivations, including education, limited productive resources, and unfavorable labor market outcomes, that make those who are most exposed to these deprivations reliant on social transfers. Indeed, inequalities in health can perpetuate the cycle of poverty and inequality, thereby limiting intergenerational social mobility. When women experience poor health during pregnancy as a result of limited access to health care, they are more likely to have low-birthweight babies, premature births, and associated health complications. Early anthropometric gaps facilitated by health inequalities can transfer to other domains later in life (Von Fintel and Richter 2019).

Novignon et al. (2019) have argued that, in Ghana, the current health status of households plays a critical role in determining their future vulnerability to poverty. Similarly, Von Fintel and Richter (2019) have provided empirical evidence showing the lasting effects of health inequalities on intergenerational outcomes in South Africa. Specifically, given that cognitive skills develop over a person's life course, cognitive inequalities due to inequalities in health and other socioeconomic dimensions can contribute to labor market opportunities and outcomes. Children who experience poor health are more likely to miss school, lag in their studies, and ultimately have reduced opportunities for higher education and employment.

Adults who have chronic poor health are more likely to be unable to work, have reduced productivity, and be absent from work. These issues have important implications for their labor market choices (the decision to work full-time or part-time, in the formal or informal sector) and outcomes (earnings). Moreover, people with poor health are less likely to upgrade their skills through continuous training to compete for higher paying jobs, thus limiting their ability to earn higher wages and leading to perpetually lower wages. The intersectionality of health and educational inequalities can compound the negative effects of inequalities in the labor market in the contexts of most African countries.

Conclusion

This chapter highlights the strong interlinkages among inequalities in education, health, and labor market outcomes, as well as the common drivers for each type of inequality. Overall, consistent and similar patterns exist in the drivers of inequality in education and health. For the African countries considered, the disparities in health care access, health outcomes, and educational attainment are mostly driven by similar factors, such as household socioeconomic circumstances and poverty, geographic location, and gender.

Poverty is an important driver of inequality, as it reinforces inequality in education and health. The relationship also works in the reverse direction, as education and health are key aspects of people's well-being and can enhance opportunities to participate in the labor market, decreasing income inequality. Individuals with low economic standing have limited access to quality health care services and education. Poor households are more likely to access health care services from health facilities that are less endowed with resources. Similarly, poor households are disproportionately disadvantaged in education. Although governments have implemented interventions to narrow the gap in educational access, the gap persists in educational quality, as access to good quality education is still determined by income, and children from low-income households have less access to critical skills.

In addition to poverty, social and cultural norms are important factors in the persistence of income disparities in Africa, leading to important inequalities in both health and education by gender, with women being severely disadvantaged. Social norms disproportionately place the burden of unpaid domestic and care work on women, as well as practices such as early marriage, which significantly reduces girls' opportunities for better economic outcomes in the future. In addition, sociocultural norms can reduce women's access to quality health care and education and constrain their ability to escape poverty through the labor market channel. More investments in women's human capital are required to overcome this historical disadvantage.

The large differences in education and health outcomes across social groups due to location reflect the disparities in infrastructure across different regions in various countries in SSA. Furthermore, rural areas in African countries often lack adequate infrastructure and are characterized by poor road networks, limited access to WASH facilities, and limited access to educational and health resources. These disparities result in suboptimal health and education outcomes for the populations residing in these areas.

A great concern is the intergenerational persistence of inequalities in health and education, which impedes economic and social mobility for some groups, particularly in labor market outcomes. It is important to turn attention to the underlying drivers of inequality in human capital—education and health—because this disparity manifests in observed income inequality. As such, to achieve the goal of leaving no one behind by 2030, governments in SSA must focus their efforts on eliminating all forms of inequalities in education and health.

Notes

1. The Capitation Grant was initiated by the government to support inclusive education by eliminating extra fees and charges at the basic school level.
2. The analysis in this section is based on research conducted in Burkina Faso, Côte d'Ivoire, the Democratic Republic of Congo, Ghana, Kenya, Senegal, and the SACU countries, including South Africa.
3. The focus here is on people's ability to pay, even if the costs are high.
4. Medical aid in South Africa is an insurance-type plan that provides financial coverage for medical expenses for members who pay a monthly contribution for this coverage.
5. The number of maternal deaths and the institutional maternal death ratio decreased in 2019 and 2020, despite an increase in total births and the COVID-19 pandemic (WHO 2023).

References

Acheampong, Alex O., Eric Evans Osei Opoku, and Godsway Korku Tetteh. 2024. "Unveiling the Effect of Income Inequality on Safe Drinking Water, Sanitation and Hygiene (WASH): Does Financial Inclusion Matter?" *World Development* 178: 106573. https://doi.org/10.1016/j.worlddev.2024.106573.

Adeniran, Adedeji, Joseph Ishaku, and Lateef Olawale Akanni. 2020. "Is Nigeria Experiencing a Learning Crisis? Evidence from Curriculum-Matched Learning Assessment." *International Journal of Educational Development* 77: 102199. https://doi.org/10.1016/j.ijedudev.2020.102199.

Adu, Joseph, Shree Mulay, and Mark Fordjour Owusu. 2021. "Reducing Maternal and Child Mortality in Rural Ghana." *Pan African Medical Journal* 39: 263. https://doi.org/10.11604/pamj.2021.39.263.30593.

Aka, Bédia François, Wadjamse Beaudelaire Djezou, Angbonon Eugène Kamalan, Ya Assanhoun Guillaume Kouassi, Gongbé Blaise Makaye, Konan Abogni Augustin Kouadio, Affia Larissa Eklau, et al. 2020. "Etat Des Lieux Des Inégalités En Côte d'Ivoire." AFD Research Paper 169. Agence Française de Développement, Paris.

Anarwat, Samuel George, Mubarik Salifu, and Margaret Atosina Akuriba. 2021. "Equity and Access to Maternal and Child Health Services in Ghana: A Cross-Sectional Study." *BMC Health Services Research* 21 (1): 864. https://doi.org/10.1186/s12913-021-06872-9.

Apanga, Paschal Awingura, and John Koku Awoonor-Williams. 2018. "Maternal Death in Rural Ghana: A Case Study in the Upper East Region of Ghana." *Frontiers in Public Health* 6: 101. https://doi.org/10.3389/fpubh.2018.00101.

Ataguba, John Ele-Ojo. 2021. "The Impact of Financing Health Services on Income Inequality in an Unequal Society: The Case of South Africa." *Applied Health Economics and Health Policy* 19 (5): 721–33. https://doi.org/10.1007/s40258-021-00643-7.

Ataguba, John Ele-Ojo, and Olufunke Alaba. 2012. "Explaining Health Inequalities in South Africa: A Political Economy Perspective." *Development Southern Africa* 29 (5): 756–64. https://doi.org/10.1080/0376835X.2012.730962.

Atta-Ankomah, Richmond, Robert Darko Osei, Isaac Osei-Akoto, Felix Ankomah Asante, Abena D. Oduro, Nkechi Owoo, Monica Lambon-Quayefio, and Stephen Afranie. 2020. *Inequality Diagnostics for Ghana*. African Center of Excellence for Inequalities Research, University of Cape Town, South Africa.

Becker, Gary S. 1964. *Human Capital: A Theoretical and Empirical Analysis, with Special Reference to Education*. New York: Columbia University Press.

Becker, Gary S. 1975. *Human Capital: A Theoretical and Empirical Analysis, with Special Reference to Education*, 2nd ed. Human Behavior and Social Institutions 5. New York: National Bureau of Economic Research.

Bintabara, Deogratius, Keiko Nakamura, and Kaoruko Seino. 2018. "Improving Access to Healthcare for Women in Tanzania by Addressing Socioeconomic Determinants and Health Insurance: A Population-Based Cross-Sectional Survey." *BMJ Open* 8 (9): e023013. https://doi.org/10.1136/bmjopen-2018-023013.

Bixby, Honor, James E. Bennett, Ayaga A. Bawah, Raphael E. Arku, Samuel K. Annim, Jacqueline D. Anum, Samilia E. Mintah, et al. 2022. "Quantifying Within-City Inequalities in Child Mortality across Neighbourhoods in Accra, Ghana: A Bayesian Spatial Analysis." *BMJ Open* 12 (1): e054030. https://doi.org/10.1136/bmjopen-2021-054030.

Bold, Tessa, Mwangi Kimenyi, Germano Mwabu, Alice Ng'ang'a, and Justin Sandefur. 2018. "Experimental Evidence on Scaling Up Education Reforms in Kenya." *Journal of Public Economics* 168: 1–20. https://doi.org/10.1016/j.jpubeco.2018.08.007.

Branson, Nicola, Julia Garlick, David Lam, and Murray Leibbrandt. 2012. "Education and Inequality: The South African Case." Southern Africa Labour and Development Research Unit, University of Cape Town, South Africa. https://EconPapers.repec.org/RePEc:ldr:wpaper:75.

Chauvet, Lisa, Siyavash Eslami, Marin Ferry, and Laure Pasquier-Doumer. 2020. "Spatial Inequality and Attitudes Towards Taxation: The Case of Sub-Saharan Africa." AFD Research Paper 122, Agence Française de Développement, Paris.

Dia, Hamidou, and Jean Alain Goudiaby. 2020. "Le Paradoxe de l'enseignement Supérieur Privé Au Sénégal: Réduire Les Inégalités Tout En Les Maintenant." AFD Research Paper 154, Agence Française de Développement, Paris.

Erikson, Martin G., and Malgorzata Erikson. 2019. "Learning Outcomes and Critical Thinking—Good Intentions in Conflict." *Studies in Higher Education* 44 (12): 2293–2303. https://doi.org/10.1080/03075079.2018.1486813.

Faye, Cheikh Mbacké, Fernando C. Wehrmeister, Dessalegn Y. Melesse, Martin Kavao Kavao Mutua, Abdoulaye Maïga, Chelsea Maria Taylor, Agbessi Amouzou, et al. 2020. "Large and Persistent Subnational Inequalities in Reproductive, Maternal, Newborn and Child Health Intervention Coverage in Sub-Saharan Africa." *BMJ Global Health* 5 (1): e002232. https://doi.org/10.1136/bmjgh-2019-002232.

Fiestas Navarrete, Lucia, Simone Ghislandi, David Stuckler, and Fabrizio Tediosi. 2019. "Inequalities in the Benefits of National Health Insurance on Financial Protection from Out-of-Pocket Payments and Access to Health Services: Cross-Sectional Evidence from Ghana." *Health Policy and Planning* 34 (9): 694–705. https://doi.org/10.1093/heapol/czz093.

Földvári, Péter, and Bas van Leeuwen. 2011. "Should Less Inequality in Education Lead to a More Equal Income Distribution?" *Education Economics* 19 (5): 537–54. https://doi.org/10.1080/09645292.2010.488472.

Fontanella, Lara, Annalina Sarra, and Simone Di Zio. 2020. "Do Gender Differences in Social Institutions Matter in Shaping Gender Equality in Education and the Labour Market? Empirical Evidences from Developing Countries." *Social Indicators Research* 147 (1): 133–58. https://doi.org/10.1007/s11205-019 -02148-2.

Grimm, M. 2005. "Educational Policies and Poverty Reduction in Côte d'Ivoire." *Journal of Policy Modeling* 27 (2): 231–47. https://doi.org/10.1016/j.jpolmod.2004.12.002.

Grossman, Michael. 1972. "On the Concept of Health Capital and the Demand for Health." *Journal of Political Economy* 80 (2): 223–55. https://doi.org/10.1086/259880.

GSS (Ghana Statistical Service). 2022. *Ghana 2022 Earnings Inequality in the Public Sector*. Accra: GSS.

Gulliford, Martin, Jose Figueroa-Munoz, Myfanwy Morgan, David Hughes, Barry Gibson, Roger Beech, and Meryl Hudson. 2002. "What Does 'Access to Health Care' Mean?" *Journal of Health Services Research & Policy* 7 (3): 186–88. https://doi.org/10.1258/135581902760082517.

Hodin, Sarah. 2017. "Maternal Health Care in Kenya: Poor Quality for Women." *MHTF Blog*, March 15, 2017. https://www.mhtf.org/2017/03/15/maternal-health-care-in-kenya-poor-quality-for-poor-women/.

Ilinca, Stefania, Laura Di Giorgio, Paola Salari, and Jane Chuma. 2019. "Socio-Economic Inequality and Inequity in Use of Health Care Services in Kenya: Evidence from the Fourth Kenya Household Health Expenditure and Utilization Survey." *International Journal for Equity in Health* 18 (1): 196. https://doi .org/10.1186/s12939-019-1106-z.

Kazungu, Jacob S., and Edwine W. Barasa. 2017. "Examining Levels, Distribution and Correlates of Health Insurance Coverage in Kenya." *Tropical Medicine & International Health* 22 (9): 1175–85. https://doi .org/10.1111/tmi.12912.

Keats, Emily Catherine, Nadia Akseer, Zaid Bhatti, William Macharia, Anthony Ngugi, Arjumand Rizvi, and Zulfiqar Ahmed Bhutta. 2018. "Assessment of Inequalities in Coverage of Essential Reproductive, Maternal, Newborn, Child, and Adolescent Health Interventions in Kenya." *JAMA Network Open* 1 (8): e185152. https://doi.org/10.1001/jamanetworkopen.2018.5152.

KNBS (Kenya National Bureau of Statistics). 2020. *Inequality Trends and Diagnostics in Kenya 2020*. Nairobi: KNBS.

Kobiane, Jean-François, Idrissa Ouilili, and Sibi Guissou. 2020. "Etat Des Lieux Des Inégalités Multidimensionnelles Au Burkina Faso." AFD Research Paper 132, Agence Française de Développement, Paris.

Kouraogo, Pierre, and Ambroise Y. Dianda. 2008. "Education in Burkina Faso at Horizon 2025." *Journal of International Cooperation in Education* 11. 23–38.

Lambon-Quayefio, Monica P., Robert D. Osei, Abena D. Oduro, and Isaac Osei Akoto. 2020. "Understanding the Relationship between Consumption Inequality, Inequality of Opportunity and Education Outcomes in Ghana." AFD Research Paper 159, Agence Française de Développement, Paris.

Levesque, Jean-Frederic, Mark F. Harris, and Grant Russell. 2013. "Patient-Centred Access to Health Care: Conceptualising Access at the Interface of Health Systems and Populations." *International Journal for Equity in Health* 12 (1): 18. https://doi.org/10.1186/1475-9276-12-18.

Lindahl, Mikael, Mårten Palme, Sofia Sandgren Massih, and Anna Sjögren. 2015. "Long-Term Intergenerational Persistence of Human Capital: An Empirical Analysis of Four Generations." *Journal of Human Resources* 50 (1): 1–33. https://doi.org/10.3368/jhr.50.1.1.

Mincer, Jacob. 1974. *Schooling, Experience, and Earnings*. Human Behavior and Social Institutions 2. New York: National Bureau of Economic Research.

Munthali, Alister C., Leslie Swartz, Hasheem Mannan, Malcolm MacLachlan, Charles Chilimampunga, and Cecilia Makupe. 2019. "'This One Will Delay Us': Barriers to Accessing Health Care Services among Persons with Disabilities in Malawi." *Disability and Rehabilitation* 41 (6): 683–90. https://doi.org/10.108 0/09638288.2017.1404148.

Mutegi, Reuben Gitonga, Genevieve Wanjala, and Moses Kinyanjui Muriithi. 2017. "Education Policies in Kenya: Does Free Secondary Education Promote Equity in Public Secondary Schools?" *International Journal of Development Research* 7 (11): 16696–16699.

Nikolai, Rita, and Marcel Helbig. 2021. "Private Schools as Drivers of Social Segregation: Why Private Schools Should Be Regulated." *On Education Journal for Research and Debate* 4 (11). https://doi.org /10.17899/on_ed.2021.11.9.

Novignon, Jacob, Bernice Ofori, Kwasi Gyabaa Tabiri, and Mohammad Habibullah Pulok. 2019. "Socioeconomic Inequalities in Maternal Health Care Utilization in Ghana." *International Journal for Equity in Health* 18 (1): 141. https://doi.org/10.1186/s12939-019-1043-x.

Ouilili, Idrissa, Abdramane Soura, Kassoum Dianou, Sibi Guissou, and Samuel Ramde. 2020. "Dynamique Des Inégalités de La Pauvreté Multidimensionnelle à Ouagadougou: Données de l'Observatoire de Population de Ouagadougou." AFD Research Paper 142, Agence Française de Développement, Paris.

Park, Kang H. 1996. "Educational Expansion and Educational Inequality on Income Distribution." *Economics of Education Review* 15 (1): 51–58. http://doi.org/10.1016/0272-7757(95)00000-3.

Pérez-Mesa, David, Gustavo A. Marrero, and Sara Darias-Curvo. 2022. "Child Health Inequality in Sub-Saharan Africa." *Economics & Human Biology* 47: 101176. https://doi.org/10.1016/j.ehb.2022.101176.

Poncelet, Marc, and Pascal Kapagama. 2020. "Des Inégalités Éducatives à La Mise En Question de l'opposition Public/Privé Dans l'enseignement Supérieur Congolais. Un Défi Documentaire et Conceptuel." AFD Research Paper 162, Agence Française de Développement, Paris.

Psacharopoulos, George. 1985. "Returns to Education: A Further International Update and Implications." *Journal of Human Resources* 20 (4): 583. https://doi.org/10.2307/145686.

Rudasingwa, Martin, Bona Mukoshya Chitah, Chrispin Mphuka, Edmund Yeboah, Emmanuel Bonnet, Valéry Ridde, Paul André Somé, Adamson Muula, and Manuela De Allegri. 2020a. "Estimating the Distributional Incidence of Healthcare Spending on Curative Health Services in Sub-Saharan Africa: Analysis in Burkina Faso, Malawi and Zambia." AFD Research Paper 140, Agence Française de Développement, Paris.

Rudasingwa, Martin, Bona Mukoshya Chitah, Chrispin Mphuka, Edmund Yeboah, Emmanuel Bonnet, Valéry Ridde, Paul André Somé, Adamson Muula, and Manuela De Allegri. 2020b. "Estimating the Distributional Incidence of Healthcare Spending on Maternal Healthcare Services in Sub-Saharan Africa: Analysis in Burkina Faso, Malawi, and Zambia." AFD Research Paper 141, Agence Française de Développement, Paris.

Rudasingwa, Martin, Manuela De Allegri, Chrispin Mphuka, Collins Chansa, Edmund Yeboah, Emmanuel Bonnet, Valéry Ridde, and Bona Mukosha Chitah. 2022. "Universal Health Coverage and the Poor: To What Extent Are Health Financing Policies Making a Difference? Evidence from a Benefit Incidence Analysis in Zambia." *BMC Public Health* 22 (1): 1546. https://doi.org/10.1186/s12889-022-13923-1.

Sefa-Nyarko, Clement, Pearl Kyei, and David Mwambari. 2018. *Transitions from Primary to Lower Secondary School: A Focus on Equity.* Mastercard Foundation, Toronto, Canada.

Sen, Amartya. 2000. *Development as Freedom.* New York: Anchor Books. https://search.library.wisc.edu /catalog/999977297202121.

Sidze, E. M., F. M. Wekesah, L. Kisia, and A. Abajobir. 2022. "Inequalities in Access and Utilization of Maternal, Newborn and Child Health Services in Sub-Saharan Africa: A Special Focus on Urban Settings." *Maternal and Child Health Journal* 26 (2): 250–79. https://doi.org/10.1007/s10995-021 -03250-z.

Smith-Greenaway, Emily. 2020. "Does Parents' Union Instability Disrupt Intergenerational Advantage? An Analysis of Sub-Saharan Africa." *Demography* 57 (2): 445–73. https://doi.org/10.1007/s13524-019 -00854-7.

Stats SA (Statistics South Africa), SALDRU (Southern Africa Labour and Development Research Unit), and AFD (Agence Française de Développement). 2019. *Inequality Trends in South Africa: A Multidimensional Diagnostic of Inequality, 2017.* Pretoria: Stats SA, SALDRU, and AFD.

Stats SA (Statistics South Africa). 2022. *Maternal Mortality Rate on the Decline in South Africa.* Pretoria: Stats SA.

UIS (UNESCO Institute for Statistics). 2023. "Data for the Sustainable Development Goals." UIS, Montreal, Canada. https://uis.unesco.org/.

UNICEF (United Nations Children's Fund). 2020. "Country Profiles." UNICEF Data, UNICEF, New York.

University of Cape Town. n.d. "Tracking South Africa's Progress Toward the 28% Attainment Goal." University of Cape Town, South Africa. https://commerce.uct.ac.za/siyaphambili.

Von Fintel, Dieter, and Linda Richter. 2019. "Intergenerational Transfer of Health Inequalities: Exploration of Mechanisms in the Birth to Twenty Cohort in South Africa." *BMJ Global Health* 4 (5): e001828. https://doi.org/10.1136/bmjgh-2019-001828.

WHO (World Health Organization). 2013. *State of Health Financing in the African Region.* Geneva: WHO.

WHO (World Health Organization). 2023. "Maternal Mortality." Data. WHO, Geneva. http://www.who .int/mediacentre/factsheets/fs348/en/.

World Bank. 2020. *World Development Indicators.* Washington, DC: World Bank. https://databank .worldbank.org/source/world-development-indicators.

Yuen, Erica. 2022. "Kenya and Maternal Health: Delivering Results." Think Global Health, Washington, DC.

Chapter **4**

Labor Market Inequalities

Vimal Ranchhod, Anda David, Damiano Kulundu Manda, Cecilia Poggi,
Claire Zanuso, and Rawane Yasser

Introduction

The labor market is a major determinant of the levels of poverty and inequality in a country.
Finding employment affects a household's general well-being and is an important determinant of
several socioeconomic welfare measures, particularly access to income (Ranchhod and Daniels
2021). Finding formal-sector employment is strongly correlated with exiting from poverty, while
precarious forms of work, such as casual employment and employment without a permanent
work contract, make up the largest share of jobs among the poor population and those who are
vulnerable to falling into poverty (Schotte, Zizzamia, and Leibbrandt 2018). With its large share
of informal and casual employment, the precariousness of youth, and a relatively small formal
sector, labor market dynamics are key to understanding the inequality dynamics in Africa.

Although the labor market has always been central to understanding welfare in developing
countries, its salience has increased recently as the COVID-19 pandemic has had a direct impact
on employment prospects. The consequences of the associated disruptions and restrictions
have varied considerably in terms of people's position in income distribution and their level of
vulnerability, with vulnerable groups experiencing disproportionate labor market effects.

This chapter explores the dynamics and characteristics of African labor markets as a key
driver of inequalities. Labor markets constitute a source of inequality through two channels:
first, by determining who does and does not get a job, and second, through the distribution of
earnings among employed people. The chapter explores these two aspects of the labor market
in the section on employment outcomes and earnings inequality, which highlights the main
findings on the levels and trends of unemployment and earnings inequality in Africa from the
recent literature. The section on informality analyzes the role of the labor market in inequality
in Africa, considering the high shares of employment in the informal sector. Understanding
horizontal inequalities is also important. The section on marginalized groups examines
the situations of marginalized people who face the most-precarious working conditions.

The chapter concludes by summarizing the lessons learned and reflecting on the future of the labor market in Africa.

Employment Outcomes and Earnings Inequality

In many African countries, the labor market is characterized by a large share of informal employment; high unemployment, particularly among youth; a relatively small formal sector; and differences in earnings across sectors and occupations. Understanding employment patterns and the associated wage distributions is a key component for understanding inequality in Africa. In South Africa, for example, labor income is the main driver of income inequality (Stats SA, SALDRU, and AFD 2019), while in Kenya, wage inequality is much higher than income inequality (KNBS 2020). Inequality in the labor market also manifests in other dimensions of employment, such as job security and conditions of employment. This section focuses on the levels and trends in unemployment and earnings inequality.

Unemployment

High unemployment and labor market segmentation are among the main drivers of labor market inequality in Africa (World Bank 2022). Unemployment is generally higher in Africa than in the rest of the world. Figure 4.1 shows that the unemployment rate in Africa is slightly above the global unemployment rate. However, this aggregate statistic masks significant regional variation. Compared to the global unemployment rate, the rate in North Africa is substantially higher, while the rate in Sub-Saharan Africa (SSA) is slightly lower. In 2022, for instance, the average unemployment rate in North African countries was 11.29 percent, while it was 6.41 percent in the SSA region.

Figure 4.1 Unemployment Rates, 2000–22

Percent

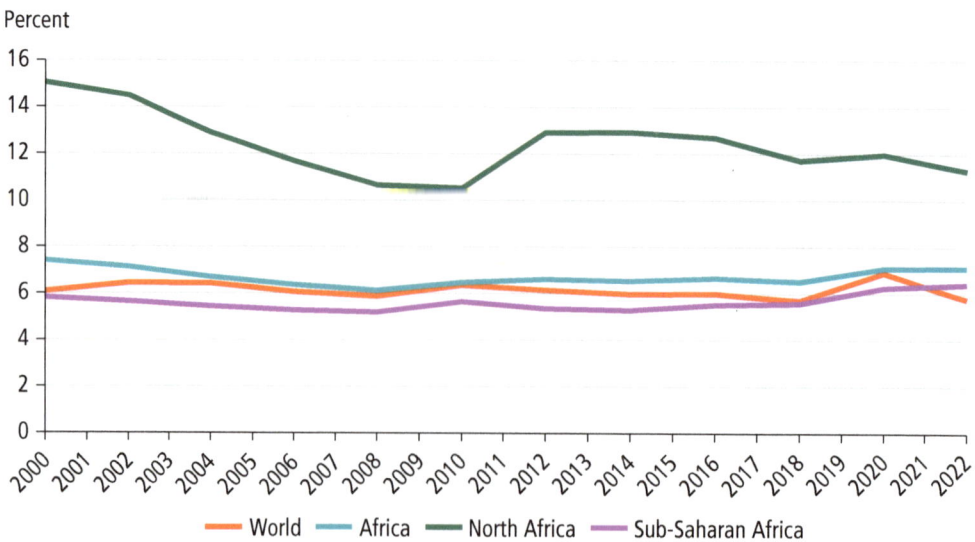

Source: Authors' elaboration using International Labour Organization modeled estimates.

Figure 4.2 Unemployment Rates in Select Countries, 2000–22

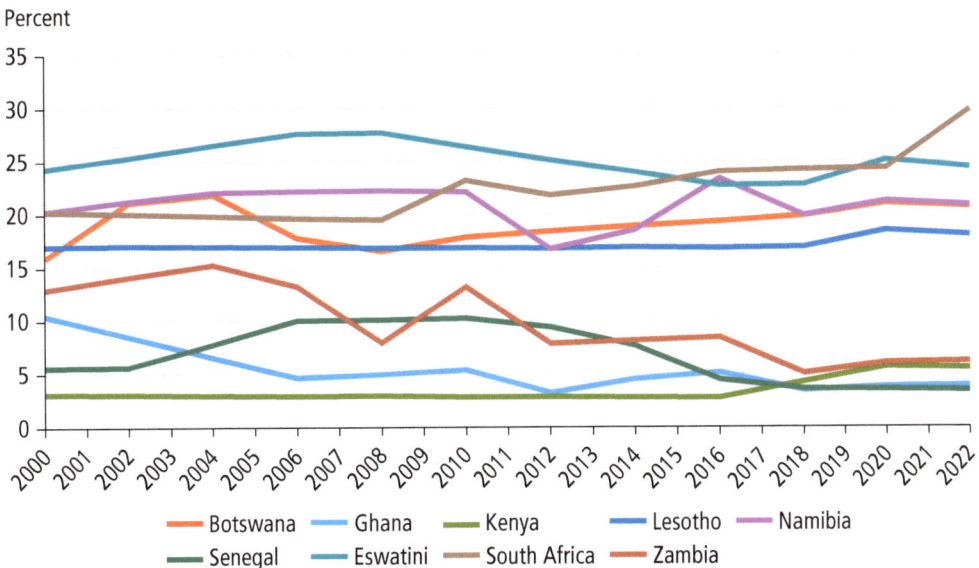

Source: Authors' elaboration using International Labour Organization modeled estimates.

The unemployment rate varies by country and within countries in the same region. For example, in Southern African countries in 2022, the national unemployment rates ranged from 18 percent in Lesotho to 29.8 percent in South Africa, as shown in figure 4.2. In contrast, the unemployment rate is much lower in countries in Western and Eastern Africa. For example, the unemployment rates were estimated to be 3.4 percent in Senegal and 6.1 percent in Zambia in 2022, with the rates for Ghana and Kenya falling within this range.

Unemployment rates also vary over time within a country. For example, the unemployment rate in South Africa has increased considerably, from 24.8 percent in 2011 to 27.5 percent in 2017 (Stats SA et al. 2019) to 29.1 percent in 2018 (ILOSTAT 2018). In Kenya, unemployment declined from 14.6 percent of the labor force in 1998 to 7.4 percent in 2016 (KNBS 2020). In Ghana, the unemployment rate declined from 8 percent in 2005/06 to 4.4 percent in 2012/13 and then increased to 7.9 percent in 2016/17 (Atta-Ankomah et al. 2020).

The increase in unemployment in South Africa is explained by factors such as low competition, high input costs, an uncertain regulatory environment, and skills mismatches, which can constrain private-sector job creation (World Bank 2022). The decline in the unemployment rate in Kenya is attributed mainly to informal-sector job creation (KNBS 2020).

Since 2020, unemployment rates have worsened due to the COVID-19 pandemic, which started in early 2020 and affected almost all the countries in Africa and around the world. For instance, in South Africa, aggregate employment decreased by 2.2 million (14 percent) in the second quarter of 2020 (Kohler et al. 2022). In addition, the share of employed workers decreased from 57 percent of working-age adults in February 2020 to 48 percent in April, with the share falling to 38 percent if temporarily absent workers are excluded (Ranchhod and Daniels 2021). According to a report released by the Kenya National Bureau of Statistics, the unemployment rate doubled to 10.4 percent in September 2020, compared to 5.2 percent in March 2020. As many as 1.7 million Kenyans lost their jobs in the first few months of the pandemic (KNBS 2020).

Unemployment rates also vary across regions, with rural areas in most African countries having higher unemployment rates than urban areas. However, in Ghana, the urban unemployment rate in 2016/17 was 10.9 percent, compared to the rural unemployment rate of 4.8 percent. Unemployment rates also varied across the different regions in Ghana in 2016/17, with the Greater Accra region having the highest unemployment rate, at 11.3 percent, followed by the Western and Central regions with unemployment rates of 8.3 and 7.0 percent, respectively (Atta-Ankomah et al. 2020). In contrast, in South Africa in 2017, the unemployment rate was 30.5 percent in rural areas compared with 26.5 percent in urban areas (Stats SA et al. 2019).

Wage Inequality

Wage inequalities in Africa are among the highest in the world. For example, the Gini coefficient for earnings inequality in South Africa increased from about 0.62 in 2011 to about 0.69 in 2015 (Stats SA et al. 2019). In Ghana, the Gini coefficient for wages from paid employment declined from about 0.67 in 2005/06 to 0.65 in 2012/13 and then dropped substantially to 0.51 in 2016/17 (Atta-Ankomah et al. 2020). In Kenya, the Gini coefficient increased from 0.50 in 1988/89 to 0.70 in 2005/06, before falling to 0.60 in 2015/16 (KNBS 2020). In Kenya, the richest 10 percent received 36 percent of the earnings share in 1998/99, and this increased to 57 percent in 2005/06, before falling to 46 percent in 2015/16. The poorest 10 percent of employees received less than 1 percent of the earnings in each of those years.

Inequality in labor market earnings contributes significantly to overall income inequality and is generally higher than overall income inequality, although the high levels of earnings inequality may partly reflect the time span over which inequality is being measured, as a positive age-earnings profile is typically observed (Zizzamia and Ranchhod 2020). For example, in South Africa, inequality arising from the labor market contributed about two-thirds of overall income inequality (Stats SA et al. 2019).

National-level earnings inequality measures tend to hide regional and group-level variations. For example, in Ghana, inequality in earnings is higher in rural areas than in urban areas and varies greatly across regions, ranging from a Gini coefficient of 0.45 in the lowest inequality region to 0.54 in the highest inequality region in 2016/17 (Atta-Ankomah et al. 2020). In South Africa, high earnings inequality is compounded by polarization at the two extremes, with employees in high-skill jobs (accounting for less than one-fifth of the total working population) earning nearly five times the average wage of those in low-skill jobs (World Bank 2022).

In addition, there are substantial gross earnings differentials of around 88 percent between workers in temporary employment services and other workers (Cassim and Casale 2022).

The earnings differentials along these lines add another dimension to understanding the high levels of labor market earnings inequality in South Africa. Important aspects of earnings inequality are also related to horizontal inequalities by race or ethnicity and gender, which are discussed later in this chapter.

Wage inequality stems from several sources, including educational attainment, with earnings increasing for higher levels of education. For instance, having completed secondary education is associated with earnings that are significantly higher than those of workers with less than a primary education. In the Southern African Customs Union, educational attainment accounts for 30.2 percent of the Gini coefficient of earnings, and worker occupation and industry contribute 44.4 percent to earnings inequality (World Bank 2022). In South Africa, employer wage setting explains about one-third of wage inequality (Bassier 2023), which is more than the share that is explained by differences in workers' characteristics. Other sources of wage inequality include gender discrimination, geographic region, and inequality of opportunity.

Much of the inequality in the labor market is due to labor market segmentation, which occurs across industrial sectors and occupations, with mining, public administration, construction, and finance having relatively higher returns than agriculture. Segmentation leads to inequality if people of a certain race, gender, or ethnicity are concentrated in low-paying sectors and occupations relative to others who are more likely to find employment in high-paying occupations and sectors. For example, in South Africa, Whites dominate professional and management positions, whereas Africans are mainly artisans and operators in service, craft, and related occupations and are in the armed forces (Gradín 2019; Van der Berg and Bhorat 1999).

African women are more likely to be in self-employment and domestic service, and more of them are unemployed, in school, or engaged in household activities. African women and Coloured women are more likely to be found in elementary occupations (Gradín 2021). In Kenya, unpaid family work and self-employment are the major sources of employment for women, while wage employment is the major source for men (KNBS 2020).

Informality

One specificity of labor markets in Africa is the high share of informal activity. The informal sector in Africa is among the largest in the world, estimated at about 85 percent of total employment on the continent (ILOSTAT 2018), and contributes about 62 percent of gross domestic product (GDP) (Ohnsorge and Yu 2022). Figure 4.3 plots the share of informal employment[1] in total employment for the world and select regions. Along with South Asia, SSA has had the highest share of informal employment over the past decade, and this share has remained stable. In contrast, the populous Southeast Asia and Pacific region has had a declining rate of informal employment, leading to the declining world share of informal employment in total employment. Only North Africa has seen significant increases in the share of informal employment in total employment.

Figure 4.3 **Share of Informal Employment**

Percent

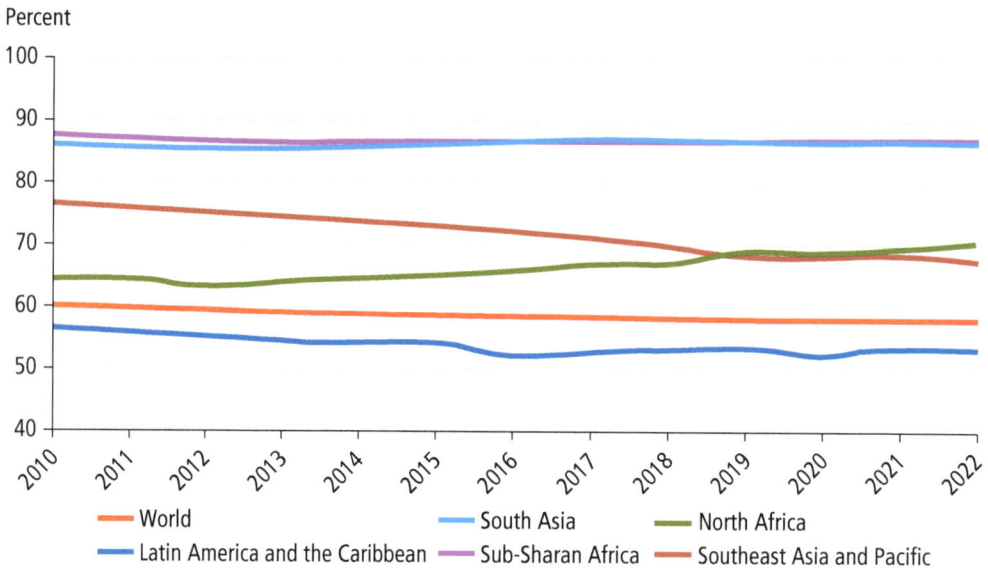

Source: Authors' elaboration using International Labour Organization modeled estimates.

The high level of informality in Africa masks significant heterogeneity between subregions (67 percent in North Africa and 89 percent in SSA) and countries (95 percent in Burkina Faso and 96 percent in Benin, compared to 46 percent in Cabo Verde and 32 percent in South Africa) (David, Diallo, and Nilsson 2023). Dell'Anno and Adu (2020) have estimated that, in Nigeria, between 38 percent and 58 percent of GDP comes from informal work.

Furthermore, although the data for the recent decade show practically no variation in the size of the informal sector, countries such as Cameroon and Kenya saw significant increases in their shares of informal employment (KNBS 2020; Zamo Akono et al. 2021). In Kenya, for instance, the structure of employment changed from formal wage work toward informal jobs, with the share of informal employment rising from 73 percent in 2001 to 83 percent in 2017. Over the same period, the share of formal wage employment declined from 21 to 12 percent of total employment (KNBS 2020).

Although untangling the linkages between informality and inequality is challenging, some channels can be delineated as follows. On the one hand, the lack of protection, high vulnerability, and low productivity that characterize the informal sector can lead to a dual labor market and a highly unequal society. This inequality can be amplified by the lower redistributive capacity of the state due to a narrow tax base, or it could be improved if the informal sector facilitates entrance into the labor market for those who would not have had the opportunity otherwise. On the other hand, the degree of inequality shapes the institutional framework of the economy and can encourage informality through high credit constraints or barriers to entry. A cross-country analysis shows that a smaller informal sector is associated with a less-unequal income distribution (David et al. 2023). A series of household surveys from African capitals confirm the findings of the cross-country analysis, with the results showing a positive correlation between having access to formal incomes and a decrease in inequality.

Labor markets in SSA are more flexible than is usually acknowledged, where varied forms of private wage employment and self-employment coexist alongside pockets of public-sector opportunities. These configurations are different across countries and urban and rural labor markets, but it is common to see informal employment across the private and public sectors. Accessing formal jobs may be dependent on both the structural traits and existing networks of the local economy (De Vreyer and Roubaud 2013), and those awaiting a salaried public-sector job opening may diversify their income by combining a part-time job in the private sector with "volunteer" work in the public sector (da Corta et al. 2021).

Some types of informal self-employment—like those based on mortgaging productive materials, such as goods given on credit—may not provide resilience to shocks or facilitate social mobility. For example, da Corta et al. (2021) examined trends in the poverty trajectories of youth entering the labor market in Niger and identified precarious forms of employment that can lead to chronic poverty, including low-paid farm labor activities combined with home-based activities in rural areas and market gardening and textile sewing in urban areas.

Not all informal activities are precarious. There is evidence of benefits for some types of small-scale entrepreneurship—such as those based on skills acquired through school or vocational training or observation—and there is also evidence of sound trajectories for return migrants (da Corta et al. 2021; De Vreyer and Roubaud 2013). The consensus is that, in Africa, some occupations in the informal sector act as a stepping stone to formal jobs (De Vreyer and Roubaud 2013). Across the continent, informal activities are also associated with the middle class. For instance, in a comparative study, Clément et al. (2022) showed that, in Côte d'Ivoire, middle-income households are both rural and urban and are employed in both formal and informal sectors. Sketching a typology of the middle class in Côte d'Ivoire, these authors found that informal workers constitute almost 40 percent of this group, working mostly in the manufacturing and wholesale and retail sectors, with many of them having entrepreneurial profiles.

The overlap between the informal and the service sectors makes the emergence of the "gig economy" of interest for what the informal sector could look like in the future. Cieslik, Banya, and Vira (2022) provided a useful framework for conceptualizing the linkages between the informal sector and the gig economy, assessing its potential to create decent jobs. Using a case study of e-hailing services in Lagos, Nigeria, they found that, despite some gains compared to regular taxiing, the gig economy does not offer secure employment or earnings. Beyond the gig economy, growing digitalization can shape the informal sector through channels that go from lowering the cost of formalization to improving market transparency and enhancing productivity, with significant returns in the agriculture sector, for instance (Nguimkeu and Okou 2020).

Several studies have reported a correlation between human capital or skills accumulation and earnings, which varies across employment types and informality status. The theory predicts that, in a highly informal labor market with a mix of formal and informal jobs, overlapping wage distributions, and changes in formality status between and within jobs, the probability of human capital upgrading is lower when working informally than formally (Bobba et al. 2021). Empirical evidence shows that, in SSA, the occupational trajectories have differentiated effects on workers' welfare according to the type of informal employment. For instance, in Ghana, education is positively correlated with earnings growth for those who are wage employed but not for those who are self-employed (Falco et al. 2014).

According to Danquah, Schotte, and Sen (2021), informal wage jobs are more likely than self-employment to be a stepping stone to formal employment relationships in Ghana, South Africa, Tanzania, and Uganda. The authors also identified job segmentation between wage employment and self-employment, with few workers exiting formal jobs or informal wage employment in occupations that have barriers to entry (like capital or training) for self-employment (Danquah et al. 2021). However, the transition from a formal occupation to an informal occupation does not always translate into a setback for the household as a whole. Evidence from urban Nigeria shows that the consumption of a household is not substantially altered across various degrees of informality experienced through its working members' job transitions (Egger, Poggi, and Rufrancos 2023).

Marginalized Groups: Women, Youth, and Ethnic and Racial Groups

The labor market inequalities highlighted in the previous sections appear even more sharply where marginalized groups are concerned. Social identities such as gender, age, or race can contribute to discrimination in the labor market and amplify the inequalities experienced by vulnerable groups. This section delves into some of the intersectional inequalities of the labor market in Africa.

Women

Across Africa, women have lower employment rates than men do. For example, in South Africa, less than 38 percent of women are employed in any year, while the corresponding statistic for men is never below 48 percent (Stats SA et al. 2019). In Ghana, the unemployment rate among women was 8.8 percent compared to 7.0 percent among men (Atta-Ankomah et al. 2020). In Kenya, youth and women have higher unemployment rates than adults and men (KNBS 2020).

Family agriculture is the major source of employment in most countries, particularly for women. Unpaid family work and self-employment are the major sources of employment for women, while wage employment is the major source for men.

Despite the decreasing gender gap in labor force participation, women in the labor market face more-precarious conditions and lower wages. Using evidence from African countries, Danquah et al. (2021) have shown that women are more likely to engage in precarious forms of informal work. Women are more likely to be in informal employment (90 percent) compared to men

(83 percent) (Houngbedji and Zanuso 2021). In Burkina Faso, for example, young women not only have less access to wage work but also are often confined to jobs that extend their domestic roles (such as small food trade or "maid" services) (Kobiane, Ouilili, and Guissou 2020). Furthermore, the average annual income of employed men is almost three times higher than that of women.

In addition, women are subject to occupational segregation, and female-dominated occupations pay lower wages, highlighting the weight of social gender norms (refer to chapter 5). While a woman's personal preferences are a key factor in determining whether she will seek paid work, these preferences are heavily skewed by social norms and constraints that lead women to conform to traditional gender roles. For example, evidence from Tanzania suggests that the social norms underpinning the gender differences in paid work are persistent (Chopra and Zambelli 2017). Most female respondents believed that men are better at paid work and women are better at care work and household tasks. In Burkina Faso, 92 percent of the population believe that men's role is to support the family financially (OECD Development Centre 2018).

Addressing gender norms is key when designing public policies to reduce the gender gap in the labor market. These issues are examined in more depth in chapter 5 on gender inequality.

Youth

The young population experiences much higher unemployment rates compared to older cohorts. For example, in South Africa, young people (ages 16–24) are highly unlikely to be consistently employed and are more likely to experience chronic unemployment (Zizzamia and Ranchhod 2020). According to the narrow definition of unemployment, 40 percent of those between ages 20 and 29 were unemployed between 2005 and 2015 (Sulla and Zikhali 2018). In Niger, young adults (ages 18–35) were found to be economically vulnerable compared to the generations preceding them, with increasingly few possibilities to access employment in the civil service or manufacturing (da Corta et al. 2021).

In a period of insecurity and low state development, the inclusion of youth in both rural and urban labor markets is increasingly precarious and takes place mostly in the informal sector. Rural areas tend to be home to even-more-vulnerable youth. Their primary occupations remain linked to agricultural production, and thus rural youth are more vulnerable to impoverishment or chronic poverty. In Kenya, young people between ages 15 and 34 make up 80 percent of the 2.3 million unemployed (Dolan and Rajak 2016), and the youth unemployment rate among those ages 20–24 is 19.2 percent, more than double the national unemployment rate of 7.4 percent (KNBS 2020).

Seeing their prospects for formal employment in Africa shrinking, youth rely on the informal or second economy (Dolan and Rajak 2016). While most studies on Africa focus on unemployment, most youth are instead working but underemployed and working in a challenging and precarious labor market (Ayele, Khan, and Sumberg 2017; Dolan and Rajak 2016).

This emphasis on youth draws attention to the current inequalities in the labor market and its inability to allow many people to contribute to the economy and development and to achieve a certain level of personal well-being. Informality and vulnerable employment[2] remain a strong reality for most employed youth around the world, and the situation is even more difficult for youth in Africa. This issue is reflected in high youth underemployment and unemployment rates; high rates of youth who are not in employment, education, or training (NEET); and a difficult transition from school to work.

There are large regional variations in NEET rates around the world, with Africa having the highest rate of NEET youth, at 26 percent (refer to figure 4.4). This rate masks the significant heterogeneity between subregions and countries. Across Africa's subregions, the highest average youth NEET rates are in Southern and Western Africa, exceeding 30 percent, and the average rate is much lower in Eastern Africa (19 percent) (refer to figure 4.4). The countries with the highest rates include Benin, Burkina Faso, Guinea, Lesotho, Mauritania, Nigeria, Senegal, and South Africa, with rates exceeding 30 percent, while those in Cameroon, Malawi, Tanzania, and Zimbabwe do not exceed 20 percent (refer to figure 4.5).

Figure 4.4 **Shares of Youth Ages 15–24 Not in Employment, Education, or Training around the World, 2022**

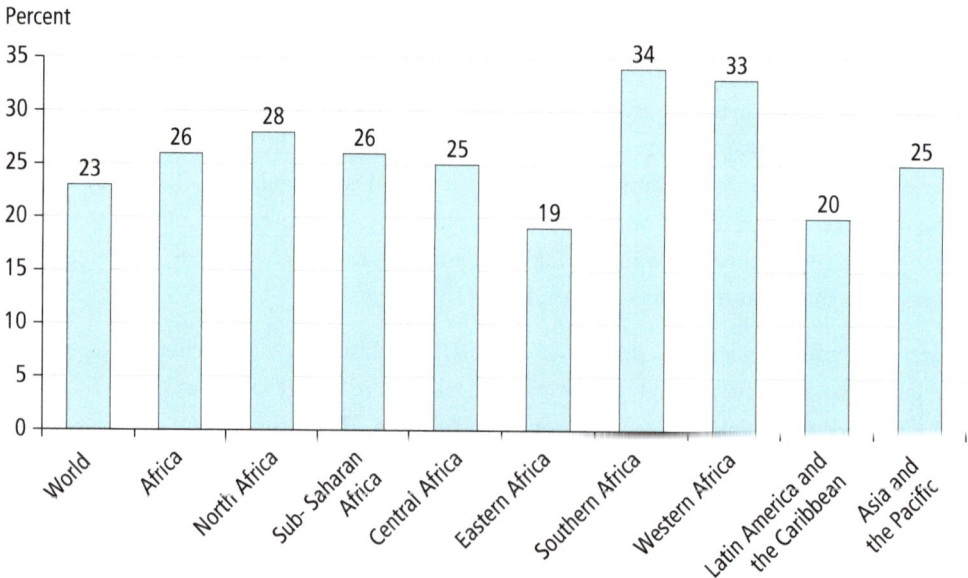

Source: Authors' elaboration using International Labour Organization modeled estimates.

Figure 4.5 Shares of Youth Ages 15–24 Not in Employment, Education, or Training in Select African Countries, 2022

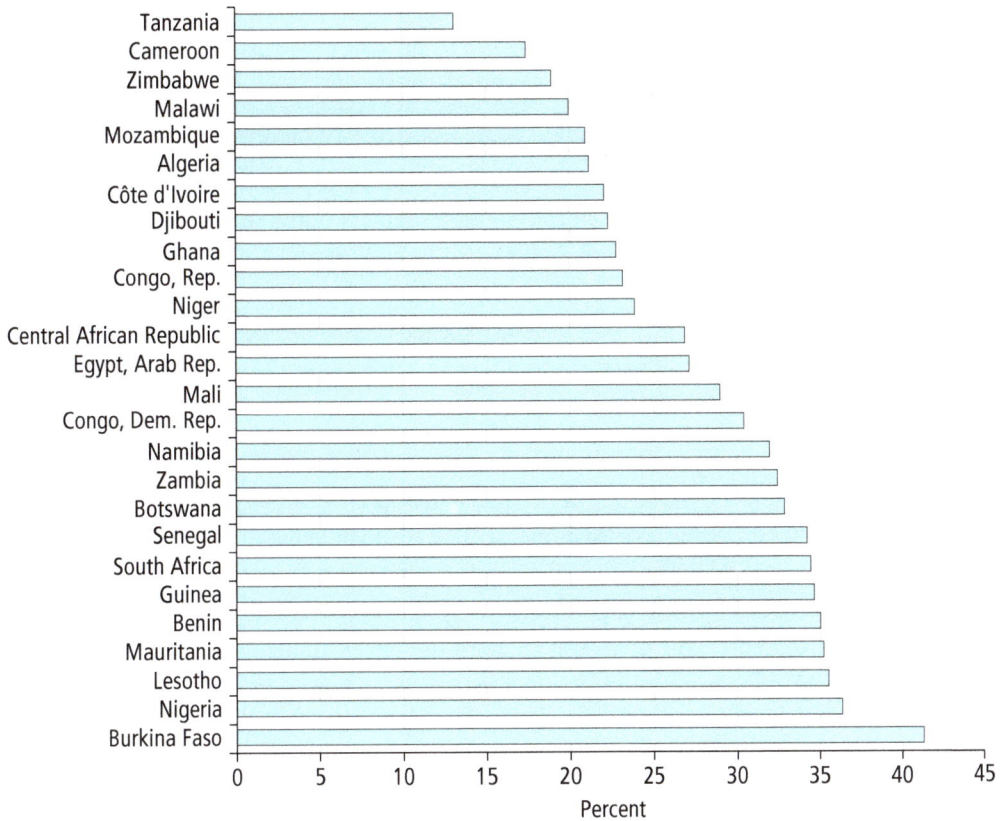

Source: Authors' elaboration using International Labour Organization modeled estimates.

Youth precariousness may be driven by several factors, including relatively low levels of educational attainment (compared with Organisation for Economic Co-operation and Development countries), low access to productive assets (land, transport vehicles, and livestock), rising costs of public services (education and health) and basic services, and lack of access to credit. As a result, youth may be trapped in farming in rural areas or may be driven to find precarious employment in local rural or urban labor markets characterized by weak contractual terms (da Corta et al. 2021).

The literature on youth in African countries has found that self-employment is prevalent, lacks decent remuneration or protection by any legal framework, and is characterized by seasonality (Carreras, Sumberg, and Saha 2021; da Corta et al. 2021; Dolan and Rajak 2016). In rural areas, employment opportunities for young people tend to be intermittent and linked to agricultural production (Nilsson 2019; Yeboah and Jayne 2018). Strong arguments have been advanced in favor of more-integrated and coherent policies across education, labor markets, and financial services (Ayele et al. 2017). Currently, the labor markets in Africa create mainly agricultural or informal nonagricultural jobs for young people, the majority of whom would prefer formal jobs in the public or private sector. This issue highlights the divergence between youth aspirations and the realities of the labor market (Yeboah and Jayne 2018).

The weight of the labor force in the agriculture sector combined with the need to design resilient and less-emissive food systems raise the need to promote policies that reconcile the aspirations of young people, the use of advanced technologies, and the challenges of sustainable agriculture (Houngbedji and Zanuso 2021). Diversification of opportunities within and outside agriculture constitutes a key channel of inclusion for rural youth (da Corta et al. 2021). Prominent channels for inclusion include informal education, vocational training, and networks, which can be designed to change gender and generational norms, thus enabling young people to have the flexibility necessary to achieve autonomy and escape poverty (da Corta et al. 2021).

Youth inclusion in the labor market is a key channel through which young adults can escape chronic poverty and experience upward mobility. Given that youth make up a dominant share of the working-age population in almost all African countries (Lam and Leibbrandt 2023), providing productive employment opportunities for young people is a key priority for the continent, especially in the transition toward a more-sustainable future. Evidence shows that Africa has great potential to create jobs through the transition toward more-sustainable green and digital economies (Dasgupta 2022). Investing in the green and digital sectors can help not only to achieve the United Nations Sustainable Development Goals but also to create additional and resilient jobs for young people.

Ethnic and Racial Groups

Differences across ethnic groups can explain differential economic outcomes, including labor market outcomes (Awaworyi Churchill and Smyth 2017). Ethnic differences have been associated with discrimination in the labor market, with groups that experience discrimination facing financial losses as a result. The existence of several ethnic groups in a society can engender a hierarchical structure, which projects one ethnic group as superior over others or prioritized in policy. This hierarchy causes economic and labor market disadvantages, leaving some ethnicities discriminated against, lacking opportunities, and relatively disadvantaged or marginalized. This labor market discrimination can also influence wages and productivity, for example, by limiting access to the formal labor market for certain groups or individuals, thus forcing them into informal or precarious employment (Awaworyi Churchill and Danquah 2022). A key channel through which ethnic differences can influence informal work is trust, which has been linked to income poverty, productivity, and wages (Awaworyi Churchill and Danquah 2022).

In Ghana, ethnic diversity is associated with a higher probability of engaging in informal work (Awaworyi Churchill and Danquah 2022). Evidence from South Africa shows that differences in labor market experiences reflect strong, persistent legacies of apartheid policies, with Black Africans having the highest unemployment rate, at 31 percent in 2017, while the unemployment rate was 6.7 percent among Whites (Stats SA et al. 2019). In addition to having worse employment outcomes, Black Africans also earn the lowest wages when employed. In pooled survey data from 2011–15, the monthly earnings of the White population were more than three times higher than those of Black Africans (Stats SA et al. 2019).

Impact of the COVID-19 Crisis

Even in periods of strong employment growth, some racial and ethnic groups, women, and youth have faced a difficult situation in the labor market. Globally, before the COVID-19 pandemic, young people were around three times more likely to be unemployed than older adults (Dasgupta 2022). The pandemic threatened to exacerbate existing inequalities within and between countries. The impact was felt more by vulnerable groups, with the distribution of job losses due to COVID-19 in South Africa being heavily skewed toward youth, those with lower levels of formal education, lower-skilled workers, and informal-sector workers (Kohler et al. 2022). Groups that have always been vulnerable, such as women, Africans or Blacks, youth, and less-educated groups, have been disproportionately negatively affected.

The employment impact of the COVID-19 crisis has been poignant among young people. The global employment deficit of young people relative to 2019 amounted to 8.2 percent (Dasgupta 2022). The deficit varies greatly among regions, with youth employment deficits of 5.6 percent in SSA and 10.1 percent in North Africa in 2020. Young women have also experienced a greater employment impact as a result of the COVID-19 crisis compared with young men. Furthermore, the COVID-19 crisis has reversed years of progress in reducing youth NEET rates.

In addition, shocks of much greater magnitude with overlapping dimensions, such as the COVID-19 pandemic, disproportionately affect informal workers and can have long-lasting negative impacts on the well-being of their households. The hard lockdowns and border closures in some African countries, combined with a global slowdown in economic activity, were estimated to have reduced GDP by 8.2 percent in South Africa, 8.9 percent in Botswana, and 15 percent in Mauritius (Anyanwu and Salami 2021), severely limiting economic opportunities (and sometimes the pursuit of activities) in the informal sector. The lack of access to social assistance or the inaccessibility of emergency measures for informal workers further increased their vulnerability.

Rogan and Skinner (2022) found that, in South Africa, job losses have been greater in the informal sector, and the recovery rate has been much slower, with even stronger negative impacts on women, thus entailing a widening of inequalities. Khambule (2022) found a similar result for a municipality in KwaZulu-Natal, with increased precariousness for informal workers due to the COVID-19 lockdown and lack of adequate policy responses. Chen et al. (2021) pointed out that, in Durban, onerous application requirements made it difficult for waste pickers to obtain support. Furthermore, some studies have indicated that the informal sector has had a negative impact on an equitable recovery in the wake of the COVID-19 pandemic (IMF 2021; Ohnsorge and Yu 2022), pointing to the need for reform of national social protection systems for greater inclusion to prevent this problem from occurring again (Barca and Alfers 2021; Bastagli and Lowe 2021).[3]

Conclusion

This chapter explored how the labor market helps explain inequality in Africa. Some of the pathways are conventional and direct, such as the implications of unemployment and wage distribution, while others are more focused on the specificities of the African context. One key is the relatively greater importance of the informal sector and informal employment in most African economies and societies. The chapter then explored horizontal inequalities by considering the labor market experiences of marginalized groups, with an emphasis on youth and women.

In all the countries considered, understanding the labor market is key to understanding the evolution of overall income inequality. Who finds employment, what type of employment they find, and whether the employment is in the formal or informal sector all contribute substantially to aggregate income inequality. In addition, a significant variation exists in the levels and trends of labor market inequality by country and for several countries and across multiple time periods. The Gini coefficient for earnings is greater than 0.5, which illustrates that wage inequality is relatively high in many African contexts and highlights the importance of situating the labor market as a key institution for understanding inequality in Africa.

In addition to wage dispersion, some countries, primarily located in Southern Africa, have very high unemployment rates. However, those with very low unemployment rates tend to have very large informal sectors, raising concerns about underemployment, precariousness, and vulnerability among the people employed in those sectors. The evidence is mixed on the dynamic welfare implications of having a large informal sector. In some cases, informal-sector employment facilitates the transfer of skills and subsequent access to formal-sector employment, which leads to upward mobility. In other contexts, informal-sector employment can generate strong, low-productivity-path dependence, leading to potential poverty traps and persistence.

For the labor market experiences of marginalized groups, significant and robust gender differentials exist in employment prospects and earnings. Women are more likely to find employment in informal jobs or to be self-employed and are disproportionately likely to be engaged in unpaid family work. These employment and wage differentials also apply to certain racial and ethnic groups in some countries.

Young people have higher unemployment rates than the rest of the working-age population, and this issue is compounded by the fact that youth who find employment tend to experience underemployment and precariousness. Furthermore, Africa has the highest levels of youth who are NEET. Considering the underlying demographic trends and that the age profile of the continent is relatively young, the NEET levels are cause for even more concern.

Labor market policies and related development policies are important for understanding how inequality in Africa will evolve in the future. The heterogeneity on the continent implies that relevant constraints and factors should be considered at smaller geographic or political levels to be meaningful. Nonetheless, at an abstract and general level, considering policy coherence across different social and economic dimensions seems sensible.

Substantial demographic, economic, and technological changes are likely to happen over the next 50 years, both globally and in Africa. The effects of climate change and corresponding measures to limit its impact will change the way economies function and evolve, and Africa is likely to have an increasingly large share of the world's working-age adults for the near future. These factors, combined with the ability to adapt to technological advances, provide a valuable, albeit imprecise, framework for thinking about how African countries could optimally manage the labor market and reduce inequality and improve welfare going forward.

Notes

1. *Informal employment* comprises persons who, in their main or secondary jobs, are (1) own-account workers, employers, or members of producers' cooperatives employed in their own informal-sector enterprises; (2) own-account workers engaged in the production of goods exclusively for their own final use by their household (for example, subsistence farming); (3) contributing family workers, regardless of whether working in formal- or informal-sector enterprises; and (4) employees holding informal jobs, whether employed by formal-sector enterprises, informal-sector enterprises, or households as paid domestic workers.
2. *Vulnerable or precarious employment* can include daywork (commission based, task based, domestic work, and so forth), self-employment, seasonal salaried work (in retail or construction), and small business ownership.
3. The COVID-19 pandemic prompted some positive, temporary experimentation on informal workers' coverage in emergency initiatives (such as Novissi in Togo; for example, refer to Bastagli and Lowe 2021; Devereux 2021). The pandemic also revealed that cash assistance alone is rarely sufficient to protect informal workers. This issue has prompted some countries, like Tanzania and Togo, to shift toward possibly wider structural changes for the inclusion of informal workers, like the progressive extension of contributory social insurance (Barca and Alfers 2021).

References

Anyanwu, John C., and Adeleke O. Salami. 2021. "The Impact of COVID-19 on African Economies: An Introduction." *African Development Review* 33 (Suppl. 1): S1–S16. https://doi.org/10.1111/1467 -8268.12531.

Atta-Ankomah, Richmond, Robert Darko Osei, Isaac Osei-Akoto, Felix Ankomah Asante, Abena D. Oduro, Nkechi Owoo, Monica Lambon-Quayefio, and Stephen Afranie. 2020. *Inequality Diagnostics for Ghana*. African Center of Excellence for Inequalities Research, University of Cape Town, South Africa.

Awaworyi Churchill, Sefa, and Russell Smyth. 2017. "Ethnic Diversity and Poverty." *World Development* 95: 285–302. https://doi.org/10.1016/j.worlddev.2017.02.032.

Awaworyi Churchill, Sefa, and Michael Danquah. 2022. "Ethnic Diversity and Informal Work in Ghana." *Journal of Development Studies* 58 (7): 1312–31. https://doi.org/10.1080/00220388.2022.2061852.

Ayele, Seife, Samir Khan, and James Sumberg. 2017. "Introduction: New Perspectives on Africa's Youth Employment Challenge." *IDS Bulletin* 47 (3). https://doi.org/10.19088/1968-2017.123.

Barca, Valentina, and Laura Alfers. 2021. "Including Informal Workers within Social Protection Systems—A Summary of Options." Social Protection Approaches to COVID-19 Expert Advice Service, DAI Global UK Ltd., Hemel Hempstead, UK.

Bassier, Ihsaan. 2023. "Firms and Inequality When Unemployment Is High." *Journal of Development Economics* 161: 103029. https://doi.org/10.1016/j.jdeveco.2022.103029.

Bastagli, Francesca, and Christina Lowe. 2021. "Social Protection Response to Covid-19 and Beyond: Emerging Evidence and Learning for Future Crises." ODI Working Paper 614, Overseas Development Institute, London. https://doi.org/10.13140/RG.2.2.10088.80641.

Bobba, Matteo, Luca Flabbi, Santiago Levy, and Mauricio Tejada. 2021. "Labor Market Search, Informality, and On-the-Job Human Capital Accumulation." *Journal of Econometrics* 223 (2): 433–53. https://doi/org/10.1016/j.jeconom.2019.05.026.

Carreras, Marco, James Sumberg, and Amrita Saha. 2021. "Work and Rural Livelihoods: The Micro Dynamics of Africa's 'Youth Employment Crisis.'" *European Journal of Development Research* 33 (6): 1666–94. https://doi.org/10.1057/s41287-020-00310-y.

Cassim, Aalia, and Daniela Casale. 2022. "Identifying the Wage Differential in the Temporary Employment Services Sector: Evidence for South Africa Using Administrative Tax Records." *Journal of Development Studies* 58 (10): 2065–88. https://doi.org/10.1080/00220388.2022.2094252.

Chen, Martha, Erofili Grapsa, Ghida Ismail, Mike Rogan, Marcela Valdivia, Laura Alfers, Jenna Harvey, Ana Carolina Ogando, Sarah Orleans Reed, and Sally Roever. 2021. "COVID-19 and Informal Work: Distinct Pathways of Impact and Recovery in 11 Cities Around the World." WIEGO Working Paper 42, Women in Informal Employment: Globalizing and Organizing, Manchester, UK.

Chopra, Deepta, and Elena Zambelli. 2017. "No Time to Rest: Women's Lived Experiences of Balancing Paid Work and Unpaid Care Work." Institute of Development Studies, Brighton, UK.

Cieslik, Katarzyna, Roland Banya, and Bhaskar Vira. 2022. "Offline Contexts of Online Jobs: Platform Drivers, Decent Work, and Informality in Lagos, Nigeria." *Development Policy Review* 40 (4): e12595. https://doi.org/10.1111/dpr.12595.

Clément, Matthieu, Eric Rougier, Jean-Philippe Berrou, François Combarnous, and Dominique Darbon. 2022. "'What's in the Middle': Scratching beneath the Surface of the Middle Class(es) in Brazil, Côte d'Ivoire, Turkey and Vietnam." *World Development* 158: 105988. https://doi.org/10.1016/j.worlddev.2022.105988.

da Corta, Lucia, Aïssa Diarra, Vidya Diwakar, Marta Eichsteller, Abdoutan Harouna, and Cecilia Poggi. 2021. "Youth Inclusion in Labour Markets in Niger: Gender Dynamics and Livelihoods." AFD Research Paper 216, Agence Française de Développement, Paris.

Danquah, Michael, Simone Schotte, and Kunal Sen. 2021. "Informal Work in Sub-Saharan Africa: Dead End or Stepping-Stone?" *IZA Journal of Development and Migration* 12 (1): 20210015. https://doi/org/10.2478/izajodm-2021-0015.

Dasgupta, Sukti. 2022. *Global Employment Trends for Youth 2022: Investing in Transforming Futures for Young People*. Geneva: International Labour Organization. https://doi.org/10.54394/QSMU1809.

David, Anda, Yoro Diallo, and Björn Nilsson. 2023. "Informality and Inequality: The African Case." *Journal of African Economies* 32 (Supplement_2): ii273–ii295. https://doi.org/10.1093/jae/ejac052.

De Vreyer, Philippe, and François Roubaud. 2013. *Urban Labor Markets in Sub-Saharan Africa*. Africa Development Forum. Washington, DC: World Bank and Agence Française de Développement.

Dell'Anno, Roberto, and Omobola Adu. 2020. "The Size of the Informal Economy in Nigeria: A Structural Equation Approach." *International Journal of Social Economics* 47 (8): 1063–78. https://doi.org/10.1108/IJSE-12-2019-0747.

Devereux, Stephen. 2021. "Social Protection Responses to COVID-19 in Africa." *Global Social Policy* 21 (3): 421–47. https://doi.org/10.1177/14680181211021260.

Dolan, Catherine, and Dinah Rajak. 2016. "Remaking Africa's Informal Economies: Youth, Entrepreneurship and the Promise of Inclusion at the Bottom of the Pyramid." *Journal of Development Studies* 52 (4): 514–29. https://doi.org/10.1080/00220388.2015.1126249.

Egger, Eva-Maria, Cecilia Poggi, and Héctor Rufrancos. 2023. "Does the Depth of Informality Influence Welfare in Urban Sub-Saharan Africa?" *Oxford Economic Papers* 76 (1): 187–206. https://doi.org/10.1093/oep/gpac052.

Falco, Paolo, Andrew Kerr, Pierella Paci, and Bob Rijkers. 2014. *Working toward Better Pay: Earning Dynamics in Ghana and Tanzania*. Washington, DC: World Bank.

Gradín, Carlos. 2019. "Occupational Segregation by Race in South Africa after Apartheid." *Review of Development Economics* 23 (2): 553–76. https://doi.org/10.1111/rode.12551.

Gradín, Carlos. 2021. "Occupational Gender Segregation in Post-Apartheid South Africa." *Feminist Economics* 27 (3): 102–33. https://doi.org/10.1080/13545701.2021.1906439.

Houngbedji, Kenneth, and Claire Zanuso. 2021. "Les jeunes et les enjeux du marché du travail en Afrique." In *Agence Française de Développement, L'économie Africaine 2021*, 75–93. Paris: La Découverte.

ILOSTAT. 2018. *ILO Modelled Estimates Database*. Geneva: ILOSTAT. https://ilostat.ilo.org/data/.

IMF (International Monetary Fund). 2021. *The Global Informal Workforce: Priorities for Inclusive Growth*. Washington, DC: IMF. https://doi.org/10.5089/9781513575919.071.

Khambule, Isaac. 2022. "COVID-19 and the Informal Economy in a Small-Town in South Africa: Governance Implications in the Post-COVID Era." *Cogent Social Sciences* 8 (1): 2078528. https://doi.org/10.1080/23311886.2022.2078528.

KNBS (Kenya National Bureau of Statistics). 2020. *Inequality Trends and Diagnostics in Kenya 2020*. Nairobi: KNBS.

Kobiane, Jean-François, Idrissa Ouilili, and Sibi Guissou. 2020. "État Des Lieux Des Inégalités Multidimensionnelles Au Burkina Faso." AFD Research Paper 132, Agence Française de Développement, Paris.

Kohler, Timothy, Haroon Bhorat, Robert Hill, and Benjamin Stanwix. 2022. "The Short-Term Labor Market Effects of South Africa's National COVID-19 Lockdown." In *The Future of the South African Political Economy Post-COVID 19*, edited by Mzukisi Qobo, Mills Soko, and Nomfundo Xenia Ngwenya, 129–49. International Political Economy Series. Cham: Palgrave Macmillan. https://doi.org/10.1007/978-3-031-10576-0_6.

Lam, David, and Murray Leibbrandt. 2023. "Demographic Challenges for Global Labour Markets in the 21st Century, Africa in a Changing World." SALDRU Working Paper 303, Southern Africa Labour and Development Research Unit, University of Cape Town, South Africa.

Nguimkeu, Pierre, and Cedric Okou. 2020. "Increasing Informal Sector Productivity." In *The Future of Work in Africa: Harnessing the Potential of Digital Technologies for All*, edited by Jieun Choi, Mark A. Dutz, and Zainab Usman, 121–62. Africa Development Forum. Washington, DC: World Bank.

Nilsson, Björn. 2019. "The School-to-Work Transition in Developing Countries." *Journal of Development Studies* 55 (5): 745–64. https://doi.org/10.1080/00220388.2018.1475649.

OECD (Organisation for Economic Co-operation and Development) Development Centre. 2018. *Burkina Faso SIGI Country Study*. Social Institutions and Gender Index. Paris: OECD Development Centre.

Ohnsorge, Franziska, and Shu Yu. 2022. *The Long Shadow of Informality: Challenges and Policies*. Washington, DC: World Bank.

Ranchhod, Vimal, and Reza Che Daniels. 2021. "Labour Market Dynamics in South Africa at the Onset of the COVID-19 Pandemic." *South African Journal of Economics* 89 (1): 44–62. https://doi.org/10.1111/saje.12283.

Rogan, Michael, and Caroline Skinner. 2022. "The COVID-19 Crisis and the South African Informal Economy: A Stalled Recovery." WIDER Working Paper 2022/40, United Nations University, World Institute for Development Economics Research, Helsinki, Finland. https://doi.org/10.35188/UNU-WIDER/2022/171-6.

Schotte, Simone, Rocco Zizzamia, and Murray Leibbrandt. 2018. "A Poverty Dynamics Approach to Social Stratification: The South African Case." *World Development* 110: 88–103. https://doi.org/10.1016/j.worlddev.2018.05.024.

Stats SA (Statistics South Africa), SALDRU (Southern Africa Labour and Development Research Unit), and AFD (Agence Française de Développement). 2019. *Inequality Trends in South Africa: A Multidimensional Diagnostic of Inequality, 2017*. Pretoria: Stats SA, SALDRU, and AFD.

Sulla, Victor, and Precious Zikhali. 2018. *Overcoming Poverty and Inequality in South Africa: An Assessment of Drivers, Constraints and Opportunities*. Washington, DC: World Bank.

Van der Berg, Servaas, and Haroon Bhorat. 1999. "The Present as a Legacy of the Past: The Labour Market, Inequality and Poverty in South Africa." Development Policy Research Unit Working Paper 99/029, Development and Poverty Research Unit, University of Cape Town, South Africa. http://hdl.handle.net/11427/7242.

World Bank. 2022. *Inequality in Southern Africa: An Assessment of the Southern African Customs Union*. Washington, DC: World Bank. https://doi.org/10.1596/37283.

Yeboah, Felix Kwame, and Thomas S. Jayne. 2018. "Africa's Evolving Employment Trends." *Journal of Development Studies* 54 (5): 803–32. https://doi.org/10.1000/00220388.2018.1430767.

Zamo Akono, Christian, Thierry Bedzeme, James Bienvenu Ebaa Ebaa, and Rosalie Niekou. 2021. "Transformation Structurelle et Inégalités de Revenus Au Cameroun: 2001–2014." AFD Research Paper, Agence française de développement, Paris. https://EconPapers.repec.org/RePEc:avg:wpaper:fr12320.

Zizzamia, Rocco, and Vimal Ranchhod. 2020. "Earnings Inequality over the Life-Course in South Africa." AFD Research Paper 160, Agence Française de Développement, Paris.

Chapter 5

Gender Inequalities

Abena D. Oduro, Serge Rabier, Jacqueline Mosomi, and Rawane Yasser

Introduction

Gender inequalities, which usually are biases against women and girls, are deep-seated in African countries. These inequalities have persisted in the economic (for example, participation in income-generating activities and access to and ownership of resources), social (for example, access to health and education), and political (for example, participation in decision-making at the community and national levels) dimensions. Gender inequalities are manifest within the household, with women often having limited voice and decision-making power; being burdened by unpaid care work; and being subjected to domestic violence, fewer political and legal rights, and more constraints on mobility.

Progress toward gender equality will not only improve women's well-being but also promote economic growth. There is less-consistent evidence on the effect of economic growth on gender equality (Kabeer and Natali 2013), because the relationship is mediated by the type of economic growth and the different ways in which patriarchy is manifested (Kabeer 2016).

This chapter focuses on the importance of gender equality in Africa, its intersectionality, and measures to reduce gender inequality in the quest to build fairer and more-inclusive African societies. The chapter discusses gender inequality along the dimensions of education, health, labor force participation (LFP), unpaid care work, and assets.

Gender Inequalities in Education

Empirical investigations have found that gender equality in literacy rates (Baliamoune-Lutz and McGillivray 2015) and in education (Altuzarra, Gálvez-Gálvez, and González-Flores 2021; Bandara 2015; Klasen and Lamanna 2009) are positively associated with economic growth in Africa. Much progress has been made on the continent in both access to education and narrowing the gender gap in enrollment (Baten et al. 2021; Evans, Akmal, and Jakiela 2021).

This progress has yielded positive spillover effects. Educated women are more likely to enroll their daughters and sons in school. Education and skills training can improve women's income earning opportunities, reduce the likelihood of early marriage, reduce fertility rates, and lead to better health outcomes for children. Still, Sub-Saharan Africa (SSA) exhibits some of the largest gender gaps in enrollment and the lowest enrollment rates at all levels of education.

Gender Gaps in School Enrollment and Performance

Although they have narrowed, gender gaps in gross primary enrollment rates (measured as the difference between male and female enrollment rates) persist despite enrollment rates of close to 100 percent in many countries (UIS 2023). In most countries, the gender gap is biased against girls; however, in some countries, such as Mauritius, the gender gap is biased against boys. There is evidence that girls outperform boys in numeracy and literacy in primary school in Kenya, Tanzania, and Uganda (Buhl-Wiggers, Jones, and Thornton 2021), and girls in grade 6 outperform boys in reading in eight countries in Southern and Eastern Africa (Welmond and Gregory 2021).

Gender gaps in secondary education occur within the context of low gross secondary enrollment rates. The gender gap is not always biased against girls. In 14 of 24 African countries for which data are available, the gender gap is biased against boys. In South Africa, for example, although enrollment is high, progress through school is slowed by high repetition rates, with boys being more likely to repeat a grade or to drop out (Lam and Branson 2014). In a few African countries, such as the Arab Republic of Egypt, Lesotho, and South Africa, secondary and tertiary enrollment rates are higher for girls and women, and there is concern about boys being left behind (Bossavie and Kanninen 2018; Spaull and Makaluza 2019).

The gender gap in enrollment rates at the different education levels differs across countries depending on their development level and the socioeconomic status of households. Therefore, it is important to consider the intersectionality of income and gender. In poorer countries, enrollment rates are lagging, and the gender gaps favor boys and men. In wealthier countries, despite the narrowing of the national gender gap, girls from poor households and those living in rural areas are more likely to be left behind.

Gender Segregation in Fields of Study

A common trend in all countries is the underrepresentation of women in the fields of science, technology, engineering, and mathematics (STEM) at the tertiary level (Hammond et al. 2020). This trend cannot be explained by gender differences in mathematics and science performance, because girls do not always perform worse than boys on standardized tests (Reddy et al. 2021; Welmond and Gregory 2021). In some countries, especially where there are wide gender gaps in enrollment, the underrepresentation of women in STEM can be explained by barriers to access to secondary school. Entrenched social norms on gender roles in society and stereotypes about male and female capabilities are another reason for the gender gaps in enrollment (Charles and Bradley 2009). For the few women who join STEM fields, other factors, such as gender discrimination, sexual harassment, and lack of mentorship, contribute to women "dropping out" of STEM fields (Hammond et al. 2020).

Interventions That Reduce the Gender Gap in Enrollment

Poverty and the direct costs and opportunity costs of education, coupled with social norms that influence perceptions of the roles and position of women in society, are important drivers of gender inequality in education. When resources are scarce, the choice sometimes can be between sending children to school and having them assist with household chores or economic activities to bring in extra income (Giacobino et al. 2022). Usually, because of patriarchal cultural norms, girls often leave school for early marriages.

Interventions to reduce the cost of schooling contribute the most to keeping girls enrolled in school. For example, in Ethiopia, the abolition of school fees increased schooling for girls and women and reduced fertility (Chicoine 2021). In Ghana, the provision of scholarships to attend senior secondary school increased tertiary enrollment rates among girls (Duflo, Dupas, and Kremer 2021). Interventions to alleviate poverty, such as conditional cash transfers in South Africa (Eyal and Woolard 2014) and Malawi (Baird et al. 2016), also have led to increased female enrollment.

Interestingly, to combat social and cultural norms, Ashraf et al. (2020) found that teaching secondary school girls in Zambia how to advocate for themselves by providing negotiation training enabled them to stay in school and improved educational outcomes in later years. In addition, providing bicycles to schoolgirls in Zambia reduced their commute time and their absenteeism from school (Fiala et al. 2022). In Kenya, improving school water, sanitation, and hygiene facilities increased school enrollment and improved gender parity (Garn et al. 2013), and the provision of feminine hygiene products to schoolgirls reduced absenteeism (Benshaul-Tolonen et al. 2020).

The high prevalence of child marriage and teenage pregnancies are additional obstacles to secondary school enrollment and completion in Africa (Giacobino et al. 2022; Male and Wodon 2018; Wodon, Nguyen, and Tsimpo 2016). Providing scholarships to girls who are about to complete primary school has been found to delay the age of marriage by 9 months in Niger (Giacobino et al. 2022).

Gender inequality in education in Africa is nuanced. The direction of the gender bias depends on the country, the education level (primary, secondary, or tertiary), and the education indicator of interest. The spillover effects of education on other dimensions of human capability and well-being suggest that education policy must be carefully designed to address the different factors that impinge on the enrollment of boys and girls in school and their progress up the education ladder.

Gender Inequalities in Health

Gender inequalities in health refer to the differences in health access and outcomes between men and women, or boys and girls, that occur because of discrimination and gender-blind prevention and treatment mechanisms. Health inequalities are usually the result of gender stereotypes and sociocultural roles, which intersect with other gender inequalities, such as in education, labor markets, and income.

This section focuses on gender inequalities in sexual and reproductive health rights because of the devastating toll that poor reproductive health and limited sexual rights have on women's well-being and society at large. Gendered social norms and gender-blind health policies and institutions contribute to the health risks and vulnerabilities that women and girls face in contrast to men and boys. The dimensions considered in this section are maternal mortality and morbidity, female genital mutilation (FGM), HIV/AIDS, and gender-based violence (GBV).

Gender Inequalities in Sexual and Reproductive Health and Rights

Although aggregate data on maternal mortality and morbidity, FGM, HIV/AIDS, and GBV show some improvements in Africa, the continent is still lagging in achieving its goals (Rabier 2021). The most recent projections for Africa show that 390 women will die in childbirth for every 100,000 live births by 2030. This issue is against the United Nations Sustainable Development Goal (SDG) target of no more than 70 deaths. Many factors explain this situation: low incomes, poor governance and funding of health systems, unmet needs in education, employment status, and place of residence. All these factors, combined with the persistence of social norms that weigh more heavily on some girls and women than on others, highlight the intersectional aspect of gender inequality. Social norms range from harmful practices (for example, FGM) or inaction to severe constraints for women seeking maternal care and services (such as being prohibited from traveling alone) and women not being allowed by custom to participate in decision-making in family planning, exposing them to risky pregnancy and delivery (Evans 2013).

Attendance at antenatal clinics and the presence of a skilled attendant at the time of childbirth can reduce the likelihood of maternal mortality. In Ghana, spatial inequality in the distribution of health facilities and income inequality combine to put poor women and women living in rural communities at higher risk of dying during childbirth. Almost all women in the highest wealth quintile deliver their children in a health facility compared to 62 percent of women in the poorest wealth quintile, and 90 percent of urban women deliver their children in a health facility compared to 69 percent of rural women (GSS, GHS, and ICF 2018).

Maternal mortality and morbidity[1] and childbirth complications due to early or unwanted pregnancies, as well as limited access to antenatal care, affect girls and young women (ages 15–19 years) who are at higher risk than adult women in countries such as Chad, Guinea, Mali, Mozambique, Niger, and Sierra Leone (Osakwe, Bharali, and Huchko 2022). Unsafe abortions are another challenge for adolescent girls' and adult women's health. Although many countries have extended the legal frameworks and conditions of safe abortions and have improved post-abortion care, unsafe abortions because of early and or unintended pregnancies remain a major challenge for the continent's 225 million women of reproductive age (Bankole et al. 2020; Bearak et al. 2020). In SSA, 520 deaths per 100,000 unsafe abortions occur, compared to 30 in developed countries and 220 in other developing regions (WHO 2021).

The issue of unintended pregnancies raises the question of women's autonomy and decision-making and is closely linked to inequalities in income and education, whereas abortion rates vary across groups (Bankole et al. 2020). The probability of induced abortion is 78 percent higher for respondents with a primary education compared to those with no formal education. Similarly, the probability of induced abortion is 68 percent higher for women in rich households compared to those in poorer households (Bankole et al. 2020).

Gender disparities in health also manifest in the high rates of FGM in Africa. More than 75 percent of girls and women ages 15–49 years in Burkina Faso, Djibouti, Egypt, Eritrea, Guinea, Mali, Sierra Leone, Somalia, and Sudan and have undergone FGM (UNICEF 2023). Maintained by social norms such as child marriage and early pregnancies (UNICEF 2021), FGM has no health justification or benefits but instead provokes death, bleeding, cysts, infections, and emotional or mental consequences. Social norms permitting violence against women and perpetuating unequal power relationships can increase women's vulnerability to practices such as FGM.

Women also carry the heaviest HIV/AIDS burden in SSA, and adolescent girls and young women accounted for 25 percent of HIV infections in 2020 despite comprising only 10 percent of the population (UNAIDS 2022). Sociocultural practices and norms, as well as economic factors, can contribute to this elevated risk (Abubakar and Kitsao-Wekulo 2015). The high risk of HIV/AIDS overlaps with gender inequalities in socioeconomic position, as women are more likely than men to have lower educational attainment, be unemployed, and be more impoverished. This economic inequality increases vulnerability to HIV/AIDS among women. In addition, unequal power relationships reinforced by social norms and cultural factors place women at a higher risk for HIV infections.

GBV affects one in three women worldwide during their lifetime, overwhelmingly due to intimate partner violence (IPV), according to the World Health Organization. The prevalence rate of IPV across Africa ranges from 10 percent to 40 percent, which is much higher than the global figures (African Development Bank 2018). Social norms that accommodate violence against women can undermine the protective effect that women's asset ownership and occupations can have on their bargaining power and fall-back positions (Oduro, Deere, and Catanzarite 2015; Owoo 2020).

Achieving Inclusiveness in Sexual and Reproductive Health Rights

Women's health needs and the challenges they face in their family and community settings are considered much less than those of men. Women are limited in their reproductive health decisions in both prevention and treatment. The existence of restrictive social norms notwithstanding, some women exercise agency and quietly take actions to prevent unwanted pregnancies (Gyan, Domfe, and Tsiboe-Darko 2023). Limited access to school and length of schooling for girls, lack of economic empowerment, low recognition of domestic violence, and weak opportunities to exercise their decision-making can have negative impacts on their reproductive health in adolescence and adulthood (Do and Kurimoto 2012; Singh, Bloom, and Brodish 2011).

By equipping young people with the appropriate knowledge, skills, and values, comprehensive sexuality education aims to limit the serious health consequences of traditional social norms and beliefs, gender inequalities, and discrimination. According to Wangamati (2020), since 2013, 20 countries in Eastern and Southern Africa have signed the "Ministerial Commitment on Comprehensive Sexuality Education and Sexual and Reproductive Health Services for Adolescents and Young People," expressing their desire to cope with health challenges such as maternal mortality, HIV/AIDS, early and unwanted pregnancies, unmet needs for contraception, and FGM.

In view of the current situation, the achievement of the health-related SDG in Africa requires two types of concrete actions. The first is to implement the commitment in the Abuja Declaration on health financing to earmark 15 percent of the annual budget for the health sector (Africa Renewal 2020). The second is to address the remaining challenges of the social standards, prejudices, and stereotypes that devalue everything related to girls and women and justify gender inequalities, discrimination, and violence (Muluneh et al. 2020).

Labor Market Inequalities

There is ample empirical evidence that gender equality in LFP is positively correlated with economic growth in Africa (Altuzarra et al. 2021). The female LFP rate in SSA of 62 percent in 2021 was higher than the global average of 53 percent but lower than SSA's male participation rate of 73 percent, resulting in a gender gap of 11 percentage points biased against women (World Bank 2023). However, the relationship between gender wage gaps and growth can be positive or negative and depends on the structure of the economy (Seguino and Were 2014). Gender inequalities permeate the labor market. This section examines gender inequalities in employment, occupational segregation, and wages, highlighting how gender inequalities in education and health can drive gender inequalities in the labor market, as do social norms that foster discrimination.

Gender Inequalities and LFP

There are stark cross-country differences in LFP rates across Africa. The gender gap in LFP is higher in North Africa, which is characterized by countries with very low female LFP rates, such as Egypt and Morocco, where the gender gap is higher than 50 percentage points. Factors such as entrenched gender norms, marital status, and a spouse with an advanced level of education can explain these low female LFP rates (Lopez-Acevedo et al. 2021; Miyata and Yamada 2016).

LFP rates do not relay information on the prevalence of decent work in these countries, but the incidence of vulnerable employment (own-account workers and contributing family members) is higher among working women than working men. Casale and Posel (2002) found that, in South Africa, the increase in LFP in the early 2000s was due to poor women (especially Black women) being pushed into the workforce as a coping mechanism due to economic need and not necessarily due to a pull (demand) from the labor market. Women's lack of education and skills, limited access to credit, and the formal sector's failure to create jobs to meet the increase in supply resulted in the increase in LFP being accompanied by an increase in informality.

The nature of women's employment, such as working in people's homes (domestic workers or caregivers), from home as own-account workers or contributing family members, or as unpaid care workers, makes women's work invisible, and their contributions are thus undercounted or excluded from national statistics. This issue results in misleading estimates of female LFP (Gaitskell et al. 1983; Standing 1999).

Gender Gaps in Employment

There are variations across countries in the gender gaps in employment ratios (refer to figure 5.1). These differences can exceed 50 percentage points in Egypt and decline to less than 5 percentage points in countries such as Angola, Burundi, Ghana, and Togo. Dieterich, Huang, and Thomas (2016) have noted that gender differentials in employment ratios that are biased against women are lower in low-income countries in SSA, due to the predominance of informal entrepreneurship and unskilled agriculture. Unsurprisingly, the share of women in subsistence agriculture is higher than that of men, because men can often migrate in search of alternative employment or are able to establish informal businesses.

Women are more likely than men to be in vulnerable employment and less likely than men to be in wage employment. The incidence of wage employment in North Africa in 2021 was much higher than that in SSA, and the gender gap was much narrower. Women in employment in North African countries are more likely to be wage employed. In Algeria, Libya, and Tunisia, the gender gap in wage employment is biased toward women (World Bank 2023). Coincidentally, these are the few countries in Africa that have reversed the gender gap in education, even at the university level.

High LFP is not synonymous with high employment rates, because those who are unemployed (searching) are included in the definition of the labor force. Some countries with high participation rates also have high unemployment rates, with women having higher unemployment rates than men. For example, in 2019, the female unemployment rate[2] in South Africa was 31.5 percent compared to the male unemployment rate of 26.8 percent (Casale, Posel, and Mosomi 2021).

Issues of intersectionality (class, race, and gender) are also important when considering employment issues. For example, poor women in South Africa are more likely to have less schooling; therefore, they are more likely to be in elementary occupations or domestic work, the lowest-paying occupations (Casale et al. 2021).

Figure 5.1 Employment-to-Population Ratio in Select African Countries, Latest Years Available, 2017–21

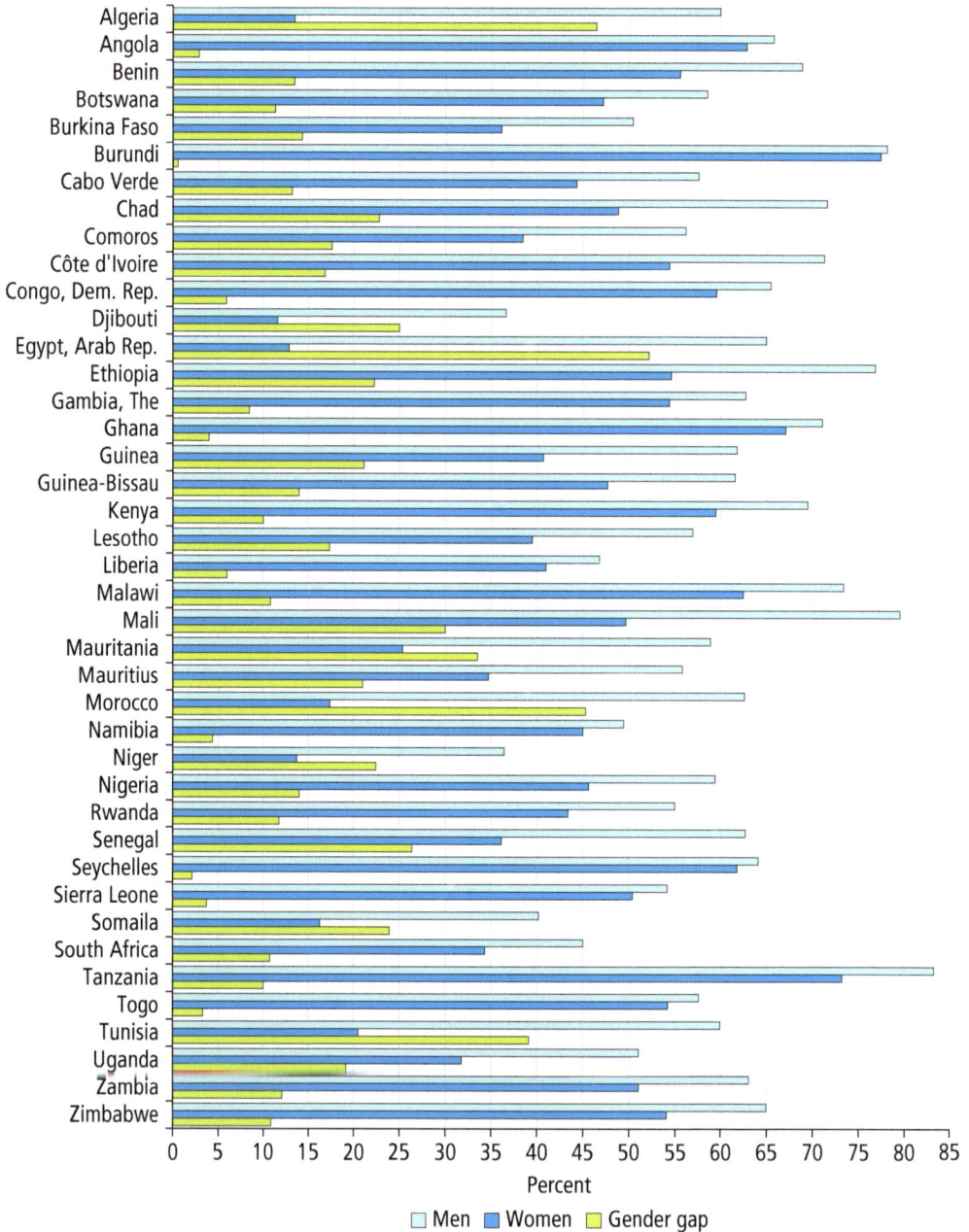

Source: Authors' calculations based on the latest available data from the International Labour Organization modeled estimate (ILOSTAT) in the World Bank's Gender database.

Occupational and Sectoral Gender Segregation

A source of the persistent gender gaps in the labor market is occupational and sectoral segregation. Men and women select into different sectors of the economy (horizontal segregation), with female-dominated occupations typically paying lower wages (Budlender 2008). Gendered social norms and stereotyping can have a pervasive influence on occupational segregation, influencing the choice of field of study in school, level of educational attainment, and choice of occupation. These norms impose restrictions on social interaction and physical mobility, thus limiting the occupations and sectors in which women can work.

Gendered perspectives on what is considered women's work and men's work can limit the occupational choices of both women and men. In addition, women's unpaid care responsibilities can influence their choice of occupation and sector of employment. Even when men and women are in similar sectors, they occupy different positions, with men more likely to be in leadership roles and women in subordinate roles (vertical segregation).

Changes in social messaging (role models) and shrinking gender inequalities in skills training can combat gender stereotyping. A study by the World Bank reported that, in the Republic of Congo, providing information to women on earnings from trade and specific trade choices led to a 28.6-percent increase in the likelihood of women joining a traditionally male-dominated field (Gassier, Rouanet, and Traore 2022). The effects are much larger for women who have technical knowledge in the field or those who have male role models. Access to tertiary education also narrows vertical occupational segregation. For example, in Egypt and Mauritius, where the gender gap in tertiary education has closed, the gender gap in skilled occupations (for example, share of managers, professionals, and technicians) has narrowed.

Gender Wage Gaps

Women in Africa, as in other countries, are, on average, paid lower wages than men (Blau and Kahn 2017; Ñopo, Daza, and Ramos 2012; Si, Nadolnyak, and Hartarska 2020). The gender wage gap is not uniform across the wage distribution, and the factors contributing to it differ (Agesa, Agesa, and Dabalen 2013; Mosomi 2019). Common factors affecting the gender wage gap include skills differences, the gender gap in education, occupational segregation, female employment levels, and family responsibilities (motherhood and marital status) (Agesa et al. 2013; Mosomi 2019).

Legislation can influence the gender wage gap. There is evidence that the gap is narrower in the regulated paid employment segment of the labor market than it is in the private self-employment segment (Nwaka, Guven-Lisaniler, and Tuna 2016) or the informal sector (Nordman and Vaillant 2014). Gender differences in access to credit and women's unpaid care responsibilities can push women into low-return activities, thus creating the conditions for a gender wage gap among those who are self-employed.

The gender wage gap is narrower in countries with low female LFP and higher gender employment gaps (Olivetti and Petrongolo 2008). This is a positive self-selection issue where wage-employed women in these labor markets tend to have better-than-average human capital characteristics compared to the rest of the population. This is the case in Egypt, where the International Labour Organization (ILO) reported that there was no gender wage gap in 2018, and in Tunisia, which has a 4-percentage-point gap in favor of women. In contrast, in South Africa, where female LFP is higher and wage-employed women are more educated, the median gender wage gap is significant, at about 30 percent (Casale et al. 2021; Mosomi 2019).

The persistent labor market gender gaps even in countries that have decreased the education gap is an indication that closing gender gaps in the labor market will require more than just closing gender gaps in education. Social norms that support negative attitudes toward female employment in particular sectors and occupations must be confronted (Humlum, Nandrup, and Smith 2019; Roethlisberger et al. 2023). Strategies to improve women's skills and educational attainment must be accompanied by efforts to create jobs and workplaces that are supportive and inclusive. The COVID-19 pandemic revealed that women's paid care work is essential, and there is no justification for lower wages in female-dominated sectors.

Paid mandatory maternity and paternity leave can contribute to reducing gender discrimination during the hiring process and shrink the "motherhood penalty." Clear laws that mandate equal remuneration for work of equal value should be introduced and reinforced.

Gender Inequalities in Unpaid Care Work

Unpaid care work comprises housework; unpaid care of sick individuals, children, and elderly people living in the household; and unpaid community services, including those provided to other households (Budlender 2008). Unpaid care work contributes to the maintenance and production of what Braunstein, Bouhia, and Seguino (2020) have described as the human capacities that determine labor productivity. Human capacities extend beyond notions of human capital to include attributes such as emotional connectedness.

This section begins by describing the relevance of unpaid care work and gender inequalities in the burden of unpaid care work to the economy. This discussion is followed by subsections on the limited evidence on gender inequality in the distribution of unpaid care work in the household and what explains gender inequality in unpaid care work. The section concludes with an explanation of the effects of gender inequality in unpaid care work and proposes interventions to reduce them. Women's unpaid care work responsibilities can limit their participation in the labor market, determine their choice of occupation, and influence their decisions about whether to be wage employed or self-employed. Thus, gender inequalities in unpaid care work are related to gender inequalities in the labor market.

Unpaid Care Work and the National Accounts

The system of national accounts excludes cooking, cleaning, and personal care for dependent family members from the production boundary. Thus, these activities are also excluded from the estimation of gross domestic product (GDP), because these activities are considered nonmarket activities, are difficult to measure, and are not perceived to be of relevance for macroeconomic policy (DeRock 2021). In the Global North, a significant proportion of unpaid care services, such as child and elder care, can be purchased or are provided by the public sector and are, therefore, captured in the national accounts. In contrast, in the Global South, these activities are usually provided by household members, particularly women, and are excluded from the national accounts.

Using different methods to value unpaid work, Budlender (2008) has estimated that the value of unpaid care work in Tanzania was between 11 percent and 30 percent of GDP in 2006 and between 35 percent and 63 percent of GDP in South Africa in 2000. This value was between 14.6 and 38.1 percent in South Africa in 2010 (Oosthuizen 2018). Estimates for Botswana have shown that the value of unpaid care services provided in the home for persons with HIV/AIDS exceeded the value of similar services provided by the state (Mmopelwa et al. 2013).

Excluding unpaid care activities from the national accounts reduces the estimated size of the economy, particularly for developing economies, and renders invisible the contributions of women and girls to the economy. It masks the effect that gender inequality in the distribution of unpaid care work has on the well-being of women and shifts the focus away from the linkages that exist between the unpaid-care sector and the economy.

Failure to consider the linkages between unpaid care work and paid work and women's inordinate responsibility for unpaid care work can have implications for the effectiveness of social and economic policy. A reduction in the time spent on unpaid care work that compromises the productivity of the unpaid-care sector can reduce productivity in the paid sector and thus can negatively impact output and growth (Vasudevan and Raghavendra 2022). Time constraints due to unpaid care work responsibilities can adversely impact women's productivity in agricultural (Carranza et al. 2017) and nonagricultural activities (Nordman and Vaillant 2014).

Gender Inequalities in Unpaid Care Work in the Household

There is limited available evidence on women's and men's participation in unpaid care work in African countries because of the dearth of time-use data. However, data from a few countries in Eastern, Western, and Southern Africa that have time-use surveys show that women and girls spend a significant amount of time each day on unpaid care work (Addati et al. 2018; Charmes, 2019). In these countries, the gender gap in the time spent on unpaid care work is biased against women. Data from South Africa, which has two time-use surveys, reveal that the amount of time spent on unpaid care work declined for both women and men between 2000 and 2010 (Floro and Komatsu 2011; Oosthuizen 2018).

However, a gender gap remains, albeit a narrower one. The amount of time spent on unpaid care work and the size of the gender gap can vary over the life cycle. The gender gap is widest among the population ages 20–35 years and narrows in later years in Ghana and South Africa (Amporfu et al. 2018; Oosthuizen 2018).

The COVID-19 pandemic drew attention to the critical importance of paid and unpaid care work for the economy. The public policy responses to the health implications of the pandemic caused an increase in both women's and men's time spent on unpaid care work. However, this reality has not always been accompanied by a narrowing of the gender gap in unpaid care work. For example, in South Africa, although men took on additional childcare responsibilities, this did not close the gender gap in unpaid childcare, because women's additional hours spent on childcare were greater than those of men (Casale and Posel 2002). As the COVID-19 restrictions eased, women's number of hours spent on childcare declined faster than men's but did not close the gender gap (Casale and Shepherd 2021).

Explaining the Gender Gap in Unpaid Work

Who participates in unpaid care work and how much time is spent on these activities are determined primarily by resources, bargaining power, available time, and gender norms. Age, education, earnings, and wealth can influence individuals' bargaining power and, therefore, their success in negotiating less time spent on unpaid care work. The evidence on the relationship between age and education, on the one hand, and the amount of time that women and men spend on unpaid care work, on the other hand, are not always consistent across studies (Herrera and Torelli 2013; Rios-Avila, Oduro, and Nassif Pires 2021; Wodon and Ying 2010). However, the evidence is fairly consistent across Ethiopia, Ghana, South Africa, and Tanzania, showing that wives in paid employment spend fewer hours on unpaid care work than wives in self-employment do (Rios-Avila et al. 2021).

As women's earnings increase, they are expected to spend less time on unpaid care work because they can outsource these services. An increase in women's earnings relative to their husbands' earnings is expected to reduce the amount of time women spend on unpaid care work because it gives women more bargaining power. However, gendered norms that define what it means to be feminine or masculine can undermine the influence of earnings, education, and wealth on women's bargaining power (Akanle, Adesina, and Ogbimi 2016; Zambelli et al. 2017).

For example, in Ghana, women's absolute earnings and their share of couple earnings are negatively associated with time spent on unpaid care work. Yet, no strong evidence supports the role of gender norms in reversing the association between women's share of couple earnings and time spent on unpaid care work (Owoo et al. 2022). In Ethiopia, women with traditional gender ideologies spend more time on unpaid care work (Getahun 2019). Furthermore, the availability of basic utilities such as electricity and water within or close to the home should reduce the time spent on unpaid care work. However, husbands appear to benefit from access to electricity in Ethiopia and Ghana, with no discernible effect on wives' time use (Rios-Avila et al. 2021). In addition, the ownership of time-saving equipment does not make a difference in the amount of time that wives spend on unpaid care work in Ghana. However, access to water does make a difference (Owoo and Lambon-Quayefio 2021).

Effects of Unpaid Care Work

A person may be described as being time poor when the difference between the person's available time (the time available after accounting for the time spent on personal care, commuting to work, and unpaid care work) and time spent on income-generating work is negative (Zacharias et al. 2021). Irrespective of women's and men's time spent on employment, women's time poverty rate exceeds that of men in Ethiopia, Ghana, South Africa, and Tanzania (Zacharias et al. 2021). This issue is largely explained by the gender gap in the amount of time spent on unpaid care work.

In an attempt to juggle both paid and unpaid work commitments successfully, women wake up early and go to bed late. This phenomenon is referred to as *time stretching,* which results in women not having enough rest, which is stressful and exhausting (Rohwerder et al. 2017; Zambelli et al. 2017) and can adversely affect their mental health (Owoo and Lambon-Quayefio 2021). The drudgery of activities such as fetching water and the amount of time spent performing these heavy-duty activities also can take a toll on women's health (Chopra 2021).

The relationship between paid work and unpaid work is bidirectional. Unpaid work reduces the time women spend on income-generating activities, and participation in income-generating activities reduces the amount of time they spend on unpaid work (Chopra 2021). The responsibility for unpaid care work not only creates a time constraint for women but also reduces their chances of being hired. Mothers who look for employment while accompanied by their young children are unlikely to be hired (Nyariro et al. 2021). Not being able to participate in income-generating activities is disempowering for women because paid employment reduces their financial dependence on their husbands, thus reducing the potential for conflict and domestic violence, which may ensue when women ask their husbands for money (Vyas, Mbwambo, and Heise 2015). Having one's own income increases the likelihood of participating in household decision-making in Ghana (Fuseini and Kalule-Sabiti 2015; Kishor and Subaiya 2008).

In Tanzania, however, gender norms can be a constraint on women's participation in decision-making despite their having their own income (Vyas et al. 2015). Unpaid care work responsibilities may cause some women to choose to exit the formal sector and work in the informal sector, because the latter offers more flexibility (Lambon-Quayefio et al. 2021).

In South Africa, increased childcare responsibilities as a result of the COVID-19 pandemic prevented more women than men from going to work or made paid work more difficult for women. It prevented women from working the same number of hours as before the lockdown and from searching for work (Casale and Shepherd 2021). Increased childcare responsibilities also increased the risk of depression among women and men, with the effect on men being greater (Nwosu 2021).

A reduction in the burden of unpaid care work on women can contribute toward improving their well-being and has the potential to enhance growth. Publicly provided infrastructure can reduce the time burden on women and increase their opportunities for participation in paid employment (Wamboye and Seguino 2015). Although gender norms are a constraint on reducing women's time poverty, norms do change over time, and statutory laws and their effective implementation are an important first step to making this happen.

Gender Inequalities in Control of and Access to Productive Resources

While studies on gender inequality have usually focused on income, employment, education, and health, recently they have also included asset or wealth inequality, despite the large gender gaps in wealth and ownership of assets. Across Africa, large differences exist between men and women in the ownership and use of assets, as well as in who has control over assets and wealth (Gaddis, Lahoti, and Swaminathan 2022; Gaddis, Lahoti, and Wenjie 2018). Gender gaps exist in land and housing ownership. Yet, the extent of gender differences in asset ownership and the factors driving these gaps are not well understood, which is mainly due to the lack of data, as household surveys traditionally collect these data for the household as a single unit. Recent efforts have addressed this issue.

This section presents the main findings from these studies in terms of the patterns and trends of gender differences in asset ownership in Africa. The section then discusses why these gender differences are important, before addressing the factors driving these gaps in the legal systems and policies.

Patterns and Trends in Gender Gaps in Asset Ownership

Across African countries, men are more likely than women to own physical assets. About 38 percent of African women report owning any land alone or jointly compared with 51 percent of African men (Beegle and Christiaensen 2019). Just under 13 percent of African women (ages 20–49 years) claim sole ownership of land compared with 36 percent of African men (refer to figure 5.2, panel a). The gender gap is smaller if joint ownership is considered, but it remains significant. A similar pattern emerges for the ownership of housing (refer to figure 5.2, panel b).

Figure 5.2 Property Ownership in Africa, 2010–16

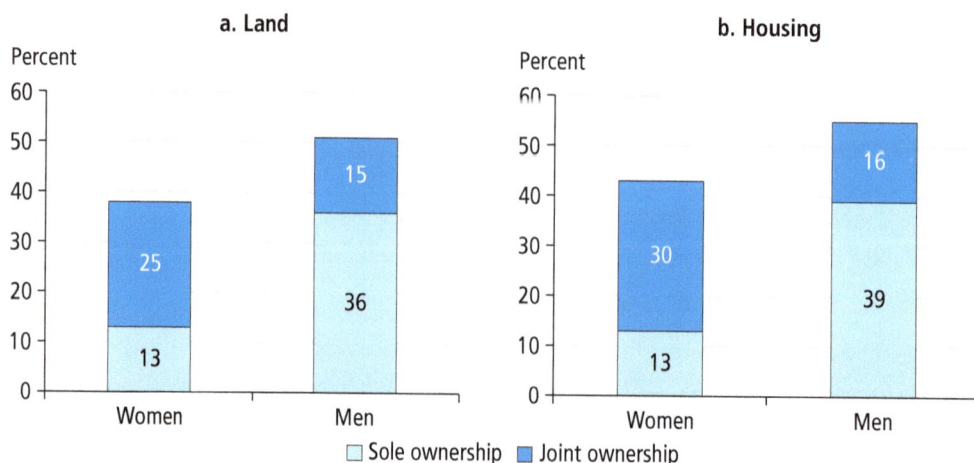

Source: Based on Beegle and Christiaensen 2019, using data from country Demographic and Health Surveys.
Note: The data are for 27 countries (panel a) and 28 countries (panel b), for the population ages 20–49 years.

Gender gaps also extend to other forms of assets, including livestock, financial assets, and savings (Doss et al. 2020). Women are less likely than men to hold financial savings. For example, worldwide, 38 percent of men have a bank account at a financial institution, compared with only 27 percent of women (Demirgüç-Kunt et al. 2018).

Gender gaps can vary across African countries. The largest gaps are in Western Africa, and much smaller gender gaps are in Southern Africa (refer to map 5.1). The gender disparity in financial assets can be observed in Tanzania, where only 5 percent of women have bank accounts compared with 11 percent of men. In countries such as Chad, Liberia, Mali, and South Sudan, men are more than twice as likely as women to have an account; however, no such gender gaps occur in Lesotho, Namibia, and South Africa. In Uganda, female entrepreneurs receive only 1 percent of the available credit in rural areas (Doss et al. 2012).

The challenges in accessing bank loans or credit can be linked to collateral. In Ghana, not only are women less likely to own assets, they also generally own less-valuable assets than those owned by men, leading to a large gender wealth gap in favor of men (Doss et al. 2014).

Within countries, gender gaps in asset ownership intersect with other types of inequalities. Gender gaps in sole ownership of assets are almost always larger in rural areas than in urban areas (Gaddis et al. 2022). Estimating gender gaps according to income, researchers have found that, in most countries, gender gaps in sole property ownership are larger for the poorest than for the richest quintile.

Gender gaps within countries also vary by marital status (Doss et al. 2012; Gaddis et al. 2018). In all countries, gender inequality in sole property ownership is largest for the married population and is higher than 40 percent in the Western African countries of Burkina Faso, Niger, and Nigeria.

Importance of Women's Asset Ownership

The intrahousehold distribution of assets matters for children's well-being. For example, in regions of Ethiopia where the marriage custom is to offer a bride price, mothers' asset ownership has a protective effect against child marriage because it increases their bargaining power (Muchomba 2022). In addition, a more-equitable distribution of property and wealth may advance economic prosperity (Gaddis et al. 2022).

Women's rights to property and other assets can be correlated with their bargaining position within the family or household (Fafchamps and Quisumbing 2005; Manser and Brown 1980; McElroy and Horney 1981). As a homeowner, a woman is less vulnerable and has much greater security in the case of marital discord. Home ownership provides women a strong fall-back position for bargaining power. In rural areas, owning agricultural land offers women a means of livelihood. In Ghana, a more-egalitarian distribution of assets between husband and wife is correlated with the wife's participation in decision-making, which is an indicator of agency (Oduro, Boakye-Yiadom, and Baah-Boateng 2012).

Map 5.1 Gender Gaps in Land and Housing Ownership in Africa, 2010–16

a. Sole ownership of property

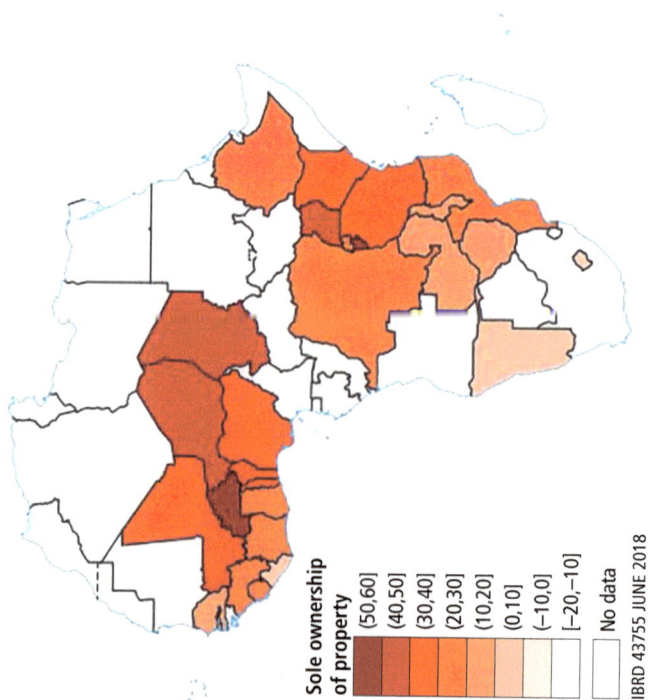

b. Sole and joint ownership of property

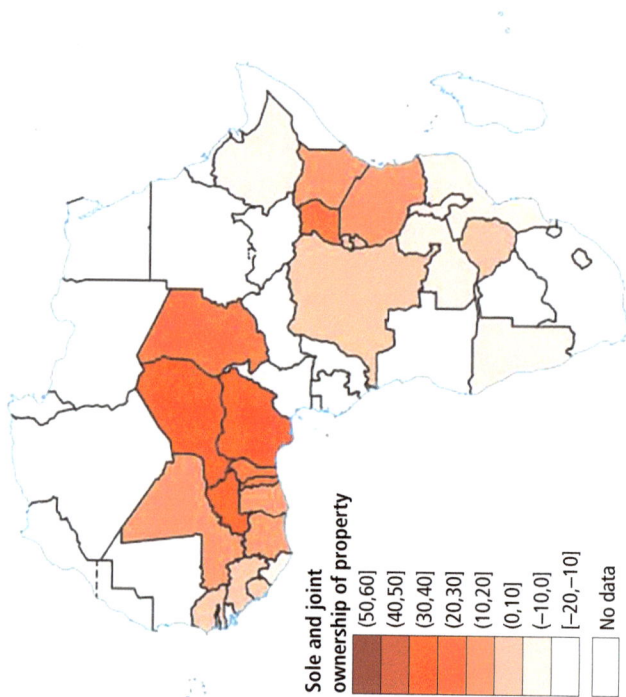

Sole ownership
of property

[50,60]
[40,50]
[30,40]
[20,30]
[10,20]
(0,10]
(−10,0]
[−20,−10]
No data

IBRD 43755 JUNE 2018

Sole and joint
ownership of property

[50,60]
[40,50]
[30,40]
[20,30]
[10,20]
(0,10]
(−10,0]
[−20,−10]
No data

Sources: Gaddis, Lahoti; and Wenjie 2018; Demographic and Health Surveys.

Note: The data are for 27 countries, for the population ages 20–49 years (excluding the Comoros). A positive (negative) value indicates that more (fewer) men than women own property.

Property ownership can also offer women protection from IPV. Women's share of couple wealth is significantly associated with lower odds of violence in Ghana (Oduro et al. 2015). However, no consistent pattern was found in the relationship between women's sole or joint ownership of assets (land, house, or both land and house) and IPV in a study of 28 countries (Peterman et al. 2017).

Ownership of assets is also permanent, as opposed to employment, which is mostly sporadic or seasonal for many African women. However, ownership that does not also imply control over the asset may undermine the empowering effect of asset ownership. Dito (2015) has found that, in Ethiopia, women's asset ownership (measured by assets brought into the marriage) is not associated with women's health status, perhaps because women contribute a minuscule share of the couple's assets at the time of marriage and so do not have control over the assets. Lack of control over the income generated by assets is a reason why rural women in southeastern Nigeria do not believe that owning assets (for example, motor transport, milling machines, and farmland) will provide them the bargaining power to decide when to become pregnant, the number of children to have, and the spacing of births. Without the economic resources that these assets would provide them, women will not have bargaining power (Omeje, Oshi, and Oshi 2011).

The protective effect of women's asset ownership is not the same along the wealth distribution and cannot be assumed in all contexts. It also depends on contextual factors, such as gender norms and inheritance and marital regimes, which are discussed in detail in the next section (Oduro et al. 2015).

Roles of Legal Systems and Social Norms

Gender inequalities are often the outcomes of gender biases in legal systems, social norms, and institutional structures. Factors such as discriminatory norms and laws on inheritance, marital regimes, and absence of protection from workplace discrimination are often associated with gender gaps in asset ownership, LFP, and time use.

In countries with more gender-egalitarian legal regimes, women generally have higher levels of property ownership, especially housing (Deere et al. 2013). Reforms to establish a more gender-equitable legislative framework could help increase women's property ownership. Many African countries are signatories to the African Union's 2005 Maputo Protocol and have enacted progressive legislation that provides women the same legal rights as men in land ownership, inheritance, and access to financial resources (Beegle and Christiaensen 2019). For example, statutory laws guarantee the same land rights to women in 46 of the 54 African countries for which data are available (Beegle and Christiaensen 2019). Studies have shown that women fare better under marital regimes that recognize women's role in the accumulation of marital property, through child rearing and other unpaid work, than under separation of property regimes, which reinforce gender gaps (Deere et al. 2013).

Women's rights in land acquisition, selling, bequeathing, or renting are key for increasing land ownership among women (Doss, Meinzen-Dick, and Bomuhangi 2014). Land formalization programs promoting the joint registration of both spouses could improve outcomes for women and narrow gender gaps (Goldstein et al. 2015; O'Sullivan 2017). Reforms to enhance financial inclusion can address women's lower savings and access to productive assets. For example, the expansion of Kenya's mobile money service benefited women disproportionately, increasing the financial savings of female-headed households and enabling women to move out of agriculture and into businesses (Suri and Jack 2016).

Legislative reforms that strengthen women's inheritance rights can improve measures of women's empowerment (Deininger et al. 2019). Laws on inheritance that do not provide equal inheritance by siblings or inheritance by spouses can play an important role in the gender gap in asset ownership. In most African countries, inheritance is the most important means of acquisition of currently owned agricultural land. In Ghana, 81 percent of agricultural land, which is more likely to have been acquired as an inheritance, belongs to individual men, reflecting the apparent male bias in inheritance regimes (Deere et al. 2013).

Women are also disadvantaged in workplace protections. For example, five countries in the Economic Community of West African States have no prohibitions against sexual harassment in the workplace, and three countries have no guarantee of equal pay to workers based on gender. Given the importance of earnings for asset acquisition, legal reforms mandating equal pay for work of equal value are key for addressing gender gaps in pay and asset ownership.

However, the effectiveness of legislative reforms is conditioned by persistent social norms in an environment where men are privileged over women (Deere et al. 2013). Across Africa, women's rights are shaped by legal pluralism,[3] which accommodates both customary and religious laws. In 43 African countries, statutory laws guarantee the same land rights for men and women, but at the same time, informal institutions discriminate against women (Beegle and Christiaensen 2019). A similar situation applies to inheritance regimes, where 39 countries have laws that guarantee the same rights for widows, widowers, sons, and daughters, but informal institutions discriminate against widows and daughters. Informal norms and institutions can be even more important than statutory laws. These social norms are usually in conflict with the statutory laws that promote equality.

Rwanda has enacted far-reaching laws to achieve a gender-equitable inheritance regime. The inheritance and land laws have provisions for joint ownership of land by spouses and require that women must be signatories to the transfer, sale, mortgage, and lease of the jointly owned land. However, the laws have not brought about much change in the day-to-day management of land. Resistance to the idea that women and men can have equal land rights remains. Some men exclude their wives from decisions concerning their jointly owned land (Abbott, Mugisha, and Sapsford 2018). Women are still unable to lay claim to what is entitled to them as stated in the laws because of the continued adherence to traditional norms and values that do not recognize women as being capable of owning land and do not value women's reproductive work and agricultural labor because these are performed within the home.

Conclusion

This discussion on gender inequality revealed four important issues. First, gender inequality in one dimension can have a domino effect on other dimensions of gender inequality, resulting in women facing multiple binding constraints that adversely impact their well-being, the well-being of their children, and the economy's growth potential. For example, gender inequality in education has implications for gender gaps in future labor market outcomes, while gender inequality in time spent on unpaid care work has implications for gender inequality in the contemporary labor market. Girls' access to education has been found to lead indirectly to positive outcomes such as better health for their children, a decline in fertility rates, and increased agency (that is, empowerment).

Second, while aggregate figures are useful summary statistics, policy makers should understand the nuances due to class, location, age, race, and ethnicity. Women are subject to multiple intersecting disadvantages.

Third, female disadvantage is not always the norm (Buhl-Wiggers et al. 2021), which has implications for policy design and interventions. A gender lens must be applied to the policy-making process to reduce the likelihood of disadvantaging a particular group. For example, education policies must be designed to promote access to and quality of education for all children. The focus on girls' education may result in boys being left behind (Evans et al. 2021; Welmond and Gregory 2021).

Fourth, gender norms and stereotypes can have a causal effect on gender inequality. Global evidence has shown a shift toward more gender-equitable norms and that economic growth is positively associated with this shift (Seguino 2007). Interventions designed to change gendered social norms have some traction (Njuki et al. 2023). An important strategy that governments must pursue is the enactment, publication, and effective implementation of national laws prohibiting discrimination against women in the social, economic, and political spheres, as well as the removal of gender-discriminatory laws.

Notes

1. WHO has defined *maternal mortality* as the death of a woman from pregnancy-related causes during pregnancy or within 42 days of pregnancy, expressed as a ratio to 100,000 live births in the population being studied, and *maternal morbidity* as any health condition attributed to or complicating pregnancy and childbirth that has a negative impact on the woman's well-being or functioning.
2. These unemployment rates, while high, significantly understate the levels of unemployment using the ILO's definition of labor force participation, as they exclude discouraged work seekers who make up a significant proportion of workers in African labor markets.
3. *Legal pluralism* is the co-existence and interaction of statutory laws with multiple legal orders such as state, customary, religious, project, and local laws, all of which provide a basis for claiming property rights (Doss et al. 2012).

References

Abbott, Pamela, Roger Mugisha, and Roger Sapsford. 2018. "Women, Land and Empowerment in Rwanda." *Journal of International Development* 30 (6): 1006–22. https://doi.org/10.1002/jid.3370.

Abubakar, Amina, and Patricia Kitsao-Wekulo. 2015. "Gender and Health Inequalities in Sub-Saharan Africa: The Case of HIV." In *Psychology of Gender through the Lens of Culture*, edited by Saba Safdar and Natasza Kosakowska-Berezecka, 395–408. Cham: Springer International Publishing. https://doi.org/10.1007/978-3-319-14005-6_19.

Addati, Laura, Umberto Cattaneo, Valeria Esquivel, and Isabel Valarino. 2018. *Care Work and Care Jobs for the Future of Decent Work*. Geneva: International Labour Organization.

Africa Renewal. 2020. "Public Financing for Health in Africa: 15% of an Elephant Is Not 15% of a Chicken." Africa Renewal, New York. https://www.un.org/africarenewal/magazine/october-2020/public-financing-health-africa-when-15-elephant-not-15-chicken.

African Development Bank. 2018. *Africa Gender Index Report 2019*. Abidjan, Côte d'Ivoire: African Development Bank.

Agesa, Richard U., Jacqueline Agesa, and Andrew Dabalen. 2013. "Sources of the Persistent Gender Wage Gap along the Unconditional Earnings Distribution: Findings from Kenya." *Oxford Development Studies* 41 (1): 76–103. https://doi.org/10.1080/13600818.2013.770304.

Akanle, Olayinka, Jimi Adesina, and A. O. Ogbimi. 2016. "Men at Work Keep Off: Male Roles and Household Chores in Nigeria." *Gender and Behaviour* 14: 7833–54.

Altuzarra, Amaia, Catalina Gálvez-Gálvez, and Ana González-Flores. 2021. "Is Gender Inequality a Barrier to Economic Growth? A Panel Data Analysis of Developing Countries." *Sustainability* 13 (1): 367. https://doi.org/10.3390/su13010367.

Amporfu, Eugenia, Daniel Sakyi, Prince Frimpong, Eric Arthur, and Jacob Novignon. 2018. "The Distribution of Paid and Unpaid Work among Men and Women in Ghana: The National Time Transfer Accounts Approach." Working Paper cwwwp3, Development Policy Research Unit, University of Cape Town, South Africa. https://EconPapers.repec.org/RePEc:ctw:wpaper:cwwwp3.

Ashraf, Nava, Natalie Bau, Corinne Low, and Kathleen McGinn. 2020. "Negotiating a Better Future: How Interpersonal Skills Facilitate Intergenerational Investment." *Quarterly Journal of Economics* 135 (2): 1095–1151. https://doi.org/10.1093/qje/qjz039.

Baird, Sarah, Joan Hamory Hicks, Michael Kremer, and Edward Miguel. 2016. "Worms at Work: Long-Run Impacts of a Child Health Investment." *Quarterly Journal of Economics* 131 (4): 1637–80. https://doi.org/10.1093/qje/qjw022.

Baliamoune-Lutz, Mina, and Mark McGillivray. 2015. "The Impact of Gender Inequality in Education on Income in Africa and the Middle East." *Economic Modelling* 47: 1–11. https://doi.org/10.1016/j.econmod.2014.11.031.

Bandara, Amarakoon. 2015. "The Economic Cost of Gender Gaps in Effective Labor: Africa's Missing Growth Reserve." *Feminist Economics* 21 (2): 162–86. https://doi.org/10.1080/13545701.2014.986153.

Bankole, Akinrinola, Lisa Remez, Onikepe Owolabi, Jesse Philbin, and Patrice Williams. 2020. *From Unsafe to Safe Abortion in Sub-Saharan Africa: Slow but Steady Progress*. New York: Guttmacher Institute.

Baten, Joerg, Michiel De Haas, Elisabeth Kempter, and Felix Meier Zu Selhausen. 2021. "Educational Gender Inequality in Sub-Saharan Africa: A Long-Term Perspective." *Population and Development Review* 47 (3): 813–49. https://doi.org/10.1111/padr.12430.

Bearak, Jonathan, Anna Popinchalk, Bela Ganatra, Ann-Beth Moller, Özge Tunçalp, Cynthia Beavin, Lorraine Kwok, and Leontine Alkema. 2020. "Unintended Pregnancy and Abortion by Income, Region, and the Legal Status of Abortion: Estimates from a Comprehensive Model for 1990–2019." *The Lancet Global Health* 8 (9): e1152–61. https://doi.org/10.1016/S2214-109X(20)30315-6.

Beegle, Kathleen, and Luc Christiaensen. 2019. *Accelerating Poverty Reduction in Africa*. Washington, DC: World Bank. https://doi.org/10.1596/978-1-4648-1232-3.

Benshaul-Tolonen, Anja, Garazi Zulaika, Marni Sommer, and Penelope A. Phillips-Howard. 2020. "Measuring Menstruation-Related Absenteeism among Adolescents in Low-Income Countries." In *The Palgrave Handbook of Critical Menstruation Studies*, edited by Chris Bobel, Inga T. Winkler, Breanne Fahs, Katie Ann Hasson, Elizabeth Arveda Kissling, and Tomi-Ann Roberts, 705–23. Singapore: Springer Singapore. https://doi.org/10.1007/978-981-15-0614-7_52.

Blau, Francine D., and Lawrence M. Kahn. 2017. "The Gender Wage Gap: Extent, Trends, and Explanations." *Journal of Economic Literature* 55 (3): 789–865. https://doi.org/10.1257/jel.20160995.

Bossavie, Laurent, and Ohto Kanninen. 2018. "What Explains the Gender Gap Reversal in Educational Attainment?" Policy Research Working Paper 8303, World Bank, Washington, DC.

Braunstein, Elissa, Rachid Bouhia, and Stephanie Seguino. 2020. "Social Reproduction, Gender Equality and Economic Growth." *Cambridge Journal of Economics* 44 (1): 129–56. https://doi.org/10.1093/cje/bez032.

Budlender, Debbie. 2008. "The Statistical Evidence on Care and Non-Care Work across Six Countries." UNRISD Gender Programme Paper 4, United Nations Research Institute for Social Development, Geneva.

Buhl-Wiggers, Julie, Sam Jones, and Rebecca Thornton. 2021. "Boys Lagging Behind: Unpacking Gender Differences in Academic Achievement across East Africa." *International Journal of Educational Development* 83: 102382. https://doi.org/10.1016/j.ijedudev.2021.102382.

Carranza, Eliana, Aletheia Amalia Donald, Rachel Winter Jones, and Léa Rouanet. 2017. "Time and Money: A Study of Labor Constraints for Female Cotton Producers in Côte d'Ivoire." Policy Brief Issue 19, Gender Innovation Lab, World Bank, Washington, DC. https://api.semanticscholar.org/CorpusID:157719900.

Casale, Daniela, and Dorrit Posel. 2002. "The Continued Feminisation of the Labour Force in South Africa: An Analysis of Recent Data and Trends." *South African Journal of Economics* 70 (1): 156–84. https://doi.org/10.1111/j.1813-6982.2002.tb00042.x.

Casale, Daniela, Dorrit Posel, and Jacqueline Mosomi. 2021. "Gender and Work in South Africa." In *The Oxford Handbook of the South African Economy*, edited by Arkebe Oqubay, Fiona Tregenna, and Imraan Valodia, 734–56. Oxford, UK: Oxford University Press. https://doi.org/10.1093/oxfordhb/9780192894199.013.32.

Casale, Daniela, and Debra Shepherd. 2021. "The Gendered Effects of the COVID-19 Crisis and Ongoing Lockdown in South Africa: Evidence from NIDS-CRAM Waves 1–5." National Income Dynamics Study–Coronavirus Rapid Mobile Survey, University of Cape Town, South Africa.

Charles, Maria, and Karen Bradley. 2009. "Indulging Our Gendered Selves? Sex Segregation by Field of Study in 44 Countries." *American Journal of Sociology* 114 (4): 924–76. https://doi.org/10.1086/595942.

Charmes, Jacques. 2019. "The Unpaid Care Work and the Labour Market: An Analysis of Time Use Data Based on the Latest World Compilation of Time-Use Surveys." ILO Working Paper, International Labour Organization, Geneva.

Chicoine, Luke. 2021. "Free Primary Education, Fertility, and Women's Access to the Labor Market: Evidence from Ethiopia." *World Bank Economic Review* 35 (2): 480–98. https://doi.org/10.1093/wber/lhz042.

Chopra, Deepta. 2021. "Paid Work and Unpaid Care Work in India, Nepal, Tanzania, and Rwanda." In *Women's Economic Empowerment*. Routledge Studies in Development and Society. Abingdon: Routledge International Development Research Centre.

Deere, Carmen Diana, Abena D. Oduro, Hema Swaminathan, and Cheryl Doss. 2013. "Property Rights and the Gender Distribution of Wealth in Ecuador, Ghana and India." *Journal of Economic Inequality* 11 (2): 249–65. https://doi.org/10.1007/s10888-013-9241-z.

Deininger, Klaus, Songqing Jin, Hari K. Nagarajan, and Fang Xia. 2019. "Inheritance Law Reform, Empowerment, and Human Capital Accumulation: Second-Generation Effects from India." *Journal of Development Studies* 55 (12): 2549–71. https://doi.org/10.1080/00220388.2018.1520218.

Demirgüç-Kunt, Asli, Leora Klapper, Dorothe Singer, Saniya Ansar, and Jake Hess. 2018. *The Global Findex Database 2017: Measuring Financial Inclusion and the Fintech Revolution*. Washington, DC: World Bank.

DeRock, Daniel. 2021. "Hidden in Plain Sight: Unpaid Household Services and the Politics of GDP Measurement." *New Political Economy* 26 (1): 20–35. https://doi.org/10.1080/13563467.2019.1680964.

Dieterich, Christine, Anni Huang, and Alun H. Thomas. 2016. *Women's Opportunities and Challenges in Sub-Saharan African Job Markets*. Washington, DC: International Monetary Fund.

Dito, Bilisuma Bushie. 2015. "Women's Intrahousehold Decision-Making Power and Their Health Status: Evidence from Rural Ethiopia." *Feminist Economics* 21 (3): 168–90. https://doi.org/10.1080/13545701.2015.1007073.

Do, Mai, and Nami Kurimoto. 2012. "Women's Empowerment and Choice of Contraceptive Methods in Selected African Countries." *International Perspectives on Sexual and Reproductive Health* 38 (1): 23–33. https://doi.org/10.1363/3802312.

Doss, Cheryl, Carmen Diana Deere, Abena D. Oduro, and Hema Swaminathan. 2014. "The Gender Asset and Wealth Gaps." *Development* 57 (3–4): 400–09. https://doi.org/10.1057/dev.2015.10.

Doss, Cheryl, Ruth Meinzen-Dick, and Allan Bomuhangi. 2014. "Who Owns the Land? Perspectives from Rural Ugandans and Implications for Large-Scale Land Acquisitions." *Feminist Economics* 20 (1): 76–100. https://doi.org/10.1080/13545701.2013.855320.

Doss, Cheryl, Hema Swaminathan, Carmen Diana Deere, J. Y. Suchitra, Abena D. Oduro, and Boaz Anglade. 2020. "Women, Assets, and Formal Savings: A Comparative Analysis of Ecuador, Ghana and India." *Development Policy Review* 38 (2): 180–205. https://doi.org/10.1111/dpr.12424.

Doss, Cheryl, Mai Truong, Gorrettie Nabanoga, and Justine Namaalwa. 2012. "Women, Marriage and Asset Inheritance in Uganda." *Development Policy Review* 30 (5): 597–616. https://doi.org/10.1111/j.1467-7679.2012.00590.x.

Duflo, Esther, Pascaline Dupas, and Michael Kremer. 2021. "The Impact of Free Secondary Education: Experimental Evidence from Ghana." NBER Working Paper 28937, National Bureau of Economic Research, Cambridge, MA. https://ideas.repec.org/p/nbr/nberwo/28937.html.

Evans, David K., Maryam Akmal, and Pamela Jakiela. 2021. "Gender Gaps in Education: The Long View." *IZA Journal of Development and Migration* 12 (1): 20210001. https://doi.org/10.2478/izajodm -2021-0001.

Evans, Emily C. 2013. "A Review of Cultural Influence on Maternal Mortality in the Developing World." *Midwifery* 29 (5): 490–96. https://doi.org/10.1016/j.midw.2012.04.002.

Eyal, Katherine, and Ingrid Woolard. 2014. "Cash Transfers and Teen Education: Evidence from South Africa." https://doi.org/10.13140/2.1.4016.1285.

Fafchamps, Marcel, and Agnes Quisumbing. 2005. "Assets at Marriage in Rural Ethiopia." *Journal of Development Economics* 77 (1): 1–25. https://doi.org/10.1016/j.jdeveco.2004.02.003.

Fiala, Nathan, Ana Garcia-Hernandez, Kritika Narula, and Nishith Prakash. 2022. "Wheels of Change: Transforming Girls' Lives with Bicycles." CESifo Working Paper 9865, Center for Economic Studies, University of Munich, Germany. https://www.ssrn.com/abstract=4175822.

Floro, Maria S., and Hitomi Komatsu. 2011. "Gender and Work in South Africa: What Can Time-Use Data Reveal?" *Feminist Economics* 17 (4): 33–66. https://doi.org/10.1080/13545701.2011.614954.

Fuseini, Kamil, and Ishmael Kalule-Sabiti. 2015. "Women's Autonomy in Ghana: Does Religion Matter?" *African Population Studies* 29 (2): 1831–42. https://doi.org/10.11564/29-2-743.

Gaddis, Isis, Rahul Lahoti, and Hema Swaminathan. 2022. "Women's Legal Rights and Gender Gaps in Property Ownership in Developing Countries." *Population and Development Review* 48 (2): 331–77. https://doi.org/10.1111/padr.12493.

Gaddis, Isis, Rahul Lahoti, and Li Wenjie. 2018. "Gender Gaps in Property Ownership in Sub-Saharan Africa." Policy Research Working Paper 8573, World Bank, Washington, DC.

Gaitskell, Deborah, Judy Kimble, Moira Maconachie, and Elaine Unterhalter. 1983. "Class, Race and Gender: Domestic Workers in South Africa." *Review of African Political Economy* 10 (27–28): 86–108. https://doi.org/10.1080/03056248308703548.

Garn, Joshua V., Leslie E. Greene, Robert Dreibelbis, Shadi Saboori, Richard D. Rheingans, and Matthew C. Freeman. 2013. "A Cluster-Randomized Trial Assessing the Impact of School Water, Sanitation and Hygiene Improvements on Pupil Enrolment and Gender Parity in Enrolment." *Journal of Water, Sanitation and Hygiene for Development* 3 (4): 592–601. https://doi.org/10.2166/washdev.2013.217.

Gassier, Marine, Lea Marie Rouanet, and Lacina Traore. 2022. "Addressing Gender-Based Segregation through Information: Evidence from a Randomized Experiment in the Republic of Congo." Policy Research Working Paper 9934, World Bank, Washington, DC. https://ideas.repec.org/p/wbk /wbrwps/9934.html.

Getahun, Chalahew. 2019. "Resources, Time and Gender: Determinants of Women's Housework in Bahir Dar and Nearby Rural Villages, Northwest Ethiopia." *Ethiopian Journal of the Social Sciences and Humanities* 14 (2). https://doi.org/10.4314/ejossah.v14i2.1.

Giacobino, Hélène, Elise Huillery, Bastien Michel, and Mathilde Sage. 2022. "Schoolgirls Not Brides: Secondary Education as a Shield Against Child Marriage." Working Papers DT/2022/01 Développement, Institutions et Mondialisation, Paris. https://ideas.repec.org/p/dia/wpaper/dt202201.html.

Goldstein, Markus, Kenneth Houngbedji, Florence Kondylis, Michael O'Sullivan, and Harris Selod. 2015. "Formalizing Rural Land Rights in West Africa: Early Evidence from a Randomized Impact Evaluation in Benin." Policy Research Working Paper 7435, World Bank, Washington, DC.

GSS (Ghana Statistical Service), GHS (Ghana Health Service), and ICF. 2018. *Ghana Maternal Health Survey 2017.* Accra, Ghana: GSS, GHS, and ICF. https://statsghana.gov.gh/gssmain/fileUpload /pressrelease/For%20website.pdf.

Gyan, Sylvia E., George Domfe, and Antoinette Tsiboe-Darko. 2023. "'I Am on a Family Planning Program, but I Have Not Told My Husband': Contraceptive Decision-Making of Child Brides in Ghana." *Journal of Family Issues* 44 (9): 2398–421. https://doi.org/10.1177/0192513X221093297.

Hammond, Alicia, Eliana Rubiano Matulevich, Kathleen Beegle, and Sai Krishna Kumaraswamy. 2020. *The Equality Equation.* Washington, DC: World Bank. https://doi.org/10.1596/34317.

Herrera, Javier, and Constance Torelli. 2013. "Domestic Work and Employment in Africa: What Is the Trade-Off for Women?" In *Urban Labor Markets in Sub-Saharan Africa*, edited by Philippe De Vreyer and François Roubaud, 221–49. Washington, DC: World Bank. https://doi.org/10.1596/9780821397817 _CH07.

Humlum, Maria Knoth, Anne Brink Nandrup, and Nina Smith. 2019. "Closing or Reproducing the Gender Gap? Parental Transmission, Social Norms and Education Choice." *Journal of Population Economics* 32 (2): 455–500. https://doi.org/10.1007/s00148-018-0692-1.

Kabeer, Naila. 2016. "Gender Equality, Economic Growth, and Women's Agency: The 'Endless Variety' and 'Monotonous Similarity' of Patriarchal Constraints." *Feminist Economics* 22 (1): 295–321. https://doi.org /10.1080/13545701.2015.1090009.

Kabeer, Naila, and Luisa Natali. 2013. "Gender Equality and Economic Growth: Is There a Win-Win?" *IDS Working Papers* 2013 (417): 1–58. https://doi.org/10.1111/j.2040-0209.2013.00417.x.

Kishor, Sunita, and Lekha Subaiya. 2008. *Understanding Women's Empowerment: A Comparative Analysis of Demographic and Health Surveys (DHS) Data.* DHS Comparative Reports 20. Calverton, MD: Macro International.

Klasen, Stephan, and Francesca Lamanna. 2009. "The Impact of Gender Inequality in Education and Employment on Economic Growth: New Evidence for a Panel of Countries." *Feminist Economics* 15 (3): 91–132. https://doi.org/10.1080/13545700902893106.

Lam, David, and Nicola Branson. 2014. "Education in South Africa since 1994." In *The Oxford Companion to the Economics of South Africa*, edited by Haroon Bhorat, Alan Hirsch, Ravi Kanbur, and Mthuli Ncube, 341–48. Oxford University Press. https://doi.org/10.1093/acprofioso/0780199689210.003.0015.

Lambon-Quayefio, Monica, Nkechi S. Owoo, Abena D. Oduro, and Sylvia E. Gyan. 2021. "The Socioeconomic and Reproductive Health Effects of Unequal Domestic Work on Women in Ghana." G²LM|LIC Policy Brief 34, Gender, Growth, and Labour Markets in Low Income Countries Programme, Institute of Labor Economics, Bonn, Germany.

Lopez-Acevedo, Gladys C., Florencia Devoto, Matías Morales, and Jaime Alfonso Roche Rodriguez. 2021. "Trends and Determinants of Female Labor Force Participation in Morocco: An Initial Exploratory Analysis." Policy Research Working Paper 9591, World Bank, Washington, DC. https://ideas.repec.org/p /wbk/wbrwps/9591.html.

Male, Chata, and Quentin Wodon. 2018. "Girls' Education and Child Marriage in West and Central Africa: Trends, Impacts, Costs, and Solutions." *Forum for Social Economics* 47 (2): 262–74. https://doi.org/10.10 80/07360932.2018.1451771.

Manser, Marilyn, and Murray Brown. 1980. "Marriage and Household Decision-Making: A Bargaining Analysis." *International Economic Review* 21 (1): 31–44. https://doi.org/10.2307/2526238.

McElroy, Marjorie B., and Mary Jean Horney. 1981. "Nash-Bargained Household Decisions: Toward a Generalization of the Theory of Demand." *International Economic Review* 22 (2): 333–49. https://doi.org/10.2307/2526280.

Miyata, Sachiko, and Hiroyuki Yamada. 2016. "Do Female Gender Role Attitudes Affect Labour Market Participation in Egypt?" *Journal of Development Studies* 52 (6): 876–94. https://doi.org/10.1080/00220388.2015.1113262.

Mmopelwa, G., B. N. Ngwenya, N. Sinha, and J. B. P. Sanders. 2013. "Caregiver Characteristics and Economic Cost of Home-Based Care: A Case Study of Maun and Gumare Villages in North West District, Botswana." *Chronic Illness* 9 (1): 3–15. https://doi.org/10.1177/1742395312449664.

Mosomi, Jacqueline. 2019. "An Empirical Analysis of Trends in Female Labour Force Participation and the Gender Wage Gap in South Africa." *Agenda* 33 (4): 29–43. https://doi.org/10.1080/10130950.2019.1656090.

Muchomba, Felix M. 2022. "Effect of Schooling on Anemia and Nutritional Status among Women: A Natural Experiment in Ethiopia." *American Journal of Epidemiology* 191 (10): 1722–31. https://doi.org/10.1093/aje/kwac111.

Muluneh, Muluken Dessalegn, Virginia Stulz, Lyn Francis, and Kingsley Agho. 2020. "Gender Based Violence against Women in Sub-Saharan Africa: A Systematic Review and Meta-Analysis of Cross-Sectional Studies." *International Journal of Environmental Research and Public Health* 17 (3): 903. https://doi.org/10.3390/ijerph17030903.

Njuki, Jemimah, Martha Melesse, Chaitali Sinha, Ruhiya Seward, Marie Renaud, Shannon Sutton, Tavinder Nijhawan, Katie Clancy, Ramata Thioune, and Dominique Charron. 2023. "Meeting the Challenge of Gender Inequality through Gender Transformative Research: Lessons from Research in Africa, Asia, and Latin America." *Canadian Journal of Development Studies/Revue canadienne d'études du développement* 44 (2): 206–28. https://doi.org/10.1080/02255189.2022.2099356.

Ñopo, Hugo, Nancy Daza, and Johanna Ramos. 2012. "Gender Earning Gaps around the World: A Study of 64 Countries." *International Journal of Manpower* 33 (5): 464–513. https://doi.org/10.1108/01437721211253164.

Nordman, Christophe Jalil, and Julia Vaillant. 2014. "Inputs, Gender Roles or Sharing Norms? Assessing the Gender Performance Gap Among Informal Entrepreneurs in Madagascar." IZA Discussion Paper 8046, Institute of Labor Economics, Bonn, Germany. https://www.ssrn.com/abstract=2412867.

Nwaka, Ikechukwu, Fatma Guven-Lisaniler, and Gulcay Tuna. 2016. "Gender Wage Differences in Nigerian Self and Paid Employment: Do Marriage and Children Matter?" *Economic and Labour Relations Review* 27 (4): 490–510. https://doi.org/10.1177/1035304616677655.

Nwosu, Chijioke O. 2021. "Childcare and Depression during the Coronavirus Pandemic in South Africa: A Gendered Analysis." *PLoS One* 16 (8): e0255183. https://doi.org/10.1371/journal.pone.0255183.

Nyariro, Milka, S. M. Hani Sadati, Claudia Mitchell, Stella Muthuri, and Milka Njeri. 2021. "Picturing Change through Photovoice Participatory Evaluation of a Daycare Intervention in an Urban Informal Context." In *Women's Economic Empowerment*, edited by Kate Grantham, Gillian Dowie, and Arjan de Haan. Routledge Studies in Development and Society. Abingdon, UK: Routledge International Development Research Centre.

Oduro, Abena D., Louis Boakye-Yiadom, and William Baah-Boateng. 2012. "Asset Ownership and Egalitarian Decision-Making among Couples: Some Evidence from Ghana." Working Paper Series No. 14, The Gender Asset Gap Project. http://rgdoi.net/10.13140/RG.2.1.2773.6084.

Oduro, Abena D., Carmen Diana Deere, and Zachary B. Catanzarite. 2015. "Women's Wealth and Intimate Partner Violence: Insights from Ecuador and Ghana." *Feminist Economics* 21 (2): 1–29. https://doi.org /10.1080/13545701.2014.997774.

Olivetti, Claudia, and Barbara Petrongolo. 2008. "Unequal Pay or Unequal Employment? A Cross-Country Analysis of Gender Gaps." *Journal of Labor Economics* 26 (4): 621–54. https://doi.org/10.1086/589458.

Omeje, Joachim C., Sarah N. Oshi, and Daniel C. Oshi. 2011. "Does Possession of Assets Increase Women's Participation in Reproductive Decision-Making? Perceptions of Nigerian Women." *Journal of Biosocial Science* 43 (1): 101–11. https://doi.org/10.1017/S0021932010000520.

Oosthuizen, Morne. 2018. "Counting Women's Work in South Africa: Incorporating Unpaid Work into Estimates of the Economic Lifecycle in 2010." Working Paper cwwwp8, Development Policy Research Unit, University of Cape Town, South Africa. https://ideas.repec.org/p/ctw/wpaper/cwwwp8.html.

Osakwe, Ekene, Ipchita Bharali, and Megan Huchko. 2022. *The Unfinished Agenda of Maternal and Child Health in Africa and Asia: Promising Directions to Address Maternal Mortality Challenges.* Durham, NC: Center for Policy Impact in Global Health.

O'Sullivan, Michael. 2017. "Gender and Property Rights in Sub-Saharan Africa: A Review of Constraints and Effective Interventions." Policy Research Working Paper 8250, World Bank, Washington, DC.

Owoo, Nkechi S. 2020. "Occupational Prestige and Women's Experience of Intimate Partner Violence in Nigeria." *Feminist Economics* 26 (4): 56–88. https://doi.org/10.1080/13545701.2020.1820064.

Owoo, Nkechi S., and Monica P. Lambon-Quayefio. 2021. "Mixed Methods Exploration of Ghanaian Women's Domestic Work, Childcare and Effects on Their Mental Health." *PLoS One* 16 (2): e0245059. https://doi.org/10.1371/journal.pone.0245059.

Owoo, Nkechi S., Monica P. Lambon-Quayefio, Sylvia E. Gyan, and Abena D. Oduro. 2022. "Women's Earnings and Domestic Work among Couples in Ghana." *African Review of Economics and Finance* 14 (1): 26–55.

Peterman, Amber, Audrey Pereira, Jennifer Bleck, Tia M. Palermo, and Kathryn M. Yount. 2017. "Women's Individual Asset Ownership and Experience of Intimate Partner Violence: Evidence From 28 International Surveys." *American Journal of Public Health* 107 (5): 747–55. https://doi.org/10.2105/AJPH .2017.303694.

Rabier, Serge. 2021. "Gender Inequalities." In *Population and Development Issues*, edited by Yves Charbit, 77–103. Hoboken, NJ: ISTE Ltd/John Wiley & Sons. Inc.

Reddy, Vijay, Lolita Winnaar, Andrea Juan, Fabian Arends, Jaqueline Harvey, Sylvia Hannan, Catherine Namome, Palesa Sekhejane, and Ncamisile Zulu. 2021. *TIMSS 2019: Highlights of South African Grade 9 Results in Mathematics and Science. Building Achievement Bridging Achievement Gaps.* Pretoria, South Africa: The Department of Basic Education, TIMSS South Africa.

Rios-Avila, Fernando, Abena Oduro, and Luiza Nassif Pires. 2021. "Intrahousehold Allocation of Household Production: A Comparative Analysis for Sub-Saharan African Countries." Working Paper Series, Levy Economics Institute, Annandale-on-Hudson, New York. https://www.ssrn.com/abstract =3780177.

Roethlisberger, Claudia, Franziska Gassmann, Wim Groot, and Bruno Martorano. 2023. "The Contribution of Personality Traits and Social Norms to the Gender Pay Gap: A Systematic Literature Review." *Journal of Economic Surveys* 37 (2): 377–408. https://doi.org/10.1111/joes.12501.

Rohwerder, Brigitte, Catherine Müller, Birasa Nyamulinda, Deepta Chopra, Elena Zambelli, and Naomi Hossain. 2017. "'You Cannot Live Without Money': Balancing Women's Unpaid Care Work and Paid Work in Rwanda." IDS Working Paper 498, Institute of Development Studies, Brighton, UK.

Seguino, Stephanie. 2007. "Plus Ça Change? Evidence on Global Trends in Gender Norms and Stereotypes." *Feminist Economics* 13 (2): 1–28. https://doi.org/10.1080/13545700601184880.

Seguino, Stephanie, and Maureen Were. 2014. "Gender, Development and Economic Growth in Sub-Saharan Africa." *Journal of African Economies* 23 (Suppl. 1): i18–i61. https://doi.org/10.1093/jae/ejt024.

Si, Chengyu, Denis Nadolnyak, and Valentina Hartarska. 2020. "The Gender Wage Gap in Developing Countries." *Applied Economics and Finance* 8 (1): 1–12. https://doi.org/10.11114/aef.v8i1.5082.

Singh, Kavita, Shelah Bloom, and Paul Brodish. 2011. "Influence of Gender Measures on Maternal and Child Health in Africa." MEASURE Evaluation Technical Report, University of North Carolina at Chapel Hill.

Spaull, Nic, and Nwabisa Makaluza. 2019. "Girls Do Better: The Pro-Female Gender Gap in Learning Outcomes in South Africa 1995–2018." *Agenda* 33 (4): 11–28. https://doi.org/10.1080/10130950.2019.1672568.

Standing, Guy. 1999. "Global Feminization through Flexible Labor: A Theme Revisited." *World Development* 27 (3): 583–602. https://doi.org/10.1016/S0305-750X(98)00151-X.

Suri, Tavneet, and William Jack. 2016. "The Long-Run Poverty and Gender Impacts of Mobile Money." *Science* 354 (6317): 1288–92. https://doi.org/10.1126/science.aah5309.

UIS (UNESCO Institute for Statistics). 2023. "Data for the Sustainable Development Goals." UIS, Montreal, Canada. https://uis.unesco.org/.

UNAIDS (Joint United Nations Programme on HIV/AIDS). 2022. "Women and Girls Carry the Heaviest HIV Burden in Sub-Saharan Africa." UNAIDS, Geneva. https://www.unaids.org/en/resources/presscentre/featurestories/2022/march/20220307_women-girls-carry-heaviest-hiv-burden-sub-saharan-africa.

UNICEF (United Nations Children's Fund). 2021. "Understanding the Relationship between Child Marriage and Female Genital Mutilation: A Statistical Overview of Their Co-Occurrence and Risk Factors." Data and Analytics, UNICEF, New York.

UNICEF (United Nations Children's Fund). 2023. "Female Genital Mutilation (FGM) Statistics." UNICEF, New York. https://data.unicef.org/topic/child-protection/female-genital-mutilation/#notes.

Vasudevan, Ramaa, and Srinivas Raghavendra. 2022. "Women's Self-Employment as a Developmental Strategy: The Dual Constraints of Care Work and Aggregate Demand." *Feminist Economics* 28 (3): 56–83. https://doi.org/10.1080/13545701.2022.2044497.

Vyas, Seema, Jessie Mbwambo, and Lori Heise. 2015. "Women's Paid Work and Intimate Partner Violence: Insights from Tanzania." *Feminist Economics* 21 (1): 35–58. https://doi.org/10.1080/13545701.2014.935796.

Wamboye, Evelyn F., and Stephanie Seguino. 2015. "Gender Effects of Trade Openness in Sub-Saharan Africa." *Feminist Economics* 21 (3): 82–113. https://doi.org/10.1080/13545701.2014.927583.

Wangamati, Cynthia Khamala. 2020. "Comprehensive Sexuality Education in Sub-Saharan Africa: Adaptation and Implementation Challenges in Universal Access for Children and Adolescents." *Sexual and Reproductive Health Matters* 28 (2): 1851346. https://doi.org/10.1080/26410397.2020.1851346.

Welmond, Michel J., and Laura Gregory. 2021. *Educational Underachievement among Boys and Men.* Washington, DC: World Bank.

WHO (World Health Organization). 2021. "Abortion Fact Sheet 2021." WHO, Geneva. https://www.who .int/news-room/fact-sheets/detail/abortion.

Wodon, Quentin, Minh Nguyen, and Clarence Tsimpo. 2016. "Child Marriage, Education, and Agency in Uganda." *Feminist Economics* 22 (1): 54–79. https://doi.org/10.1080/13545701.2015.1102020.

Wodon, Quentin, and Yvonne Ying. 2010. "Domestic Work Time in Sierra Leone." In *Gender Disparities in Africa's Labor Markets*, edited by Jorge Saba Arbache, Alexandre Kolev, and Ewa Filipiak, 333–56. Washington, DC: World Bank.

World Bank. 2023. "World Bank Database." World Bank, Washington, DC. https://data.worldbank.org /indicator.

Zacharias, Ajit, Thomas Masterson, Fernando Rios-Avila, and Abena D. Oduro. 2021. "Scope and Effects of Reducing Time Deficits via Intrahousehold Redistribution of Household Production." Levy Economics Institute, Annandale-on-Hudson, New York.

Zambelli, Elena, Keetie Roelen, Naomi Hossain, Deepta Chopra, and Jenipher Twebaze Musoke. 2017. *"My Mother Does a Lot of Work": Women Balancing Paid and Unpaid Care Work in Tanzania.* Brighton, UK: Institute of Development Studies, BRAC Research and Evaluation Unit.

Chapter 6

Spatial Inequality—Multidimensional Inequalities across Space

Nkechi Owoo, Muna Shifa, Vimal Ranchhod, and Mary Zhang

Introduction

Despite the strong recovery in economic growth in most Sub-Saharan African (SSA) economies since the mid-1990s, economic growth has not been inclusive. The extent to which economic growth alleviates poverty in SSA is limited due to, among other factors, high levels of initial and persistent inequality (Clementi, Fabiani, and Molini 2019; Fosu 2018). Within-country spatial inequality measures inequality within a country's geographic units (for example, regions or districts) and is a key component of national inequality in most SSA countries (Beegle et al. 2016; Shifa and Leibbrandt 2022). Several factors contribute to the emergence and persistence of spatial inequality in SSA, including initial conditions and colonial legacies, as well as the nature of post-independence political settlements (Abdulai 2017).

This chapter provides an overview of the nature and patterns of spatial inequality in access to basic services in SSA. The chapter focuses on basic services, such as access to electricity, safe sanitation, and clean water, as they play a key role in observed inequalities across the continent. In addition, these services form the infrastructure across individuals' life course, with implications for their health, education, and employment (that is, participation in the economy).

Map 6.1 provides a general overview of the distribution of these services across the continent, revealing two important aspects. First, the lack of access to basic services across SSA is visible, and second, the differences in access across countries are substantial. For example, more than 80 percent of the population in countries such as the Central African Republic and Chad are deemed multidimensionally poor, with limited access to basic services such as improved sanitation, but only 20 percent of the population in South Africa is similarly deprived.[1]

Map 6.1 Multidimensional Poverty and Deprivations in Basic Services in Sub-Saharan Africa

a. Multidimensional Poverty

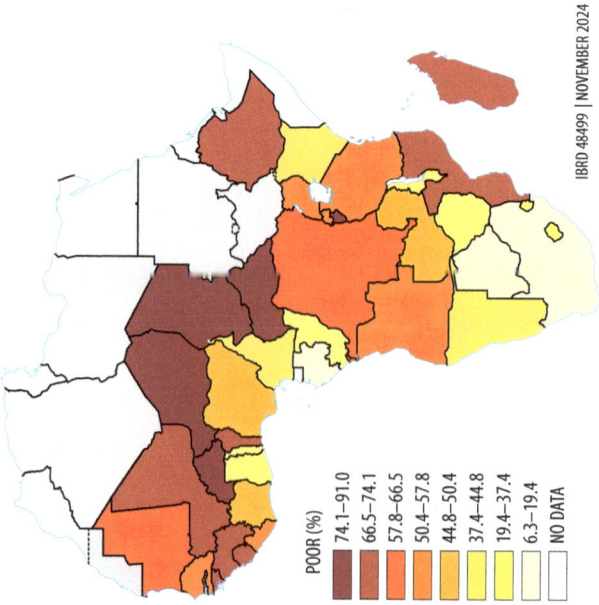

POOR (%)
- 74.1–91.0
- 66.5–74.1
- 57.8–66.5
- 50.4–57.8
- 44.8–50.4
- 37.4–44.8
- 19.4–37.4
- 6.3–19.4
- NO DATA

IBRD 48499 | NOVEMBER 2024

b. Deprived in Santation

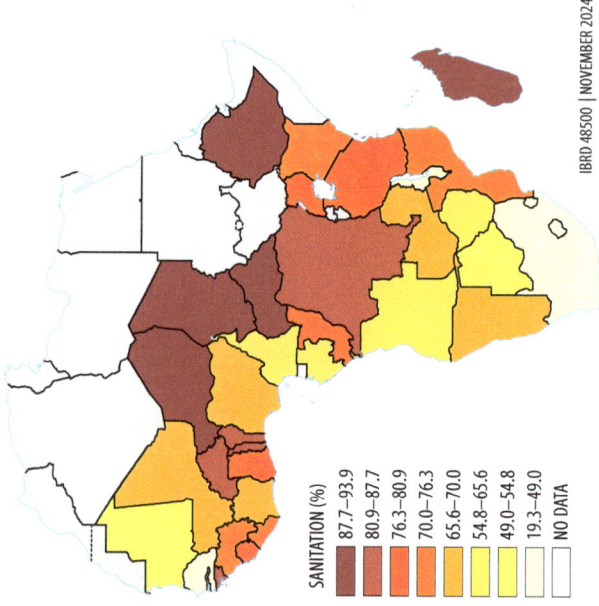

SANITATION (%)
- 87.7–93.9
- 80.9–87.7
- 76.3–80.9
- 70.0–76.3
- 65.6–70.0
- 54.8–65.6
- 49.0–54.8
- 19.3–49.0
- NO DATA

IBRD 48500 | NOVEMBER 2024

(continued next page)

Map 6.1 Multidimensional Poverty and Deprivations in Basic Services in Sub-Saharan Africa (*continued*)

c. Deprived in water

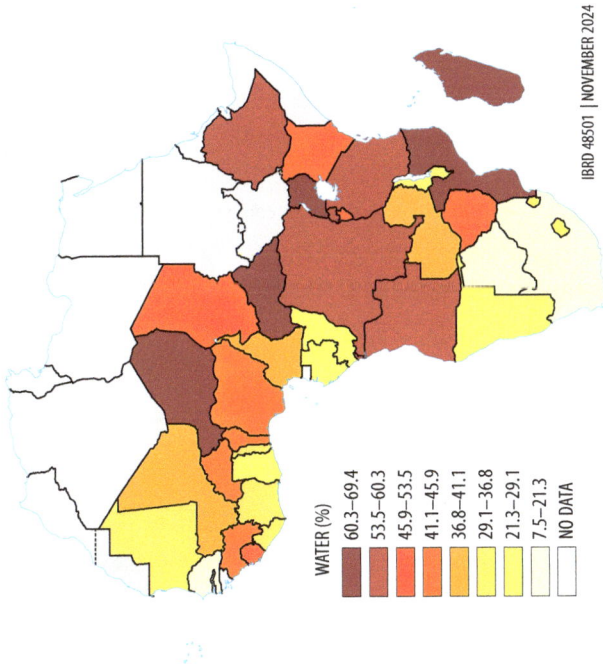

WATER (%)
- 60.3–69.4
- 53.5–60.3
- 45.9–53.5
- 41.1–45.9
- 36.8–41.1
- 29.1–36.8
- 21.3–29.1
- 7.5–21.3
- NO DATA

IBRD 48501 | NOVEMBER 2024

d. Deprived in electricity

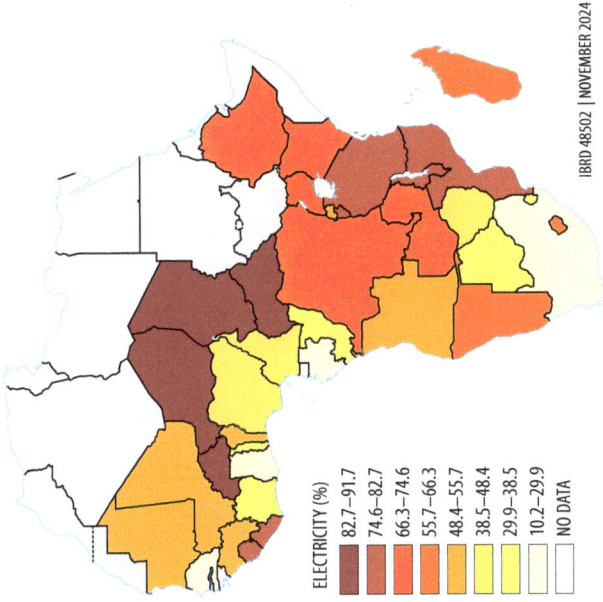

ELECTRICITY (%)
- 82.7–91.7
- 74.6–82.7
- 66.3–74.6
- 55.7–66.3
- 48.4–55.7
- 38.5–48.4
- 29.9–38.5
- 10.2–29.9
- NO DATA

IBRD 48502 | NOVEMBER 2024

Source: Authors' calculations using data from Alkire, Kanagaratnam, and Suppa 2022.

Note: The legends show the percentage of the population in multidimensional poverty or lacking access to safe sanitation, clean water, or electricity.

The remainder of the chapter is organized as follows. The first section on heterogeneities in spatial inequalities presents evidence on within-country differences (regional and provincial differences) in access to basic services across countries in SSA and discusses contributing factors. The following section discusses micro-level demographic and socioeconomic factors that affect access to basic services within countries across the continent. The final section provides concluding remarks and policy implications.

Spatial Inequalities across Settings in SSA

Spatial inequalities refer to "the uneven distribution of income or other variables across different locations" (Kanbur, Venables, and Wan 2006, 2). United Nations Sustainable Development Goals 6 and 7 specify that providing safe water, sanitation, hygiene, and sustainable modern energy to everyone should be achieved by 2030. Multidimensional spatial inequality is "a significant challenge in promoting inclusive growth in the SSA countries" (Shifa and Leibbrandt 2022, 13). This chapter uses the deprivation of electricity, safe sanitation, and clean water to illustrate the inequalities in accessing basic services across and within the SSA regions.

Using data on Ghana, Kenya, and South Africa (refer to figure 6.1), the highest level of electricity deprivation is observed in Kenya (70 percent), which is attributable to the country's high and rising cost of electricity (Njiru and Letema 2018). Among the three countries, the highest levels of deprivation in sanitation (76 percent) and water (85 percent) are observed in Ghana. This situation is explained by limited resources, staff, and implementation of programs (UNICEF 2023), particularly in rural areas.

South Africa has the lowest levels of deprivation among the three countries (Shifa and Leibbrandt 2022). However, despite its better electricity infrastructure, access is not uniformly distributed across South Africa. For example, a recent Afrobarometer report indicates that only 41 percent and 51 percent of urban and rural residents, respectively, believed that the country had a reliable electricity supply (Oyuke, Penar, and Howard 2016). Since 2007, South Africa has continued to experience widespread national blackouts of electricity supply, largely attributed to insufficient generation capacity. This situation highlights the need to contrast "measured" access to basic services with "realized access."

In addition to between-country differences, within countries, access to basic services may also vary across regions, districts, and provinces. The following subsections discuss these variations in deprivations in electricity, safe sanitation, and clean water.

Figure 6.1 Basic Service Deprivations in Ghana, Kenya, and South Africa

Percent

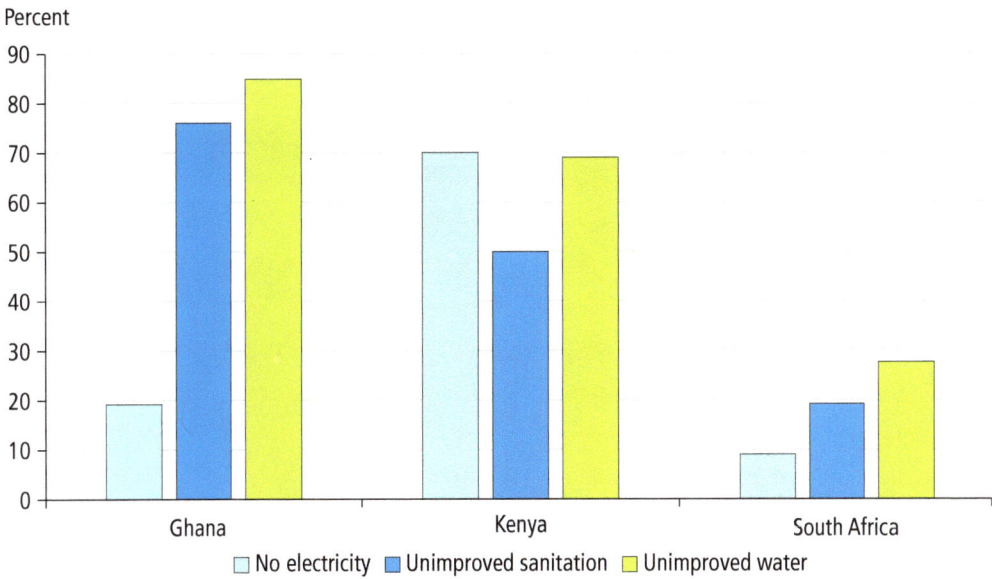

Source: Authors' calculations based on data from Multiple Indicator Cluster Surveys (MICS) and Demographic and Health Surveys (DHS).
Note: Calculations for Ghana are from the MICS6 for 2018, for Kenya from the DHS for 2014, and for South Africa from the DHS for 2016.

Electricity

Inequalities in electrification and electricity supply and consumption are critical issues in most SSA countries (Falchetta et al. 2020; Sarkodie and Adams 2020). Electricity deprivation shows substantial variations across regions and provinces within countries (refer to map 6.2). In Kenya, although around 70 percent of the population does not have access to electricity (refer to figure 6.1), this varies across counties. While the level of deprivation is as high as 92 percent in Western Kenya, it is only 12 percent in Nairobi, the country's capital city. A similar situation is observed in Ghana—although around 19 percent of the population is estimated to be deprived of electricity, the lowest level of deprivation is observed in the Greater Accra region (about 6 percent). In comparison, the highest level is observed in the Upper East region (about 53 percent). In South Africa, around 9 percent of the general population lacks access to electricity; the highest level of deprivation is in the Eastern Cape (20 percent), and the lowest level is in the Western Cape (0.3 percent).

Map 6.2 Electricity Deprivation in Ghana, Kenya, and South Africa

a. Ghana

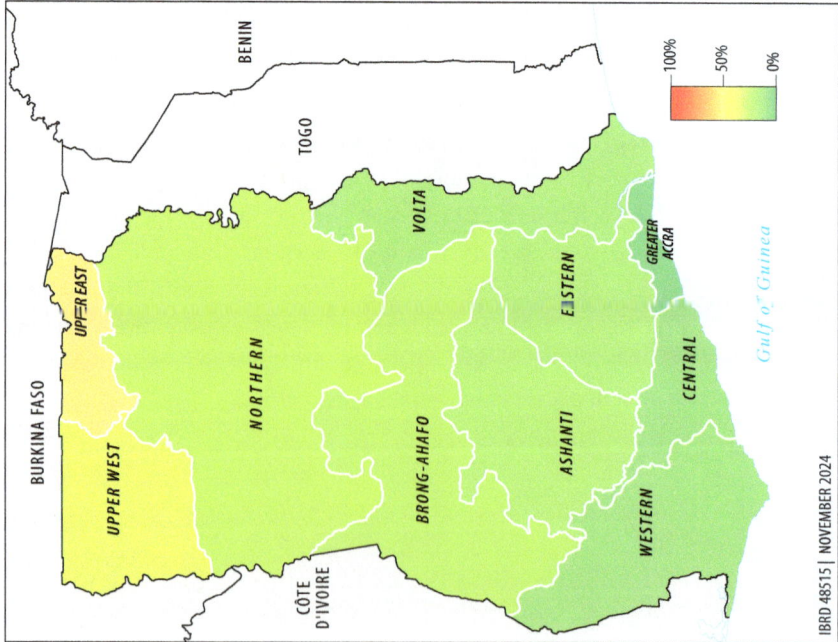

b. Kenya

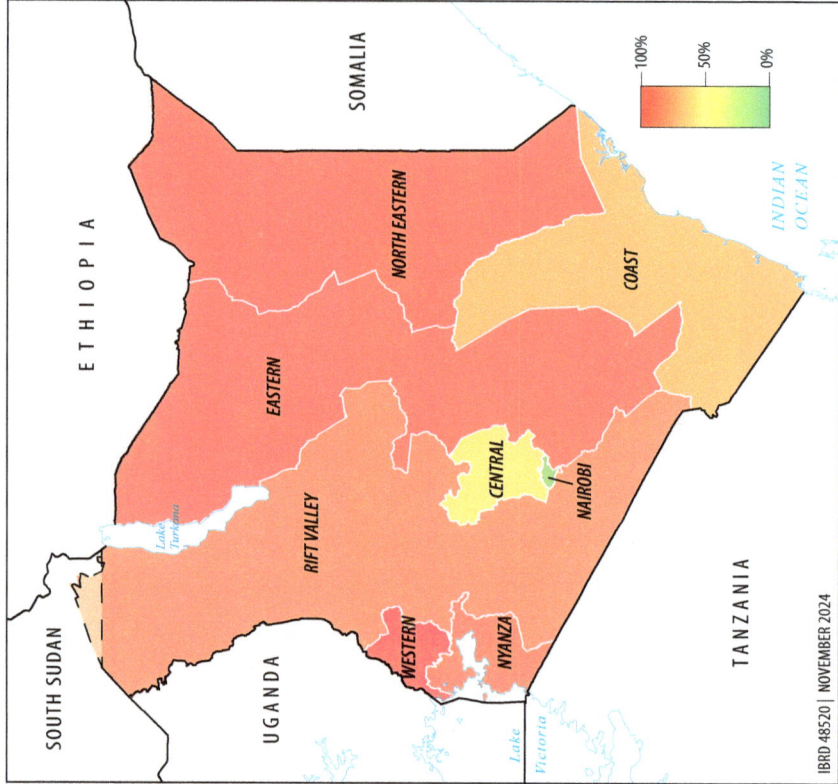

IBRD 48515 | NOVEMBER 2024

IBRD 48520 | NOVEMBER 2024

(continued next page)

Map 6.2   Electricity Deprivation in Ghana, Kenya, and South Africa *(continued)*

c. South Africa

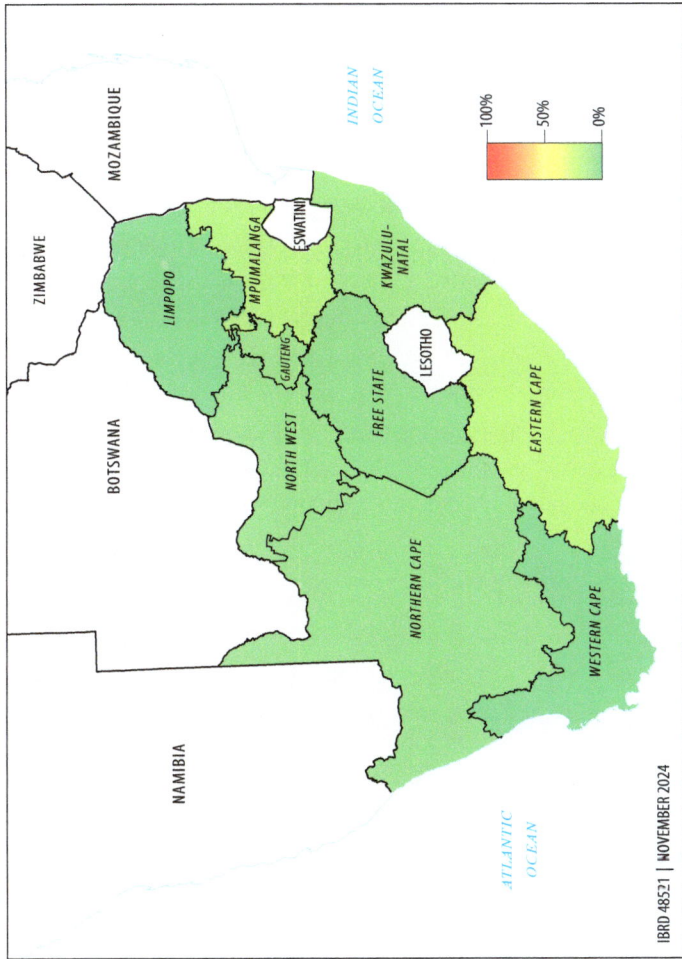

IBRD 48521 | NOVEMBER 2024

Sources: Authors' calculations using data from UNICEF Multiple Indicator Cluster Surveys (MICS) and Demographic and Health Surveys (DHS).

Note: The maps show the percentage of households that lack access to electricity. Calculations for Ghana are from the UNICEF MICS6 for 2018 (raw sample size, 61,254), for Kenya from the DHS for 2014 (raw sample size, 151,093), and for South Africa from the DHS for 2016 (raw sample size, 37,925). Normalized post stratification weight applied.

Safe Sanitation

Similar to electricity, deprivations in access to improved sanitation vary across regions and provinces within each country (refer to map 6.3). Overall, 76 percent of the population in Ghana is sanitation deprived. In Kenya and South Africa, 50 percent and 19 percent of the population, respectively, are sanitation deprived. Within Ghana, only three regions (Ashanti, Eastern, and Greater Accra) have deprivation levels below the country average. In Kenya, sanitation deprivation varies from as low as 40 percent (Western) to as high as 75 percent (North Eastern). In Kenya, despite Nairobi being the country's capital city, about 70 percent of the population there is sanitation deprived. In South Africa, the level of sanitation deprivation in most regions is lower than the national average, except for that in Gauteng (29 percent) and North West (23 percent).

Clean Water

Similar to electricity and sanitation deprivation, the distribution of households without access to clean drinking water in their dwelling or yard (water deprivation) varies across regions within each country (refer to map 6.4). Overall, 85 percent of the households in Ghana are clean water deprived, followed by about 69 percent in Kenya and 28 percent in South Africa. In Kenya, clean water deprivation is lowest in the Central and Nairobi regions (35–36 percent) and highest in the Coast (82 percent), Nyanza (90 percent), and Western (92 percent) regions. In South Africa, the percentage of households experiencing clean water deprivation is double the national average in the Eastern Cape (52 percent) and Limpopo (57 percent) regions. In contrast, the Free State (7 percent) and Western Cape (7 percent) provinces have the lowest levels of clean water deprivation.

Several factors can explain the regional and provincial differences in access to basic services like electricity, safe sanitation, and clean drinking water in countries across SSA. In Ghana, Kenya, and other countries, colonial factors play an important role in the regional divide in access to basic services. In Ghana, during colonial times, the North and South of the country were designated as the "periphery" and "core," respectively, so that Northern Ghana's interests and development were sidelined (Brukum 1998; Grischow 1999; Plange 1979; Songsore 2003). Thus, colonial investments and expenditures in the northern regions were kept to a minimum, just adequate to keep the administration running. In Kenya, colonial administrators perceived the climate in the country and in Mombasa to be conducive and, therefore, developed railways and other infrastructure (such as banking) in these areas (Morgan 1963). These uneven spatial development patterns continued even after colonialism ended (Bernards 2022; Kimari and Ernstson 2020). Other factors that explain regional variations in access to basic services may include extreme weather events (for example, droughts), limited infrastructure, poor planning, and the high costs of maintenance and services (Hope and Ballon 2021).

Map 6.3 Sanitation Deprivation in Ghana, Kenya, and South Africa

a. Ghana

b. Kenya

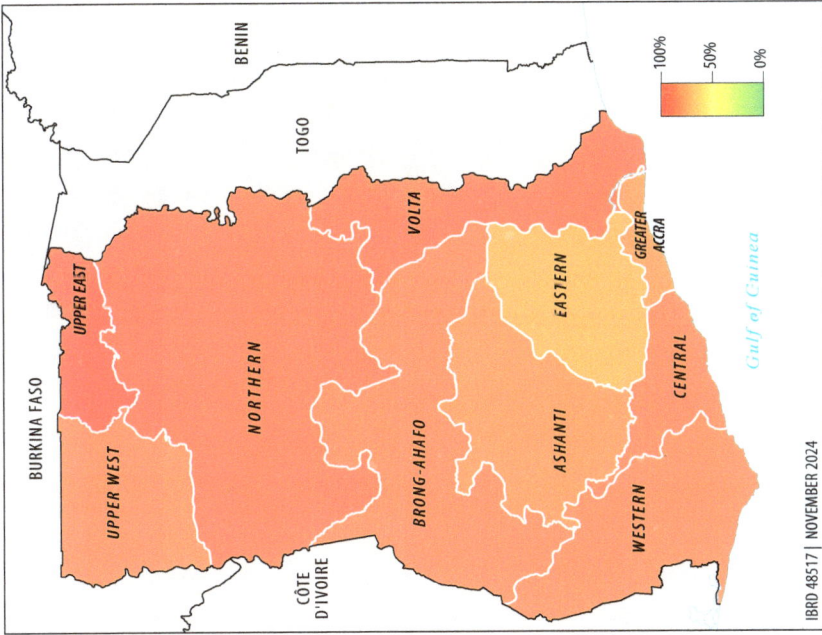

IBRD 48517 | NOVEMBER 2024

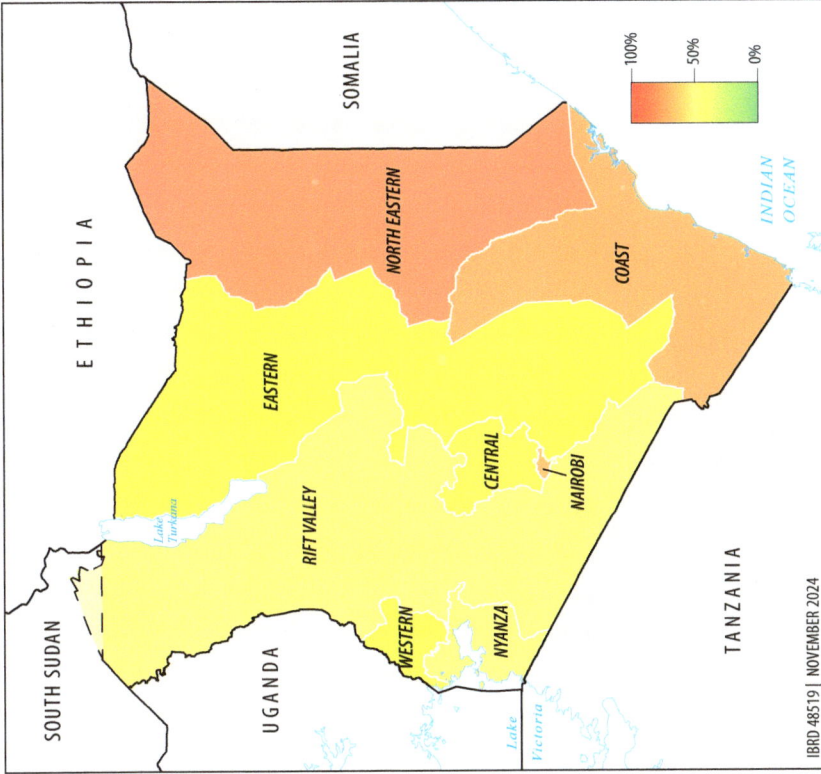

IBRD 48519 | NOVEMBER 2024

(continued next page)

Map 6.3 Sanitation Deprivation in Ghana, Kenya, and South Africa *(continued)*

c. South Africa

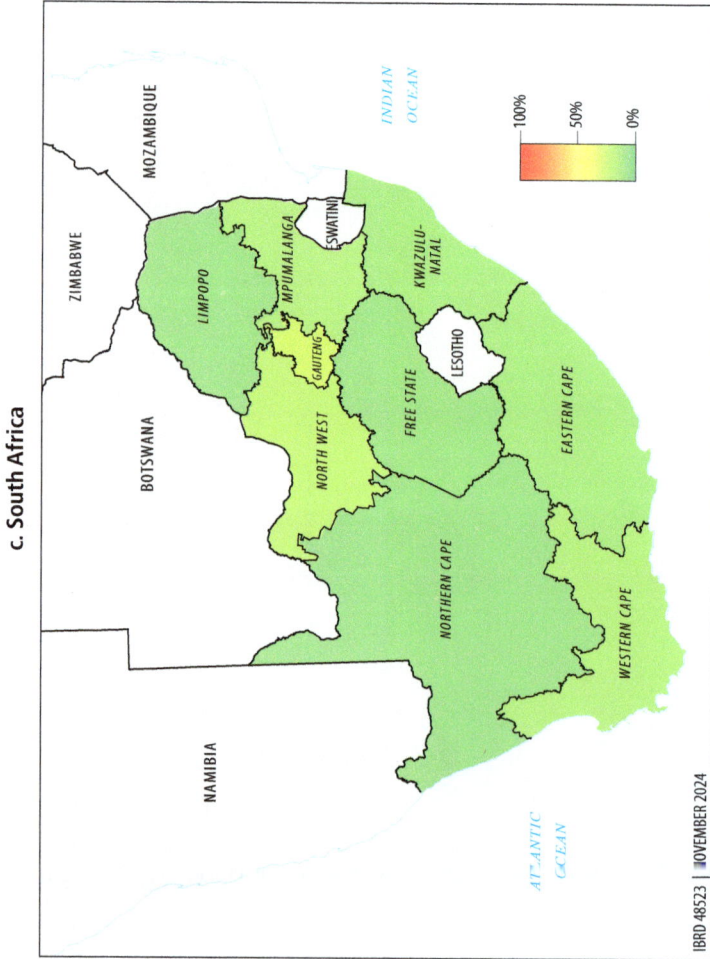

IBRD 48523 | NOVEMBER 2024

Sources: Authors' calculations using data from UNICEF Multiple Indicator Cluster Surveys (MICS) and Demographic and Health Surveys (DHS).

Note: The maps show the percentage of households that lack access to improved sanitation. Calculations for Ghana are from the UNICEF MICS6 for 2018 (raw sample size, 61,254), for Kenya from the DHS for 2014 (raw sample size, 151,093), and for South Africa from the DHS for 2016 (raw sample size, 37,925). Normalized post stratification weight applied.

Map 6.4 Clean Water Deprivation in Ghana, Kenya, and South Africa

a. Ghana

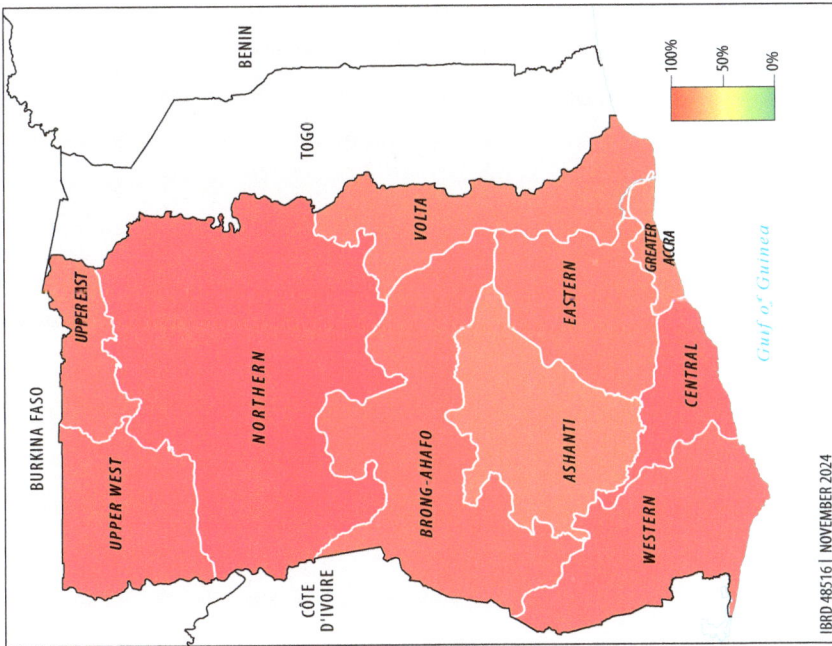

IBRD 48516 | NOVEMBER 2024

b. Kenya

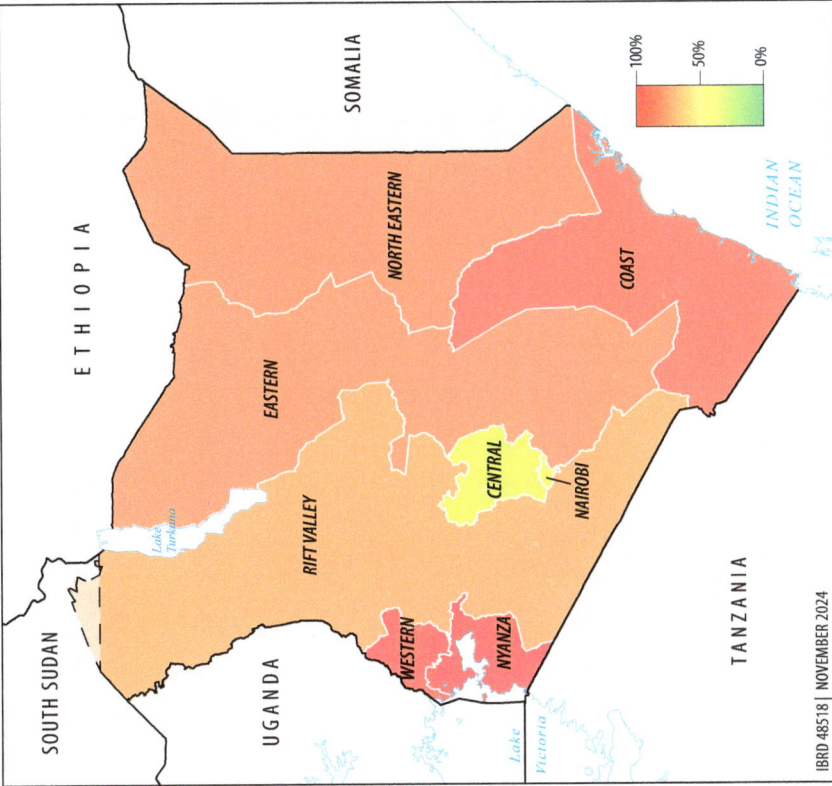

IBRD 48518 | NOVEMBER 2024

(continued next page)

Map 6.4 **Clean Water Deprivation in Ghana, Kenya, and South Africa** (*continued*)

c. South Africa

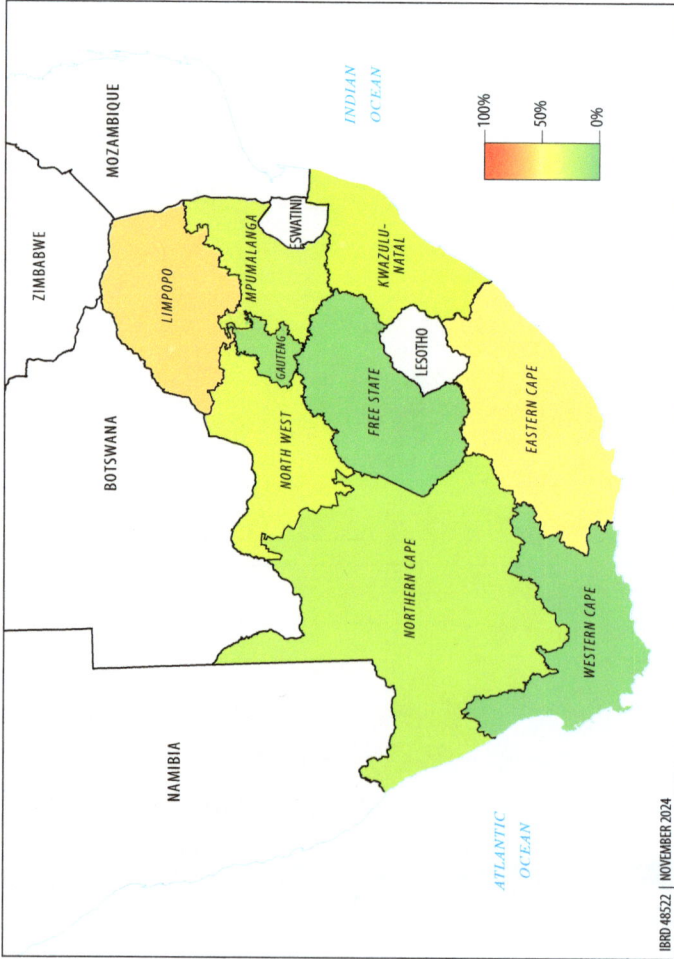

IBRD 48522 | NOVEMBER 2024

Sources: Authors' calculations using data from UNICEF Multiple Indicator Cluster Surveys (MICS) and Demographic and Health Surveys (DHS).

Note: The maps show the percentage of households that lack access to clean water. Calculations for Ghana are from the UNICEF MICS6 for 2018 (raw sample size, 61,254), for Kenya from the DHS for 2014 (raw sample size, 151,093), and for South Africa from the DHS for 2016 (raw sample size, 37,925). Normalized post stratification weight applied.

Heterogeneities in Spatial Inequalities

This section discusses factors that explain differences in access to basic services in SSA at more-disaggregated levels than regions or provinces. It explores the contributions of factors such as poverty, education, urbanization, gender, race, and ethnicity to explain differential access to basic services within countries in SSA. In map 6.5, for example, although provinces such as Limpopo and Eastern Cape in South Africa have higher levels of water deprivation compared to other provinces, like the Western Cape, within these deprived provinces, some districts are better off (for example, Waterberg) than others (for example, Vhembe and Mopani).

These within-region or province heterogeneities in access to basic services can be explained by certain individual- and household-level factors, which are discussed in the following subsections.

Poverty Status

In countries in SSA, such as Ghana and South Africa, the poorest households generally have the least access to basic amenities and public services (Atta-Ankomah et al. 2020; Stats SA, SALDRU, and AFD 2019). According to Parienté (2017), given the monopoly-like structure of service providers, the failure of governments to regulate the market properly can result in inadequate or poorly maintained services, as well as limited contract enforcement. In map 6.6, the counties in Kenya with the highest monetary poverty levels, like Mandera and Turkana, also have the highest levels of multidimensional poverty as measured by deprivations in access to education, health facilities, electricity, safe sanitation, and water, among other deprivations (Shifa and Leibbrandt 2017). Poorer households may also demonstrate a lower willingness and ability to pay for basic services, with the situation being exacerbated in the absence of credit facilities, which further constrains their demand (Devoto et al. 2012).

Urbanization

Urbanization also affects access to basic services like water, sanitation, and electricity in SSA. According to agglomeration economy arguments, a bigger pool of providers may lower the costs and improve the variety and quality of service provision through competition and specialization. In addition, there is better connectivity between customers and suppliers in urban areas as a result of more-efficient transport systems, making it easier to access services. Martine (2008) found that it is generally more efficient to provide public services and infrastructure, such as sewage treatment facilities and electricity, in large cities than in dispersed settlements where densities are low and distances are large. Therefore, urbanization is also a factor in explaining spatial heterogeneities within regions in a country.

Map 6.5 Access to Clean Water in Provinces and District Municipalities in South Africa

a. Provinces

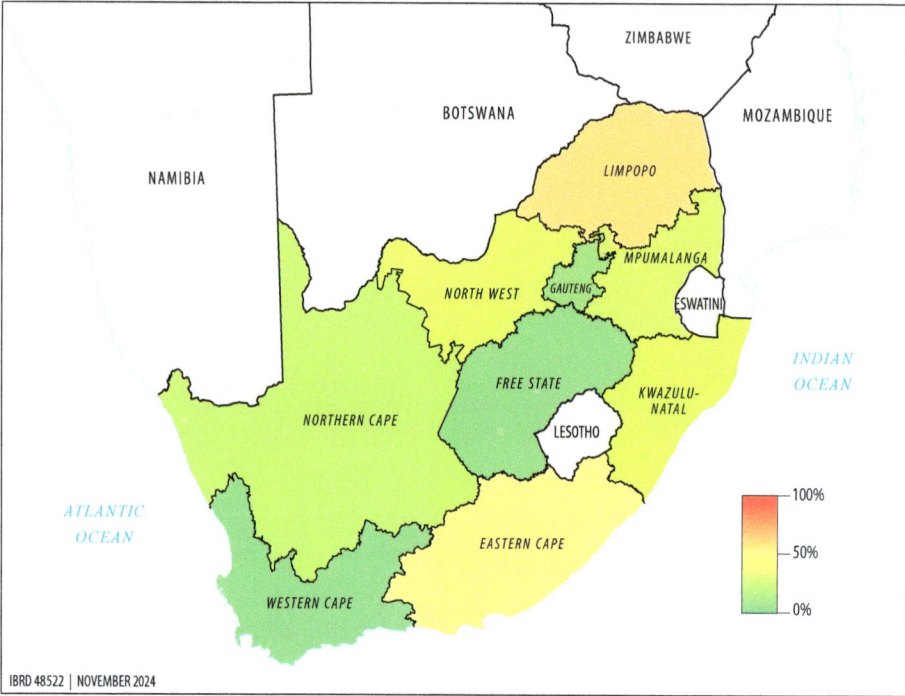

IBRD 48522 | NOVEMBER 2024

b. District municipalities

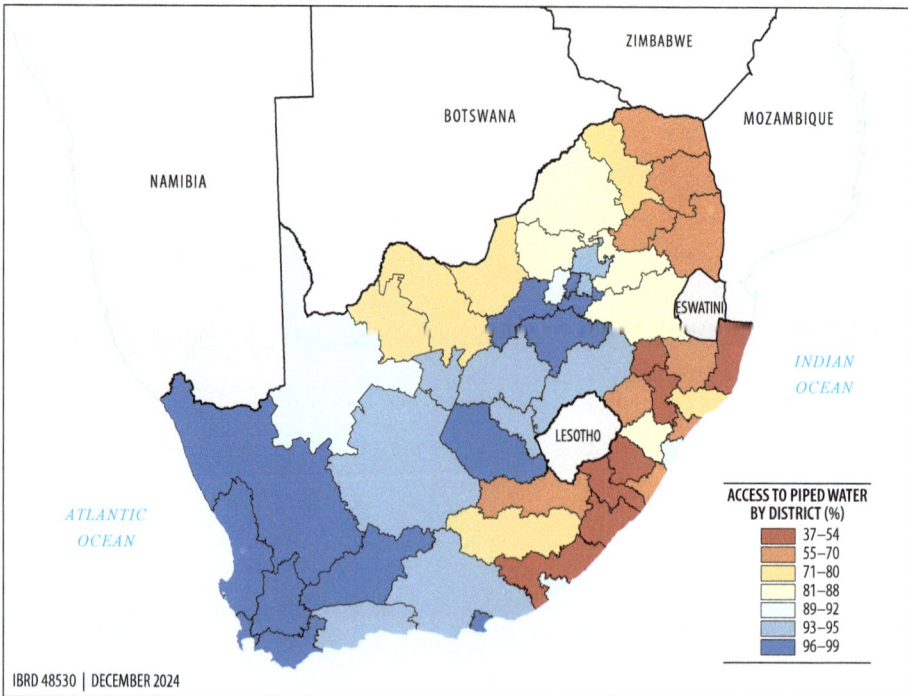

IBRD 48530 | DECEMBER 2024

Sources: Panel a is original to this publication; panel b is based on the 2011 census in Stats SA et al. 2019.

Map 6.6 Poverty and Access to Improved Water Sources, Kenya, 2009

a. Multidimensional poverty

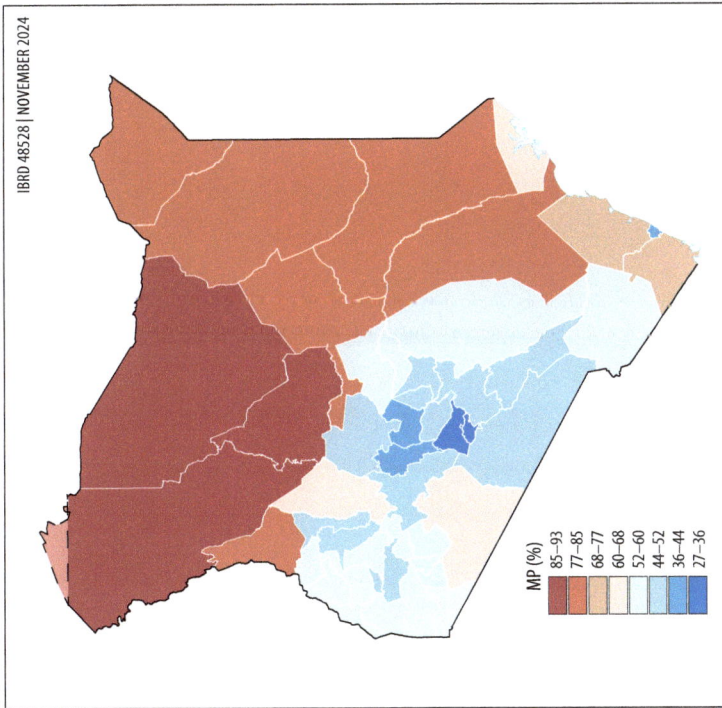

IBRD 48528 | NOVEMBER 2024

MP (%)
- 85–93
- 77–85
- 68–77
- 60–68
- 52–60
- 44–52
- 36–44
- 27–36

b. Monetary poverty

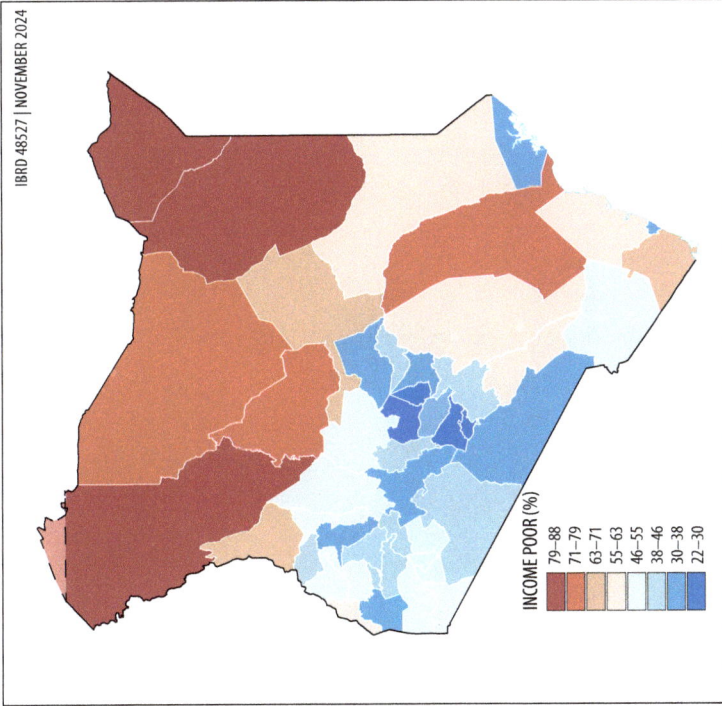

IBRD 48527 | NOVEMBER 2024

INCOME POOR (%)
- 79–88
- 71–79
- 63–71
- 55–63
- 46–55
- 38–46
- 30–38
- 22–30

Source: Based on Shifa and Leibbrandt 2017.

Map 6.7 indicates areas with access to electricity, with darker shades of green indicating greater access. Access to electricity is relatively high in the urban cities of Bagoue, Gbeke, and Poro, while less-urbanized areas, like San Pedro, appear to have lower access. This phenomenon suggests that the higher concentration of people within an area of a country is correlated with greater access to basic services, albeit with distinguishable variations between the urban rich and urban poor populations (Kuddus, Tynan, and McBryde 2020).

Map 6.7 Access to Electricity in the Largest Cities in Côte d'Ivoire, 2015

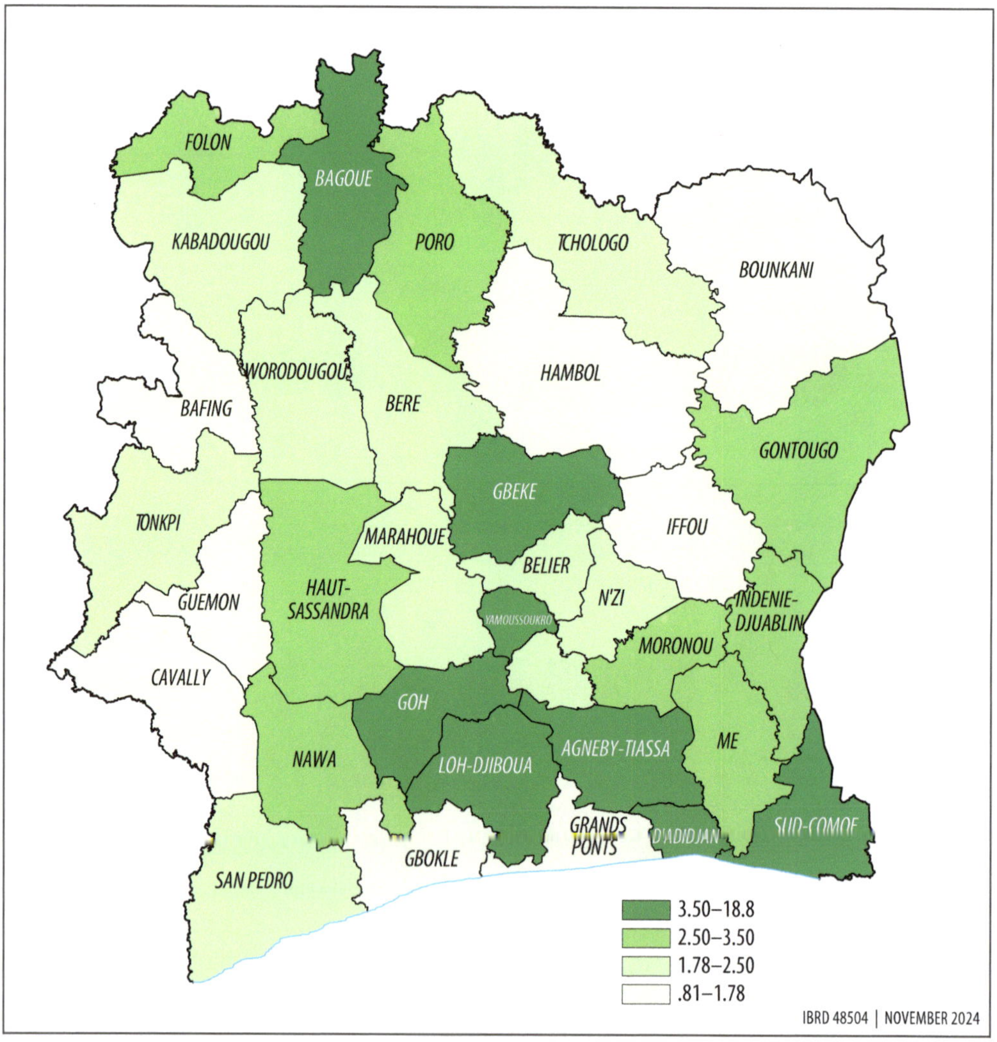

Source: Map used under Creative Commons Attribution 4.0 International License; Aka et al. 2020.
Note: Map shows the distribution of access to electricity, with darker shades of green representing areas with greater access.

Despite the likely benefits of agglomeration economies in urban centers, which increase the provision of and access to basic services, rising congestion, overcrowding, pressure on ecosystems, and other related challenges can counterbalance these if public investment is insufficient to preserve and expand essential infrastructures (Turok and McGranahan 2013).

Data from other countries, like Ghana and South Africa, also show that urban households have greater access to basic services, compared to their rural counterparts (refer to table 6.1). An explanation for the lower access in less-urbanized areas is that, on the supply side, rural dwellers may not be well organized and are, therefore, more likely to be neglected in or excluded from national development agendas (Kumar 2015). On the demand side, in rural areas, where property rights may not be effective, households may be reluctant to make housing improvements by procuring services such as safe water, safe sanitation, and electricity.

Gender

Gender also contributes to heterogeneities in access to basic services within geographic units in SSA. In many households, the burden of water collection and household hygiene rests on women and girls. Nonetheless, water and sanitation projects traditionally fail women and girls because the projects often do not systematically factor gender considerations into resource allocation decisions and, therefore, overlook women in water and sanitation planning. Because community development stakeholder meetings often have few women in attendance (and when present, women rarely speak up), men usually dominate the discussions and decision-making, leading to distributions of resources that are frequently skewed in favor of men (UN Habitat 2013).

The different statuses of women and men in many SSA households, which are influenced by historical, religious, economic, and cultural realities, are responsible for the unequal access to resources and amenities (Pouramin, Nagabhatla, and Miletto 2020). In South Africa, for example, 77 percent of male-headed households have access to safe water compared to 70 percent of female-headed households. Furthermore, 69.2 percent of male-headed households have access to refuse removal by local authorities compared to 60.6 percent of female-headed households (Stats SA et al. 2019).

Table 6.1 Basic Services by Rural and Urban Residence in Ghana, Kenya, and South Africa

Country	Safe water (%)		Safe sanitation (%)		Electricity (%)	
	Rural	**Urban**	**Rural**	**Urban**	**Rural**	**Urban**
Ghana	67.5	55.0	60.3	91.7	63.5	91.7
Kenya	61.8	86.7	48.8	86.2	20.0	73.9
South Africa	40.4	88.8	62.8	90.6	85.8	83.7

Sources: Ghana Living Standards Survey (2016/17); Kenya Integrated Household Budget Survey (2015/16); South Africa General Household Survey (2017).

Note: The values in the table are the percentage of households with access to safe water, safe sanitation, and electricity.

In contrast, in Ghana, female-headed households tend to fare better than male-headed households, with a larger proportion of female-headed households having access to clean water (62.1 versus 61.9 percent), safe sanitation (83.9 versus 71.4 percent), and electricity (81.6 versus 74.4 percent) (Atta-Ankomah et al. 2020). Brown and van de Walle (2020) stated that the nature of female headship may explain their better performance. Generally, female household heads who are married or in nonresident polygynous households with remitting husbands or male contributory workers may be better off.

Racial and Ethnic Groups

Spatial heterogeneities in access to basic services within regions may also be explained by racial and ethnic backgrounds. According to Akramov and Asante (2008), the ethnic diversity of individuals within a particular geographic area in Ghana significantly impacts their access to local public services. For example, in South Africa, Black African–headed households experience more interruptions to the water supply, have lower access to improved sanitation, and show the lowest rates of electricity and internet access compared to households headed by other population groups (Stats SA et al. 2019). Furthermore, the parts of South Africa with the highest population of Blacks are found to have the least access to safe water (Brdar et al. 2016; Stats SA et al. 2019).

Walters, Bittencourt, and Chisadza (2023) have shown that South African municipalities that are coethnic with the president are associated with better provision of water infrastructure relative to other municipalities. Where regulation is inefficient, the decision to provide basic services to certain areas may be based on ethnicity (Burgess et al. 2015). Furthermore, ethnic and racial differences in tastes and preferences for basic services may also explain heterogeneities in access to these local public goods, as well as the lack of politically independent institutions to oversee the allocation of funding and provision of local infrastructure (Walters et al. 2023). Similar influences of ethnicity on the distribution of basic services are observed in Kenya, with districts that share a common ethnicity with the president receiving double the amount of expenditure on roads and possessing five times the length of paved roads built (Burgess et al. 2015).

Education

Educational attainment also can explain the spatial heterogeneities in access to basic services between and within countries' geographic units. Higher education can contribute to more-effective use of basic services like water and sanitation. Akpakli et al. (2018) found that education is an important determining factor in rural districts' access to safe sanitation in Ghana. Furthermore, educational attainment can lead to greater awareness of the implications of, for instance, clean water and safe sanitation for welfare outcomes. Education may also be correlated with greater resource endowments, leading to the use of resources to secure needed amenities and services (Agbadi, Darkwah, and Kenney 2019).

Figure 6.2 shows that access to electricity and safe sanitation increases with the attainment of at least a secondary school education across Ghana's regions. In Greater Accra, where about 45 percent of the population has at least a secondary school education, access to safe sanitation and electricity is highest, compared to the Upper East region, where only 18 percent of the population has at least a secondary school education.

Figure 6.2 **Educational Attainment and Access to Electricity and Safe Sanitation in Ghana, by Region, 2017**

Percent

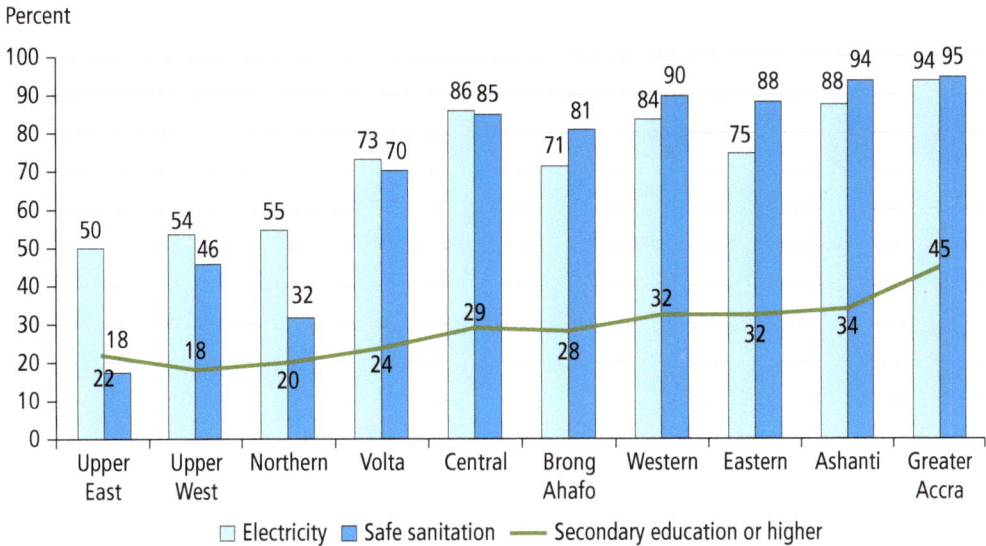

Source: Authors' calculations using the Ghana Living Standards Survey 2017.

Figure 6.3 shows that, although the Greater Accra region in Ghana has the highest levels of educational attainment and access to basic services like electricity (94 percent) and safe sanitation (95 percent), there is some variation in access based on educational attainment within the region. Access to safe sanitation is lowest among those with only primary education (92 percent) and highest among those with a post-secondary education (99.99 percent). In the Upper East region, where access to electricity and safe sanitation is the lowest in the country, households with at least a secondary education have greater access, compared to those with only primary education.

Education can also benefit from the provision of basic services, such as electricity, safe sanitation, and clean water, with increased provision of these services increasing school enrollment (Adamba 2018; Sharma and Adhikari 2022).

Spatial clustering in access to basic services is visible in the maps in this chapter. Recent research has tested the significance of these spatial clustering patterns across several African countries. For example, using a series of multidimensional poverty indicators in South Africa, Shifa, David, and Leibbrandt (2021) found hot spots of deprivations around the KwaZulu-Natal and Eastern Cape provinces, suggesting that households in these provinces have lower access to basic services and are surrounded by other households with similarly low services. However, cold spots (with better access) are observed around the Western Cape province, suggesting that households with better access are often surrounded by other households with similarly good access to basic services in this province.

Figure 6.3 Educational Attainment and Access to Basic Services in the Greater Accra and Upper East Regions of Ghana, 2017

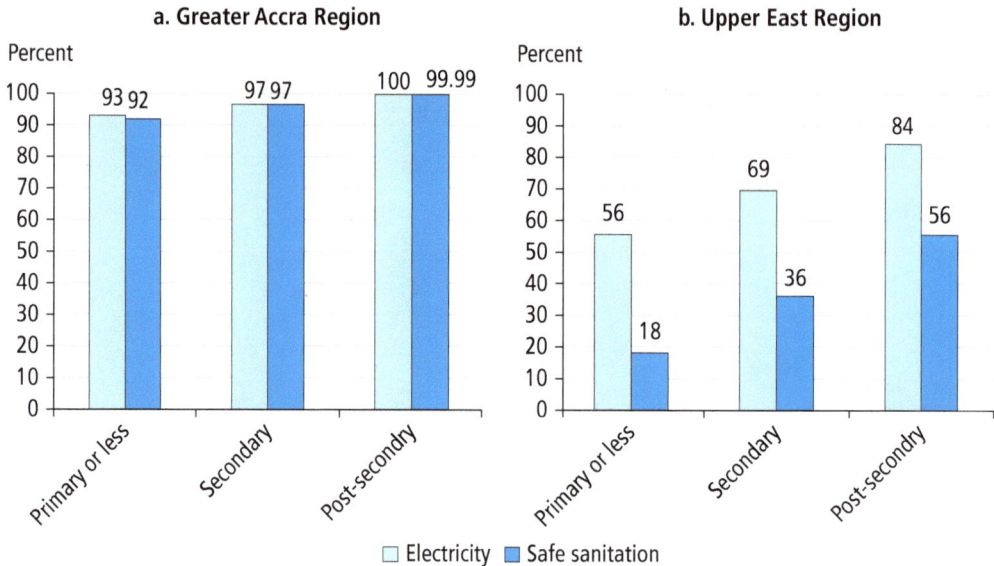

Source: Authors' calculations using the Ghana Living Standards Survey 2017.

Geremew and Damtew (2020) found evidence in Ethiopia of significant localized spatial autocorrelation in unsafe water access in the Afar, Amhara, Somalia, and Southern Nations Nationalities and People regions. There are cold spots with better access to safe water in the country's central, southern, and western regions. In Ghana, Moulds et al. (2022) found that districts with high rates of sachet water consumption tend to be spatially clustered, particularly in the southern part of the country around Accra and Kumasi. Nduhuura, Garschagen, and Zerga (2021) also found evidence of spatial autocorrelation in access to reliable electricity in Ghana, with hot and cold spots in different localities.

Beyond the continent, studies on other developing countries have shown that geographic access to basic services is not spatially random. Evidence of spatial nonrandomness in access to basic services suggests that other processes (for example, socioeconomic, political, demographic, and other factors) may influence the distribution of basic services in many African countries. Information gleaned from hot/cold spot analyses may be useful in identifying priority neighborhoods for implementing targeted interventions to improve access to water, electricity, sanitation, and other basic services.

Conclusions and Policy Implications

This chapter highlights significant differences in several dimensions of inequalities across geographic spaces in Africa. This issue is commonly observed for a single multidimensional poverty index or subcomponents of such an index, such as access to clean water, sanitation, or electricity. In addition, these spatial disparities occur across countries and regions within countries.

Even within regions, systematic differences are clear between urban and rural households. Evidence suggests that these differences are generated or sustained by households' demographic characteristics, such as gender of the household head, levels of educational attainment within the household, and racial or ethnic composition of the area.

In addition, spatial correlations mean that closer proximity to areas with better access to services also independently increases the chance of an area having greater access to services. This issue reflects the costs of the infrastructure investments required to establish access to services. For example, extending an existing electric grid for distribution is easier and more cost-effective than setting up a new distribution center in a different town.

Various policies can alleviate spatial inequalities. One policy that has been attempted in South Africa is the creation of special economic zones (SEZs). These geographic areas are designated for targeted economic activities to promote national economic growth and exports by using tax breaks and other fiscal support. In theory, SEZs could lead to enough economies of scale and agglomeration to become self-sustaining over time. They can also develop enough population density to make the infrastructure costs associated with service provision financially feasible.

Most empirical research on the effects of SEZs has focused on economic outcomes such as employment or various aspects of firm performance, and few studies have considered individuals' access to services. Aggarwal's (2007) study in India found that employment in SEZs has improved access to sanitation conditions, safe drinking water, and electricity. However, the sample was relatively small, and it would be difficult to generalize from this study. Alkon (2018) argued that, although there is evidence of the successful use of SEZs to stimulate local and regional socioeconomic development in China, an analysis of Indian census data shows that SEZs have failed to create local socioeconomic development.

Zeng (2015) attempted to draw out lessons for Africa from the Chinese experience with SEZs, noting that the SEZs in SSA have performed poorly, with a few exceptions. Zeng also highlighted some longer-term lessons from the Chinese cases, including environmental degradation and an imbalance between industrial and social development. Thus, the evidence on the efficacy of SEZs for social upliftment and local development is mixed, and SEZs should not be contemplated without considering the local economic, social, and political environments.

As an alternative to SEZs, the policy of implementing fiscal rules that allocate funds for development based on regional needs can be contemplated. This approach would remove some of the discretionary budgetary decisions, thus mitigating against the worst forms of political clientelism, which the research discussed in this chapter indicates is potentially important.

Finally, when considering welfare and attempting to maximize it dynamically, recognizing the dynamic nature of populations in terms of their size, composition, and spatial distributions is critical. This understanding has significant implications for both research and related policy design. A well-conceived urbanization plan, developed in conjunction with the planned expansion of access to services, is likely to be more efficacious than related policies designed in isolation. Ideally, information on the evolution of the distribution of people over time, as well as the historical and planned future development of the spatial distribution of services, should inform such a plan.

Note

1. Multidimensional poverty is calculated here by aggregating indicators from three dimensions: (1) education (years of schooling and school attendance), (2) health (child mortality and nutrition), and (3) living standards (access to basic services and assets). Each dimension is equally weighted, as are the indicators within each dimension (Alkire et al. 2022).

References

Abdulai, Abdul-Gafaru. 2017. "Rethinking Spatial Inequality in Development: The Primacy of Power Relations." *Journal of International Development* 29 (3): 386–403. https://doi.org/10.1002/jid.3265.

Adamba, Clement. 2018. "Effect of School Electrification on Learning Outcomes: A Subnational Level Analysis of Students' Pass Rate in English and Mathematics in Ghana." *Educational Research for Policy and Practice* 17 (1): 15–31. https://doi.org/10.1007/s10671-017-9215-1.

Agbadi, Pascal, Ernest Darkwah, and Paul L. Kenney. 2019. "A Multilevel Analysis of Regressors of Access to Improved Drinking Water and Sanitation Facilities in Ghana." *Journal of Environmental and Public Health* 2019: 1–11. https://doi.org/10.1155/2019/3983869.

Aggarwal, Aradhna. 2007. "Impact of Special Economic Zones on Employment, Poverty and Human Development." Working Paper No. 194, Indian Council for Research on International Economic Relations, New Delhi, India. https://EconPapers.repec.org/RePEc:ess:wpaper:id:1111.

Aka, Bédia François, Wadjamse Beaudelaire Djezou, Angbonon Eugène Kamalan, Ya Assanhoun Guillaume Kouassi, Gongbé Blaise Makaye, Konan Abogni Augustin Kouadio, Affia Larissa Ekian, et al. 2020. "Etat Des Lieux Des Inégalités En Cote d'Ivoire." AFD Research Paper 169. Agence Française de Développement.

Akpakli, David Etsey, Alfred Kwesi Manyeh, Jonas Kofi Akpakli, Vida Kukula, and Margaret Gyapong. 2018. "Determinants of Access to Improved Sanitation Facilities in Rural Districts of Southern Ghana: Evidence from Dodowa Health and Demographic Surveillance Site." *BMC Research Notes* 11 (1): 473. https://doi.org/10.1186/s13104-018-3572-6.

Akramov, Kamiljon T., and Felix Ankomah Asante. 2008. "Decentralization and Local Public Services in Ghana: Do Geography and Ethnic Diversity Matter?" IFPRI Discussion Paper No. 872, International Food Policy Research Institute, Washington, DC.

Alkire, Sabina, Usha Kanagaratnam, and Nicolai Suppa. 2022. "The Global Multidimensional Poverty Index (MPI) 2022 Country Results and Methodological Note." OPHI MPI Methodological Note 52, Oxford Poverty and Human Development Initiative, University of Oxford, UK.

Alkon, Meir. 2018. "Do Special Economic Zones Induce Developmental Spillovers? Evidence from India's States." *World Development* 107 (C): 396–409. https://doi.org/10.1016/j.worlddev.2018.02.028.

Atta-Ankomah, Richmond, Robert Darko Osei, Isaac Osei-Akoto, Felix Ankomah Asante, Abena D. Oduro, Nkechi Owoo, Monica Lambon-Quayefio, and Stephen Afranie. 2020. "Inequality Diagnostics for Ghana." African Center of Excellence for Inequalities Research, University of Cape Town, South Africa.

Beegle, Kathleen, Luc Christiaensen, Andrew Dabalen, and Isis Gaddis. 2016. *Poverty in a Rising Africa.* Washington, DC: World Bank. https://doi.org/10.13140/RG.2.1.2111.8167.

Bernards, Nick. 2022. "Colonial Financial Infrastructures and Kenya's Uneven Fintech Boom." *Antipode* 54 (3): 708–28. https://doi.org/10.1111/anti.12810.

Brdar, Sanja, Katarina Gavrić, Dubravko Ćulibrk, and Vladimir Crnojević. (2016). "Unveiling Spatial Epidemiology of HIV with Mobile Phone Data." *Scientific Reports*, 6 (1): 19342. https://www.nature.com/articles/srep19342.

Brown, Caitlin, and Dominique van de Walle. 2020. "Headship and Poverty in Africa." Working Paper 531, Center for Global Development, Washington, DC. https://ideas.repec.org/p/cgd/wpaper/531.html.

Brukum, N. J. K. 1998. "Studied Neglect or Lack of Resources? The Socio-Economic Underdevelopment of Northern Ghana under British Colonial Rule." *Transactions of the Historical Society of Ghana* 1998 (2): 117–31.

Burgess, Robin, Remi Jedwab, Edward Miguel, Ameet Morjaria, and Gerard Padró i Miquel. 2015. "The Value of Democracy: Evidence from Road Building in Kenya." *American Economic Review* 105 (6): 1817–51. https://doi.org/10.1257/aer.20131031.

Clementi, Fabio, Michele Fabiani, and Vasco Molini. 2019. "The Devil Is in the Detail: Growth, Inequality and Poverty Reduction in Africa in the Last Two Decades." *Journal of African Economies* 28 (4): 408–34. https://doi.org/10.1093/jae/ejz003.

Devoto, Florencia, Esther Duflo, Pascaline Dupas, Vincent Pons, and William Parienté. 2012. "Happiness on Tap: Piped Water Adoption in Urban Morocco." *American Economic Journal: Economic Policy* 4 (4): 68–99. https://doi.org/10.2139/ssrn.1803576.

Falchetta, Giacomo, Shonali Pachauri, Edward Byers, Olha Danylo, and Simon C. Parkinson. 2020. "Satellite Observations Reveal Inequalities in the Progress and Effectiveness of Recent Electrification in Sub-Saharan Africa." *One Earth* 2 (4): 364–79. https://doi.org/10.1016/j.oneear.2020.03.007.

Fosu, Augustin Kwasi, 2018. "Economic Structure, Growth, and Evolution of Inequality and Poverty in Africa: An Overview." *Journal of African Economies* 27: 1–9. https://doi.org/10.1093/jae/ejx036.

Geremew, Abraham, and Yohannes Tefera Damtew. 2020. "Household Water Treatment Using Adequate Methods in Sub-Saharan Countries: Evidence from 2013–2016 Demographic and Health Surveys." *Journal of Water, Sanitation and Hygiene for Development* 10 (1): 66–75. https://doi.org/10.2166/washdev.2019.107.

Grischow, Jeff D. 1999. "A History of Development in the Northern Territories of the Gold Coast, 1899–1957." PhD thesis, Department of History, Queen's University, Kingston, Ontario, Canada.

Hope, Rob, and Paola Ballon. 2021. "Individual Choices and Universal Rights for Drinking Water in Rural Africa." *Proceedings of the National Academy of Sciences* 118 (40): e2105953118. https://doi.org/10.1073/pnas.2105953118.

Kanbur, Ravi, Anthony J. Venables, and Guanghua Wan. 2006. "Spatial Disparities in Human Development: An Overview of the Asian Evidence." In *Spatial Disparities in Human Development: Perspectives from Asia,* edited by Ravi Kanbur, Anthony J. Venables, and Guanghua Wan, 1–6. New York: United Nations University Press.

Kimari, Wangui, and Henrik Ernstson. 2020. "Imperial Remains and Imperial Invitations: Centering Race within the Contemporary Large-Scale Infrastructures of East Africa." *Antipode* 52 (3): 825–46. https://doi.org/10.1111/anti.12623.

Kuddus, Md Abdul, Elizabeth Tynan, and Emma McBryde. 2020. "Urbanization: A Problem for the Rich and the Poor?" *Public Health Reviews* 41 (1): 1. https://doi.org/10.1186/s40985-019-0116-0.

Kumar, Arjun. 2015. "Rural Households' Access to Basic Amenities in India: Deprivation and Socio-Economic Exclusions." *Social Change* 45 (4): 561–86. https://doi.org/10.1177/0049085715602789.

Martine, George, ed. 2008. *The New Global Frontier: Urbanization, Poverty and Environment in the 21st Century*. London: Earthscan.

Morgan, W. T. W. 1963. "The 'White Highlands' of Kenya." *Geographical Journal* 129 (2): 140–55. https://doi.org/10.2307/1792632.

Moulds, Simon, Anson C. H. Chan, Jacob D. Tetteh, Honor Bixby, George Owusu, Samuel Agyei-Mensah, Majid Ezzati, Wouter Buytaert, and Michael R. Templeton. 2022. "Sachet Water in Ghana: A Spatiotemporal Analysis of the Recent Upward Trend in Consumption and Its Relationship with Changing Household Characteristics, 2010–2017." *PLoS One* 17 (5): e0265167. https://doi.org/10.1371/journal.pone.0265167.

Nduhuura, Paul, Matthias Garschagen, and Abdellatif Zerga. 2021. "Impacts of Electricity Outages in Urban Households in Developing Countries: A Case of Accra, Ghana." *Energies* 14 (12): 3676. https://doi.org/10.3390/en14123676.

Njiru, Christine W., and Sammy C. Letema. 2018. "Energy Poverty and Its Implication on Standard of Living in Kirinyaga, Kenya." *Journal of Energy* 2018: 1–12. https://doi.org/10.1155/2018/3196567.

Oyuke, Abel, Peter Halley Penar, and Brian Howard. 2016. "Off-Grid or 'Off-On': Lack of Access, Unreliable Electricity Supply Still Plague Majority of Africans." *Afrobarometer Dispatch* No. 75, March 14.

Parienté, William. 2017. "Urbanization in Sub-Sharan Africa and the Challenge of Access to Basic Services." *Journal of Demographic Economics* 83 (1): 31–39. https://doi.org/10.1017/dem.2017.3.

Plange, Nii-K. 1979. "Underdevelopment in Northern Ghana: Natural Causes or Colonial Capitalism?" *Review of African Political Economy* 6 (15–16): 4–14. https://doi.org/10.1080/03056247908703393.

Pouramin, Panthea, Nidhi Nagabhatla, and Michela Miletto. 2020. "A Systematic Review of Water and Gender Interlinkages: Assessing the Intersection with Health." *Frontiers in Water* 2: 6. https://doi.org/10.3389/frwa.2020.00006.

Sarkodie, Samuel Asumadu, and Samuel Adams. 2020. "Electricity Access and Income Inequality in South Africa: Evidence from Bayesian and NARDL Analyses." *Energy Strategy Reviews* 29: 100480. https://doi.org/10.1016/j.esr.2020.100480.

Sharma, Mohan Kumar, and Ramesh Adhikari. 2022. "Effects of Water, Sanitation, and Hygiene on the School Absenteeism of Basic Level Students in the Government School of Nepal." *Frontiers in Education* 7: 869933. https://doi.org/10.3389/feduc.2022.869933.

Shifa, Muna, Anda David, and Murray Leibbrandt. 2021. "Spatial Inequality through the Prism of a Pandemic: Covid-19 in South Africa." *Scientific African* 13: e00949. https://doi.org/10.1016/j.sciaf.2021.e00949.

Shifa, Muna, and Murray Leibbrandt. 2017. "Profiling Multidimensional Poverty and Inequality in Kenya and Zambia at Sub-National Levels." Project Working Paper 3, Consuming Urban Poverty, University of Cape Town, South Africa.

Shifa, Muna, and Murray Leibbrandt. 2022. "Spatial Inequality in Sub-Saharan Africa." *African Geographical Review* 43: 1–17. https://doi.org/10.1080/19376812.2022.2099916.

Songsore, Jacob. 2003. *Regional Development in Ghana: The Theory and the Reality*. Accra, Ghana: Woehli Publishing Services.

Stats SA. 2013. "File: South Africa 2011 dominant population group map.svg." Wikimedia Commons. https://commons.wikimedia.org/wiki/File:South_Africa_2011_dominant_population_group_map.svg.

Stats SA (Statistics South Africa), SALDRU (Southern Africa Labour and Development Research Unit), and AFD (Agence Française de Développement). 2019. *Inequality Trends in South Africa: A Multidimensional Diagnostic of Inequality, 2017*. Pretoria: Stats SA, SALDRU, and AFD.

Turok, Ivan, and Gordon McGranahan. 2013. "Urbanization and Economic Growth: The Arguments and Evidence for Africa and Asia." *Environment and Urbanization* 25 (2): 465–82. https://doi.org/10.1177/0956247813490908.

UN Habitat. 2013. *Gender Issue Guide: Gender Responsive Urban Basic Services*. Nairobi, Kenya: UN Habitat.

UNICEF (United Nations Children's Fund). 2023. *Water, Sanitation and Hygiene (WASH)*. 2023. New York: UNICEF. https://www.unicef.org/wash.

Walters, Leoné, Manoel Bittencourt, and Carolyn Chisadza. 2023. "Public Infrastructure Provision and Ethnic Favouritism: Evidence from South Africa." *Economics of Transition and Institutional Change* 31 (1): 33–65. https://doi.org/10.1111/ecot.12325.

Zeng, Douglas Zhihua. 2015. *Global Experiences with Special Economic Zones: With a Focus on China and Africa*. Washington, DC: World Bank. https://www.worldbank.org/content/dam/Worldbank/Event/Africa/Investing%20in%20Africa%20Forum/2015/investing-in-africa-forum-global-experiences-with-special-economic-zones-with-a-focus-on-china-and-africa.pdf

Chapter 7

Migration and Inequality

Anda David, Murray Leibbrandt, Muna Shifa, and Rawane Yasser

Introduction

Africa is characterized by rich flows of internal and international migration. While migration has long been identified as a pathway out of poverty (Galbraith 1979), few studies have examined how migration and inequality are interlinked. Indicator 10.7 of the United Nations Sustainable Development Goal 10, "Reduce inequality within and among countries," focuses on the facilitation of safe, orderly, regular, and responsible migration and mobility of people, placing migration policies and inequality at the center of global discussions.

Migration is one mechanism that can shape inequality (Safi 2020), as people often migrate when they are unable to satisfy their aspirations in their locality or country (Cirillo et al. 2022). However, the relationship between migration and inequality is complex, because inequality is both a driver and an outcome of human migration (World Bank 2023). Depending on its nature and context, migration has the potential to reduce inequalities, generate new inequalities, or exacerbate existing inequalities.

Migration and inequality are interlinked through the development process (Dao et al. 2018; Sjaastad 1962; Zelinsky 1971). Migration is an integral part of structural transformation, which entails the movement of workers across sectors of a given economy (for example, from rural to urban sectors). In this process, migration first increases and then decreases as a country experiences economic development. Studies of migration and income inequality have noted that inequality is low at the early stages of migration, but it rises as migration rises until a threshold where no further rise in inequality occurs with increased migration (Clemens 2014).

Most studies on migration and inequality have focused on international migration, featuring migration flows between Mexico and the United States or between the Global North and the Global South. Limited research analyzes the welfare and distributional implications of intracontinental migration in Africa. Yet, understanding the drivers and outcomes of intracontinental migration is crucial for Africa, where more than 85 percent of migration occurs within the continent (OECD and AFD 2019; Williams 2024).

This chapter discusses migration in Sub-Saharan Africa (SSA) through the lens of inequality and explores how migration shapes livelihoods and also how migration is shaped by aspects of inequality, such as spatial inequality, income inequality, and overall inequality of opportunity. The first section provides an overview of the patterns of migration in SSA, examining both internal and international mobility. The next section details the migration–inequality nexus, focusing on how inequality can drive migration, as well as how international migration patterns influence inequalities. This section focuses on remittances and labor markets as the channels through which migration can impact within-country inequality. Finally, the chapter explores new frontiers in issues related to migration, such as norms and institutions and climate change.

Migration Patterns in SSA

In developing countries in SSA or elsewhere where a large share of the population resides in rural areas, internal migration flows from rural to urban areas are significant (Brueckner and Lall 2015). However, internal migration, especially among rural areas, remains much less documented due to the lack of harmonized data. Therefore, the extent of internal migration remains largely underestimated, according to Selod and Shilpi (2021). Despite the data challenge, Cattaneo and Robinson (2019) have shown that rural-to-rural migration is the most-prevalent migration pattern in SSA, especially in low-income countries. In countries that have undergone some structural transformation, rural-to-urban migration is predominant. Cattaneo and Robinson (2019) also found evidence of extensive stepwise migration, with more than one-third of those who have moved once moving a second time or more.

Within Africa, internal migration intensities (rates of movement) are heterogeneous. Bell et al. (2015) provided estimates of permanent migration intensities during 2000–10, finding high migration intensities in parts of Eastern and Western Africa (Cameroon, Guinea, Kenya, Senegal, and Tanzania) and Southern Africa (South Africa and Zambia) but low migration intensities in the rest of the continent.

Rural-to-urban migration can lead to international migration given that urban migrants can migrate internationally as they earn more and discover job opportunities (Williams 2024). In SSA, most international migrations take place within the region (refer to figure 7.1). Migration patterns are more intense in corridors such as from Burkina Faso to Côte d'Ivoire or those that go to regional economic poles, such as Nigeria or South Africa (World Bank 2023). In addition, recent conflicts in Ethiopia, Sudan, and other countries have led to an increase in emigrants moving toward neighboring countries. Large refugee movements originate from the Central African Republic, the Democratic Republic of Congo, Somalia, South Sudan, and Sudan.

Figure 7.1 Key Figures on Migration in Africa, 2000–25

Migrants (millions)

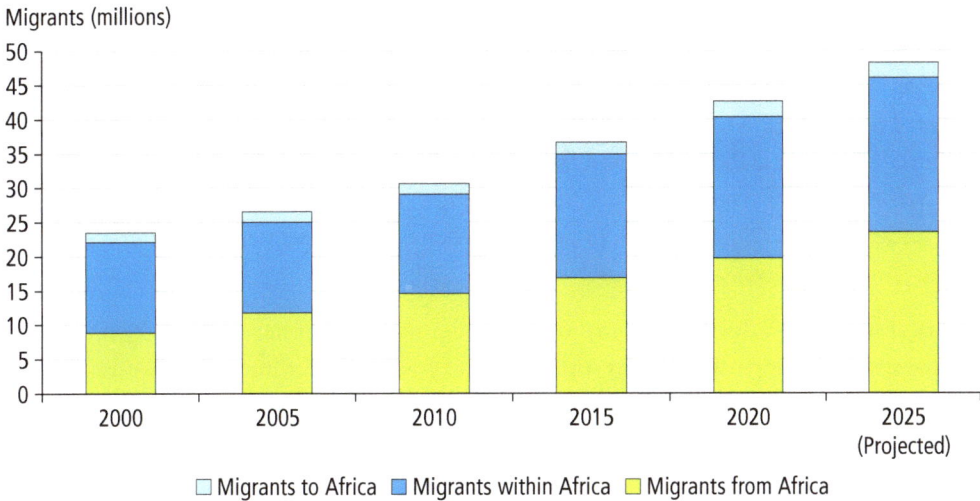

Legend: ☐ Migrants to Africa   ■ Migrants within Africa   ☐ Migrants from Africa

Sources: Williams 2024; data are from the United Nations Department of Economic and Social Affairs. Figure used with permission of the Africa Center, Washington, DC. Further permission required for additional reuse.

Emigration to non-African countries is mainly directed to the Middle East and Europe, although Africans represent only 6.6 and 8.2 percent of all migrants in those regions, respectively (World Bank 2023). Recent migration flows to these regions have largely involved migrants from Senegal toward the Canary Islands and Spain due to the social unrest in Senegal (Ratha, Chandra, et al. 2023). Ratha, Chandra, et al. (2023) also noted an increase in migrants from Burkina Faso, Cameroon, Côte d'Ivoire, Guinea, and Mali toward Italy, where they accounted for 40 percent of arrivals in 2023, compared to around 5 percent during the same period in 2022.

A combination of factors have been proposed as the main drivers of both internal and international migrations in SSA. Spatial earnings disparities and inequalities in other development outcomes are key among these. In addition, climate shocks and violent conflicts, notably in the Middle East and SSA, are driving migration.

The Migration–Inequality Nexus

Inequality plays an important role as a driver of migration, determining both the level of migration and who migrates (McKenzie 2018). However, the relationship between inequality in the origin country or sending region and migration is not straightforward, because inequality can affect migration in several opposing ways. Migration is driven by access to opportunities, resulting in who can migrate and to where. The differential in opportunities is where inequality can shape migration. This section discusses the evidence suggesting that inequality is a determinant of both internal and international mobility.

Inequality as a Driver of Migration

Studies have focused on the role of labor market income differentials between urban and rural areas as the main driver of internal migration. In accounting for rural-to-urban migration, the Lewis model (Lewis 1954) and the Harris–Todaro model (Harris and Todaro 1970) have presented migration as a response to economic incentives that offer the prospect of higher income in urban areas. The neoclassical theory of migration argues that people migrate from regions with low wages to those with higher wages according to a cost-benefit analysis (Harris and Todaro 1970). This theory states that, when wage inequalities in a country decrease, migration levels also decrease.

Empirical studies have documented that economic development is often associated with unequal spatial development patterns within a country, leading to income and wage disparities between urban and rural areas. This issue creates a positive relationship between migration and development, where increased development accentuates urban-rural wage gaps and fosters increased migration between these areas (World Bank 2023). According to the World Bank (2023), the urban-rural wage gap accounts for 40 percent of mean country inequality. One of every four or five individuals raised in rural areas moves to an urban area as a young adult, where they earn much higher incomes, as compared to nonimmigrant permanent rural residents (Young 2013).

Differentials between rural and urban amenities can be a driving force in rural-urban migration (Selod and Shilpi 2021), including access to electricity, paved roads, and social and educational opportunities. Food insecurity is also an important determinant of both migration intentions and preparations (Sadiddin et al. 2019; Smith and Floro 2020). Youth in SSA, facing higher unemployment rates than those of other age groups (refer to chapter 4 in this book), often see migration as their only chance for social mobility (David and Nilsson 2021).

An increasing number of studies have highlighted drivers of internal migration other than differences in labor market outcomes between destination and origin areas. Based on observations of rural-to-urban migration in Africa, Migration Systems Theory argues that the broader environment influences the decisions of individual migrants (Mabogunje 1970). Environmental factors influencing the decision to migrate include the social welfare system, including education and health; wages; prices; the level of industrial development; and technological development (Muyonga, Odipo, and Agwanda 2020).

Another potential mechanism is that inequality within origin areas increases migration; therefore, individuals living in unequal areas tend to migrate (Lipton 1980). As a result, the remittances sent from richer migrants can negatively impact rural income distribution, exacerbating income inequality between migrant and nonmigrant households. Over time, there is a neutralizing impact on intrahousehold inequality in the origin regions as migration grows between rural and urban areas.

For international migration, a combination of factors, including inequalities in earnings and well-being outcomes, may be its main drivers in Africa. The literature has long dwelled on the nexus between migration and development, gradually moving away from the theoretical underpinnings proposed by Sjaastad (1962), according to which migration is the result of a wage differential, toward a more-comprehensive view including geography, culture, information asymmetries, and policies (Dao et al. 2018).

According to the neo-classical view, there are significant global disparities between developed and developing countries (McKenzie 2018). Therefore, international migration arises as a response to the global disparities in income and well-being across countries, motivated by prospects of higher wages and access to better services (World Bank 2023).

The idea that labor mobility is shaped by real or expected differentials in wages and productivity dates to the Lewis model of development of a dual economy (Lewis 1954) and the Harris–Todaro model (1970) of rural-urban migration. These dynamics exist beyond national borders, too. Özden, Packard, and Wagner (2017) showed how international migration flows respond to wage differentials between countries, along with geographic characteristics, such as distances and country size. Studies have extensively documented how the economic benefits of migration manifest through wage gains for migrants (Clemens, Montenegro, and Pritchett 2019; McKenzie, Stillman, and Gibson 2010; Özden et al. 2017). More than 80 percent of migrants move in search of better opportunities in the destination country, mainly driven by the potential for higher wages and access to better services (World Bank 2018, 2023).

The global view is especially important. Milanovic (2015) showed that, globally, more than half of the variability in income is explained by individuals' country of residence and circumstances at birth, implying that, for the world's distribution of income, migration is a key factor for individuals to improve their position. This view is also in line with Galbraith's (1979) observation that migration is the oldest action against poverty in history. These income maximization theories of migration imply that migration from the poorest countries would be high (Sjaastad 1962). However, this prediction does not apply in practice, as most migrants are not among the poorest in their country of origin; they are largely from middle-income countries, which hold the largest share of emigrants, therefore prompting a more comprehensive view on the nexus between migration and development (World Bank 2023).

Dao et al. (2018) identified an inverted U-shaped relationship between migration and development, meaning that emigration first increases and then decreases as a country experiences economic development. These results suggest that, in the short term, a rise in income induces small effects on low-skilled and average emigration rates, as financial constraints prevent low-skilled workers from realizing their migration aspirations. In the long run, a rise in income may relax financial constraints and increase the share of college graduates among emigrants and the average emigration rate. A reason why migration rates start to fall at a certain level of wealth or income is that the opportunity cost of migrating grows with the income-earning prospects at home, as well as the presence of risks in migrating and incomplete information about opportunities abroad (McKenzie 2018). However, as rising incomes are not uniformly distributed, they can be accompanied by rising inequality.

Clemens (2014) suggested that within-country income inequality tends to be more pronounced during the initial stages of development, marked by a rise in inequality and, therefore, by a rise in the number of those who are relatively deprived. During this period, worse-off individuals feel relatively deprived, prompting them to migrate to improve their position relative to other households (Dao et al. 2018). As such, inequality can impact migration through the lens of aspirations. This phenomenon would predict that emigration is positively associated with inequality in the country of origin. However, at low levels of income, inequality has a limited effect on migration due to financial constraints that make the costs of migration too high for poor individuals (McKenzie 2018).

McKenzie (2018) identified two effects of inequality on the rate of migration. The first is a mechanical effect, in which higher inequality for a given income results in a higher number of poor people, which can lower migration rates if poor people cannot afford to migrate. The second is an indirect effect, by which inequality reflects unequal returns to skills. Therefore, more-unequal countries with higher returns to skills will see lower rates of migration among wealthy people and skilled people and relatively higher rates among poor people and those with an intermediate level of wealth, if they can afford to migrate.

Poverty and critical income thresholds to underwrite migration are, therefore, strong determinants of how inequality impacts migration. Emigration rates are lower still for the regions with the poorest people. In SSA, emigrants are only 2.5 percent of the population (World Bank 2023). Wouterse (2010) showed that intercontinental migration from Burkina Faso is most common among the households that own the most land, whereas intra-African migration is less biased toward rich households. Dao et al. (2018) found that low rates of migration at low levels of per capita income can be attributed to two factors. First, in low-income countries, educated workers comprise a much lower share of the labor force, and people who are less educated are less likely to want or be able to migrate, compared with those who are more educated (Docquier, Peri, and Ruyssen 2014; Kerr et al. 2017). Migration from lower-income countries is characterized by a significantly higher share of high-skilled workers, in what is known as the "brain drain."

Second, low-income countries have smaller migration networks than slightly richer countries, and the likelihood of migrating increases with network size. Therefore, poor individuals are more likely to move when migration costs are low, networks exist, and policy makes it possible for them to do so (Dao et al. 2018; McKenzie 2024).

These findings and proposed models are based on the hypothesis that migration is voluntary. However, 20 percent of the 184 million migrants worldwide are refugees (a percentage that increases to 34 percent for low- and middle-income countries; World Bank 2023). From this perspective of forced migration, the conceptualization of the linkages with economic inequality is more strenuous. Forced displacement entails a loss of assets and also of human capital and networks, thus increasing individuals' vulnerability and trapping them in a cycle of poverty (World Bank 2018). As forced displacement often occurs for the most-vulnerable populations, it could be inferred that it can potentially increase global inequality or, if the displacement occurs within national borders, it can increase national inequality.

Should studies focus on inequality between refugees and host populations, even though their contexts are extremely different, or should they consider inequality between those who have left and those who have not? Research outside Africa has shown that the arrival of refugees negatively impacts low-skilled, low-wage earners, but this issue can be offset by tax redistribution, as tax revenue and profits per earner increase (World Bank 2023). In a review of the impact of refugees on host communities in Africa, Ruiz and Vargas-Silva (2018) found mixed evidence of the effects on well-being, as often labor market outcomes decline due to increased competition, while households' assets may increase due to the provision of public services or disbursement of international aid.

How Migration Shapes Inequality: Channels of Transmission

Studies have examined the causal impacts of migration on poverty and inequality. Although the macro-level impacts of migration are ambiguous, these impacts are much larger at the micro level on the individuals and households engaging in migration. Most studies have found important gains in income for individuals who voluntarily migrate from developing to developed countries, which lowers poverty and inequality at the global level (McKenzie 2018). However, evidence on the impact on the origin countries is mixed, because it depends on who can migrate. Although within-country inequality may rise at first if skill-selective policies and liquidity constraints prevent poor individuals from benefiting from migration, poverty falls more when networks are large or migration policies provide more options for unskilled workers to migrate. Ebeke and Le Goff (2011) highlighted that the impact of migration on inequality depends on the cost of migration and the levels of development and human capital in origin communities.

Migration can have direct and indirect effects on inequality (Muyonga et al. 2020). The direct effect occurs through remittances sent to migrant households who change their patterns of household expenditure. The indirect effect can occur through labor market shifts within the sending communities as a result of these new patterns of expenditure and investments, as well as the receiving communities.

Role of Remittances

Remittances are the most-highly-visible impact of migration in the origin countries. However, a dilemma identified in research on the impact of migration on inequality is that remittances have increased significantly over the past three decades without a visible impact on economic growth or poverty in the countries that send the most migrants and receive the most remittances (McKenzie 2018). However, Clemens and McKenzie (2018) pointed to the unreliability of such a relationship, as the growth of remittances reflects changes in measurement rather than genuine growth of remittances. Furthermore, as many factors drive growth and poverty at the macro level, a regression would have insufficient power to detect change in the relationship, suggesting that a reliable estimate of the impact of international migration on growth (or poverty) at the macro level is not possible at present.

Remittances to low- and middle-income countries have increased over the past two decades (World Bank 2023), representing a large and growing share of external financing flows to these countries, including those in SSA (refer to figure 7.2). In SSA, remittances have grown steadily and are considered a reliable source of support (refer to figure 7.3), and they are projected to rise by 3.7 percent in 2024 (Ratha, Plaza, et al. 2023).

It has been estimated that remittance flows to SSA increased by about 1.9 percent in 2023, driven by the growth of remittances to Mozambique (48.5 percent), Rwanda (16.8 percent), and Ethiopia (16.0 percent). Nigeria is the largest remittance recipient country in SSA. In The Gambia, remittances accounted for 28 percent of gross domestic product (GDP) in 2022 (World Bank 2023), which was the largest share of remittances as a share of GDP, followed by Lesotho, the Comoros, Cabo Verde, and Zimbabwe (Ratha, Plaza, et al. 2023). Intra-Africa remittance flows are also important. Kenya has seen a strong increase in remittances due to a doubling of remittances from Uganda and Zambia and increases from Côte d'Ivoire and Nigeria in 2023 (Ratha, Plaza, et al. 2023).

Figure 7.2 **Personal Remittances Received as a Percentage of GDP in Sub-Saharan Africa, 1977–2023**

Percentage of GDP

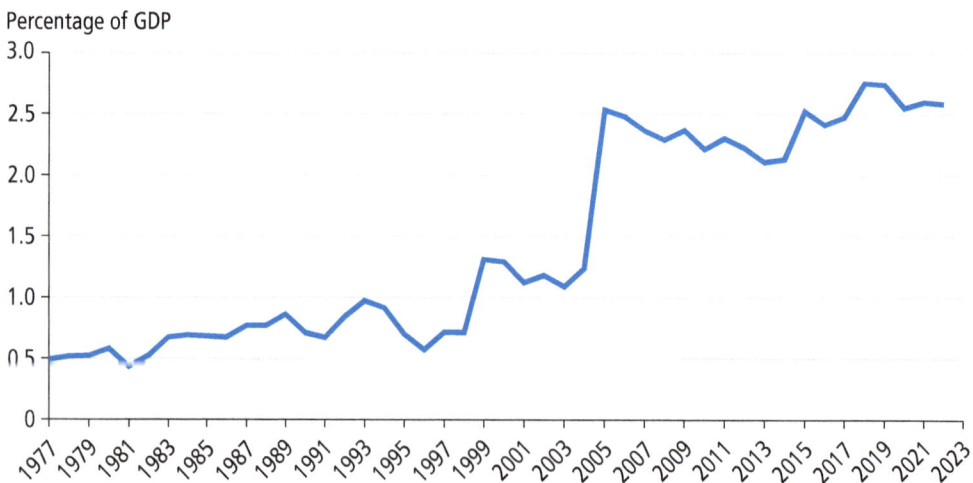

Source: Authors' calculations using data from the World Development Indicators, World Bank.
Note: GDP = gross domestic product.

Figure 7.3 Personal Remittances Received in Current US$ Billions in Sub-Saharan Africa, 1970–2022

Remittances (current US$, billions)

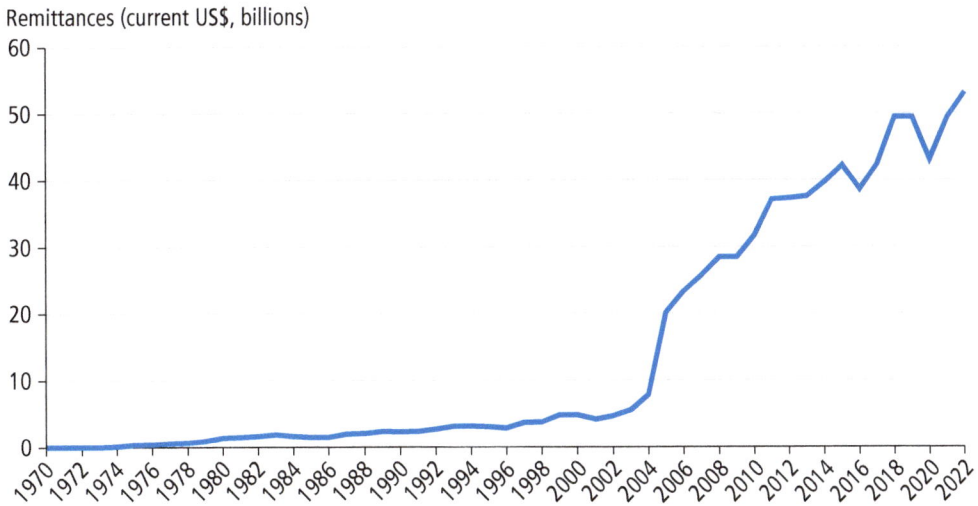

Source: Authors' calculations using data from the World Development Indicators, World Bank.
Note: Personal remittances comprise personal transfers and compensation of employees. Personal transfers consist of all current transfers in cash or in-kind made or received by resident households to or from nonresident households. Personal transfers thus include all current transfers between resident and nonresident individuals. Compensation of employees refers to the income of border, seasonal, and other short-term workers who are employed in an economy where they are not a resident and of residents employed by nonresident entities. The data are the sum of the two items as defined in the sixth edition of the International Monetary Fund's Balance of Payments and International Investment Position Manual (IMF 2009). The data are in current US dollars.

At the macroeconomic level, remittances can provide a stable source of foreign exchange to the receiving country, which can support macroeconomic stability and increase the foreign exchange reserves available to pay external debt (World Bank 2023). Remittances also tend to be more resilient than other capital inflows, even in periods of crisis. They remained stable during the global financial crisis of 2008–10 and during the COVID-19 pandemic. However, the evidence is mixed on their impact on economic growth (Clemens and McKenzie 2018).

At the micro level, the remittances that migrants send their families are a main motivation for people to migrate due to the funds' poverty-reducing impact. In some countries, remittances boost the economic and social mobility of poor individuals, such as in Morocco (De Haas 2009). By increasing household income, remittances can serve as a lifeline for certain households and act as insurance (Bossavie and Özden 2023).

Remittances can increase consumption and food security. For example, in Ethiopia, farm households that receive remittances are less worried about food insecurity and have a lower risk of malnutrition (Abadi et al. 2018). Remittances allow households to spend more on human capital investments for education and health care. For example, migration from Malawi to South Africa has increased the educational attainment of children in rural areas in Malawi

(Dinkelman and Mariotti 2016). Remittances can also ease financial constraints and thus facilitate entrepreneurship. In Morocco, the Sahel, and Tunisia, households are more likely to expand into commercial agriculture when they receive remittances (Konseiga 2004). In Nigeria, investment in agrochemicals and modern agricultural equipment is higher among households that receive remittances, which increases their yields (Iheke 2014).

Furthermore, remittances can impact poverty reduction, even for households that do not receive them. The increase in consumption by households receiving remittances can boost local economic activity and create local jobs, thereby increasing the incomes of other households and reducing inequality (World Bank 2023).

However, the dynamics of remittances are complex; their effect on inequality depends on which households receive them and how much they receive (Koczan et al. 2021). If the receiving families are disadvantaged and low income, remittances can lower inequality. However, if the receiving households are wealthy, remittances can increase inequality. Furthermore, by increasing the incomes of the households that receive them, remittances can create new inequalities between receiving and nonreceiving households in the same community (World Bank 2023).

Moreover, the effectiveness of the increases in income and consumption in alleviating poverty and their impact on inequality also depend on the participation of the poor population in migration and the migration patterns of the rich population. As wealthier households can more easily afford to migrate and thus send higher remittances, they can initially increase inequality. However, the level of inequality can decline over time as the costs of migration decrease through migrant networks, making it possible for poorer households to benefit as well (Koczan et al. 2021; World Bank 2023). Margolis et al. (2015) pointed to larger inequality-reducing effects in regions of Algeria that have more migrants and remittance-receiving households.

The impact of remittances on inequality can also depend significantly on the costs of sending and receiving them. These costs are high, especially in SSA, which has the highest costs (Ratha, Chandra, et al. 2023). The costs of sending and receiving remittances vary, with the most-expensive corridors being intra-Africa, such as Tanzania to Uganda or South Africa to Angola, as opposed to remittances from France to Côte d'Ivoire or the United States to Ethiopia. Studying the role of financial development in how remittances affect inequality in 42 African countries, Ofori et al. (2022) found that remittances increased income inequality in Africa due to inefficiencies in the continent's financial institutions. They argued that the presence of a well-developed financial sector in terms of access, depth, and efficiency can result in remittances being allocated efficiently and at lower costs, contributing to a more-equitable distribution of income.

The impact of remittances in Africa also depends on the migrant destinations. A distinction between intercontinental migration to Europe and internal migration within the African continent is necessary. Wouterse (2010) found that remittances from intercontinental migration contributed to increased income inequality at the village level in Burkina Faso, as opposed to intra-African remittances. Given the higher costs and risks, migration to intercontinental destinations will initially involve wealthier households. Remittances from these households will, therefore, accrue to the already wealthy households and would increase income inequality.

Adams, Cuecuecha, and Page (2008) found that, in Ghana, international remittances increased income inequalities more than domestic remittances did, reflecting the challenges that poorer households face in overcoming the costs of intercontinental migration. However, when poor individuals participate in migration, the impacts on poverty and inequality reduction in the sending regions can be substantial. Olowa et al. (2013) found that, in Nigeria, both internal and international remittances reduced poverty and inequality among rural households. Anyanwu (2011), using data from 1960–2006 for African countries, found that remittances had different impacts on income inequality between North African regions, where it fueled higher inequality, and SSA, where the reverse was true. Gubert, Lassourd, and Mesplé-Somps (2010) found that remittances reduced both poverty and inequality in Mali, estimating that more people would be in poverty if there were no remittances.

Thus, despite a positive impact on poverty and the living conditions of households, the effect of remittances on inequality remains ambiguous and largely depends on the characteristics of the migrants, the migrants' destinations, and the costs of migration. It can also depend on the extent to which remittances compensate for the loss of labor from a member moving abroad, highlighting the need to examine the impact of the labor market.

Role of the Labor Market

While remittances can impact economic inequalities by changing the allocation of financial resources, human mobility itself shapes labor markets and, thus, economic inequalities, albeit with different outcomes for origin and destination countries.

Origin Countries

Migration can shape inequality in origin countries through its impact on labor markets. The emigration of a significant number of workers can reduce the size of the labor force, which can reduce the risk of unemployment and underemployment (Koczan et al. 2021). However, it can also reduce demand, human capital, and entrepreneurship and be a sign of brain drain, where the most-productive individuals of a community disappear (World Bank 2023).

Brain drain involves the emigration of highly-skilled and -productive individuals and can be an important source of negative effects on inequality in origin countries (Koczan et al. 2021). Highly-educated people are more likely to migrate than less-educated people. In SSA, people with a tertiary education are 30 times more likely to emigrate than those who are less educated (Kerr et al. 2017). In 2018, almost 25 percent of the doctors trained in SSA were working in Organisation for Economic Co-operation and Development countries (Socha-Dietrich and Dumont 2021).

While destination countries benefit from this high-skilled immigration from low-income countries, it can inflict losses on the countries of origin in many ways. First, it produces a shortage of high-skilled labor, thereby reducing productivity and hampering development when the costs of losing a highly-qualified worker outweigh the benefits from remittances (Koczan et al. 2021; World Bank 2023). Second, brain drain aggravates the shortage of skilled workers who provide essential services such as health care. Third, it can have a damaging impact on the quality of institutions in the origin countries, as high-skilled workers often constitute a political force demanding improvements in business and better control of corruption (Koczan et al. 2021). Fourth, brain drain can increase wage and income inequality.

Using a panel of 110 developing countries with data for 1980–2010, Uprety (2020) found that high-skilled migration increases income inequality, while low-skilled migration appears to have no effect on inequality. An increase of 10 percent in high-skilled migration is associated with a 5 percent increase in income inequality. This finding is due to a decrease in the supply of skilled labor, which raises their earnings, along with an increase in the relative supply of low-skilled labor, which lowers their earnings. Furthermore, if high-skilled and low-skilled labor are complementary, the demand for low-skilled labor would decrease with high-skilled emigration, which would further depress the wage rate.

However, these results are only significant in the short term and disappear in the long term. In the long term, the labor market can respond by increasing demand for low-skilled labor or increasing investment, schooling, and job training, thereby increasing the supply of educated people and balancing skilled emigration. However, these responses are very long adjustments. Short-run adjustments to compensate for brain drain include the immigration of skilled labor from elsewhere.

The impacts of migration on inequality in origin countries can be noted through return migration, which usually impacts labor markets through an increase in entrepreneurial activities, as return migrants are more likely to engage in self-employment and entrepreneurship (Bossavie and Özden 2023; David and Nilsson 2021; World Bank 2023). Highly-skilled return migrants can also help develop industries in their countries of origin (Kerr et al. 2017). However, the impact of return migration is highly dependent on the skill levels of emigrants relative to the working-age population in the origin country, as well as the economic conditions in the origin and destination countries (Bossavie and Özden 2023).

Migration can contribute to integrating origin countries into global networks through knowledge transfers from the diasporas. Furthermore, migration can increase international trade between origin and destination countries by linking sellers and buyers across countries (Kerr et al. 2017; World Bank 2023).

Policies in the countries of origin can play a crucial role in how migration impacts inequality. Policies can help maximize the positive impacts of migration on inequality by facilitating remittances and knowledge transfers, building skills, and mitigating brain drain to reduce the impact of high-skilled migration on inequality (Uprety 2020; World Bank 2023).

Destination Countries

The effects of migration on inequality are shaped by the demand for labor in the destination country. The outcomes depend on migrants' skills, gender, age, and language ability. While high-skilled workers gain larger benefits than low-skilled workers, low-skilled workers also experience an increase in their income. For example, low-skilled Nigerians moving to the United States can increase their earnings by 15 times (Clemens et al. 2019).

The impact of migration on inequality also depends on the extent to which migrants' skills match the needs of the destination countries. When there is a match between migrants' skills and the needs of the destination countries, the migrants can gain significant benefits, such as higher wages and access to better services. These income gains are shared with their families and communities in their countries of origin through remittances, which means better living conditions for many migrants and their families (Clemens et al. 2019).

Migrants' skills can complement those of the national workers in the destination countries. The presence of low-skilled workers can provide complementary skills in high-income countries, where education levels have increased and workforces have aged. Immigration can, therefore, make it possible for employers to meet their needs for low-skilled workers (World Bank 2023). The presence of high-skilled migrants, through a positive effect on innovation and productivity, can, in the long run, increase the relative wages of low-skilled workers and reduce inequality (Altındağ, Bakış, and Rozo 2020; Koczan et al. 2021).

In the destination countries, although migration can benefit complementary workers, it can have negative effects on workers whose skills are similar to those of the migrants (Dustmann, Glitz, and Frattini 2008). Different outcomes have been observed for wage gains or losses. In South Africa, the arrival of migrant workers led to lower wages and caused national workers to move to areas with better employment opportunities (Biavaschi et al. 2018). Compared with higher-skilled workers, lower-skilled workers tend to have skills that are closer to those of migrants, and lower-skilled workers tend to be negatively affected more often.

Migrants' gains and inclusion also depend on labor market regulations, and the rights they receive in labor market access can significantly impact their wages, employment levels, and job quality (Slotwinski, Stutzer, and Uhlig 2019). Undocumented migrants are often relegated to the informal labor market, with lower wages and fewer opportunities. They are more easily exploited, underpaid, and also are in competition with other informal workers. When migrants have documented status, their wages are close to those of nationals (World Bank 2023). The recognition of degrees and skill certifications is also crucial in facilitating migrants' inclusion.

The question of how migration shapes inequality is closely linked to social inclusion and cohesion in destination countries. By avoiding the emergence of a marginalized population, both migrants and destination societies can benefit. Children of undocumented migrants face specific challenges and are only able to access education of lower quality. They are also less likely to have access to health care services. Migrant networks are important, as they can help reduce the costs of migration through resources and information, making migration less risky.

How migration shapes inequality has, therefore, been found to have mixed effects, considering the different channels of transmission. Migration can present some benefits for the origin countries, such as remittances, knowledge transfers, and positive impacts on the labor market that help alleviate poverty and inequality. However, migration can have a downside when high-skilled workers emigrate and countries must endure the impacts of brain drain. Thus, the effects of the different impacts highly depend on the context. De Haas (2010) has highlighted the role of structural factors, such as the political, institutional, economic, social, and cultural contexts in which migration occurs and that might explain the differences in outcomes between countries.

Beyond Economic Inequalities

Migration has cultural, social, and anthropological dimensions, but it is also dynamic and reacts swiftly to new challenges. This section focuses on two important strands of literature that indirectly shape the linkages between migration and inequalities: norms and institutions and climate change.

Norms and Institutions

Norms and institutions, defined as formal and informal laws, social norms, and practices, are central to defining gender roles and, therefore, to migration choices and pathways, acting as both incentives and barriers to migration. Perceived gender discrimination can explain migration intentions, with migration as a way for women to escape discrimination, but inequalities in economic and political opportunities can prevent women from migrating (Ferrant et al. 2014; Ruyssen and Salomone 2018). Migration patterns, choices, and outcomes are not gender neutral.

The percentage of female migrants has been increasing since the 1960s, driven by the feasibility for women to travel and the nature of the demand for migrant labor, such as domestic work, for example (World Bank 2023). Women are overrepresented among some groups of migrants, especially among refugees. In 2022, 62 percent of Ethiopian adult refugees in South Sudan were women (World Bank 2023).

Gender norms and discrimination determine the education and employment options and opportunities available for women in their countries of origin. Gender inequality in familial, societal, and cultural structures, accompanied by unequal access to paid employment and public life, can be considered as both barriers and incentives to migrate (Ferrant et al. 2014). For example, while being married with children reduces the probability that women will migrate, the opposite is true for men (Ferrant et al. 2014). Education levels also have different impacts on the migration decision. Men with higher levels of education are found to be less likely to migrate, which is not the case for educated women, for whom the probability increases.

Restrictive gender norms can play a role, especially for highly-educated women. Many highly-educated women migrate to seek more inclusive gender norms through work or further education. These women often prefer destinations with smaller gender gaps and less gender discrimination. Among highly-educated women, the probability of migrating is higher when they originate from countries that are in the mid-range of gender discrimination, where they have both the opportunity and incentives to move. In contrast, women with a lower education have lower levels of migrating on their own (Ferrant et al. 2014; World Bank 2023).

While restrictive gender norms can be an incentive to migrate for highly-skilled women, they can also be an obstacle (Ferrant et al. 2014). Social norms and expectations can prevent women from traveling under the same conditions as men and place higher burdens on women to fulfill family duties. Women's economic dependence on their husbands and women's low skills and level of education all limit the opportunity for them to migrate.

Ferrant et al. (2014) found that discriminatory social institutions in the origin country can be an incentive for women to migrate, but only to the point where the discrimination starts to become an obstacle (refer to figure 7.4). When the level of discrimination increases from low to moderate, female emigration flows increase. Therefore, emigration is a way for women to escape discriminatory institutions. However, when the level of discrimination becomes too high, female emigration decreases, as their abilities are hampered by discriminatory laws and institutions.

Discriminatory policies and attitudes in destination countries can also play a key role. Ferrant et al. (2014) found that female immigration flows are negatively correlated with discriminatory social institutions in the destination country. Low levels of discrimination, such as in inheritance rights, protection from violence, and reproductive rights, appear to be attractive for female migrants, especially those from countries with low levels of gender discrimination. Among women from such countries, 62 percent of their main destination countries also have a low level of discrimination, reflecting their preference for gender equality.

However, discriminatory policies and attitudes can present other challenges. Darker skin color and foreign names can affect migrants' ability to access the labor market, as well as can housing, education, health care, and social services (World Bank 2023). Many migrant women face obstacles in accessing the labor market in the destination country, pushing many women into precarious conditions in the informal and service sectors where they work as domestic or care workers (World Bank 2023).

Figure 7.4 Discriminatory Social Institutions as Both an Incentive to and Constraint on Female Migration

Female migration (% of female population)

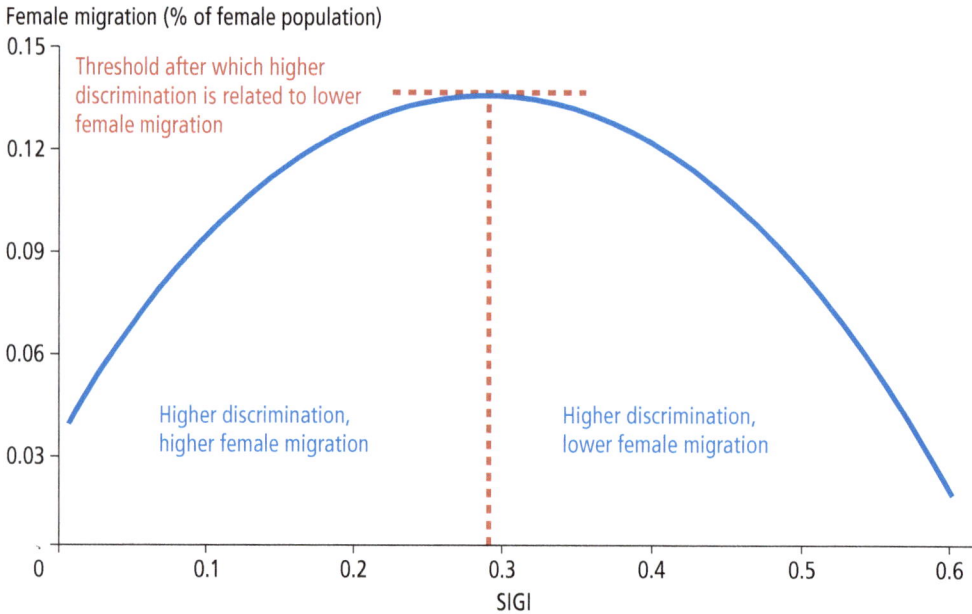

Source: Based on Ferrant et al. 2014.
Note: Female migration flows are the estimated share of female migrants in the female population. The SIGI measures discriminatory social institutions in non–Organisation for Economic Co-operation and Development countries. The scale is from 0 (low discrimination) to 1 (high level of discriminatory social institutions). SIGI = Social Institutions and Gender Index.

Social inclusion and social support programs can reduce the risk of isolation and tackle issues of gender and labor discrimination. Policies can include childcare, skills matching, and vocational training, which can support women's access to labor markets.

Violence against women is also a major determinant of mobility, as some women and girls migrate to escape sexual and gender-based violence (GBV) in their origin countries. GBV increases in the context of armed conflict. For example, in the Democratic Republic of Congo, 40,000 cases of GBV were registered between 2003 and 2006 (Dallman 2009). However, women and girls also encounter violence in the various stages of migration and along migration routes, especially as forced migrants.

Finally, climate change brings new dimensions and challenges to these patterns. In low-income countries, women are often engaged in activities that are disproportionately affected by the impacts of climate change, such as small, independent-production agriculture. As they lack other skills that are in demand in the labor market or have more family constraints than their male counterparts, women may not always be able to move, which traps them in a situation of maladaptation (Šedová, Čizmaziová, and Cook 2021). In Mali and Nigeria, men are more likely to migrate when facing climate shocks versus in Bangladesh, where women are more likely to migrate in cases of crop failure (Miletto et al. 2017).

Migration, especially for women, can lead to better opportunities for education, employment, and empowerment. However, for women to benefit from migration, discrimination must be addressed in education and employment opportunities.

Climate Change and Migration

The impacts of climate change are manifested in a wide range of outcomes, such as health, income, food security, water supply, and overall security. As a result, climate change is compounding the economic drivers of migration, with about 40 percent of the world's population living in places that are highly exposed to the impacts of climate change, such as the Sahel (World Bank 2023). With economic opportunities decreasing in these affected regions, vulnerabilities are increasing, along with the pressures for migration. The extent to which climate change will impact international migrations in the future depends on the global and national policies for mitigation and adaptation.

Climate change amplifies existing patterns of movements, accelerating internal rural-urban migration. Climate change also affects people unequally, depending on their skills and human capital. People who lack the means to move are further impoverished and trapped in place, which is the case for poorer households in locations highly exposed to climate change (Cattaneo et al. 2019).

SSA faces a combination of vulnerabilities. In SSA, poverty, state fragility, population growth, and climate change are drivers of migration that reinforce one another. SSA faces pressures in all these dimensions. The region has the lowest income per capita in the world, the fastest demographic growth, and the highest vulnerability to climate change. The depletion of natural resources due to climate impacts leads to a rise in poverty. Climate change has led to a 34 percent reduction in agricultural productivity since 1961 (WMO 2022), severely impacting food security (refer to chapter 10 for more details).

The Sahel illustrates these challenges, with countries such as Burkina Faso, Chad, Mali, Mauritania, and Niger being among the world's poorest countries. Their fertility rates are also among the highest globally. Rising temperatures have aggravated the Sahel's climate vulnerability, and conflicts in Burkina Faso and Mali have accelerated the region's fragility, resulting in the displacement of millions of people as a coping strategy.

Studying 73 countries between 1960 and 1990, Barrios, Bertinelli, and Strobl (2006) found that the decline in rainfall accelerated urbanization in SSA. However, while examining the impact of rainfall in Mali between 1981 and 2009, Grace et al. (2018) found no increase in migration, which they explained by the reduction in available resources and lack of destinations with better economic prospects. Henderson, Storeygard, and Deichmann (2017) studied 29 SSA countries between 1960 and 2009, finding a strong impact of adverse climate change on migration from rural areas to neighboring urban areas. Hauer et al. (2019) predicted that involuntary migration due to droughts is expected to increase in Africa.

Defrance, Delesalle, and Gubert (2023) estimated the volume of migration induced by the droughts in Mali since the late 1980s, finding that net migration rates have decreased in the affected localities due to droughts. The effect of drought episodes is determined by the capacity of localities and households to adapt to climatic constraints, with the effect fading in localities characterized by diversified crops and areas that receive more rainfall. Climate shocks have also had an impact on international mobility, with additional departures attributed to droughts. The authors projected that drought-induced mobility will grow substantially in the next decades.

The extent to which climate change will lead to large cross-border movements depends largely on climate mitigation and adaptation policies.

Conclusion

In SSA, substantial rural-to-urban migration happens in many countries, and substantial international migratory movements occur, most of which are within the region. Because the population is aging rapidly in most high- and middle-income countries and SSA will be the only region with population growth, the flows of migration are expected to increase for all countries, which might trigger changes in the region's migration dynamics.

This chapter provides an overview of the complex linkages between migration and inequalities. The World Bank (2023) identified four intertwined drivers of mobility: (1) poverty, (2) demographic pressures, (3) state fragility, and (4) climate change. As pressure is mounting on each driver, migration is expected to rise, and it is important to consider its impacts on inequalities and other welfare outcomes.

The evidence is mixed on migration's impacts on inequality in origin or destination countries and regions within countries, because these effects depend on the state of the labor market at both ends of the migration decision. In line with a long tradition in development economics, there will be incentives or pull factors to migrate as long as people or households improve their situation by migrating. Once they migrate, this reality will have implications for both the sending and receiving labor markets. Therefore, analyzing the impact of migration on labor market outcomes and relative earnings in both the sending and receiving countries is crucial.

Migration offers high returns for skilled labor in more lucrative labor markets across and within countries, and, therefore, strong incentives exist for those who are better-off to migrate. With international migration, this issue is the basis of brain drain. In the receiving labor markets, such migration is generally positive for economic activity (growth) and aggregate labor demand, tempering earnings at the upper end of the receiving labor market and taking away the highest earners from the sending labor market. These forces, therefore, tend to lower inequality.

People who are less skilled, who often are poor and vulnerable, face similar incentives across and within countries, and migration would seem to offer mobility toward a better life.

However, at least initially, less-skilled individuals have neither the resources nor the networks to respond by migrating. Yet, push factors can prompt migration if situations in sending areas become untenable due to war, rampant unemployment, or discrimination in many formal and informal institutional factors, including gender, ethnicity, race, religion, or spatial social and development policies. Initially, such types of migration can put downward pressure on wages at the bottom end of labor markets in receiving countries and areas and can be a source of increasing inequality within receiving countries or regions. However, this impact depends on whether the work of these migrants complements or substitutes for local labor. The empirical evidence is mixed on this key issue. Given the sensitivity around such migration, further research adapted to each context is urgently needed.

This chapter also discusses some key factors contributing to migration, emphasizing inequality as a key driver of migration. This perspective is important for assessing the impacts of migration policies on reducing inequality. Migration has high fixed costs and often requires access to networks and social capital. These financial and social constraints are correlated with inequalities in receiving areas and, without horrendous push factors, poor people, vulnerable individuals, and those subject to discrimination are often unable to migrate. The evidence clearly indicates that aggregate migration rates depend on the initial poverty rates, and financial and social constraints significantly hamper mobility. These important inequalities of opportunity can constrain large sections of African populations from changing their lives for the better and, therefore, can hamper an important channel of inclusive development.

References

Abadi, Nigussie, Ataklti Techane, Girmay Tesfay, Daniel Maxwell, Bapu Vaitla, and UNU-WIDER. 2018. "The Impact of Remittances on Household Food Security: A Micro Perspective from Tigray, Ethiopia." WIDER Working Paper 40/2018, United Nations University, World Institute for Development Economics Research, Helsinki, Finland. https://doi.org/10.35188/UNU-WIDER/2018/482-7.

Adams, Richard H., Alfredo Cuecuecha, and John Page. 2008. "The Impact of Remittances on Poverty and Inequality in Ghana." Policy Research Working Paper 4732, World Bank, Washington, DC.

Altındağ, Onur, Ozan Bakış, and Sandra V. Rozo. 2020. "Blessing or Burden? Impacts of Refugees on Businesses and the Informal Economy." Journal of Development Economics 146: 102490. https://doi.org/10.1016/j.jdeveco.2020.102490.

Anyanwu, John. 2011. "International Remittances and Income Inequality in Africa." Review of Economic and Business Studies 4 (1): 117–48.

Barrios, Salvador, Luisito Bertinelli, and Eric Strobl. 2006. "Climatic Change and Rural–Urban Migration: The Case of Sub-Saharan Africa." Journal of Urban Economics 60 (3): 357–71. https://doi.org/10.1016/j.jue.2006.04.005.

Bell, Martin, Elin Charles-Edwards, Philipp Ueffing, John Stillwell, Marek Kupiszewski, and Dorota Kupiszewska. 2015. "Internal Migration and Development: Comparing Migration Intensities around the World." Population and Development Review 41 (1): 33–58. https://doi.org/10.1111/j.1728-4457.2015.00025.x.

Biavaschi, Costanza, Giovanni Facchini, Anna Maria Mayda, and Mariapia Mendola. 2018. "South–South Migration and the Labor Market: Evidence from South Africa." *Journal of Economic Geography* 18 (4): 823–53. https://doi.org/10.1093/jeg/lby010.

Bossavie, Laurent, and Çağlar Özden. 2023. "Impacts of Temporary Migration on Development in Origin Countries." *World Bank Research Observer* 38 (2): 249–94. https://doi.org/10.1093/wbro/lkad003.

Brueckner, Jan K., and Somik V. Lall. 2015. "Cities in Developing Countries: Fueled by Rural–Urban Migration, Lacking in Tenure Security, and Short of Affordable Housing." In *Handbook of Regional and Urban Economics*, edited by Gilles Duranton, J. Vernon Henderson, and William C. Strange, vol. 5, 1399–1455. Amsterdam: Elsevier. https://doi.org/10.1016/B978-0-444-59531-7.00021-1.

Cattaneo, Andrea, and Sherman Robinson. 2019. "Economic Development and the Evolution of Internal Migration: Moving in Steps, Returnees, and Gender Differences." FAO Agricultural Development Economics Working Paper 2019/03, Food and Agriculture Organization, Rome. https://doi.org/10.18356/763a233f-en.

Cattaneo, Cristina, Michel Beine, Christiane J. Fröhlich, Dominic Kniveton, Inmaculada Martinez-Zarzoso, Marina Mastrorillo, Katrin Millock, Etienne Piguet, and Benjamin Schraven. 2019. "Human Migration in the Era of Climate Change." *Review of Environmental Economics and Policy* 13 (2): 189–206. https://doi.org/10.1093/reep/rez008.

Cirillo, Marinella, Andrea Cattaneo, Meghan Miller, and Ahmad Sadiddin. 2022. "Establishing the Link between Internal and International Migration: Evidence from Sub-Saharan Africa." *World Development* 157: 105943. https://doi.org/10.1016/j.worlddev.2022.105943.

Clemens, Michael A. 2014. "Does Development Reduce Migration?" In *International Handbook on Migration and Economic Development*, edited by Robert E. B. Lucas, 152–85. Cheltenham, United Kingdom: Edward Elgar Publishing. https://doi.org/10.4337/9781782548072.00010.

Clemens, Michael A., and David McKenzie. 2018. "Why Don't Remittances Appear to Affect Growth?" *Economic Journal* 128 (612): F179–F209. https://doi.org/10.1111/ecoj.12463.

Clemens, Michael A., Claudio E. Montenegro, and Lant Pritchett. 2019. "The Place Premium: Bounding the Price Equivalent of Migration Barriers." *Review of Economics and Statistics* 101 (2): 201–13. https://doi.org/10.1162/rest_a_00776.

Dallman, Ashley. 2009. "Prosecuting Conflict-Related Sexual Violence at the International Criminal Court." SIPRI Insights on Peace and Security 2009/1, Stockholm International Peace Research Institute, Solna, Sweden.

Dao, Thu Hien, Frédéric Docquier, Chris Parsons, and Giovanni Peri. 2018. "Migration and Development: Dissecting the Anatomy of the Mobility Transition." *Journal of Development Economics* 132: 88–101. https://doi.org/10.1016/j.jdeveco.2017.12.003.

David, Anda, and Björn Nilsson. 2021. "Migration and Rural Development in NENA Countries." *Region et Developpement* 53: 147–65.

De Haas, Hein. 2009. "Remittances and Social Development." In *Financing Social Policy: Mobilizing Resources for Social Development*, edited by Katja Hujo and Shea McClanahan, 293–318. London: Palgrave Macmillan UK.

De Haas, Hein, 2010. "Migration and Development: A Theoretical Perspective." *International Migration Review*, 44(1): 227–64.

Defrance, Dimitri, Esther Delesalle, and Flore Gubert. 2023. "Migration Response to Drought in Mali: An Analysis Using Panel Data on Malian Localities over the 1987–2009 Period." *Environment and Development Economics* 28 (2): 171–90. https://doi.org/10.1017/S1355770X22000183.

Dinkelman, Taryn, and Martine Mariotti. 2016. "The Long-Run Effects of Labor Migration on Human Capital Formation in Communities of Origin." *American Economic Journal: Applied Economics* 8 (4): 1–35. https://doi.org/10.1257/app.20150405.

Docquier, Frédéric, Giovanni Peri, and Ilse Ruyssen. 2014. "The Cross-Country Determinants of Potential and Actual Migration." *International Migration Review* 48 (1 Suppl.): 37–99. https://doi.org/10.1111/imre.12137.

Dustmann, Christian, Albrecht Glitz, and Tommaso Frattini. 2008. "The Labour Market Impact of Immigration." *Oxford Review of Economic Policy* 24 (3): 477–94. https://doi.org/10.1093/oxrep/grn024.

Ebeke, Christian, and Maëlan Le Goff. 2011. "Why Migrants' Remittances Reduce Income Inequality in Some Countries and Not in Others?" CERDI, Working Papers. HAL Open Science. https://shs.hal.science/halshs-00554277.

Ferrant, Gaëlle, Michele Tuccio, Estelle Loiseau, and Keiko Nowacka. 2014. "The Role of Discriminatory Social Institutions in Female South-South Migration." Issues Paper, OECD Development Centre, Organisation for Economic Co-operation and Development, Paris.

Galbraith, John Kenneth. 1979. *The Nature of Mass Poverty*. Cambridge, MA: Harvard University Press. https://doi.org/10.4159/harvard.9780674333109.

Grace, Kathryn, Véronique Hertrich, Djeneba Singare, and Greg Husak. 2018. "Examining Rural Sahelian Out-Migration in the Context of Climate Change: An Analysis of the Linkages between Rainfall and Out-Migration in Two Malian Villages from 1981 to 2009." *World Development* 109: 187–96. https://doi.org/10.1016/j.worlddev.2018.04.009.

Gubert, Flore, Thomas Lassourd, and Sandrine Mesplé-Somps. 2010. "Do Remittances Affect Poverty and Inequality? Evidence from Mali." Working Paper DT/2010/08, Unité Mixte de Recherche DIAL (Développement, Institutions et Mondialisation), Institut de Recherche pour le Développement, Université Paris-Dauphine, Paris. https://EconPapers.repec.org/RePEc:dia:wpaper:dt201008.

Harris, John R., and Michael P. Todaro. 1970. "Migration, Unemployment and Development: A Two-Sector Analysis." *American Economic Review* 60 (1): 126–42.

Hauer, Mathew E., Elizabeth Fussell, Valerie Mueller, Maxine Burkett, Maia Call, Kali Abel, Robert McLeman, and David Wrathall. 2019. "Sea-Level Rise and Human Migration." *Nature Reviews Earth & Environment* 1 (1): 28–39. https://doi.org/10.1038/s43017-019-0002-9.

Henderson, J. Vernon, Adam Storeygard, and Uwe Deichmann. 2017. "Has Climate Change Driven Urbanization in Africa?" *Journal of Development Economics* 124: 60–82. https://doi.org/10.1016/j.jdeveco.2016.09.001.

Iheke, Onwuchekwa Raphael. 2014. "Impact of Migrant Remittances on the Output of Arable Crop Farm Households in South Eastern Nigeria." *American Journal of Experimental Agriculture* 4 (10): 1209–18. https://doi.org/10.9734/AJEA/2014/6502.

Kerr, Sari Pekkala, William Kerr, Çağlar Özden, and Christopher Parsons. 2017. "High-Skilled Migration and Agglomeration." *Annual Review of Economics* 9 (1): 201–34. https://doi.org/10.1146/annurev-economics-063016-103705.

Koczan, Zsoka, Giovanni Peri, Magali Pinat, and Dmitriy Rozhkov. 2021. "The Impact of International Migration on Inclusive Growth: A Review." IMF Working Paper WP/21/88, International Monetary Fund, Washington, DC.

Konseiga, Adama. 2004. "Adoption of Agricultural Innovations in the Sahel: The Role of Migration in Food Security." Paper presented at the 38th Annual Meeting of the Canadian Economics Association, Toronto, Ontario.

IMF (International Monetary Fund). 2009. *Payments and International Investment Position Manual*, 6th ed. Washington, DC: IMF. https://www.imf.org/external/pubs/ft/bop/2007/pdf/bpm6.pdf

Lewis, W. Arthur. 1954. "Economic Development with Unlimited Supplies of Labour." *Manchester School* 22 (2): 139–91. https://doi.org/10.1111/j.1467-9957.1954.tb00021.x.

Lipton, Michael. 1980. "Migration from Rural Areas of Poor Countries: The Impact on Rural Productivity and Income Distribution." *World Development* 8 (1): 1–24. https://doi.org/10.1016/0305-750X(80)90047-9.

Mabogunje, Akin L. 1970. "Systems Approach to a Theory of Rural-Urban Migration." *Geographical Analysis* 2 (1): 1–18. https://doi.org/10.1111/j.1538-4632.1970.tb00140.x.

Margolis, David N., Luis Miotti, El Mouhoub Mouhoud, and Joel Oudinet. 2015. "'To Have and Have Not': International Migration, Poverty, and Inequality in Algeria." *Scandinavian Journal of Economics* 117 (2): 650–85. https://doi.org/10.1111/sjoe.12103.

McKenzie, David. 2018. "Poverty, Inequality, and International Migration: Insights from 10 Years of Migration and Development Conferences." *Revue d'économie Du Développement* 25 (3): 13–28. https://doi.org/10.3917/edd.313.0013.

McKenzie, David. 2024. "Fears and Tears: Should More People Be Moving within and from Developing Countries, and What Stops This Movement?" *World Bank Research Observer* 39 (1): 75–96. https://doi.org/10.1093/wbro/lkac009.

McKenzie, David, Steven Stillman, and John Gibson. 2010. "How Important Is Selection? Experimental vs. Non-Experimental Measures of the Income Gains from Migration." *Journal of the European Economic Association* 8 (4): 913–45. https://doi.org/10.1111/j.1542-4774.2010.tb00544.x.

Milanovic, Branko. 2015. "Global Inequality of Opportunity: How Much of Our Income Is Determined by Where We Live?" *Review of Economics and Statistics* 97 (2): 452–60. https://doi.org/10.1162/REST_a_00432.

Miletto, Michela, Martina Angela Caretta, Francesca Maria Burchi, and Giulia Zanlucchi. 2017. *Migration and Its Interdependencies with Water Scarcity, Gender and Youth Employment*. Paris: United Nations Educational, Scientific, and Cultural Organization.

Muyonga, Mary, George Odipo, and Alfred O. Agwanda. 2020. "Interlinkages between Migration and Inequality in Africa: Review of Contemporary Studies." *African Human Mobility Review* 6 (1): 6–26. https://doi.org/10.14426/ahmr.v6i1.779.

OECD (Organisation for Economic Co-operation and Development) and AFD (Agence Française de Développement). 2019. *Migration Data Brief*. Number 5. Paris: OECD and AFD.

Ofori, Isaac K., Emmanuel Y. Gbolonyo, Toyo Amègnonna M. Dossou, and Richard K. Nkrumah. 2022. "Remittances and Income Inequality in Africa: Financial Development Thresholds for Economic Policy." *Research in Globalization* 4: 100084. https://doi.org/10.1016/j.resglo.2022.100084.

Olowa, Olatomide Waheed, Taiwo Timothy Awoyemi, Musediku Adebayo A. Shittu, and Omowumi Ayodele Olowa. 2013. "Effects of Remittances on Poverty among Rural Households in Nigeria." *European Journal of Sustainable Development* 2 (4): 263–84. https://doi.org/10.14207/ejsd.2013.v2n4p263.

Özden, Çağlar, Michael Packard, and Mathis Wagner. 2017. "International Migration and Wages." *Revue d'économie du développement* 25 (3–4): 93–133. https://doi.org/10.3917/edd.313.0093.

Ratha, Dilip, Vandana Chandra, Eung Ju Kim, Sonia Plaza, and William Shaw. 2023. *Migration and Development Brief 39: Leveraging Diaspora Finances for Private Capital Mobilization*. Washington, DC: World Bank.

Ratha, Dilip, Sonia Plaza, Eung Ju Kim, Vandana Chandra, Nyasha Kurasha, and Baran Pradhan. 2023. *Migration and Development Brief 38: Remittances Remain Resilient but Are Slowing*. Washington, DC: World Bank.

Ruiz, Isabel, and Carlos Vargas-Silva. 2018. "The Consequences of Forced Migration for Host Communities in Africa." *Revue d'économie Du Développement* 25 (3): 135–54. https://doi.org/10.3917/edd.313.0135.

Ruyssen, Ilse, and Sara Salomone. 2018. "Female Migration: A Way Out of Discrimination?" *Journal of Development Economics* 130: 224–41. https://doi.org/10.1016/j.jdeveco.2017.10.010.

Sadiddin, Ahmad, Andrea Cattaneo, Marinella Cirillo, and Meghan Miller. 2019. "Food Insecurity as a Determinant of International Migration: Evidence from Sub-Saharan Africa." *Food Security* 11 (3): 515–30. https://doi.org/10.1007/s12571-019-00927-w.

Safi, Mirna. 2020. "Migration and Inequality." *Social Forces* 99 (2): e1–e3. https://doi.org/10.1093/sf/soaa084.

Šedová, Barbora, Lucia Čizmaziová, and Athene Cook. 2021. "A Meta-Analysis of Climate Migration Literature." CEPA Discussion Paper 29, Center for Economic Policy Analysis, Universität Potsdam, Potsdam, Germany. https://publishup.uni-potsdam.de/49982.

Selod, Harris, and Forhad Shilpi. 2021. "Rural-Urban Migration in Developing Countries: Lessons from the Literature." *Regional Science and Urban Economics* 91: 103713. https://doi.org/10.1016/j.regsciurbeco.2021.103713.

Sjaastad, Larry A. 1962. "The Costs and Returns of Human Migration." *Journal of Political Economy* 70 (5): 80–93. https://doi.org/10.1086/258726.

Slotwinski, Michaela, Alois Stutzer, and Roman Uhlig. 2019. "Are Asylum Seekers More Likely to Work with More Inclusive Labor Market Access Regulations?" *Swiss Journal of Economics and Statistics* 155 (17): 1–15. https://doi.org/10.1186/s41937-019-0046-2.

Smith, Michael D., and Maria S. Floro. 2020. "Food Insecurity, Gender, and International Migration in Low- and Middle-Income Countries." *Food Policy* 91: 101837. https://doi.org/10.1016/j.foodpol.2020.101837.

Socha-Dietrich, Karolina, and Jean-Christophe Dumont. 2021. "International Migration and Movement of Doctors to and within OECD Countries—2000 to 2018: Developments in Countries of Destination and Impact on Countries of Origin." OECD Health Working Paper 126 (February 19), vol. 126, Organisation for Economic Co-operation and Development, Paris. https://doi.org/10.1787/7ca8643e-en.

Uprety, Dambar. 2020. "Does Skilled Migration Cause Income Inequality in the Source Country?" *International Migration* 58 (4): 85–100. https://doi.org/10.1111/imig.12661.

Williams, Wendy. 2024. *African Migration Trends to Watch in 2024*. Washington, DC: Africa Center for Strategic Studies.

WMO (World Meteorological Organization). 2022. *State of the Climate in Africa 2021*. Geneva: WMO.

World Bank. 2018. *Moving for Prosperity: Global Migration and Labor Markets*. Washington, DC: World Bank. https://doi.org/10.1596/978-1-4648-1281-1.

World Bank. 2023. *World Development Report 2023: Migrants, Refugees, and Societies*. Washington, DC: World Bank. https://www.worldbank.org/en/publication/wdr2023.

Wouterse, Fleur 2010. "Remittances, Poverty, Inequality and Welfare: Evidence from the Central Plateau of Burkina Faso." *Journal of Development Studies* 46 (4): 771–89. https://doi.org/10.1080/00220380903019461.

Young, Alwyn. 2013. "Inequality, the Urban-Rural Gap, and Migration." *Quarterly Journal of Economics* 128 (4): 1727–85. https://doi.org/10.1093/qje/qjt025.

Zelinsky, Wilbur. 1971. "The Hypothesis of the Mobility Transition." *Geographical Review* 61 (2): 219–49. https://doi.org/10.2307/213996.

Chapter 8

Social Mobility and the Persistence of Inequality

Murray Leibbrandt, Rawane Yasser, Robert Osei, and Mike Savage

Introduction

Since the 1950s, the analysis of social mobility has become a central area of social sciences research that considers the extent to which people's fates are shaped by their birth circumstances. This analysis can play a vital role in assessing how far structural divides, such as those of class, gender, and race, determine individuals' life chances and well-being, as well as to what extent individuals can mold their own futures.

Social mobility has increasingly become a major political issue, as governments seek to justify economic inequalities—which have often intensified and become harsher due to cuts in the provision of public welfare—by emphasizing that it is possible for all their citizens with the right skills and aptitudes to have realistic chances to get ahead. It is in these terms that the idea of *meritocracy* has gained almost universal support across capitalist nations (Mijs 2021).

Research on social mobility has been strongly biased toward the Global North. This situation is changing, reflecting two ways in which the paradigms of the Global North have run their course. First, the standard toolkit of mobility research uses measures rooted in the industrial capitalist systems that have predominated in these nations. These measures notably focus on the influential class structural perspectives that were popularized, for example, by Erikson and Goldthorpe (1992), and rely on measures of status premised on affluent consumer societies in the United States, as codified by Blau, Duncan, and Tyree's (1967) status attainment models.

A major theme in both perspectives is the role of formal education in mediating the relations between origins and destinations, which thus assumes norms of high levels of the provision of education. These two competing perspectives, and others drawn from the same broad family, have dominated Global North research agendas. Yet, it is uncertain whether these can illuminate the mobility dynamics in nations marked by colonial histories, the predominance of work in primary (for example, agriculture and mining) and informal sectors, historically restricted to the provision of education and limited bureaucratized employment.

Second is the social mobility research developed as a means of empirically exploring the reality of the "American Dream" and the visions of upward mobility held out by educational credentialism (for example, Chetty et al. 2014). A major theme in recent research has been that these dreams are increasingly failing. Chetty posed fundamental questions such as, "Is the United States Still a Land of Opportunity?" (Chetty et al. 2014), and has shown dramatic declines in absolute income mobility since 1940 (Chetty et al. 2017). The same theme of social mobility decline has been influential in the United Kingdom (Blanden et al. 2002), and the decline of absolute mobility, especially upward, was confirmed by Bukodi and Goldthorpe (2018).

Given that analysis of social mobility has been rooted in Global North framings and experiences, what can be learned from focusing on African nations? Appeals to meritocracy have been made in Africa, as with the South African dream of a post-apartheid society that transforms itself away from race-based rewards to one that flourishes through maximizing the potential of all. In South Africa and other countries, a commitment to building such a society is written into the constitution. Across the African continent, the long-run aspiration has been, and remains, to shake off the shackles of colonialism and build inclusive and flourishing post-colonial African societies that are better for each successive generation.

Does the evidence on social mobility in Africa suggest a realistic support for these aspirations? Social mobility is closely linked to inequality. The social and economic forces that facilitate or impede social mobility are the drivers of change or persistence of inequality across and within generations. The distribution of physical and human assets undergirds inequalities in access to opportunities, which, in turn, shape outcomes in the future. Formal and informal policies, rules, and social norms also shape inequalities in opportunities and outcomes in the future.

This chapter distinguishes between intergenerational and intragenerational findings. The former allows a long-run view by comparing the education, labor market, or household income situations of children relative to those of their parents at comparable times in their lives. As is shown throughout this book, inequalities intersect, strengthen each other, and change very slowly. However, if the situations of children are better than those of their parents, this intergenerational improvement is a sign of some progress and a better society. The chapter also considers intragenerational mobility, which takes place over the life course of specific individuals and can be more salient to people as they examine their prospects and reflect on their life trajectories.

Although, in the perspectives of the Global North, intragenerational mobility is often downplayed compared to intergenerational mobility, the chapter discusses and reviews the available African evidence on both. The chapter concludes by assessing the importance of policies that seek to improve social mobility as part of policies to address inequality.

Intergenerational Mobility

Intergenerational mobility is the extent to which people's life outcomes (such as educational achievement, earnings, and occupation) are correlated with those of their parents (World Bank 2022). Inherited circumstances, such as gender, race, birth location, and family background, can limit opportunities for children and, therefore, can hamper intergenerational mobility (Brunori, Ferreira, and Neidhöfer 2023). This inequality of opportunity hampers intergenerational mobility through different pathways, including unequal access to private assets and wealth; public services, including water, energy, health care, and education; and information and communications technology. There are often stark spatial inequalities in these patterns of access to resources and opportunities.

These concerns are high in Africa, where the future of children is still strongly linked to the socioeconomic status (SES) of their parents, including being limited at the start of their lives by deprivations in pregnancy and the early years (Narayan et al. 2018). These inequalities of opportunities can have a strong negative correlation with levels of mobility (World Bank 2022). Research has highlighted the central role played by equality of opportunity in the relationship between inequality and growth (Aiyar and Ebeke 2020). In societies where inequality of opportunity is high, income inequality is more persistent, constraining investment opportunities and growth. Clearly, the extent to which socioeconomic outcomes are transmitted from one generation to another is consequential.

To study such mobility, or the lack thereof, requires comparing parents with children at comparable points in their lives. Due to the lack of appropriate data, such studies on Africa are scarce. However, some research exists on intergenerational mobility in Africa, and this section reviews its findings about the persistence of inequality on the continent. The section explores the patterns of intergenerational educational, occupational, and earnings mobility, before focusing on the drivers and correlates of these mobilities.

Evolution and Patterns of Intergenerational Mobility in Education

Given the methodological challenges and data limitations in estimating intergenerational earnings and occupational and income mobility, research has tended to focus on mobility in education (Alesina et al. 2021; Azomahou and Yitbarek 2021; Narayan et al. 2018; Van der Weide et al. 2021). Methodologically, parents' schooling and educational attainment are more reliably reported by children, compared to income, wealth, or consumption. In addition, unlike income, education level does not vary across an individual's lifecycle, presenting fewer measurement challenges. Finally, data on education are more available in developing countries, compared to income or wealth. Educational mobility is important on its own and constitutes an important pathway to economic mobility, as human capital and schooling tend to be strong predictors of earnings and economic well-being as important drivers of labor market outcomes.

To measure intergenerational educational mobility, it is important to distinguish between absolute and relative mobility. The former measures the share of individuals who surpass the education of their parents; the latter captures the degree to which individuals' socioeconomic success is independent of the socioeconomic success of their parents.

Many African countries have undergone a sustained period of expansion of primary schools and reduced or even removed school fees. This issue has been reflected in gross primary school enrollment rates in Sub-Saharan Africa (SSA) of 97.3 percent in 2016, an increase of 20 percentage points since 1990 (Razzu and Wambile 2022). However, SSA stands out as the region with some of the lowest rates of absolute and relative intergenerational mobility in education.

For absolute mobility, less than 20 percent of the respondents in some of the poorest or most-fragile countries have more education than their parents, compared to more than 80 percent in parts of East Asia (Van der Weide et al. 2021). Among the 15 countries in the bottom decile of absolute mobility, 10 are in SSA. In SSA, on average, 36 percent of those born in the 1980s have a higher level of education than their parents, compared to 57 percent of the same generation in the average country in East Asia and the Pacific. For relative educational mobility,[1] about 12 percent of adults born in the 1980s in some low-income countries in SSA had more education than their parents, compared with 80 percent of the same generation in the East Asia and Pacific region (Narayan et al. 2018).

The picture for Africa has been augmented by country-level research. Examining the evolution of intergenerational mobility in educational attainment in 27 African countries since independence, Alesina et al. (2021) found that the likelihood that children born to parents with no education go on to complete primary schooling exceeds 70 percent in South Africa and Botswana, compared to less than 20 percent in Sudan (4 percent), Ethiopia, Mozambique (11 percent), Burkina Faso, Guinea, and Malawi. Ouedraogo and Syrichas (2021) and Razzu and Wambile (2022) confirmed this strong variation across countries.

Focusing on the intergenerational persistence of years of schooling over a 50-year period, Azomahou and Yitbarek (2021) highlighted a declining cohort trend after the 1960s in the intergenerational persistence of education in nine SSA countries, implying greater educational mobility for more-recent birth cohorts. Once more, heterogeneity is apparent between countries, with Ghana, Guinea, Nigeria, and Uganda experiencing the highest intergenerational mobility, and the Comoros and Madagascar experiencing the lowest.

Heterogeneity is also prevalent within countries. For example, in Kenya, the likelihood that children of illiterate parents will complete primary education ranges from 5 percent (in the Northwest) to 85 percent (in Westlands in Nairobi) (Alesina et al. 2021). In general, upward mobility is higher for urban households. The rural-urban gap is the highest in countries with low levels of mobility and literacy. For example, a gap of about 40 percentage points exists between rural and urban places in Burkina Faso and Ethiopia (countries with the lowest mobility). The gap is less than 10 percentage points in Botswana and South Africa (which have high mobility). In some regions in Mali, children's probability of being less educated than their parents is more than 70 percent, while in other regions, it is about 18 percent (refer to map 8.1).

Map 8.1 Intergenerational Education Elasticities in Mali

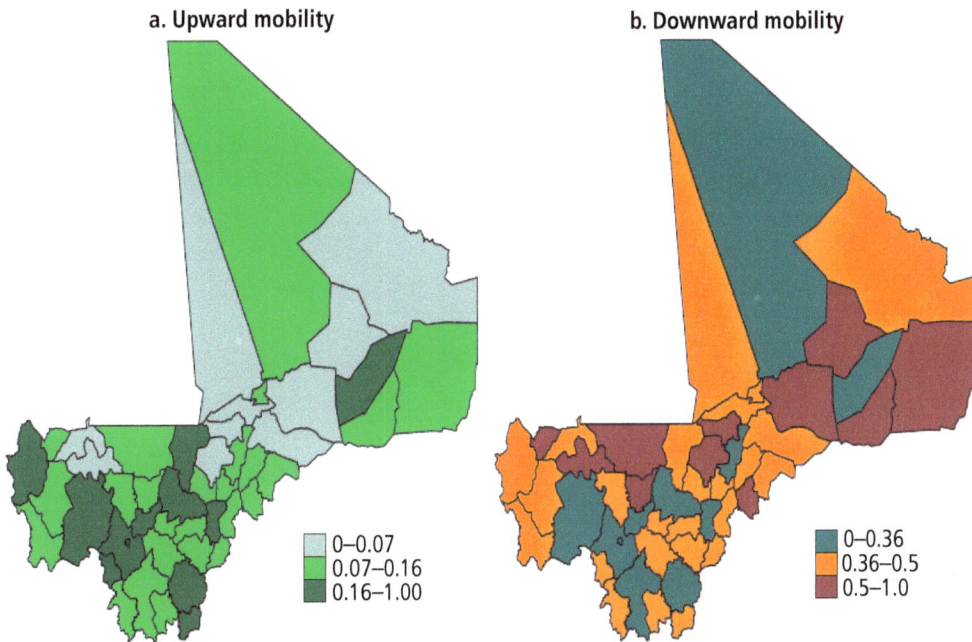

a. Upward mobility

b. Downward mobility

Upward mobility legend:
- 0–0.07
- 0.07–0.16
- 0.16–1.00

Downward mobility legend:
- 0–0.36
- 0.36–0.5
- 0.5–1.0

Source: Used with permission from Ouedraogo and Syrichas 2021, IMF Working Paper 2021/215 "Intergenerational Social Mobility in Africa Since 1920," © International Monetary Fund. https://doi.org/10.5089/9781513593807.001.
Note: The maps show the shares of children's probabilities of upward (panel a) and downward (panel b) intergenerational mobility in education. *Upward mobility* is the average probability of completing primary school among children ages 14+ whose parents are not educated. *Downward mobility* is the average probability of failing to complete primary school among children whose parents are educated.

Within countries, gender gaps in educational mobility are closing, with girls acquiring more education than boys in recent decades (Razzu and Wambile 2022). However, for this progress to translate into income mobility for girls, it is important to tackle the gender disparities in the labor market. The same is true of other horizontal inequalities, such as race and ethnicity.

A common finding in Europe is that, whereas the children of non-White migrants often perform well in education, and sometimes better than the White native-born populations, this finding does not translate into subsequent advances in employment and earnings (Heath and Schneider 2021; Van De Werfhorst and Heath 2019). Similar patterns are evidenced in Africa. For example, in South Africa, children's considerably greater educational attainment versus that of their parents has not reduced the high level of intergenerational earnings immobility (Finn, Leibbrandt, and Ranchhod 2017). The chances of finding work depend on unequal parental labor market experience and earnings, resulting in high levels of persistence between the earnings of parents and those of their children. This leads substantively into a discussion of intergenerational earnings and occupational mobility in Africa.

Evolution and Patterns of Intergenerational Earnings and Occupational Mobility

Measuring intergenerational earnings and occupational mobility in most African countries is constrained by data availability, with evidence on these intergenerational mobilities scarce.

South Africa is among the few countries that have gathered survey data that allow estimating intergenerational earnings mobility. This research has shown that the opportunities available to South Africans are still closely related to the SES of their parents (Finn et al. 2017; Piraino 2015), with a high degree of persistence at both the top and bottom of the earnings distribution (refer to figure 8.1).

Disadvantage is passed on to the next generation, with 9 in 10 children from the poorest families occupying the same place in the earnings distribution as their parents. Advantage is also "inherited," with the children of top-earning fathers having a 70 percent chance of finding themselves at the top of the earnings distribution. Those in the middle of the earnings distribution are the most vulnerable and the least stable, facing both upward and downward mobility. The strong transmission of disadvantage and advantage from parents to children is an alarming metric of a post-apartheid South Africa as it is a far cry from the South African dream referred to at the start of this chapter.

Intergenerational earnings immobility is high in other African countries, too, with a strong correlation between earnings across two generations found in Botswana, Eswatini, Lesotho, Namibia, and South Africa (World Bank 2022).[2] Using a rich data set on intergenerational occupational mobility in 26 African countries, Ouedraogo and Syrichas (2021) found that, on average, upward occupational mobility increased for children born before independence, around the 1960s, but then fell until the most-recent cohort. This finding covers significant

Figure 8.1 Intergenerational Earnings Elasticities across the Earnings Distribution in South Africa

Strength of relationship between parent's earnings and children's earnings

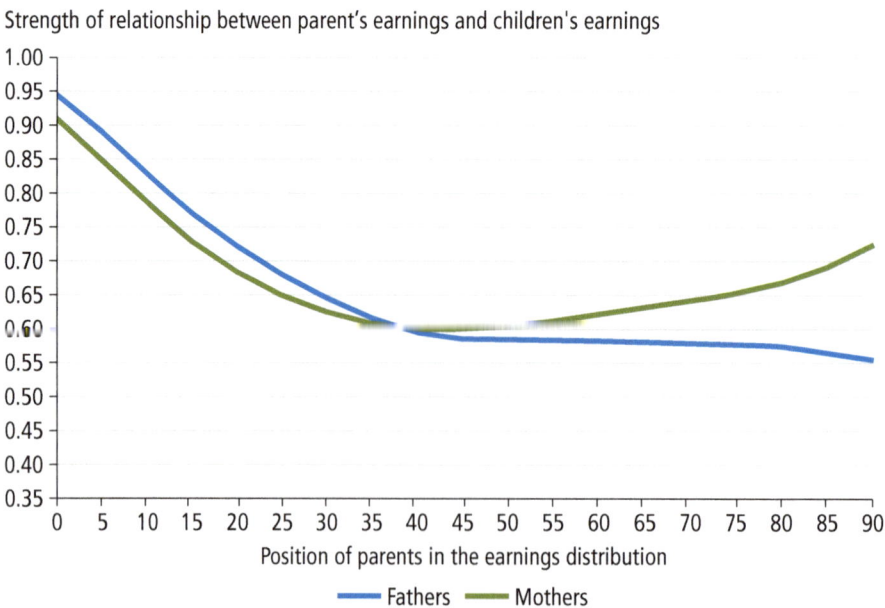

Position of parents in the earnings distribution

—— Fathers —— Mothers

Source: Authors' calculations based on Finn et al. 2017, figure 6.
Note: The strength of the relationship between parent's and children's earnings is measured by intergenerational elasticity earnings (the elasticity of children's earnings to their parents' earnings) over earnings quantiles.

variation across countries. On average, less than 20 percent of children climbed up the occupational ladder. However, around 30 percent of the children born to parents employed in nonagriculture sectors ended up in agricultural work. The top three countries for upward mobility are Botswana, the Arab Republic of Egypt, and South Africa, and the bottom three are Burkina Faso, Ethiopia, and Mali (Ouedraogo and Syrichas, 2021)).

Caution is required when examining earnings and occupational mobility in Africa, as the analysis needs to consider unemployment (zero earnings) and informal-sector earnings and occupations (Iversen, Krishna, and Sen 2021). In addition, the same occupation can mean a different kind and quality of job for children in the more-contemporary labor market than it did for their parents.

Channels of Persistence and Determinants of Intergenerational Mobility

There is a wealth of evidence on the importance of education and educational inequalities as essential elements in explaining economic mobility in Africa (Alesina et al. 2021; Azomahou and Yitbarek 2021; Narayan et al. 2018; Ouedraogo and Syrichas 2021; Razzu and Wambile 2022). Narayan et al. (2018) suggested that, across SSA, parents' educational attainment levels are among the most-important factors explaining their children's educational outcomes.

However, intergenerational mobility is less pronounced for daughters than for sons. In a compelling example of intersecting inequalities, a daughter's educational attainment is more strongly correlated with her parents' education than that of a son, yet significant differences exist between countries and, within countries, by gender (Azomahou and Yitbarek 2021; Razzu and Wambile 2022). In countries in the Central Africa and Southern Africa regions and in countries with historical links to former British colonies, intergenerational mobility in education is relatively higher. This phenomenon indicates the importance of accessible schooling systems to breaking the persistence of intergenerational earnings.

In Guinea, Nigeria, and Rwanda, parental education and occupation contribute the most to inequality of opportunity (Brunori, Palmisano, and Peragine 2016). However, it is clear that the quality and affordability of schooling are important given the concerningly low earnings mobility in Africa despite increased levels of educational attainment. The content and quality of the years of education that children receive at the primary and secondary levels are crucial (Finn et al. 2017; also refer to chapter 3 of this book).

These trends appear cross-nationally, too. Absolute educational mobility is correlated with levels of national income in an inverted U-shaped relationship—the lowest rates of absolute mobility are observed in the poorest and best-off countries, suggesting a national poverty trap in the poorest countries and a ceiling effect in the best-off countries, where it becomes harder for children to surpass their parents' level of education (Van der Weide et al. 2021). As countries move from poorer to richer, public expenditures on interventions that aim to equalize opportunities for children of parents with different backgrounds, especially the quality of education, are key channels through which mobility can increase (Azomahou and Yitbarek 2021; Ouedraogo and Syrichas 2021; Van der Weide et al. 2021).

That said, factors other than education are strongly positively correlated with intergenerational earnings and income mobility, including good child health indicators, ethnolinguistic fractionalization, and population size (Van der Weide et al. 2021). A decomposition of the channels through which parental income influences the income of the next generation finds that parental characteristics, other than education, constitute the strongest channel. Labor markets and birthplace are important contributors.

First, many labor markets reward children with parental connections, legacies, or social privileges. Second, richer parents tend to live in places that allow better access to information, services, jobs, and networks. Therefore, a child's birthplace is identified as the primary circumstance variable determining inequality of opportunity, for example, in the Comoros and Niger (Brunori et al. 2016).

Ethnicity and race are inherited circumstances that also play an important role in children's futures (Brunori et al. 2016; Funjika and Getachew 2022; Piraino 2015). In South Africa, where a limited set of inherited circumstances explains a significant fraction of earnings inequality among male adults, race can play an important role (Piraino 2015). Ethnicity plays a dominant role in inequality of opportunity in the Democratic Republic of Congo and Uganda (Brunori et al. 2016).

This subsection has highlighted the role of historical and geographical factors in intergenerational educational mobility (Funjika and Getachew 2022). Alesina et al. (2021) and Razzu and Wambile (2022) broadened the analysis of educational mobility to include factors such as proximity to the coast and the capital, colonial transportation investments, and missionary activity. Upward mobility is higher in regions that are close to the coast and the capital. An extra year spent in a high-mobility region before age 12 (and after age 5) significantly increases the likelihood of completing primary school among children of uneducated parents (Alesina et al. 2021). Of the historical factors, colonial investments in transportation and missionary activity are strong determinants of educational mobility. In contrast, natural resources, proximity to borders, and precolonial statehood seem to play a minor role in explaining educational mobility in Africa.

Intergenerational educational mobility, earnings, occupations, and incomes provide crucial metrics of the long run progress of societies in increasing the equality of opportunities and reducing inequalities in outcomes. This section examined the mechanisms correlated with improvements in these long-run metrics. These drivers can influence the lives of parents, children, and others, day-by-day and year-by-year, to result in intergenerational outcomes. The next section examines intragenerational mobility, which measures and explains people's relative trajectories over time.

Intragenerational Mobility

Major and Machin (2018) called *intragenerational mobility* "class mobility" because it tracks movements of individuals across and within key socioeconomic categories. In an African context, it seems useful to partition society into three such categories—poor, middle class, and elite—and to examine the evidence on movements into and out of each group. This evidence includes information on the size and drivers of the groups who are trapped in poverty over time, those who escape from poverty, those who fall into poverty, those who move up within the middle class (perhaps even into the elite), and mobility into and out of the elite. These dynamics provide an essential lens for understanding changes in inequalities as well as the information base for designing effective policies to tackle chronic poverty, supporting the growth of a stable middle class, or changing tax policy toward the elite in tackling inequality.

However, the measurement of such intragenerational dynamics requires data that track people over time. Such longitudinal or panel data are costly to collect and scarce in Africa. In recent years, the collection of panel data has expanded somewhat in Africa, allowing for some assessment of these processes, including transitions into and out of poverty, the middle class, and the elite.[3] In addition, systematic efforts have created synthetic panel data sets that track, across a set of cross-sectional data sets, the progress of comparable cohorts as they age.[4] The following subsections review the state of knowledge about poverty, middle-class, and elite dynamics and their channels of persistence in Africa.

Poverty Dynamics

Although there is substantial research on the trends in African poverty, much less is known about the dynamics of poverty. Is it chronic or transient? Chronic poverty occurs when the same individuals are consistently poor over time and seem to be trapped in poverty. Identifying which people are more likely to remain in poverty over their lifetime or experience downward or upward mobility out of or into poverty directs a lens on the lower, vulnerable sections of any society and, therefore, is key for addressing inequalities on the continent.

A review of various studies showed that the incidence of chronic (persistent) poverty in certain African countries, such as Malawi and South Africa, remains remarkably high (Himanshu and Lanjouw 2021). In the absence of panel household survey data, Dang and Dabalen (2019) constructed synthetic panel data to estimate poverty dynamics for 21 SSA countries. While the results showed that one-third of the population in Africa is chronically poor, Dang and Dabalen (2019) pointed to great disparities across countries. Some countries, such as Ethiopia, Ghana, Malawi, Mauritania, Mozambique, Tanzania, Togo, and Uganda, have lower levels of chronic poverty because of their pro-poor growth.[5] Other countries, such as Burkina Faso, Cameroon, Madagascar, Nigeria, Senegal, and Zambia, have experienced growth that is not pro-poor, leaving high numbers in chronic poverty.

Although the results point to a 28-percent increase in the size of the middle-class population across the region, and, therefore, to some upward mobility out of poverty, chronic poverty remains high, particularly in countries such as the Democratic Republic of Congo, Madagascar, and Malawi. In the Democratic Republic of Congo, the poverty rate was 80 percent in 2012, and the chronically-poor population represented almost 75 percent of this group. In Madagascar, the chronically-poor population represented 60 percent. In terms of dynamics, 17 percent of the population in Africa has emerged from poverty but remains vulnerable to falling back into poverty.

Using a synthetic panel approach, an analysis of poverty dynamics in multiple African countries highlighted the characteristics associated with movements of people into and out of poverty in Ethiopia, Mozambique, and Tanzania (Lanjouw and Tarp 2021). Mekasha and Tarp (2021) focused on poverty dynamics in Ethiopia, showing a high rate of poverty persistence and a high risk of downward mobility, with a high probability of moving from vulnerable nonpoor to poor status. The COVID-19 pandemic aggravated this downward mobility. Dynamic poverty profiling analysis has shown that the rate of downward mobility increases when the household head is less educated, engaged in the services sector, self-employed, or a domestic worker. Similar results were found for Tanzania, where 12.5 percent of the population remained in persistent poverty between 2012 and 2018, and 30 percent experienced transient poverty (Aikaeli, Garcés-Urzainqui, and Mdadila 2021).

Education beyond the primary level and employment in the nonfarm sector were found to effectively protect households from poverty. Rural areas have higher levels of persistent poverty and downward mobility. In Mozambique, Salvucci and Tarp (2021) found a greater proportion of people moving out of poverty than falling into poverty. However, they noted that Mozambique is characterized by a high rate of immobility, with a large portion of the population remaining in poverty or out of poverty and a smaller portion moving upward or downward. They observed that poverty dynamics seem to be more related to intrayear shocks, as a higher percentage of individuals move into poverty between the dry and rainy seasons, and a nonnegligible proportion of vulnerable people do not move out of poverty in the following dry season, pointing to a high degree of immobility.

These synthetic panel data sets cover the start of the COVID-19 pandemic. As such, these country studies highlight how the pandemic expanded faster in countries with high levels of chronic poverty and increased the number of nonpoor people facing a high risk of falling back into poverty (Aikaeli et al. 2021; Mekasha and Tarp 2021; Salvucci and Tarp 2021).

A model of poverty transitions that estimates the risk of future poverty given an individual's current poverty status and household characteristics was applied to South Africa by Schotte, Zizzamia, and Leibbrandt (2018). These authors differentiated between persistent and transient poverty, finding that chronic-poor individuals, those with below-average chances of exiting poverty, made up 50 percent of the South African population and accounted for 80 percent of total poverty in South Africa between 2008 and 2017. They observed that only 16.5 percent of initially-poor individuals escaped poverty between one wave and the next. The average probability of falling into poverty for initially-nonpoor individuals was 25.9 percent.

These results are similar to those of Atta-Ankomah and Osei (2021), who found that, for Ghana, about 18 percent of the poor population escaped poverty during 2010–14. They also showed that an even higher proportion, about 60 percent, of the nonpoor population fell into poverty over the same period. This result is consistent with the idea that a large proportion of the middle class may be vulnerable (for instance, refer to Thurlow, Resnick, and Ubogu 2015). A study by Zizzamia, Schotte, and Ranchhod (2016) found that 80 percent of the poor population in South Africa is chronically poor, and the vulnerable nonpoor population is vulnerable because of the high downward mobility into poverty.

Africans living in rural locations are highly likely to be in persistent or transient poverty. In urban areas, difficulty in accessing labor market income similarly leads to vulnerability and poverty among those predominantly located on the informal fringes of urban society. Successful assimilation into the labor market is strongly related to structural inequalities and inherited and socially determined characteristic (Zizzamia et al. 2019).

Middle-Class Dynamics

A recent business briefing states that, "Historically, a nation's middle class has been representative of its overall economic health. A growing mid-income segment typically signals higher levels of wealth and well-being. It also can support a strong financial outlook for the country" (Amdani 2023). A small middle class often inhibits economic mobility and reflects a society with a high level of income polarization, with a concentration of poor people and a few very high-income and wealthy people. Empirical evidence suggests that a larger and faster-growing middle class is associated with economic stability and mobility. As people gain middle-class status, they tend to accumulate savings and acquire higher education. They consume high-quality goods and services, thus fostering economic stability. Thus, the emergence of a middle class in Africa can play an important social, political, and economic role (Resnick 2015).

The growth of the middle class and its statistical representation, the swelling of the middle section of the income distribution, are central for inclusive, inequality-reducing economic development. Hence, understanding the causes and limitations of the expansion of the middle is imperative. However, little is known about the actual dynamics of the African middle class. Who among the poor population are more likely to transition into the middle class, and what constraints are preventing this from happening?

Since independence, the rise of the middle class in Africa has often occurred through nationalization initiatives that helped transfer assets, property ownership, and employment from foreigners to locals (Resnick 2015). Later, additional policies on land ownership and abolishing private land holdings also were important. The structural adjustment programs of the 1990s were purported to shape the growth of the middle class by offering potential opportunities for the expansion of the private sector and a working middle class. However, in practice, this privatization often served to enrich the population of political elites, as they would acquire the state-owned enterprises.

The growth resurgence that has occurred since the 2000s, accompanied by employment growth in the services sector, has increased the share of the middle class in total employment and played a role in its growth. However, recent research on the continent provides little evidence of an expanding middle class in Africa (Corral, Molini, and Oseni 2015; Giesbert and Schotte 2016; Visagie and Posel 2013; Zizzamia et al. 2016). For example, Schotte et al. (2018) estimated that, in South Africa, only 24 percent of the people could be classified as stably middle class or elite. In Mozambique, while an upward transition from poor to vulnerable is a likely transition (30 percent), the transition from vulnerable to middle class or from poor to middle class is extremely unlikely (Salvucci and Tarp 2021).

That said, the precise definitions of middle class are fraught with countless criteria and alternative approaches, which can affect how much social mobility is claimed to be occurring. An income-based definition raises the question of whether those who are no longer starving automatically enter the middle class. If not, then what is the income threshold into the middle class? Using an income- and consumption-based approach, AFDB (2011) classified one-third of Africa's population as being in the middle class. Many studies have pointed out that this approach is problematic, by highlighting the large share within this middle class of the vulnerable population who have a high risk of falling back into poverty (Melber 2022; Thurlow et al. 2015).

An income-based approach is, therefore, insufficient for defining the middle class, unless it is accompanied by other factors, such as asset ownership, education levels, occupation, social attitudes, and political consciousness, which can facilitate possibilities for upward mobility (Giesbert and Schotte 2016; Němečková, Harmáček, and Schlossarek 2020). One asset-based study showed how the middle class in Africa is growing in size but at a slower rate than suggested by income-based estimations (Shimeles and Ncube 2015). An approach based on political attitudes and behavior pointed to SSA's youth who, alienated by high unemployment rates and persistent inequality, are at the crossroads between upward and downward mobility and do not exhibit any kind of shared middle-class identity (Giesbert and Schotte 2016).

A more-promising vulnerability-based approach[6] defines the middle class as an "empowered class" that is reasonably secure against falling into poverty (López-Calva and Ortiz-Juarez 2014). This approach helps understand the poor and middle-class populations as dynamic phenomena. To qualify as middle class, the risk of falling into poverty should remain below a specific threshold.[7] Using such a low vulnerability to poverty to define the middle class and the National Income Dynamics Study panel data set, the middle class in South Africa was found to be relatively small and has grown sluggishly since 1993 (Schotte et al. 2018, 2022; Zizzamia et al. 2016).

The pattern of growth over this period has implied a decline in poverty, but one that lifted households into a vulnerable middle class and not a stable situation that would be a marker of an enduring middle-class position. Instead, this vulnerable middle-class population is far closer in its incomes and characteristics to the transient-poor population, implying a sizable South African precariat that straddles the poverty line.

Nonetheless, studies have noted some transformation in the racial composition within the stable middle class in South Africa, with Black Africans outnumbering Whites by a significant margin. As there has been negligible downward mobility of White South Africans out of the middle class, this evidence accords with the upward mobility of some Africans into the middle class since 2010/11. However, race remains a strong predictor of poverty and precariousness, and Black Africans are at a far higher risk of being poor.

Using the same low vulnerability to poverty approach, Corral et al. (2015) showed growth in the size of the middle class in Nigeria, with people moving out of poverty between 2003 and 2013. Poverty decreased from 45 percent to 33 percent, and the middle class increased from

13 percent to 19 percent. However, most of the population that moved out of poverty still lives with high levels of vulnerability to poverty.

Studying middle-class dynamics in Ghana, Rougier, et al. (2023) pointed to the heterogeneity of trajectories within the middle class,[8] with a lower middle class of uneducated and vulnerable informal workers and an upper middle class of informal but successful entrepreneurs with lower vulnerability. Education seems to be an important determinant of social mobility toward the middle class. A period of sustained growth accompanied by structural changes that allowed workers to move from agriculture into services and industry, along with important progress in education, offered new opportunities and contributed to the emergence of a new middle class in the 1990s. Patterns of social mobility and movement of educated professionals into the middle class also have been observed (Lentz and Noll 2023).

However, this upward mobility started to sag in the 2000s and, although many individuals managed to escape poverty, most of those in the new middle class have remained vulnerable to shocks. Even within the middle-class population, upward mobility remains constrained by an unequal distribution of opportunities that confine those starting their working life to low-paying and low-skilled occupations, such as urban informal services, and, often, to low earnings during their entire working life. Using a mixed-methods approach and a definition combining income, employment, and education characteristics, Berrou et al. (2018) found that the middle-class population in Côte d'Ivoire represents only 26.4 percent of the total population. However, they showed that it has a dual composition, with an upper stratum (around one-fifth of its composition) representing the "inheritors" of the previous generation of the middle class and a lower stratum (making up around 80 percent) who are "newcomers" characterized by high vulnerability and composed of urban and agricultural informal workers.

In several African cities in Angola, Ethiopia, Kenya, Mozambique, South Africa, and Tanzania, studies have indicated the emergence of an urban middle class among the younger generations. Urbanization has offered young people opportunities for upward mobility in large African cities such as Addis Ababa, Dar es Salaam, Luanda, Maputo, and Nairobi (Gastrow 2020; Mercer 2020; Nielsen and Jenkins 2021; Spronk 2014). Similar trends have been suggested for the younger, urban, Black middle-class population in South Africa (Ndlovu 2020).

This repositioning of the younger generations toward an urban middle class seems to be an aspirational rather than monetary category of belonging and the accompanying lifestyle. However, this process of rapid urbanization highlights the concept of "ideal of urban living," which is limited within the economic realities (Melber 2022). The unfulfilled aspirational desires of this young generation can undermine their idealized urban middle class and highlight the polarization caused by the rapid growth of the urban population. In some cities, the surge in urban population has been accompanied by rising inequality, with large cities being home to both extreme poverty and extreme wealth.

Elite Dynamics

Previous evidence on the persistent barriers to middle-class growth shows high levels of income polarization in African countries, with a concentration of poor people and few very-high-income and wealthy people, usually referred to as the "elite." In chapter 11 of this book (refer to figure 11.3), an African version of Milanovic's famous elephant diagram gives considerable credence to this trend as a stylized fact of the texture of economic growth in Africa over the past few decades. This issue reflects wider arguments that point out how enhanced elite formation is a major force in contemporary societies across the globe (Savage 2021).

A common theme in the Global North literature notes that, although substantial mobility exists in the middle levels of the social structure, it is harder to gain entry to the elite levels (O'Brien 2024; Reeves et al. 2017). These transitions have received far less attention than poverty and middle-class dynamics, although there is good reason to signal their importance. For example, in South Africa, the National Income Dynamics Study survey showed that the incomes at the top of the distribution grew significantly faster than those in the upper middle of the distribution (Zizzamia and Ranchhod 2019). Combined with very low upward mobility from the stable middle class into the elite class, this finding suggests that the elite class is structurally distinct from the middle class.

Evidence from South African tax data provides additional support for this view. Table 8.1, a transition matrix reflecting transitions across personal real-income percentiles between 2011 and 2021, is derived from a panel of real personal incomes produced by merging company tax data with personal income tax data. The table focuses on mobility into and within the top decile. Therefore, the table examines transitions from the bottom nine deciles into the top decile; from the top decile into the bottom nine deciles; and then details transitions within the top decile, including into and out of the top 1 percent and the top 0.01 percent. The table shows that 95 percent of those who were in deciles 1 to 9 in 2011 were still there in 2021. There has been little upward mobility into the top decile and none at all from the lower deciles into the top 1 percent. There has been some downward mobility out of the top decile, but this movement has been especially low for those who were in the top 1 and 0.1 percent groups in 2011.

Table 8.1 South African Personal Income Mobility in the Top Income Groups, 2011 and 2021

Income group in 2011	Income group in 2021 (percent)				
	p0–p90	p90–p99	p99–p99.9	p99.9–p100	Total
p0–p90	95	5	0	0	100
p90–p99	46	49	4	0	100
p99–p99.9	31	34	30	4	100
p99.9–p100	22	21	29	27	100

Source: Jacobs et al. 2024.
Note: p = percentile.

Jacobs et al. (2024) showed that labor market earnings remain the dominant form of income, even in the top decile. However, capital gains, dividends, pensions, and interest income grew in importance to a maximum of 40 percent of total income in the 10th decile, suggesting that the structural discreteness of the elite population and elite dynamics involves labor market dynamics as well as wealth dynamics and their intersections.

The African literature on elite individuals recognizes the importance of wealth, inheritance, and human and social capital in addition to the labor market in understanding social mobility and inequality (Lentz 2015). Even in long-run analyses, historical factors, such as colonization, can explain the emergence and growth of an elite population concentrating high levels of wealth in Africa. For those who study African elite groups, the analytic focus has been on Africans who received a Western education and worked in colonial and post-colonial administrations, as well as on African politicians who held high positions in post-colonial governments (Lentz 2015; Michalopoulos and Papaioannou 2020; Sumich 2018). Colonial institutions, such as indirect rule via local chiefs, and concessionary agreements with private corporations have played an important role in concentrating political and economic power in the hands of a small group (Michalopoulos and Papaioannou 2020).

Institutional and social traits, such as political centralization, also is important. Sumich (2018) argued that, as elite individuals held key positions in political and economic domains of society, they perpetuated inequalities to keep their privilege, hindering opportunities for upward mobility. In Mozambique, the cleavage between the middle class and the elite class increased, as the elite class was able to manage networks to maintain their hold on socioeconomic and political power, in contrast to the poor or vulnerable populations, who fell through the safety net and were unable to escape (Sumich 2018).

Branson et al. (2024) showed how economic, social, and cultural capital combined in South Africa to produce two kinds of elite groups: (1) an inheritor group, which shows high levels of intergenerational persistence, and (2) an upwardly mobile group, which has used credentialed routes to enter elite positions. The elite class is strongly racialized, with White South Africans showing enduring persistence and few prospects of downward mobility, but some upward mobility into elite positions exists, especially for Asian and Coloured South Africans.

Another historical factor is housing ownership. The privatization policies of previously nationalized property in the 1990s are often cited as a pivotal point in the growth of African elites (Resnick 2015; Sumich 2018). Although offering a possibility for the development of the private sector and working middle class, privatization mainly benefited the political elite, with state-owned enterprises sold to ministers and political leaders (Taylor 2012).

Channels of Persistence

Middle-income countries and the most-resource-rich countries have more upward than downward intragenerational mobility. Education is a main determinant of upward mobility toward the upper-middle-class population in Africa (Rougier et al. 2023). Post-secondary education, in particular, is strongly associated with higher upward mobility

(Dang and Dabalen 2019). In several African countries, education and employment can effectively shield households from falling into poverty, while rural and large households are the most likely to slip into poverty (Aikaeli et al. 2021; Mekasha and Tarp 2021; Schotte et al. 2018). For example, in South Africa, those classified as chronically poor live in households of five members on average, which is almost twice the size of middle-class households (Schotte et al. 2018).

Occupation also can explain the persistence of poverty during a person's lifetime. Zizzamia, Schotte, and Ranchhod (2016) found that occupational categories strongly align with social class, with almost all the poor-working population in service and elementary occupations and the elite population in managerial and professional occupations. However, although occupation may be a strong determinant of class for the elite and poor populations, no dominant occupational category exists for the middle class, suggesting that occupation has become less important in determining mobility toward or out of the middle class.

Nonetheless, access to the labor market remains an important determinant of mobility, with 75 percent of the middle-class and elite populations in South Africa in employment, versus only 30.8 percent of the chronic-poor population (Schotte et al. 2018). Households that are resilient to poverty and considered as middle class often have household heads who are formally employed with a permanent contract or union coverage.

Another key determinant of social mobility is geographic location. For example, in South Africa, one-half of the chronic-poor population resided in traditional villages and on communally owned land, and only 17.8 percent of the transient-poor population resided in these areas (Schotte et al. 2018).

In countries such as South Africa, race remains a strong predictor of poverty and a barrier to social mobility, with Black Africans being at the highest risk of falling into poverty (Zizzamia, Schotte, and Ranchhod 2016). The chronically-poor population is almost exclusively comprised of Black Africans, while Whites constitute two in three members of the elite (Schotte et al. 2018).

Overall, most of the findings point to poverty immobility: A large social class vulnerable to falling back into poverty; a thin, stable middle class; and a small elite, which is hard to access. This issue is an important lens on the unfolding livelihoods of Africans over their lifetimes.

Importance of Targeting Social Mobility in Policies That Tackle Inequalities

Recent discussions about the relationship between inequality and mobility have been systematized around the idea of the "Great Gatsby Curve." This idea draws out the association between high levels of income or wealth inequality and intergenerational immobility (Durlauf, Kourtellos, and Tan 2022) and, thus, disputes the argument that social mobility can be a realistic prospect in highly-unequal nations. The Great Gatsby Curve was first used by Alan Kruger, Chairman of the President's Council of Economic Advisors in the United States, when he predicted that the persistence of the advantages and disadvantages of income passed from parents to their children would "rise by about a quarter for the next generation as a result of the rise in inequality that the U.S. has seen in the last 25 years. It is hard to look at these figures and not be concerned that rising inequality is jeopardizing our tradition of equality of opportunity" (Krueger 2012, 4).

The African evidence on intergenerational mobility suggests levels of immobility that are at least as high as those that Alan Kruger was concerned about in the United States and far higher in some countries, such as South Africa. Therefore, all should be extremely concerned about the limitations on opportunities that this issue implies for many African societies. As Kruger emphasized, this issue has negative consequences for stifled growth and development. Although income, earnings, and wealth inequalities in many African countries may not be rising, they are not decreasing, and this persistence is correlated with low mobility and low equalities of opportunity.

The evidence on the drivers of intragenerational mobility draws out the inequality dynamics in African societies that undergird long-run intergenerational metrics. As such, this perspective offers a unique bridge between shorter-run and longer-run policies to overcome inequalities. The mobility literature highlights the imperative to focus policy attention on the structural factors underlying inequalities of opportunity and consequent inequalities in earnings, income, and wealth (Hackl 2018). These factors include formal laws and informal norms that affect both equitable access to quality health care and education as well as the distribution of labor market opportunities, assets, and wealth across generations (for example, laws and norms on inheritance).

Several policies are claimed to affect upward mobility. Research points to education and social protection policies as important for increasing the chances of upward mobility out of poverty (Salvucci and Tarp 2021). These are orthodox policy instruments, but in the mobility context, the evidence shows that improvements in the quality rather than quantity of schooling and health from the earliest years are essential for providing the platform for better employment opportunities and sustainably tackling the intergenerational persistence of inequality (Finn et al. 2017).

Van der Weide et al. (2021) highlighted the importance of targeted public investments, with higher public spending of this sort being strongly associated with higher mobility in education. Azomahou and Yitbarek (2021) also illuminated the importance of targeted redistributive policies for expanding access to quality secondary education to improve mobility.

This chapter's review of mobility within and between chronic and transitory poverty, the vulnerable and stable middle classes, and the elite class emphasizes the same important point. The review clearly distinguishes between policies needed to provide buffering or insurance to protect existing livelihoods and prevent downward absolute mobility within sluggish and unstable economies, alongside policies required to build upward mobility. Both are important, but, as an example, while social grants are important for the survival of chronic-poor individuals, they do not address the structural barriers to sustainable upward mobility (Zizzamia et al. 2019).

For poor individuals, social grants must be complemented with policies that change access to labor markets and ownership of land and other assets or that change the spatial distribution of economic opportunities. Much of the African population is trapped in chronic poverty, and these complementary policies must be put in place to break poverty traps as a means of boosting upward mobility. The low levels of upward mobility across the continent make it clear that this challenging policy mandate will require doing things differently.

The vulnerability approach shows that poverty reduction policies should not only target the existing poor population but also the vulnerable nonpoor population with a high risk of falling into poverty (Mekasha and Tarp 2021). This broad group straddles the poverty line, and many impediments are in the way of upward mobility for this group to move into a stable middle class. This review shows that those individuals below the stable middle class are two-thirds or more of the population in many African societies. Promoting upward mobility for this group requires quality education and health care, along with an array of supportive public and private assets. For example, affordable housing policies can positively impact upward mobility (Visagie, Turok, and Scheba 2020). In addition, upward mobility requires the provision of water; sanitation; passable roads; affordable transport; and safe, functional communities.

This is not a wish list. The stable middle-class and the elite populations rely on these provisions when responding to opportunities or challenges. Certainly, stable middle-class individuals would not be stable without them. Elite individuals can draw on their human and financial capital to buffer themselves through sluggish and even crisis-ridden economies and through shocks such as the COVID-19 pandemic. This ability has given elite individuals far stronger real income growth than even that of stable middle-class individuals. This reality is exponentially true of the top percentiles in the income distribution and, in general, the elite population is a narrow group with weak links to the broader society while accruing up to 50 percent of a country's total income.

Such African societies are not sustainable for the reasons that Alan Kruger alluded to in the United States (Krueger 2012). Modest prospects for mobility in the middle levels of society, especially those facilitated by educational provision, can be more than offset by the pulling away of the elite population and the institutionalization of entrenched privilege, including that originating in colonial experiences (Branson et al. 2024). Therefore, a dynamic, welfare-maximizing argument for carefully designed redistribution of this income is needed to fund the human and physical infrastructure to give most African populations real opportunities for upward mobility.

Notes

1. *Relative mobility* is measured by the extent to which the educational attainment of individuals is independent of their parents' education, using the coefficient from a regression of children's years of education on the parents' education. Higher values indicate greater persistence and thus lower relative mobility (Narayan et al. 2018).

2. The intergenerational elasticity of earnings is measured for young people (ages 21–25) and their parental household head using household survey data.

3. Dang and Dabalen (2018) showed that the coverage of panel data in African countries remains limited. Panel data with national coverage exist in only seven countries in SSA and, where panel data were available, were collected for relatively short periods.

4. Refer to Garcés-Urzainqui, Lanjouw, and Rongen (2021) and Dang and Lanjouw (2023) for a technical introduction to the creation of synthetic panel data. Chapter 2 of this book provides a more in-depth discussion of these data.

5. *Pro-poor growth* is defined as the dynamics most beneficial to the lowest-income, middle-income, and top-income categories. In the most-positive pro-poor growth scenario, both the poor and vulnerable categories decrease while the middle-class category expands.

6. *Vulnerability* is the condition of being at risk of remaining or becoming poor over time.

7. This approach is similar to the modeling of poverty dynamics, except the focus is on the probability of falling into poverty rather than staying in or escaping from poverty.

8. Their approach to defining the middle class combines the definition of the middle class as a socioeconomic category inherited from the sociology of European and American middle classes (Goldthorpe, Llewellyn, and Payne 1980), with an approach of social stratification captured through qualitative and subjective information on those in the middle of the consumption expenditure range.

References

AFDB (African Development Bank). 2011. "The Middle of the Pyramid: Dynamics of the Middle Class in Africa." AFDB Market Brief 20, AFDB, Tunis, Tunisia.

Aikaeli, Jehovaness, David Garcés-Urzainqui, and Kenneth Mdadila. 2021. "Understanding Poverty Dynamics and Vulnerability in Tanzania: 2012–2018." *Review of Development Economics* 25 (4): 1869–94. https://doi.org/10.1111/rode.12829.

Aiyar, Shekhar, and Christian Ebeke. 2020. "Inequality of Opportunity, Inequality of Income and Economic Growth." *World Development* 136: 105115. https://doi.org/10.1016/j.worlddev .2020.105115.

Alesina, Alberto, Sebastian Hohmann, Stelios Michalopoulos, and Elias Papaioannou. 2021. "Intergenerational Mobility in Africa." *Econometrica* 89 (1): 1–35. https://doi.org/10.3982/ECTA17018.

Amdani, Yusuf. 2023. "5 Benefits of a Growing Middle Class." *Forbes Books Author Post* (blog), June 6, 2023. https://www.forbes.com/sites/forbesbooksauthors/people/yusufamdani/?sh=33b279486274.

Atta-Ankomah, Richmond, and Robert Darko Osei. 2021. "Structural Change and Welfare: A Micro Panel Data Evidence from Ghana." *Journal of Development Studies* 57 (11): 1927–44. https://doi.org/10.1080 /00220388.2021.1939864.

Azomahou, Théophile T., and Eleni Yitbarek. 2021. "Intergenerational Mobility in Education: Is Africa Different?" *Contemporary Economic Policy* 39 (3): 503–23. https://doi.org/10.1111/coep.12495.

Berrou, Jean-Philippe, Dominique Darbon, Anne Bekelynck, Christian Bouquet, Matthieu Clément, François Combarnous, and Éric Rougier. 2018. "Le réveil des classes moyennes ivoiriennes? Identification, caractérisation et implications pour les politiques publiques." AFD Research Paper, Agence Française de Développement, Paris. https://doi.org/10.3917/afd.berro .2018.01.0001.

Blanden, Jo, Alissa Goodman, Paul Gregg, and Stephen Machin. 2002. "Changes in Intergenerational Mobility in Britain." Centre for Economic Performance, London School of Economics.

Blau, Peter Michael, Otis Dudley Duncan, and Andrea Tyree. 1967. *The American Occupational Structure*. New York: Wiley.

Branson, Nicola, Johs Hjellbrekke, Murray Leibbrandt, Vimal Ranchhod, Mike Savage, and Emma Whitelaw. 2024. "The Socioeconomic Dimensions of Racial Inequality in South Africa: A Social Space Perspective." *British Journal of Sociology* 74 (4): 613–632. https://doi.org/10.1111/1468-4446.13034.

Brunori, Paolo, Francisco H. G. Ferreira, and Guido Neidhöfer. 2023. *Inequality of Opportunity and Intergenerational Persistence in Latin America*. Washington, DC: Inter-American Development Bank. https://doi.org/10.18235/0005207.

Brunori, Paolo, Flaviana Palmisano, and Vito Peragine. 2016. "Inequality of Opportunity in Sub-Saharan Africa." Policy Research Working Paper 7782, World Bank, Washington, DC. https://documents .worldbank.org/en/publication/documents-reports/documentdetail/522541470317691539 /inequality-of-opportunity-in-sub-saharan-africa.

Bukodi, Erzsébet, and John H. Goldthorpe. 2018. *Social Mobility and Education in Britain: Research, Politics and Policy*. Cambridge, UK: Cambridge University Press. https://doi.org/10.1017/978110 8567404.

Chetty, Raj, David Grusky, Maximilian Hell, Nathaniel Hendren, Robert Manduca, and Jimmy Narang. 2017. "The Fading American Dream: Trends in Absolute Income Mobility since 1940." *Science* 356 (6336): 398–406. https://doi.org/10.1126/science.aal4617.

Chetty, Raj, Nathaniel Hendren, Patrick Kline, Emmanuel Saez, and Nicholas Turner. 2014. "Is the United States Still a Land of Opportunity? Recent Trends in Intergenerational Mobility." *American Economic Review* 104 (5): 141–47. https://doi.org/10.1257/aer.104.5.141.

Corral, Paul, Vasco Molini, and Gbemisola O. Oseni. 2015. "No Condition Is Permanent: Middle Class in Nigeria in the Last Decade." Policy Research Working Paper 7214, World Bank, Washington, DC. https://ideas.repec.org/p/wbk/wbrwps/7214.html.

Dang, Hai-Anh H., and Andrew L. Dabalen. 2018. "Is Poverty in Africa Mostly Chronic or Transient? Evidence from Synthetic Panel Data." *Journal of Development Studies* 55 (7): 1527–47. https://doi.org/10 .1080/00220388.2017.1417585.

Dang, Hai-Anh H., and Peter F. Lanjouw. 2023. Measuring Poverty Dynamics with Synthetic Panels Based on Repeated Cross Sections. *Oxford Bulletin of Economics and Statistics* 85 (3): 599–622.

Durlauf, Steven N., Andros Kourtellos, and Chih Ming Tan. 2022. "The Great Gatsby Curve." *Annual Review of Economics* 14 (1): 571–605. https://doi.org/10.1146/annurev-economics-082321-122703.

Erikson, Robert, and John Harry Goldthorpe. 1992. *The Constant Flux: A Study of Class Mobility in Industrial Societies*. Oxford, UK: Clarendon Press.

Finn, Arden, Murray Leibbrandt, and Vimal Ranchhod. 2017. "Patterns of Persistence: Intergenerational Mobility and Education in South Africa." SALDRU Working Paper 175, Southern Africa Labour and Development Research Unit, University of Cape Town, South Africa.

Funjika, Patricia, and Yoseph Y. Getachew. 2022. "Colonial Origin, Ethnicity and Intergenerational Mobility in Africa." *World Development* 153: 105841. https://doi.org/10.1016/j.worlddev.2022.105841.

Garcés-Urzainqui, David, Peter Lanjouw, and Gerton Rongen. 2021. "Constructing Synthetic Panels for the Purpose of Studying Poverty Dynamics: A Primer." *Review of Development Economics* 25 (4): 1803–15. https://doi.org/10.1111/rode.12832.

Gastrow, Claudia. 2020. "Housing Middle-Classness: Formality and the Making of Distinction in Luanda." *Africa* 90 (3): 509–28. https://doi.org/10.1017/S0001972020000054.

Giesbert, Lena, and Simone Schotte. 2016. "Africa's New Middle Class: Fact and Fiction of Its Transformative Power." *GIGA Focus Africa*. Mannheim, Germany: Infrastructure and Research for Social Sciences.

Goldthorpe, John H., Catriona Llewellyn, and Clive Payne. 1980. *Social Mobility and Class Structure in Modern Britain*. Oxford, UK: Clarendon Press.

Hackl, Andreas. 2018. "Mobility Equity in a Globalized World: Reducing Inequalities in the Sustainable Development Agenda." *World Development* 112: 150–62. https://doi.org/10.1016/j.worlddev.2018.08.005.

Heath, Anthony F., and Silke L. Schneider. 2021. "Dimensions of Migrant Integration in Western Europe." *Frontiers in Sociology* 6: 510987. https://doi.org/10.3389/fsoc.2021.510987.

Himanshu, and Peter Lanjouw. 2021. "Income Mobility in the Developing World: Recent Approaches and Evidence." In *Social Mobility in Developing Countries: Concepts, Methods, and Determinants*, edited by Vegard Iversen, Anirudh Krishna, and Kunal Sen, 115–38. Oxford, UK: Oxford University Press. https://doi.org/10.1093/oso/9780192896858.003.0006.

Iversen, Vegard, Anirudh Krishna, and Kunal Sen. 2021. *Social Mobility in Developing Countries*. Oxford, UK: Oxford University Press. https://global.oup.com/academic/product/social-mobility-in-developing-countries-9780192896858?prevNumResPerPage=20&prevSortField=1&sortField=8&resultsPerPage=20&start=0&lang=en&cc=gb.

Jacobs, Chandré, Amina Ebrahim, Murray Leibbrandt, Jukka Pirttilä, and Marlies Piek. 2024. "Income Inequality in South Africa: Evidence from Individual-Level Administrative Tax Data." UNU-WIDER Working Paper, United Nations University, World Institute for Development Economics Research, Helsinki, Finland.

Krueger, Alan B. 2012. "The Rise and Consequences of Inequality in the United States." Speech at the Center for American Progress, January 12, Washington, DC.

Lanjouw, Peter F., and Finn Tarp. 2021. "Poverty, Vulnerability and Covid-19: Introduction and Overview." *Review of Development Economics* 25 (4): 1797–1802. https://doi.org/10.1111/rode.12844.

Lentz, Carola. 2015. "Elites or Middle Classes? Lessons from Transnational Research for the Study of Social Stratification in Africa." Working Paper 161, Department of Anthropology and African Studies, Johannes Gutenberg University, Mainz, Germany.

Lentz, Carola, and Andrea Noll. 2023. "Across Regional Disparities and beyond Family Ties: A Ghanaian Middle Class in the Making." *History and Anthropology* 34 (3): 455–72. https://doi.org/10.1080/02757206.2021.1885400.

López-Calva, Luis F., and Eduardo Ortiz-Juarez. 2014. "A Vulnerability Approach to the Definition of the Middle Class." *Journal of Economic Inequality* 12 (1): 23–47. https://doi.org/10.1007/s10888-012-9240-5.

Major, Lee Elliot, and Stephen Machin. 2018. *Social Mobility and Its Enemies*. London: Pelican.

Mekasha, Tseday Jemaneh, and Finn Tarp. 2021. "Understanding Poverty Dynamics in Ethiopia: Implications for the Likely Impact of COVID-19." *Review of Development Economics* 25 (4): 1838–68. https://doi.org/10.1111/rode.12841.

Melber, Henning. 2022. "Africa's Middle Classes." *Africa Spectrum* 57 (2): 204–19. https://doi.org/10.1177/00020397221089352.

Mercer, Claire. 2020. "Boundary Work: Becoming Middle Class in Suburban Dar es Salaam." *International Journal of Urban and Regional Research* 44 (3): 521–36. https://doi.org/10.1111/1468-2427.12733.

Michalopoulos, Stelios, and Elias Papaioannou. 2020. "Historical Legacies and African Development." *Journal of Economic Literature* 58 (1): 53–128. https://doi.org/10.1257/jel.20181447.

Mijs, Jonathan J. B. 2021. "The Paradox of Inequality: Income Inequality and Belief in Meritocracy Go Hand in Hand." *Socio-Economic Review* 19 (1): 7–35. https://doi.org/10.1093/ser/mwy051.

Narayan, Ambar, Roy Van der Weide, Alexandru Cojocaru, Christoph Lakner, Silvia Redaelli, Daniel Gerszon Mahler, Rakesh Gupta N. Ramasubbaiah, and Stefan Thewissen. 2018. *Fair Progress? Economic Mobility across Generations around the World*. Washington, DC: World Bank. https://doi.org/10.1596/978-1-4648-1210-1.

Ndlovu, Thabisani. 2020. "Shuttling between the Suburbs and the Township: The New Black Middle Class(es) Negotiating Class and Post-Apartheid Blackness in South Africa." *Africa* 90 (3): 568–86. https://doi.org/10.1017/S000197202000008X.

Němečková, Tereza, Jaromír Harmáček, and Martin Schlossarek. 2020. "Measuring the Middle Class in Africa—Income Versus Assets Approach." *Africa Spectrum* 55 (1): 3–32. https://doi.org/10.1177/0002039720916087.

Nielsen, Morten, and Paul Jenkins. 2021. "Insurgent Aspirations? Weak Middle-Class Utopias in Maputo, Mozambique." *Critical African Studies* 13 (2): 162–82. https://doi.org/10.1080/21681392.2020.1743190.

O'Brien, Shay. 2024. "The Family Web: Multigenerational Class Persistence in Elite Populations." *Socio-Economic Review* 22 (1): 1–27. https://doi.org/10.1093/ser/mwad033.

Ouedraogo, Rasmane, and Nicolas Syrichas. 2021. "Intergenerational Social Mobility in Africa Since 1920." IMF Working Paper 2021/15, International Monetary Fund, Washington, DC.

Piraino, Patrizio. 2015. "Intergenerational Earnings Mobility and Equality of Opportunity in South Africa." *World Development* 67: 396–405. https://doi.org/10.1016/j.worlddev.2014.10.027.

Razzu, Giovanni, and Ayago Wambile. 2022. "Four Decades of Intergenerational Educational Mobility in Sub-Saharan Africa." *Journal of Development Studies* 58 (5): 931–50. https://doi.org/10.1080/00220388.2021.2008366.

Reeves, Aaron, Sam Friedman, Charles Rahal, and Magne Flemmen. 2017. "The Decline and Persistence of the Old Boy: Private Schools and Elite Recruitment 1897 to 2016." *American Sociological Review* 82 (6): 1139–66. https://doi.org/10.1177/0003122417735742.

Resnick, Danielle. 2015. "The Political Economy of Africa's Emergent Middle Class: Retrospect and Prospects." *Journal of International Development* 27 (5): 573–87. https://doi.org/10.1002/jid.3110.

Rougier, Eric, Matthieu Clément, François Combarnous, Robert Darko Osei, and Stephen Arfanie. 2023. "'Multiple, Polarized, and Vulnerable': A Socio-Economic Exploration of Ghana's Middle Class." AFD Research Paper 287, Agence Française de Développement, Paris. https://www.afd.fr/en/ressources/multiple-polarized-and-vulnerable-socio-economic-exploration-ghanas-middle-class.

Salvucci, Vincenzo, and Finn Tarp. 2021. "Poverty and Vulnerability in Mozambique: An Analysis of Dynamics and Correlates in Light of the Covid-19 Crisis Using Synthetic Panels." *Review of Development Economics* 25 (4): 1895–1918. https://doi.org/10.1111/rode.12835.

Savage, Michael. 2021. *The Return of Inequality: Social Change and the Weight of the Past*. Cambridge, MA: Harvard University Press.

Schotte, Simone, Rocco Zizzamia, and Murray Leibbrandt. 2018. "A Poverty Dynamics Approach to Social Stratification: The South African Case." *World Development* 110: 88–103. https://doi.org/10.1016/j.worlddev.2018.05.024.

Schotte, Simone, Rocco Zizzamia, and Murray Leibbrandt. 2022. "Snakes and Ladders and Loaded Dice: Poverty Dynamics and Inequality in South Africa between 2008 and 2017." *South African Journal of Economics* 90 (2): 214–42. https://doi.org/10.1111/saje.12308.

Shimeles, Abebe, and Mthuli Ncube. 2015. "The Making of the Middle-Class in Africa: Evidence from DHS Data." *Journal of Development Studies* 51 (2): 178–93. https://doi.org/10.1080/00220388.2014.968137.

Spronk, Rachel. 2014. "Exploring the Middle Classes in Nairobi: From Modes of Production to Modes of Sophistication." *African Studies Review* 57 (1): 93–114. https://doi.org/10.1017/asr.2014.7.

Sumich, Jason. 2018. *The Middle Class in Mozambique: The State and the Politics of Transformation in Southern Africa.* Cambridge, UK: Cambridge University Press. https://doi.org/10.1017/9781108659659.

Taylor, Scott D. 2012. *Globalization and the Cultures of Business in Africa: From Patrimonialism to Profit.* Bloomington: Indiana University Press.

Thurlow, James, Danielle Resnick, and Dumebi Ubogu. 2015. "Matching Concepts with Measurement: Who Belongs to Africa's Middle Class?" *Journal of International Development* 27 (5): 588–608. https://doi.org/10.1002/jid.3105.

Van De Werfhorst, Herman G., and Anthony Heath. 2019. "Selectivity of Migration and the Educational Disadvantages of Second-Generation Immigrants in Ten Host Societies." *European Journal of Population* 35 (2): 347–78. https://doi.org/10.1007/s10680-018-9484-2.

Van der Weide, Roy, Christoph Lakner, Daniel Gerszon Mahler, Ambar Narayan, and Rakesh Ramasubbaiah. 2021. "Intergenerational Mobility around the World." Policy Research Working Paper 9707, World Bank, Washington, DC. https://www.ssrn.com/abstract=3981372.

Visagie, Justin, and Dorrit Posel. 2013. "A Reconsideration of What and Who Is Middle Class in South Africa." *Development Southern Africa* 30 (2): 149–67. https://doi.org/10.1080/0376835X.2013.797224.

Visagie, Justin, Ivan Turok, and Andreas Scheba. 2020. "Social Housing and Upward Mobility in South Africa." AFD Research Paper 191, Agence Française de Développement, Paris.

World Bank. 2022. *Inequality in Southern Africa: An Assessment of the Southern African Customs Union.* Washington, DC: World Bank. https://doi.org/10.1596/37283.

Zizzamia, Rocco, and Vimal Ranchhod. 2019. "Measuring Employment Volatility in South Africa Using NIDS: 2008–2017." SALDRU Working Paper 246, NIDS Discussion Paper, Southern Africa Labour and Development Research Unit, University of Cape Town, South Africa.

Zizzamia, Rocco, Simone Schotte, Murray Leibbrandt, and UNU-WIDER. 2019. "Snakes and Ladders and Loaded Dice: Poverty Dynamics and Inequality in South Africa, 2008–2017." UNU-WIDER Working Paper 235, United Nations University, World Institute for Development Economics Research, Helsinki, Finland. https://doi.org/10.35188/UNU-WIDER/2019/659-3.

Zizzamia, Rocco, Simone Schotte, and Vimal Ranchhod. 2016. "Vulnerability and the Middle Class in South Africa." SALDRU Working Paper 188, Southern Africa Labour and Development Research Unit, University of Cape Town, South Africa.

Chapter 9

Policies to Tackle Inequality in Africa

Fabio Andrés Díaz Pabón, Annalena Oppel, Murray Leibbrandt, Mike Savage, and Anda David

Introduction

Whether in the words of John Schmitt (Schmitt 2009), Alan Krueger (Krueger 2012), Oxfam (Lawson and Martin 2017), or the World Bank and International Monetary Fund (IMF; Mohieldin and Sanchez-Paramo 2019), there is agreement that inequality is a policy choice. The urgency of the challenges of inequality and the need to tackle them require no underscoring here. Indeed, it is difficult to address inequalities because of the multiple axes on which they operate, ranging over the material dimensions of life—income, wealth, access, and opportunities—and extending to experiential, cultural, and symbolic aspects, which can generate powerful forms of stigmatization, marginalization, and exclusion (Savage 2021; Therborn 2013; Tyler 2020).

Thus, in addition to asking about inequality of *what*, it is important to understand inequality among *whom* (Stewart 2004). The mechanisms driving inequalities, which allocate opportunities and rewards and bring different outcomes for different individuals within the same society, overlap and operate via tangible and intangible ways and visible and less-visible markers that vary across place and time. Despite their specific inequality lenses, each of the preceding chapters flagged these intersections whereby, for example, the level and quality of education can make a huge difference in employment and earnings, but even for people who share the same level and quality of education, these outcomes can differ by gender, location, or access to social networks.

This situation challenges any "magic-bullet" or "single-binding-constraint" approach claiming that a specific policy intervention, however bold, can be expected to tackle the full range of inequalities. In particular, strategies designed to tackle unequal distributions of resources are needed, as well as those for norms and cultural values (Lamont et al. 2016; Tilly 2009). In addition, Africa has 54 countries, and this book shows that they exhibit substantial variation. Therefore, impactful policies must be grounded in the distinctive mechanisms at work in each context.

However, commonalities in inequality exist across countries in Africa. An important example is that it is not the case that high levels of poverty on the continent mean that inequality is not an issue or that "Africa is too poor to be unequal." All African contexts are unequal, and understanding and addressing these inequalities is central to any sustainable and inclusive development policy. For example, chapter 11 shows that economic growth is directly hampered by inequalities in almost all African contexts, and these inequalities can dampen the impacts of growth on poverty reduction in Africa relative to elsewhere in the world.

Multiple pressures from demographic shifts, economic turmoil, and the prospect of climate breakdown bring a sense of urgency to understanding how different policies can address inequalities, including the pressures created on peoples' livelihoods by these systemic shocks. Recently, the COVID-19 pandemic and the shocks associated with increasing interest rates, food prices, and inflation have highlighted the vulnerabilities of African economies and their citizens to ongoing crises. Also, the risk of external shocks and their effects on people's livelihoods remain, as illustrated by the impacts of droughts in driving famine and poverty and deepening preexisting inequalities in Eastern Africa. The worsening of well-being can fuel instability and lead to tensions and the emergence of or support for a political economy of war and armed conflict (such as in the Central African Republic, Mali, and Mozambique) (UNDP 2023). Many African countries are severely fiscally constrained in dealing with these shocks. Of the world's 39 Heavily Indebted Poor Countries, 34 are in Africa.

Thus, addressing inequalities in every African context through impactful policies is needed. The multidimensional and intersecting nature of inequalities makes crafting these policies daunting. Yet, the policy responses to the COVID-19 pandemic made it clear that it is possible to think innovatively. The declarations of national disasters have enabled creative improvisations and elaborations of existing policies. Attaching these policies to existing programs and schemes was necessary in the moment, but it did not address their weaknesses in design and coverage. Instead, such emergency responses opened the window of opportunity to fashion new policy proposals and adaptive policy systems that can more adequately respond to crises.

There is a momentum of institutional learning about what works, what does not, and under which circumstances in tackling inequality. Consolidating this learning is the task of this chapter.

Atkinson's (2015) framework for thinking inside and outside the box is useful for presenting a clear typology of policies to reduce inequality. He focused on incomes and the three elements that constitute them: wages, capital, and subsidies or state transfers (refer to figure 9.1). Broadly, Atkinson classified whether policies fall inside or outside a conventional policy box based on how they aim to reduce income inequalities.

Policies that change incomes directly (via direct changes in wages or through social transfers or taxes) can be understood as policies "inside the box" of conventional economic policy-making. A wealth of international evidence supports the framing of these policies in any context. Atkinson considered policies aimed at changing the social relations that condition incomes, but that leave existing social structures in place, "outside the box." For example, strengthening the protection of unions changes the relationship between workers and employers, which can impact wages and the distribution of income between labor and capital. Competition policy can also influence this relationship as well as output prices. Hence, outside-the-box policies have a more-indirect effect on incomes by shaping how they are produced in a capitalist economy. Outside-the-box proposals include those that influence technological change and its impacts on labor and capital, public employment programs, the strengthened role of unions and guilds, competition policies that shape how input and output markets work, and the possibilities for a guaranteed minimum income for all individuals or a more-targeted endowment payable to young people as they move from adolescence into further training or employment (Atkinson 2015).

Figure 9.1 Policies That Are Inside, Outside, and Beyond the Box

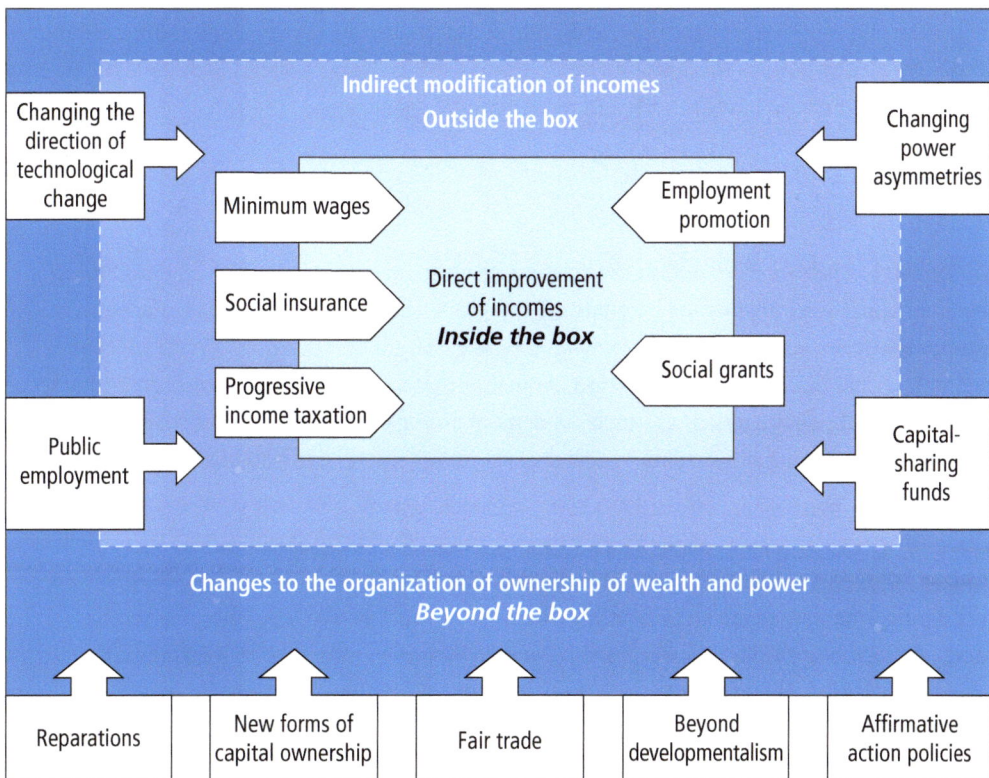

Source: Original figure for this book, based on Atkinson 2015.

This is a useful organizing framework, and most of this chapter discusses options that are inside or outside the box. However, this framework is built from a developed, Global North perspective and makes assumptions, such as about the power of trade unions, the dominance of formal employment, and high levels of state capacity, which might not apply everywhere— or indeed anywhere—in Africa. In addition, it is crucial to recognize the long-term historical forces of colonialism, which have shaped economies and generated inequalities.

These forces continue to shape the structures of African economies and the restrictions on their inclusion in the globalizing world today. They cannot be wished away or defined as beyond the scope of contemporary policies to confront African inequalities. Policies that pay more attention to wealth inequalities and these long-term historical forces are needed to overcome structural legacies (Savage 2021). Because social structures and social relations drive existing inequalities, thinking boldly about how they can be changed is needed. This chapter discusses policies implemented on the continent that are directed at shifting the direction of historical inequalities in Africa under the outside-the-box banner, although they push beyond the boundaries of Atkinson's framework.

The chapter begins with inside-the-box policies, then examines outside-the-box policies, reflecting on their broader economic and political rationales, and concludes by summarizing and highlighting policies that push further beyond the box. These policies include some aspects that are yet to be adequately reflected in most national agendas.

Inside-the-Box Policies

Inside-the-box policies work within the existing structure of an economy, directly modifying incomes and, therefore, income inequality. Examples include the promotion of employment, minimum wages, social insurance, social grants, and tax policy. Such policies can affect an individual's net income in a given period. Arguably, these are the most-common components of a conventional policy agenda, and their implementation globally and within Africa has a long history. The following subsections review these types of policies and note their challenges in the African context.

Labor Market Policies

For a long time in the mainstream policy discourse, it was asserted that labor market deregulation always leads to lower unemployment. However, more and more studies have shown that this is seldom the case in either Northern or Southern contexts (Brancaccio, Garbellini, and Giammetti 2018; Ernst, Merola, and Reljic 2022). Among the labor market policies that countries have at their disposal, the minimum wage is perhaps the most widely used. Of the 54 African countries, 40 have a minimum wage in place, although the level varies widely (refer to map 9.1).

Map 9.1 Minimum Wages in African Countries, 2022

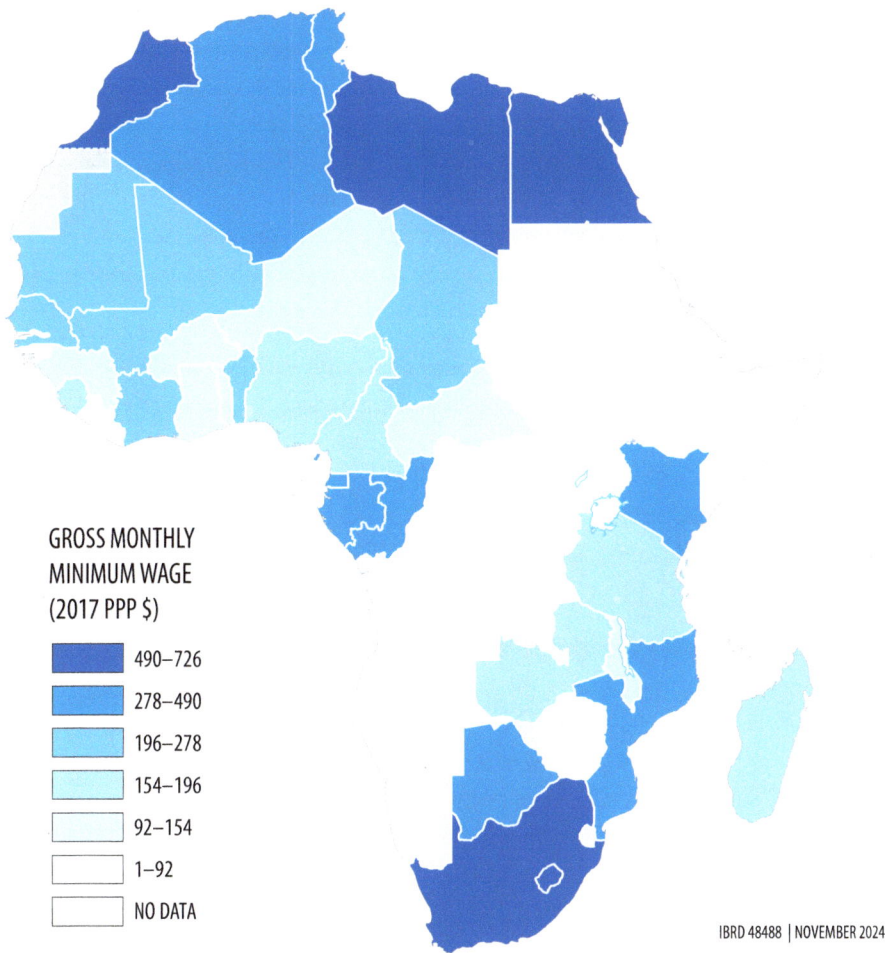

GROSS MONTHLY
MINIMUM WAGE
(2017 PPP $)

- 490–726
- 278–490
- 196–278
- 154–196
- 92–154
- 1–92
- NO DATA

IBRD 48488 | NOVEMBER 2024

Source: Original map for this book, using data from the International Labour Organization.
Note: The map shows the statutory nominal gross monthly minimum wage (in 2017 PPP US dollars).
PPP = purchasing power parity.

In a study on minimum wages in Sub-Saharan Africa (SSA), Bhorat, Kanbur, and Stanwix (2017) showed that higher levels of the minimum wage are positively linked to higher levels of gross domestic product per capita when the minimum wage is set significantly lower than average wages. The level of the minimum wage is, therefore, always a consideration. So, too, is compliance with the minimum wage. An International Labour Organization study on select African countries showed that significant shares of wage employees are paid below 80 percent of the minimum wage and pointed to the prevalence of the informal sector as one determinant of low compliance (ILO 2019).

Collective bargaining also can have a significant impact on wage disparities and, thus, on inequalities. In Africa, 48 countries have ratified the Freedom of Association and Protection of the Right to Organize Convention of 1948, yet only 19 countries have ratified the Labor Inspection Conventions or the Employment Policy Convention of 1964 (ILO 2023). Overall, on issues of occupational safety and health, migration, human resources development, and policies targeted at supporting Indigenous people, the degree of ratification is mostly absent. A study on collective bargaining agreements in 12 developing countries, of which 8 are in Africa, found large variations in clauses, which usually are weak on issues such as social security and maternity leave (Besamusca and Tijdens 2015). Again, this is correlated with informality, and Lapeyre and Barussaud (2019) showed that the density of trade unions in informal employment is less than half that observed in formal employment. This issue highlights the need for expansion of labor rights to informal workers on the continent.

Beyond institutions, active labor market policies (ALMPs), such as employment incentives, trainings, and public employment programs, also can reduce inequality by enabling vulnerable individuals to participate in the labor market. McKenzie (2017) and Lam and Elsayed (2021) conducted thorough reviews of ALMP evaluations in the Global South, and both concluded that, on their own, these policies have a poor track record, with little significant impact on earnings or even employment. However, some have succeeded, and both papers drew lessons from these cases.

Policies that address labor market failures related to location are important. In South Africa, for example, the high cost of transportation has been identified as a key obstacle to job search and employment (Kerr 2017; Loewald, Makrelov, and Wörgötter 2021). Appropriate policies include subsidizing transport or job search. In South Africa, too, is emerging evidence that cash transfer and public employment programs are facilitating transitions into work. Indeed, while many of the evaluations of ALMPs pre-date 2020, these interventions have seen significant expansion in response to the COVID-19 pandemic (Gentilini et al. 2021), and further investigations are needed.

Given the underwhelming performance of many conventional ALMPs when implemented on their own, experimenting with bolder initiatives, for example, around guaranteed public employment policies, is needed. Atkinson and Bourguignon (2015, 140) proposed to "[...] adopt an explicit target for preventing and reducing unemployment [...] by offering guaranteed public employment at the minimum wage to those who seek it." There is no guaranteed public employment in Africa. Nonetheless, there is some promising evidence from large-scale public employment interventions.

For example, a large South African public employment program, the Presidential Employment Stimulus, was launched in response to the COVID-19 pandemic in October 2020. A recent evaluation of the program noted that it directly created 1.8 million temporary jobs from its launch through December 2023 (Bassier and Budlender 2024). Those employed were paid the national minimum wage, and the evaluation showed that the Presidential Employment Stimulus's largest program, the Basic Education Employment Initiative, had significant, positive indirect effects on community retailers.

According to the World Bank, unemployment in SSA is less than 7 percent (World Bank 2023b). South Africa is an obvious exception, with unemployment levels of around 30 percent. However, it could be claimed that, outside Southern Africa and North Africa, the continent does not have an unemployment problem but rather a problem of precarious and informal employment. Nonetheless, public employment programs have been implemented across Africa to build a pipeline between the formal and informal sectors and improve the conditions of informal employment. At present, 27 labor market or employment programs are listed for the continent, including job training, economic inclusion programs, and public work programs (socialprotection.org 2023). There also are 19 public work programs, including cash and in-kind benefits for work.

One prominent example is the Productive Safety Net Program (PSNP), launched in 2005 in Ethiopia. The program's fourth round was implemented in July 2015 for a 5-year period, at a total cost of GBP 2.216 billion, funded by the Ethiopian government (14 percent) and nine donors (DFID 2016). The scale of these programs raises earlier considerations of sufficient domestic revenue for national financing capacities. After its implementation, the PSNP was said to increase the number of beneficiaries to 10 million in 2015, reaching about 18 percent of Ethiopia's working-age population. The program also provided the beneficiary list for piloting new social protection measures to reduce poverty and inequality.

Social Expenditure Policies

For social expenditures, cash transfers are a popular tool used for reducing poverty in Africa. Of the 70 social transfer programs listed in Africa, a majority (57 percent) are unconditional cash transfers (socialprotection.org 2023), because the implementation of such policies tends to be more straightforward than structural reforms. More recently, because of their reach (and expansion) and existing targeting, social grants have become an important mechanism to alleviate the impact of the COVID-19 pandemic, as illustrated in South Africa (Bassier et al. 2021).

Cash transfers can be a crucial tool for establishing universal social protection in African countries and have been shown to reduce or ameliorate poverty. During the COVID-19 pandemic, many crisis-induced social transfer programs used existing schemes through vertical and horizontal expansions. According to the United Nations (UN) COVID-19 Stimulus Tracker, 35 African countries implemented cash transfers or other income support as social assistance measures, followed by 26 countries that implemented in-kind transfers and vouchers as well. This issue highlights governments' capacity to respond to crises when needed, and, although vulnerable groups were left out, the cash transfers reached many people who were in need.

Particularly for targeted policies, comprehensive social registries are a vital component. These registries serve a key purpose in outreach, intake, registration, and determination of the individuals and households eligible for social programs (Leite et al. 2017). This issue again raises the challenge of including and reaching informal workers, who often are missing from such registers. Although social registries expanded significantly between 2020 and 2022, the percentage of the total population covered by at least one social protection benefit in 2020 was only 17.4 percent of the continent's population (ILO 2021). Thus, systematic gaps exist in accounting for the most-vulnerable groups in the population, including informal workers.

Doubts also remain about the effectiveness of social protection benefits in reducing inequalities, with cash transfers often designed with poverty alleviation rather than inequality reduction in mind. The latter requires explicit recognition of the links between social protection policies and labor market policies and the need to harmonize both. Many African countries have no unemployment insurance schemes. The predominance of informal employment and difficult transitions into employment for labor market entrants make it difficult to design self-financing and sustainable unemployment insurance schemes.

Tax Policies

Taxation has long been promoted for financing public expenditures through domestic revenue (Modica, Laudage, and Harding 2018; Oppel, McNabb, and Chachu 2022). Tax policy is also a central component of the distributive role of the state. However, in Africa, many tax systems have not been designed to be progressive and with a focus on reducing inequality (McNabb and Oppel 2023). Even when the tax systems are designed to achieve these ends, institutional capacity is required for efficient tax collection and, particularly, to counter tax nonpayment and avoidance and ensure that income taxation systems that are designed to be progressive are progressive in practice.

Thus, taxation is central for financing inside-the-box policies. Such policies can modify disposable incomes for individuals, for example, through financing social insurance and social grants, or design tax breaks, exemptions, and allowances. Yet, the design of such policies requires understanding the capacities and weaknesses of current governments' abilities to rely on a diversified stream of domestic revenue. Revenues may come from the extraction of mineral resources; service industries, including emerging models such as Uber; or the financial services economy, including newer developments such as crypto currencies.

Fiscal space, or the amount of resources available for progressive policies inside the box, is determined by the tax revenue streams and also by the tax base. In several African countries, the income tax base remains limited, leaning mostly on the formal sector.

Moreover, indirect taxation, which is almost always regressive, remains dominant (Lustig, Jellema, and Martinez Pabon 2019). Often in countries with highly informal economies, there is a dependency on the taxation of natural resources for the generation of public revenues (Devarajan and Do 2023; Shaxson 2007; Siakwah 2017). In addition, tax rates can be limited by international competition. For example, higher corporate tax rates can result in disincentives for foreign direct investment. Overall, limited fiscal space reduces states' capacity for taxation and redistribution.

Tax policies were important during the recent COVID-19 crisis, primarily for crisis relief, including for businesses. For example, during 2020, according to the UN COVID-19 Stimulus Tracker, 37 countries in Africa introduced tax exemptions, reductions, or measures for small and medium-size enterprises and other businesses to ease economic contractions and prevent layoffs. In South Africa, Köhler, Bhorat, and Hill (2023) showed that the rapidly implemented Temporary Employer/Employee Relief Scheme increased the probability of remaining employed in the short term by 15.6 percentage points, thereby arguably saving or at least buffering 2.7 million jobs. The policy involved companies applying for tax relief on behalf of their workers through the mandatory unemployment insurance payment system that was in place.

This scheme is an impressive example of the flexible use of existing policies. However, it excluded workers hired informally within formal firms, for example, through labor brokers. Even among eligible workers, the effects were marginally regressive across the earnings distribution. Alongside corporate taxation, other measures included price controls for essential goods and waivers of customs duties for businesses.

These and other measures highlight a window of opportunity for policy innovation. While some of the measures are primarily geared toward dealing with a crisis, they might create a pathway for more long-lasting changes or renegotiations, for example, in the area of trade agreements.

Clearly, inside-the-box policies have their place—and an important one. These policies define lower bounds for protecting those on the bottom rungs of the income distribution. However, although temporary employment and relief from hunger and poverty are crucial, they do not systematically reduce vulnerability and instability. Concerns about precariousness are not exclusive to Africa or the Global South. Indeed, the Global North is grappling with many of the same issues, and it was such grappling that prompted Atkinson (2015) to argue for policies that lie outside the conventional policy toolkit box as essential complements in tackling inequality.

Outside-the-Box Policies

Outside-the-box policies aim to modify the workings of national economies to bring about systemic change in income flows (Atkinson and Bourguignon 2015). These policies focus on technological change, guaranteed public employment, countervailing power asymmetries between employers and employees due to market power in factor and product markets, capital-sharing funds, and citizens' incomes. The policies also have a common focus on shifting the rewards derived from capital and labor. Such considerations are relevant for Africa.

However, a persistent challenge and key difference in the African context is the high degree of economic informality. At present, informality amounts to 83 percent of the workforce in Africa (ILO 2022). The COVID-19 pandemic illuminated the economic volatility, precariousness, uncertainty, and hardship that informal workers face. Furthermore, in many cases, formal employees have fallen into informality due to economic contractions.

Although informality is continuously discussed in policy-making in Africa, the effects of the COVID-19 crisis brought the informal sector to the forefront of policy dialogues and debates (David, Diallo, and Nilsson 2023). The discussion included exploring new pathways for generating better integration of informal workers into systems of formal social protection, which is vital for protecting the well-being of informal workers in the face of economic shocks. More broadly, the conversation has highlighted the importance of creating avenues for enabling pathways from the informal sector into more-secure work and living conditions. Such a discussion is long overdue.

However, it is important to ensure that a problem-based focus on informality per se does not crowd out broader policy engagement on alternative modes of inclusive economic structures and practices for African economies within the contemporary global economy. For example, the issue of informality should not be isolated from discussions of industrial restructuring or export policies. Grappling with these issues at scale can give rise to new and innovative modes of economic organization. Within such a framing, informality may also present an outside-the-box field of opportunities from which to learn, for example, for green growth agendas (Amis 2016).

Policy interventions must respond to new technologies that affect the distribution of employment and earnings. Atkinson argued that the direction of technological change is not exogenously given; it needs to be and can be shaped through national policies that encourage innovation in a form that increases the employability of local workers and emphasizes the human dimensions of service provision (Atkinson and Bourguignon 2015). From the outset, such an approach focuses explicitly on the workers, who must be included in the growth process (Atkinson and Bourguignon 2015). To support this policy framing, understanding the processes of technological innovation is essential. It is not only the usage of technology but also the production, ownership, and regulation of technology that must be tackled.

The use of mobile applications to transfer money is an important African example. More than 50 percent of the population of Africa resides in rural areas (World Bank 2023a). Until the past decade, this population was largely disconnected from financial offices. The established financial systems have not accommodated informal urban populations either. These are consequential financial market failures.

The introduction of M-Pesa, a system that allows payments and transfers between individuals using mobile phones, has been an important innovation. M-Pesa operates in Afghanistan, the Democratic Republic of Congo, the Arab Republic of Egypt, Ethiopia, Ghana, Kenya, Mozambique, South Africa, and Tanzania. In Kenya alone, M-Pesa had a cash flow of around KSh 15 billion (approximately US$149 million) in 2015 (Payments Industry Intelligence 2016).

A body of evidence shows that M-Pesa has been breaking the credit constraints confronting many people not served by the existing formal, noncompetitive private and public financial institutions.

This new technology has creatively disrupted old, noninclusive markets, leading to many positive development outcomes (Dupas and Robinson 2013; Jack and Suri 2014; Suri and Jack 2016).

However, M-Pesa has also resulted in new inequalities in access (Van Hove and Dubus 2019) and could be much more effective than it has been. Change requires confronting underlying corporate structures, including the ownership of such platforms, as well as current tax systems. For example, understanding where the corporations' operating apps in Africa have their headquarters and where they pay their taxes is needed to assess their role in supporting or undermining innovation driven by Indigenous need. There is always the danger that regulation of mobile platforms is shaped in a way that brokers new forms of collusion between international business and local political elites. Further research on the ownership, structure, and organization of such companies internationally and at the country level in Africa can provide insight into how such technological developments influence inequalities, in this case, at the important intersection of financial markets.

There is a need to reflect not only on the role of technology in incomes but also on how mobile platforms affect working conditions. For example, the experience of Uber workers is precarious: Employees are uninsured and do not have guaranteed minimum wages, and unions are weak or absent. Furthermore, the power in the relationship is characterized by a direct employer-employee link that is somewhat obscured due to minimum engagement via mobile applications that tend to prioritize a consumer focus over employees' right to decent work (Anwar and Graham 2021). Again, this issue is not solely an African phenomenon—all countries are trying to manage how to regulate such platforms. This reality does not take away from the fact that such casualization intersects differently with the broad range of African regulatory frameworks for labor. Each country must engage with these issues.

Policy and regulation associated with new technologies usually emerge in a reactive manner. For example, regulation associated with the locomotive—which was invented early in the 19th century—was passed only in 1860. The lag between the rollout of technologies and their regulation continues to apply in the 21st century. For example, Uber began to operate in Africa in 2013, but the first memorandum of understanding between Uber and an African government took place in 2016 (United Nations 2017). It is important to reflect on how states can learn and adapt faster, proactively if possible, to the rollout of technologies, to guide technological developments to ensure they support inclusive economic development.

This issue has bearing on the significant policy debate around the role of the Fourth Industrial Revolution in Africa (Signé and Ndung'u 2020). Technological advancement presents possibilities for economic growth on the continent. However, it is important to reiterate Atkinson's (2015) insistence on creating policy space to reflect on the directions in which these changes can maximally promote equitable growth.

Relatedly, there is significant momentum around the role of industrial policies (Aiginger and Rodrik 2020). In their collective volume on industrialization in SSA, Abreha et al. (2021) argued that it is not useful to assert that SSA as a whole has experienced premature deindustrialization. There is much variation in actual trends that require understanding and response. Within this diversity, Abreha et al. (2021) highlighted some generic priorities for policy makers to act, focusing on upgrading into high-skill tasks, increasing the value-added content of current exports, and creating comparative advantages in knowledge-intensive industries.

This section has reviewed outside-the-box labor market policies. However, Atkinson also considered policies related to rebalancing power relations between employers and employees, arguing that strengthening countervailing power is envisioned as "[…] introduc[ing] an explicitly distributional dimension into competition policy; […] ensur[ing] a legal framework that allows trade unions to represent workers on level terms; and […] establish[ing], where it does not already exist, a Social Economic Council involving the social partners and other nongovernmental bodies" (Atkinson 2015, 131). Such a vision is designed to give workers voice and bargaining power at all levels of the economy, including within firms, sectoral councils, and national policy discussions.

Also important is capital-sharing, which is directed at broadening historical capital and asset ownership and accumulation patterns that have been restricted to a highly exclusive number of individuals. This issue is of obvious relevance in Africa given its colonial histories and post-colonial political economies. Possible vehicles for underwriting capital-sharing funds to direct them toward the wider population include extraction of natural resources as well as rents from state-owned capital-sharing funds.

There are examples of ambitious capital-sharing policies in Africa. South Africa's Black Economic Empowerment and Broad-Based Black Economic Empowerment affirmative action policies aim to redress racial and gender inequalities by changing the structure of capital ownership in the country. Although there has been an important transfer of stock and capital to Black South Africans, such policies have not reduced income inequality in the country. Manning (2014) found that the limited success of the Black Economic Empowerment strategy is due to its narrow scope and the fact that, instead of creating entrepreneurship, it has created a cluster of rent-seeking individuals.

Another set of affirmative action and capital redistribution policies are related to land redistribution, restitution, and tenure. In South Africa, where millions of hectares have been redistributed, the structure of land ownership—and its inequality—seems to have been mostly unaffected (Díaz Pabón et al. 2021). Indeed, these outcomes seem to result from implementations that have created and reproduced capital and land ownership inequalities along gendered, racial, and ethnic lines (Hall and Kepe 2017). This issue serves as another example highlighting the role of elite individuals, both existing and emerging, in capturing the policy agenda, thereby often distorting its initial purpose and implementation (Acemoglu, Gelb, and Robinson 2007; De Wet 1997).

Data on the nature and composition of private wealth in Africa are growing, but they are still sparse and limited because a lens on ownership beyond national boundaries is needed. This issue is linked to the difficulties of establishing and maintaining accurate registries that account for domestic and foreign assets and the weak coordination of national and international tax policies. Individual cases—some of which have been brought to court—indicate the degree to which wealth is shifted to tax havens and the need for an accounting of the public wealth extracted from the continent that can be taxed. These factors make it difficult to formulate concrete proposals for taxing wealth.

However, these pragmatic concerns do not diminish the importance of considering wealth tax options as possible pathways to tackle structural inequality and raise domestic revenues. Complexities in implementation do not imply that it is unfeasible or that such policies cannot be considered on the policy menu. A wealth tax on stock has been in place in countries in the past. Indeed, some wealth taxes remain in place, and some have been removed; for example, Germany had one until 1977.

Atkinson's final outside-the-box policy proposes the creation of a citizen's income or the payment of a guaranteed minimum income to all individuals (Atkinson and Bourguignon 2015). Although this type of policy is often considered as a nontargeted, broad, universal social protection policy, it can represent more than that. As Ferguson (2015) argued, it can also present a political reorientation toward shared national resources and wealth. In addition, he argued, it provides a way to acknowledge and compensate for the shortcomings in the operation of labor markets that fail to accommodate qualified labor or that relegate most employed workers to precarious informal labor. Social protection is an attractive vision.

However, Lustig et al. (2019) modeled the fiscal feasibility of such a "universal" transfer in select countries in SSA, finding that direct taxes would be far from sufficient to establish an income floor equivalent to the international poverty line. Furthermore, if the income floor were equal to the country-specific poverty line, this infeasibility is further exacerbated.

That said, the COVID-19 pandemic has brought a new momentum to some of these discussions (refer to Marais [2022] for a debate on South Africa). During the crisis, everyone was affected, although in different ways, leading to renewed recognition of the value of universality. Universal basic incomes represent a way to link a form of social spending to the rationale of shared capital funds. They also were a viable pathway for introducing adaptive social protection with a broad-based horizontal coverage in place (the number of beneficiaries) on which crisis measures can "piggyback" through vertical expansions (increasing benefit levels).

In sum, this section introduced a menu of outside-the-box policies that seek to confront key processes that generate income inequalities. These policies are directed at creating pathways to greater security and improved well-being for people at the bottom of the distribution of income and resources, including capital and asset ownership. A benefit of drawing on Atkinson's (2015) framework is that it makes clear that these policies require attention because of how inequalities are perpetuated in contemporary national and global factor and output markets. If they are not considered, then the effectiveness of conventional, inside-the-box policies is dampened.

Some aspects of implementation in Africa are daunting. Weak legislated institutional voice and protections are often accompanied by large-scale informality, which undermines the effectiveness of these institutions even when they are in place. The political economy of policy implementation contains the risk of counteracting forces that seek to turn back these policies. Against this backdrop, the chapter concludes by taking stock of the art of the possible.

Art of the Possible for Policies to Overcome Inequality

The Atkinson (2015) framework is useful for understanding the prevailing policy discussions in many African contexts despite the fact that the framework and, therefore, these policy discussions, are drawn from a Global North perspective and do not address important stylized facts evident in Africa.

Most policies to tackle income inequalities in Africa are part of the conventional toolkit of social safety nets, labor markets, and tax policies. However, there has been much useful thinking, sharpened by the COVID-19 pandemic, around better-integrated approaches that improve social protection and the incomes of beneficiaries in a way that is harmonized with labor market interventions. Such thinking confronts the intersecting nature of inequalities not with magic bullets but with coordinated interventions that have aggregate impacts greater than the sum of their parts. However, coordination depends on strengthening social registries to track and link individuals across social protection, education, health, and labor market databases.

This work is difficult but especially important for those who are marginalized and in informal work. The pandemic showed clearly that, without strengthened social registries and coordination, preexisting inequalities widened between those who were accounted for and those who were not. As Atkinson pointed out, more-ambitious policies, such a as minimum inheritance endowment paid to all at adulthood, require the capacity to account for and reach out to all citizens (Atkinson 2015). Renewed attention has been given to understanding country-specific tax and revenue systems so that prioritized policy design can be twinned to revenue collection from those who benefit from national growth.

Yet, if the goal is to achieve the UN Sustainable Development Goals (SDGs) or the objectives of Africa's Agenda 2063 associated with reducing inequality, the toolset must be extended with attention to African specificities. The overwhelmingly informal nature of labor markets in most African contexts has been noted a few times in this chapter, and the limited presence of competitive markets in the formal-sector demands direct consideration, too. Sectoral and industrial policies must focus on breaking barriers and building bridges between the formal and informal sectors. Similarly, large percentages of economically active individuals are marginalized, and a platform is needed for cash transfers and labor market interventions that underwrite engagement and participation in the economy.

As Atkinson's framework focused on income flows, it paid little attention to pre-market inequalities of opportunity based on health, education, and location that drive income and wealth inequality. Atkinson (2015) acknowledged that these broader societal inequalities are important and must be addressed. However, for him, this work should not be done through income and tax policies. Although Atkinson rightly wanted to be pragmatic about what can be expected from specific policies, the analysis of African inequalities in this book makes it clear that the intersections among social, labor market, and income policies must be considered explicitly if policies are to change rather than nudge the structures that perpetuate inequality.

Indeed, in such an integrated approach to policy, it is difficult to include the social and cultural divides prominent in the sociological perspectives of inequality (Bourdieu 1986; Savage 2021). Despite these difficulties, the chapters in this book on gender (chapter 5), education and health (chapter 3), and labor markets (chapter 4) make it clear that such formal and informal norms are prevalent in many African contexts and, as discussed in chapter 11, are discriminatory and highly unproductive. Narrowly put, they impede growth by unfairly excluding many people.

It is both possible and desirable to ensure that laws define such discrimination as illegal, and many African countries now have such laws in place. However, ensuring compliance is difficult because of the high levels of informality in the economy and social norms that often lag behind legislated norms. Nonetheless, it is crucial to recognize the extent to which such discriminations can blunt the effectiveness of all policies to overcome inequalities, whether they are inside or outside the box.

Furthermore, despite their merits, neither the SDGs nor Africa's Agenda 2063 sufficiently addresses imbedded structures of exploitation that drive within- and between-country inequalities. Centuries of globalization have integrated African economies and societies into the global economic system in extractive ways. Today, when African societies confront the new dimensions of globalization, they do so with the inertia of these historically set patterns of integration and international power asymmetries. This is the international policy environment within which African countries interact with the broader international community, including on future covariate shocks induced by the climate breakdown, external economic shocks, pandemics, and political tensions that arise due to competing global and regional hegemons.

Such an environment sets a severely limited policy space for adjustments and reforms within African contexts. However, as this chapter describes, shocks such as the COVID-19 pandemic can induce policy innovation within countries that can expand social protection networks and strengthen policy complementarities within coordinated national responses. With climate change as a good example, policies can also prompt productive discussion of coordinated global responses, including financing needed structural reforms. For example, the payment of compensation and reparations, which was off limits previously, is now frequently discussed in the climate change "loss-and-damage" narrative (WEF 2022). A breakthrough moment here presents the establishment of the loss-and-damage climate change fund that provides funding for vulnerable countries (UNFCCC 2022).

While this innovation may be politically feasible now due to a currently shared sense of urgency about the climate breakdown, lessons and actions should be taken beyond climate damage. Proposals within the Group of 20 and even the World Economic Forum have sought to establish a global fund for universal social protection. These regained momentum during the COVID-19 crisis (OHCHR 2021). Trade flow data show that flows to the Global North exceed aid and foreign assistance flows to African economies (Hickel 2017). However, addressing this inequity does not need to be limited to global funds with earmarked spending availability; it can also occur in bilateral arrangements to rebalance the effects of former colonial relations by renegotiating existing trade agreements that currently do not favor African economies (Rodney et al. 2018).

Thinking beyond the box prompts a policy agenda that confronts inequality through a coordinated, coherent set of policies that collectively reduce income inequality by broadening the ownership of wealth and social capital. Fiscal prioritization and constraints should be addressed through complementary approaches so that fiscal revenue from all who benefit from the current system can be maximized and used to leverage the productivity of all within these societies. Such an approach will maximize the societal returns to each increment of economic growth and maximize sustainability more generally. There are too many intersecting binding constraints here for prioritization to imply narrow magic bullets. A creatively radical approach is required to challenge the deep-rooted historical inequalities that confront 21st-century African nations.

This work includes radical reform not only within the African context but also—perhaps even more so—in the Global North, such as policies on reparations, global financial architecture reforms, and fairer trade agreements. A long-standing and growing critique of development "as is" exists, with recent voices emphasizing the need for alternatives that move beyond Western-centric models (Ndlovu-Gatsheni 2015). For instance, critics of the Grand Bargain, an agreement to improve aid efficiency, have highlighted its failure to meet key targets, particularly in localization and funding commitments (Matcalfe-Hough et al. 2021). In general, a mapping of global agendas versus realized partnership building often exposes systemic issues within the current aid architecture.

One response to this issue is seen in trust-based development gaining traction, advocating for a shift toward equitable partnerships where local communities hold fundamental decision-making power and resources (Trust-Based Philanthropy 2024). More broadly, concrete steps toward decolonial partnership building also include prioritizing Indigenous knowledge systems (Smith 2022), ensuring meaningful participation of marginalized groups, and restructuring financial flows to support self-determined development paths. These approaches aim to dismantle power imbalances and foster more-sustainable and -inclusive development outcomes.

The current global policy moment evidences some acceptance of these policy realities. Recent efforts on global financial architecture reform address significant imbalances in international governance, focusing on enhancing equity considerations, restructuring debt mechanisms, and increasing representation of the Global South. Central to these reforms is the push for equitable distribution of resources and opportunities, seeking to mitigate the disproportionate impacts of global economic policies on marginalized and developing nations. These reforms advocate for a comprehensive overhaul of debt frameworks, emphasizing sustainable and fair debt relief practices that prevent economic exploitation and ensure long-term financial stability for indebted countries.

They also include modernizing the global tax architecture, which is essential for boosting public-sector revenues to finance development agendas and global public goods. The UN General Assembly's resolution to commence work toward a UN Tax Convention marks a pivotal step in promoting more-equitable and -progressive global tax structures. The resolution addresses critical areas such as corporate taxation, the prevention of tax evasion by wealthy individuals, and appropriate taxation of carbon emissions. In addition, reforming global economic governance emphasizes the need to make international financial institutions—such as the International Monetary Fund and the World Bank—more inclusive and effective.

A critical component of reform is amplifying the voices from the Global South in these key institutions to foster more-inclusive decision-making processes that reflect the diverse realities and needs of all nations. Reforms to change the allocation of voices in the governing bodies of these institutions are critical to enhance their legitimacy and efficacy, but such reforms may take time to build consensus. Although they aim to create a more-balanced and -just global economic system, these reforms face substantial resistance from established powers that benefit from the status quo.

References

Abreha, Kaleb G., Woubet Kassa, Emmanuel K. K Lartey, Taye A. Mengistae, Solomon Owusu, and Albert G. Zeufack. 2021. *Industrialization in Sub-Saharan Africa: Seizing Opportunities in Global Value Chains.* Africa Development Forum. Washington, DC: World Bank. https://openknowledge.worldbank.org /entities/publication/a7fcc389-e024-5a8a-841c-4b32ad1b4ffe.

Acemoglu, Daron, Stephen Gelb, and James Robinson. 2007. "Black Economic Empowerment and Economic Performance in South Africa." Center for Economic Development Working Paper. https:// www.researchgate.net/publication/228416806_Black_Economic_Empowerment_and_Economic _Performance_in_South_Africa.

Aiginger, Karl, and Dani Rodrik. 2020. "Rebirth of Industrial Policy and an Agenda for the Twenty-First Century." *Journal of Industry, Competition and Trade* 20 (2): 189–207. https://doi.org/10.1007/s10842 -019-00322-3.

Amis, Mao. 2016. "Lessons from the Informal Sector." *International Institute for Environment and Development* (blog), February 24, 2016. https://www.iied.org/lessons-informal-sector.

Anwar, Mohammad Amir, and Mark Graham. 2021. "Between a Rock and a Hard Place: Freedom, Flexibility, Precarity and Vulnerability in the Gig Economy in Africa." *Competition & Change* 25 (2): 237–58. https://doi.org/10.1177/1024529420914473.

Atkinson, Anthony B. 2015. *Inequality: What Can Be Done?* Cambridge, MA: Harvard University Press. http://www.jstor.org/stable/j.ctvjghxqh.

Atkinson, Anthony B., and François Bourguignon, eds. 2015. *Handbook of Income Distribution*, volume 2b. Amsterdam: Elsevier.

Bassier, Ihsaan, and Joshua Budlender. 2024. "Stimulus Effects of a Large Public Employment Programme." AFD Research Paper 305, Agence Française de Développement, Paris.

Bassier, Ihsaan, Joshua Budlender, Rocco Zizzamia, Murray Leibbrandt, and Vimal Ranchhod. 2021. "Locked Down and Locked Out: Repurposing Social Assistance as Emergency Relief to Informal Workers." World Development 139: 105271. https://doi.org/10.1016/j.worlddev.2020.105271.

Besamusca, Janna, and Kea Tijdens. 2015. "Comparing Collective Bargaining Agreements for Developing Countries." International Journal of Manpower 36 (1): 86–102. https://doi.org/10.1108/IJM-12-2014 -0262.

Bhorat, Haroon, Ravi Kanbur, and Benjamin Stanwix. 2017. "Minimum Wages in Sub-Saharan Africa: A Primer." World Bank Research Observer 32 (1): lkw007. https://doi.org/10.1093/wbro/lkw007.

Bourdieu, Pierre. 1986. "The Forms of Capital." In Handbook of Theory and Research for the Sociology of Education, edited by John G. Richardson, 241–58. New York: Greenwood.

Brancaccio, Emiliano, Nadia Garbellini, and Raffaele Giammetti. 2018. "Structural Labour Market Reforms, GDP Growth and the Functional Distribution of Income." Structural Change and Economic Dynamics 44: 34–45. https://doi.org/10.1016/j.strueco.2017.09.001.

David, Anda, Yoro Diallo, and Björn Nilsson. 2023. "Informality and Inequality: The African Case." Journal of African Economies 32 (Suppl. 2): ii273–ii295. https://doi.org/10.1093/jae/ejac052.

De Wet, Chris. 1997. "Land Reform in South Africa: A Vehicle for Justice and Reconciliation, or a Source of Further Inequality and Conflict?" Development Southern Africa 14 (3): 355–62. https://doi.org /10.1080/03768359708439970.

Devarajan, Shantayanan, and Quy-Toan Do. 2023. "Taxation, Accountability, and Cash Transfers: Breaking the Resource Curse." Journal of Public Economics 218: 104816. https://doi.org/10.1016/j.jpubeco.2022 .104816.

DFID (Department for International Development). 2016. "Impact Assessment—Ethiopia Productive Safety Net Programme Phase 4 (PSNP 4)." DFID, London.

Díaz Pabón, Fabio Andrés, Murray Leibbrandt, Vimal Ranchhod, and Michael Savage. 2021. "Piketty Comes to South Africa." British Journal of Sociology 72 (1): 106–24. https://doi.org/10.1111/1468 -4446.12808.

Dupas, Pascaline, and Jonathan Robinson. 2013. "Savings Constraints and Microenterprise Development: Evidence from a Field Experiment in Kenya." American Economic Journal: Applied Economics 5 (1): 163–92. https://doi.org/10.1257/app.5.1.163.

Ernst, Ekkehard, Rossana Merola, and Jelena Reljic. 2022. Labour Market Policies for Inclusiveness: A Literature Review with a Gap Analysis. Geneva: International Labour Organization.

Ferguson, James. 2015. Give a Man a Fish: Reflections on the New Politics of Distribution. Duke University Press. https://doi.org/10.2307/j.ctv1198xwr.

Gentilini, Ugo, Mohamed Bubaker Alsafi Almenfi, Yuko Okamura, John Austin Downes, Pamela Dale, Michael Weber, David Locke Newhouse, et al. 2021. "Social Protection and Jobs Responses to COVID-19: A Real-Time Review of Country Measures." Working Paper 168386, World Bank, Washington, DC. https:// documents.worldbank.org/en/publication/documents-reports/documentdetail/110221643895832724 /social-protection-and-jobs-responses-to-covid-19-a-real-time-review-of-country-measures.

Hall, Ruth, and Thembela Kepe. 2017. "Elite Capture and State Neglect: New Evidence on South Africa's Land Reform." Review of African Political Economy 44 (151): 122–30. https://doi.org/10.1080/03056244 .2017.1288615.

Hickel, Jason. 2017. *The Divide: A Brief Guide to Global Inequality and Its Solutions.* London: William Heinemann.

ILO (International Labour Organization). 2019. *Wages in Africa: Recent Trends in Average Wages, Gender Pay Gaps and Wage Disparities.* Geneva: ILO.

ILO (International Labour Organization). 2021. *Africa Regional Social Protection Strategy, 2021–2025.* Geneva: ILO.

ILO (International Labour Organization). 2022. "Informal Economy in Africa: Which Way Forward? Making Policy Responsive, Inclusive and Sustainable." Concept Note. ILO, Geneva.

ILO (International Labour Organization). 2023. *Labour Standards in Africa.* Geneva: ILO.

Jack, William, and Tavneet Suri. 2014. "Risk Sharing and Transactions Costs: Evidence from Kenya's Mobile Money Revolution." *American Economic Review* 104 (1): 183–223. https://doi.org/10.1257/aer.104.1.183.

Kerr, Andrew. 2017. "Tax(i)ing the Poor? Commuting Costs in South African Cities." *South African Journal of Economics* 85 (3): 321–40. https://doi.org/10.1111/saje.12161.

Köhler, Timothy, Haroon Bhorat, and Robert Hill. 2023. "The Effect of Wage Subsidies on Job Retention in a Developing Country: Evidence from South Africa." WIDER Working Paper 2023/114, United Nations University, World Institute for Development Economics Research, Helsinki, Finland. https://doi.org/10.35188/UNU-WIDER/2023/422-9.

Krueger, Alan B. 2012. "The Rise and Consequences of Inequality in the United States." Speech at the Center for American Progress, January 12, Washington, DC.

Lam, David, and Ahmed Elsayed. 2021. *Labour Markets in Low-Income Countries: Challenges and Opportunities.* Oxford, UK: Oxford University Press. https://doi.org/10.1093/oso/9780192897107.003.0001.

Lamont, Michèle, Graziella Moraes Silva, Jessica Welburn, Joshua Guetzkow, Nissim Mizrachi, Hanna Herzog, and Elisa Reis. 2016. *Getting Respect: Responding to Stigma and Discrimination in the United States, Brazil, and Israel.* Princeton, NJ: Princeton University Press.

Lapeyre, Frédéric, and Simon Barussaud. 2019. *La formalisation vue d'en bas: enjeux pour la transition vers l'économie formelle.* Espace Afrique 22. Louvain-la-Neuve, Belgium: Academia-l'Harmattan.

Lawson, Max, and Matthew Martin. 2017. *The Commitment to Reducing Inequality Index: A New Global Ranking of Governments Based on What They Are Doing to Tackle the Gap between Rich and Poor.* Nairobi, Kenya: Oxfam: Development Finance International. https://doi.org/10.21201/2017.0131.

Leite, Pereira Guimaraes, Phillippe George, Tina George, Changqing Sun, Theresa Jones, and Kathy A. Lindert. 2017. "Social Registries for Social Assistance and Beyond : A Guidance Note and Assessment Tool." Social Protection and Labor Discussion Paper 1704, World Bank, Washington, DC. https://ideas.repec.org/p/wbk/wbrwps/117971.html.

Loewald, Christopher, Konstantin Makrelov, and Andreas Wörgötter. 2021. "Addressing Low Labour Utilisation in South Africa." Working Paper 21/09, South African Reserve Bank, Pretoria, South Africa.

Lustig, Nora, Jon Jellema, and Valentina Martinez Pabon. 2019. "Leaving No One Behind: Can Tax-Funded Transfer Programs Provide Income Floors in Sub-Saharan Africa?" Commitment to Equity Working Paper Series 85, Department of Economics, Tulane University, New Orleans, LA. https://ideas.repec.org/p/tul/ceqwps/85.html.

Manning, Claudia. 2014. "Origins, Trends and Debates in Black Economic Empowerment." In *The Oxford Companion to the Economics of South Africa*, edited by Haroon Bhorat, Alan Hirsch, S. M. Ravi Kanbur, and Mthuli Ncube, 313–21. Oxford, UK: Oxford University Press.

Marais, Hein. 2022. *In the Balance: The Case for a Universal Basic Income in South Africa and Beyond*. Johannesburg, South Africa: Wits University Press. https://doi.org/10.18772/12022077724.

Matcalfe-Hough, Victoria, Wendy Fenton, Barnaby Willitts-King, and Barbara Spencer. 2021. "The Grand Bargain at Five Years: An Independent Review." Overseas Development Institute, London. https://odi .org/en/publications/the-grand-bargain-at-five-years-an-independent-review/.

McKenzie, David. 2017. "How Effective Are Active Labor Market Policies in Developing Countries? A Critical Review of Recent Evidence." *World Bank Research Observer* 32 (2): 127–54. https://doi.org /10.1093/wbro/lkx001.

McNabb, Kyle, and Annalena Oppel. 2023. "Personal Income Tax Reforms and Income Inequality in African Countries." ODI Working Paper, Overseas Development Institute, London.

Modica, Emmanuelle, Sabine Laudage, and Michelle Harding. 2018. "Domestic Revenue Mobilisation: A New Database on Tax Levels and Structures in 80 Countries." OECD Taxation Working Papers 36, Organisation for Economic Co-operation and Development, Paris. https://www.oecd-ilibrary.org /content/paper/a87feae8-en.

Mohieldin, Mahmoud, and Carolina Sanchez-Paramo. 2019. "Tackling Inequality Is a Political Choice." *Project Syndicate*, July 15. https://www.project-syndicate.org/commentary/inequality-political -not-economic-by-mahmoud-mohieldin-and-carolina-sanchez-paramo-2019-07?barrier=accesspaylog.

Ndlovu-Gatsheni, Sabelo J. 2015. "Decoloniality as the Future of Africa." *History Compass* 13 (10): 485–96. https://doi.org/10.1111/hic3.12264.

OHCHR (Office of the High Commissioner for Human Rights). 2021. "World Needs to Prepare for the Next Crisis by Setting Up Global Fund for Social Protection Now." Press Release. OHCHR, United Nations, Geneva. https://www.ohchr.org/en/press-releases/2021/06/world-needs-prepare-next-crisis -setting-global-fund-social-protection-now-un.

Oppel, Annalena, Kyle McNabb, and Daniel Chachu. 2022. "The Dynamics of Domestic Revenue Mobilization across Four Decades." WIDER Working Paper Series wp-2022-1, United Nations University, World Institute for Development Economics Research, Helsinki, Finland. https://ideas.repec .org/p/unu/wpaper/wp-2022-1.html.

Payments Industry Intelligence. 2016. "M-Pesa: The Good and the Bad News." Payments Industry Intelligence, Norfolk, UK. https://www.paymentscardsandmobile.com/m-pesa-good-bad-news/.

Rodney, Walter, Angela Y. Davis, Vincent Harding, Robert A. Hill, William Strickland, and Abdul Rahman Mohamed Babu. 2018. *How Europe Underdeveloped Africa*. London: Verso.

Savage, Michael. 2021. *The Return of Inequality: Social Change and the Weight of the Past*. Cambridge, MA: Harvard University Press.

Schmitt, John. 2009. "Inequality as Policy." *Real Word Economics Review* 51 (1): 2–9.

Shaxson, Nicholas. 2007. "Oil, Corruption and the Resource Curse." *International Affairs* 83 (6): 1123–40. https://doi.org/10.1111/j.1468-2346.2007.00677.x.

Siakwah, Pius. 2017. "Political Economy of the Resource Curse in Africa Revisited." *Development and Society* 46 (1): 83–112.

Signé, Njuguna, and Landry Ndung'u. 2020. "Capturing the Fourth Industrial Revolution: A Regional and National Agenda." In *Brookings Foresight Africa*, 61–66. Washington, DC: Brookings Institution.

Smith, Linda Tuhiwai. 2022. *Decolonizing Methodologies: Research and Indigenous Peoples*, 3rd edition. London: Bloomsbury Academic.

socialprotection.org. 2023. "Social Protection Profiles." socialprotection.org, United Nations Research Institute for Social Development, Geneva.

Stewart, Mark B. 2004. "The Employment Effects of the National Minimum Wage." *Economic Journal* 114 (494): C110–C116. https://doi.org/10.1111/j.0013-0133.2003.00200.x.

Suri, Tavneet, and William Jack. 2016. "The Long-Run Poverty and Gender Impacts of Mobile Money." *Science* 354 (6317): 1288–92. https://doi.org/10.1126/science.aah5309.

Therborn, Göran. 2013. *The Killing Fields of Inequality*. Cambridge, UK: Polity.

Tilly, Charles. 2009. *Durable Inequality*. Berkeley: University of California Press.

Trust-Based Philanthropy. 2024. "Trust-Based Philanthropy." Trust-Based Philanthropy, San Francisco, CA. https://www.trustbasedphilanthropy.org.

Tyler, Imogen. 2020. *Stigma: The Machinery of Inequality*. London: Zed Books Ltd. https://doi.org /10.5040/9781350222809.

UNDP (United Nations Development Programme). 2023. *Journey to Extremism in Africa: Pathways to Recruitment and Disengagement*. New York: UNDP.

UNFCCC (United Nations Framework Convention on Climate Change). 2022. "COP27 Reaches Breakthrough Agreement on New 'Loss and Damage' Fund for Vulnerable Countries." UNFCCC, New York. https://unfccc.int/news/cop27-reaches-breakthrough-agreement-on-new-loss-and -damage-fund-for-vulnerable-countries.

United Nations. 2017. "Africa's App-Based Taxis Battle Uber over Market Share." *Africa Renewal* (blog). https://www.un.org/africarenewal/magazine/august-november-2017/africa%E2%80%99s-app-based -taxis-battle-uber-over-market-share#:~:text=Many%20African%20governments%20seem%20 to,Ministry%20of%20Transport%20and%20Uber.

Van Hove, Leo, and Antoine Dubus. 2019. "M-PESA and Financial Inclusion in Kenya: Of Paying Comes Saving?" *Sustainability* 11 (3): 568–94. https://doi.org/10.3390/su11030568.

WEF (World Economic Forum). 2022. "Loss and Damage: Why Climate Reparations Are Top of the Agenda at COP27." WEF, Geneva. https://www.weforum.org/agenda/2022/10/cop27-why-climate reparations-are-one-of-the-biggest-issues/.

World Bank. 2023a. "Rural Population (% of Total Population)—Sub-Saharan Africa." World Bank, Washington, DC. https://data.worldbank.org/indicator/SP.RUR.TOTL.ZS?locations=ZG.

World Bank. 2023b. "Unemployment, Total (% of Total Labor Force)—Sub-Saharan Africa." World Bank, Washington, DC. https://data.worldbank.org/indicator/SL.UEM.TOTL.ZS?locations=ZG.

PART 3
Pushing the Knowledge Frontier and Policy Actions

Chapter **10**

Climate Change, Poverty Reduction, and Inequality between and within Countries

Anda David, Murray Leibbrandt, Hélène Djoufelkit, and Rawane Yasser

Introduction

Climate change has become the most-challenging development issue of our time, and Africa is the continent most vulnerable to its consequences. United Nations Sustainable Development Goal 13 focuses on urgent action to combat climate change and its impacts. To this end, the Paris Agreement was adopted in 2015 with the goal to limit global warming. However, one question remains: How compatible is containing climate change with reducing poverty and increasing the consumption levels of the poor population? Answering this question places inequality and distribution at the center of the discussion. Since the beginning of the Paris Agreement negotiations, questions about inequality of development and inequality of emissions between countries has shaped the tone of these discussions.

There is an urgent need to move beyond discussion, as the consequences of the climate crisis are now materializing. These consequences include reduced food and water security in many regions due to extreme weather events. Such shocks can directly reduce agricultural outputs and disrupt the livelihoods of agricultural households. In turn, these effects can contribute to the volatility of food prices, putting low-income households at risk of food insecurity. Therefore, climate change contributes to economic and material inequality by aggravating water and food scarcity.

The latest Intergovernmental Panel on Climate Change (IPCC) report has shown that countries and residents within countries neither contribute to nor are affected by climate change in the same ways (IPCC 2022). Climate impacts are not equally distributed across the world, with low- and middle-income countries experiencing greater impacts than their richer counterparts. The Global South, and Africa in particular, is disproportionately affected by temperature change and extreme weather events. Scientific evidence indicates that Africa will be drastically impacted by climate change due to high levels of vulnerability, low adaptive capacity, and overdependence on natural-resource-based livelihoods. Although the continent contributes less than 5 percent of global carbon emissions, it will experience most of the worst impacts (Davis-Reddy and Vincent 2017). The climate crisis is also marked by significant inequalities within countries. Here, too, vulnerability to climate impacts is strongly linked to income and wealth.

In recent years, climate change has been responsible for increasing inequalities both between and within countries. Therefore, it is imperative to gain a better understanding of climate change inequalities when designing adaptation and mitigation actions. While the connection between inequality and climate change impacts has been well documented (Ayanlade et al. 2022; Chancel, Bothe, and Voituriez 2023; IPCC 2022; Taconet, Méjean, and Guivarch 2020), these distributional concerns are not always central in policies tackling climate change, and evidence for Africa is lacking.

This chapter argues that, although there is a growing acknowledgment that reduction of inequality is intertwined with the fight against climate change, the necessary tools and frameworks to bring the two topics together are lacking. This issue is particularly troubling, as country climate change commitments and within-country internal policies are being made anyway. By reviewing the latest research on climate change inequalities, the chapter aims to offer a better understanding of climate inequalities in Africa, both between and within countries, and to point to the necessary tools for designing climate policies.

Inequalities between Countries

A driving force of climate inequalities is how climate change negatively impacts inequalities between countries. Global inequality manifests in relative emissions contributions, the growth and development losses resulting from these emissions, and the capacity to finance effective responses.

Unequal Contributions to Climate Change

Current and historical emissions are unequal between countries. Comparing the bottom 50, middle 40, and top 10 percent by losses, emissions, and capacity to finance global climate actions provides a clear image of climate inequality. The top 10 percent of global carbon emitters generate almost one-half of all greenhouse gas emissions. Meanwhile, the bottom 40 percent account for 75 percent of the total losses and only 12 percent of emissions, compared to 3 percent of total losses accounted for by the top 10 percent, whose share of emissions is 48 percent (Chancel et al. 2023).

According to Chancel (2022), the total carbon emissions of the top 1 percent largely exceed the emissions of the bottom half of the global population. The top 1 percent per capita emission levels were more than 16 times the global average in 2019. Between 1990 and 2019, the top 1 percent of global emitters were responsible for 23 percent of the total growth in emissions (Chancel 2022).

Bruckner et al. (2022) highlighted the unequal emissions between countries and analyzed the contributions of different groups to global emissions, finding a strong concentration of emissions at the top of the income distribution and negligible contributions at the bottom half of the global income distribution. Countries such as Australia, Canada, the Russian Federation, and the United States have among the highest per capita emissions, while in many of the countries in Sub-Saharan Africa (SSA)—such as the Central African Republic, Chad, and Niger—the average footprint is around 0.1 tonnes per year (refer to map 10.1).

SSA is the only region where average per capita emissions currently meet the levels to achieve the target of limiting the temperature increase to less than 1.5 degrees Celsius by 2030. Emissions in SSA could increase by almost 20 percent and still meet the target, while all the other regions in the world largely exceed the target (Chancel et al. 2023). Moreover, the carbon footprint of the bottom half of the population in SSA is the smallest in the world (Chancel 2022), indicating that the current emissions of low-income countries are often near the targets set by high-income countries for 2030.

Map 10.1 Per Capita CO_2 Emissions, 2021

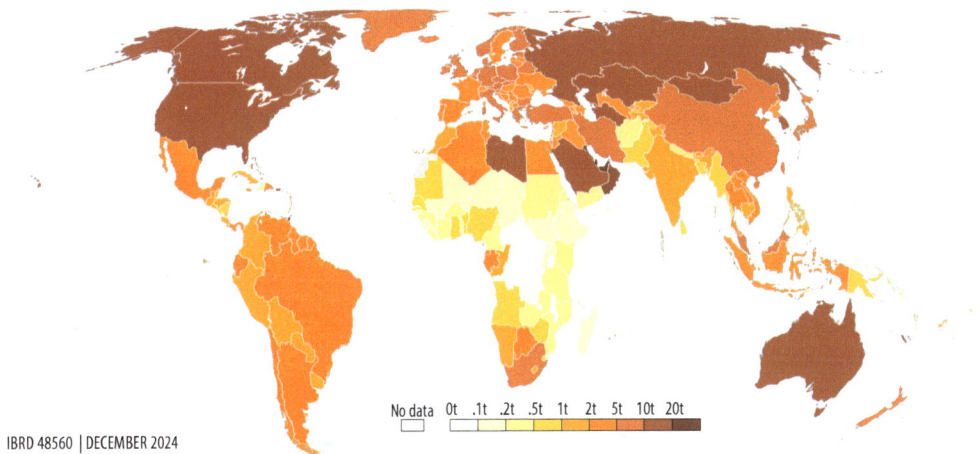

IBRD 48560 | DECEMBER 2024

Source: Our World in Data, based on the Global Carbon Project 2023 (OurWorldinData.org/co2-and-greenhouse -gas-emissions).
Note: Fossil emissions measure the quantity (tonnes) of CO_2 emitted from the burning of fossil fuels and directly from industrial processes such as cement and steel production. Fossil CO_2 includes emissions from coal, oil, gas, flaring, cement, steel, and other industrial processes. Fossil emissions do not include land use change, deforestation, soils, or vegetation. CO_2 = carbon dioxide.

Unequal Impacts of Climate Change

Inequality is significant at the country level, and the Global South is disproportionately affected by temperature change and extreme weather events (Ayanlade et al. 2022; Chancel et al. 2023; IPCC 2022; Taconet et al. 2020). These climate changes affect inequalities between countries in two ways. First, rising temperatures and extreme weather events cause direct effects that more heavily impact low-income countries. Second, the costs to poorer countries of mitigating climate change through reduced emissions could hamper their economic catch-up.

Economic Losses

As chapter 1 in this book shows, on aggregate, income inequalities between countries have declined in recent decades (Bourguignon 2015; Gradín 2021; Milanovic 2016). However, this issue has mostly been due to strong convergence in China and East Asia. This convergence has been much more muted in poorer countries, which are predominantly in Africa. The impact of climate change can reverse this aggregate course and will primarily impact the poorest countries. While high-income countries, which are relatively cold, may profit from climate change, low-income countries in warmer regions will face significant losses (Diffenbaugh and Burke 2019; Taconet et al. 2020). Diffenbaugh and Burke (2019) combined counterfactual historical temperature trajectories with empirical evidence on the relationship between historical temperature fluctuations and economic growth, finding that global warming has increased economic inequality between countries, with warming increasing growth in relatively cool (typically high-income) countries and decreasing growth in low-income countries in warm regions.[1]

Many low-income countries are significantly poorer today than they would have been in the absence of climate change, to which they have contributed very little. Meanwhile, many rich countries that bear the highest responsibility for climate change have benefited in terms of income. This reality can be explained by the Global North's extractive processes of fossil fuel–based production, consumption, and wealth accumulation, which largely continue today.

In addition to fossil fuel benefits not being shared equally, the warming arising from wealthy countries' energy consumption has significantly harmed many poor countries (Diffenbaugh and Burke 2019). For example, it has been estimated that, in Mozambique, the impacts of climate change on the economy will reduce the gross domestic product (GDP) by about 13 percent by 2050 (Arndt and Thurlow 2015). Similar results were obtained in other countries in Southern Africa, such as Angola, Mozambique, Namibia, and Zambia (Ayanlade et al. 2022).

It seems that differential levels of vulnerability to climate change and the ability to adapt across countries are the main drivers of the unequal impacts of climate change (Taconet et al. 2020). Some countries, mostly in SSA, depend more on the sectors that will be most affected by exposure to extreme climate events.

Exposure to Extreme Weather Events

In addition to long-run exposure, some effects of global warming materialize in extreme weather events such as heatwaves, droughts, and flooding. These events do not have the same types or extents of impacts across countries. Poor countries will face the highest volatility in temperature levels, with significant effects on agriculture, while the regions with the highest contributions to global warming may experience reduced temperature volatility (Bathiany et al. 2018).

Southern Africa is among the regions disproportionately affected by adverse climate consequences such as droughts and floods (Ayanlade et al. 2022; Davis-Reddy and Vincent 2017). Many extreme events have been observed in the region, leading to reduced quality and quantity of crop yields, with greater impact on smallholder farmers' livelihoods as shown in the current IPCC report (Trisos et al. 2022). From 1970 to recent years, African populations have been among the most affected in the world by extreme weather events such as droughts, extreme heat events, volatility in weather patterns, and varying amounts of rainfall. Drought disasters account for almost 20 percent of the disaster occurrences in all regions in Africa, particularly affecting rural communities and contributing to famine and loss of livestock, and the Sahel and Savannah zones are most vulnerable to severe droughts (Ayanlade et al. 2022). Projections have indicated that about 43.5 percent of the agricultural land in SSA will be affected by dry conditions, in contrast to the world average of 29.0 percent (Ayanlade et al. 2022).

Many of these climate effects are not independent of each other, and some are more likely to occur simultaneously, aggravating the impacts on social and environmental systems, which is referred to as a *compound event*. More than 780 million people globally are currently exposed to the combined risk of poverty and serious flooding (Chancel et al. 2023). Zimbabwe faced such a compound event in 2020 when the country was hit by a severe drought and heatwave while trying to contain the COVID-19 pandemic. This event increased the pressure on public health authorities due to malnutrition, disease, and excess mortality. It also triggered migration in some regions, which caused further challenges to curbing the pandemic (Phillips et al. 2020).

Clearly, such negative, compounding interactions can aggravate the social and environmental challenges of climate change. These events must be better understood to design suitable policy packages and adaptation strategies.

Effect on Food Security and Agriculture

Studies have reported that extreme weather events can have significant consequences for the agriculture sector and have intensified in recent years, affecting people's activities and livelihoods. However, these risks affect world regions disproportionately, with poor countries facing the most-adverse effects and SSA being the most-vulnerable region (Ajetomobi 2016; Ayanlade et al. 2022; Emediegwu, Wossink, and Hall 2022; Fuller et al. 2018; Trisos et al. 2022). It has been estimated that 55 percent to 62 percent of the workforce in SSA is employed in agriculture, and 95 percent of the region's cropland is rainfed (Trisos et al. 2022).

Scientific studies have highlighted impacts such as reduced crop yields and quality of crops, dried-up streams and rivers, heat fluxes, loss of land, reduced vegetation and biodiversity, decreased incomes for farm households, and other socioeconomic impacts (Apraku, Morton, and Gyampoh 2021; Ayanlade et al. 2022; Ayanlade, Radeny, and Akin-Onigbinde 2018; Emediegwu et al. 2022; Serdeczny et al. 2017).

Relatedly, SSA is the second-most-likely region to be confronted with the challenge of insufficient food as an impact of drought (Ayanlade et al. 2022). Chancel et al.'s (2023) recent estimates have shown that, in Africa, average agricultural productivity is estimated to be 35 percent below its potential value because of drought. In contrast, other countries such as Canada and Russia have seen their productivity increase as a consequence of climate change. Countries such as Mali, Niger, and Sudan face the most-extreme adverse effects, with losses of as much as 40 percent due to climate change. The latest IPCC report has highlighted these adverse effects (Bezner Kerr et al. 2022). Trisos et al. (2022) estimated that agricultural productivity growth in Africa has been reduced by 34 percent since 1961 due to climate change, more than any other region in the world.

In summary, SSA, the region with the highest poverty levels and highest rates of food insecurity, must cope with significant yield losses. This issue increases the incidence of hunger among the populations who rely on agricultural incomes or are vulnerable to the volatility of food prices. In Africa, climate change also poses a significant threat to marine and freshwater fisheries, which provide the main source of protein for around 200 million people (Trisos et al. 2022).

Exposure to Rising Sea Levels and Floods

Exposure to rising sea levels and floods is also unequal, and poorer countries are disproportionately exposed to rising sea levels. Almost 43 percent of the people exposed to flood risk are trying to cope with poverty simultaneously, and poverty undermines the capacity to adapt to and recover from natural disasters (Chancel et al. 2023). The combined risk of flooding and poverty is the largest in SSA, where 28 percent of the population is exposed to both challenges. According to the latest IPCC report, flood risks will increase significantly even under moderate climate change, highlighting the importance of implementing effective adaptation measures, particularly for the most-exposed and vulnerable populations (IPCC 2022).

Exposure to Diseases

Climate change has significantly increased the risk of diseases such as malaria, dengue fever, and Zika virus, especially in poor countries. The burden of malaria is greatest in Africa, where more than 90 percent of all malaria-related deaths occur. In the latest IPCC report, Cissé et al. (2022) showed that these impacts are unevenly distributed across countries, and wider geographic areas are becoming more suitable for transmission.

More-frequent flooding contributes to increases in water-borne diseases such as cholera, especially in areas where water, sanitation, and hygiene deficiencies are significant.

In Ethiopia, Mozambique, Senegal, and South Africa, increases in temperatures and rainfall are associated with increases in diarrhea and childhood diarrhea (Cissé et al. 2022). The relationship between poor sanitation infrastructure and increased risk of outbreaks in low-income countries illustrates the interlinkages of different climate impacts. Drawing on individual data from 30 SSA countries from 1991 to 2017, Cissé et al. (2022) found that Central Africa is projected to face the greatest temperature-induced risk of diarrheal episodes (Flückiger and Ludwig 2022).

Unequal Mitigation Costs

Climate mitigation policies are key to limiting the rise of future inequalities between countries. However, trying to limit the impacts of climate change through greenhouse gas reduction policies can have severe consequences for inequalities, as these mitigation policies can hamper the development of low-income countries. Few studies have explored the impact of reduced climate change on inequalities between countries via mitigation costs, but Taconet et al. (2020) have analyzed how mitigating climate change affects future inequalities, showing that the costs of reducing greenhouse gas emissions vary across countries and can be more burdensome for low-income countries, which can lose a greater share of GDP for the same amount of reduced emissions. Similarly, low-income economies are often characterized by higher energy and carbon intensities. Therefore, raising the price of energy as a mitigation policy can be more burdensome in these countries. However, the impact of mitigation costs depends largely on how the burden of reducing emissions will be distributed among countries, which is explored later in this chapter.

The relative national costs of mitigation are unequally high for poorer countries, and this issue must be addressed explicitly in framing collective, cross-national mitigation strategies. This consideration is important, as weaker economic conditions and significant debt burdens in poorer countries make it difficult to budget for and spend money on self-financed mitigation policies. Thus, there are short-term incentives to postpone the implementation of mitigation; however, the long-run costs of such inaction are very high. These costs reinforce path dependencies and lock the poorest countries into production and energy systems that further increase their vulnerability (Fouquet 2016).

Although many projections are predictions for the future of the continent as a whole, the impacts of climate change may differ across the regions of Africa and, indeed, within each country. The next section describes within-country inequalities.

Inequalities within Countries

The pattern of inequalities also holds within each country, as the link between exposure to climate risks and socioeconomic conditions is strong. Within-country inequalities present a vicious cycle, whereby initial inequality causes disadvantaged groups to disproportionately experience the adverse effects of climate change, resulting in greater subsequent inequality (Ayanlade et al. 2022; Islam and Winkel 2017; Winsemius et al. 2018; World Bank 2022).

Unequal Contributions

For emissions, although cross-country inequalities remain significant, the unequal shares across income groups are mostly driven by within-country inequalities in emissions. Inequalities within countries appear to be greater than inequalities between countries, especially for carbon inequalities. Chancel (2022) estimated that, while in 1990 almost two-thirds of global carbon inequality was due to between-country inequalities (62 percent), in 2019 global carbon inequality was driven mostly by differences in emission levels within countries, with 64 percent of the global inequality in emissions due to differences within countries (refer to figure 10.1). A geographical breakdown reveals that the top global emitters stretch across all world regions. Even within African countries, income groups do not contribute equally to carbon emissions.

The high concentration of income, wealth, and carbon-intensive activities in a small population group leads to a significant degree of carbon inequality in most countries in Africa. In contemporary SSA, the bottom 50 percent emit around 0.5 tonnes per capita of carbon dioxide each year, compared to 7.5 tonnes per capita by the top 10 percent in 2019 (Chancel 2022). In Nigeria, the per capita emissions of the top 10 percent are five times higher than those of the bottom 50 percent (Chancel et al. 2023).

Unequal Impacts

Based on the IPCC conceptual framework, this subsection explores the unequal impacts within countries based on the three dimensions of exposure, vulnerability, and resilience. Within countries, not all people are equally exposed or vulnerable to the effects of extreme weather events, as different degrees of vulnerability are highly correlated with existing patterns of income inequality.

Figure 10.1 Global Inequality of Carbon Emissions between and within Countries, 1990–2019

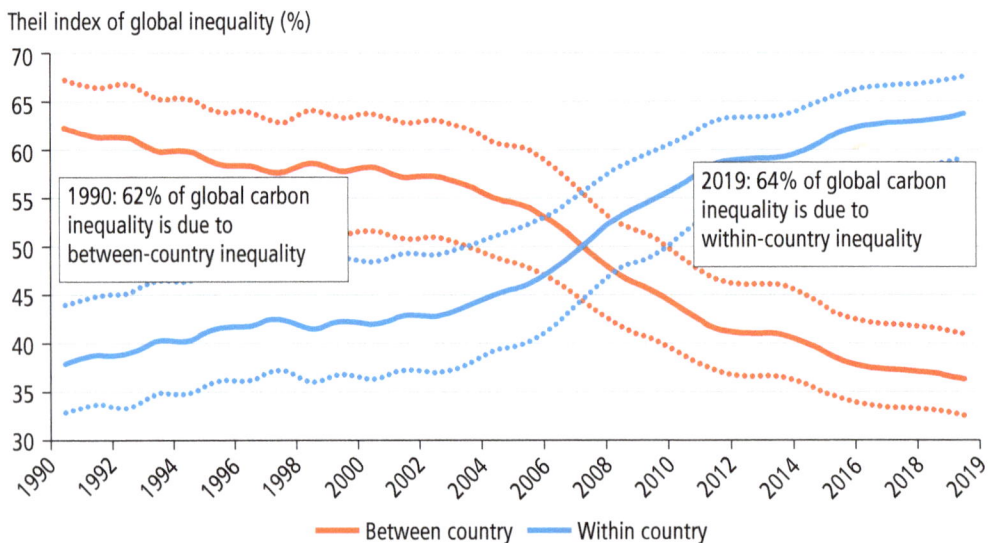

Theil index of global inequality (%)

1990: 62% of global carbon inequality is due to between-country inequality

2019: 64% of global carbon inequality is due to within-country inequality

Between country   Within country

Source: Based on Chancel 2022.
Note: Dotted lines represent scenarios with alpha = 0.4 and alpha = 0.8. For between country, the dotted line above the solid line is alpha = 0.4, and the dotted line below the solid line is alpha = 0.8. For within country, the dotted line above the solid line is alpha = 0.8, and the dotted line below the solid line is alpha = 0.4.

Studies have pointed to strong relationships between climate change exposure and vulnerability on the one hand and socioeconomic living conditions on the other. Those who are worst off are more affected than the rest. Different mechanisms include weather conditions that affect agriculture and the informal sector more than other activities, increased susceptibilities to damage caused by climate change, and decreased abilities to cope with and recover from the damage experienced (Hallegatte et al. 2017; Islam and Winkel 2017).

Similar to the unequal distribution of climate impacts across the world, poor populations within countries live in more-exposed areas or are more likely to work in jobs with higher exposure, such as agricultural work. Moreover, poorer populations are more vulnerable when exposed to adverse climate effects, as their housing is likely to be more prone to storm and flood damage. Finally, the losses incurred by the poorer populations can also undermine their *resilience,* which is their capacity to adapt to and recover from the damages.

Exposure

Poor households tend to be more exposed to the effects of climate change than nonpoor households. Hallegatte et al. (2017) have estimated that poor households are unequally exposed to three types of hazards: droughts, floods, and heat stress. For food security, smallholder farmers are exposed to prolonged droughts that lead to crop losses and livestock deaths. This issue reduces the agricultural outputs of rural farmers, who are mostly poor and vulnerable, especially in the Sudan–Sahel zone (Ayanlade et al. 2022). In Ethiopia, South Africa, and other countries in SSA, farming households are exposed to rainfall variability without the necessary means to reduce their exposure.

For example, in South Africa, rural areas with agriculture as their main economic activity, such as the Eastern Cape Provinces, KwaZulu-Natal, and Limpopo, have the highest exposure to droughts and increased and variable temperatures (Zhou et al. 2022). In Ethiopia, most farm households are recurrently exposed to drought (Gebrehiwot et al. 2021). In Mauritania during the 2014 drought, households living in the districts where the drought was more intense had a higher likelihood of falling below the poverty line, compared to households that faced less-intense drought (Ba and Mughal 2022). Thus, across many African contexts, vulnerable populations are frequently and persistently exposed to weather shocks, which can lead them into poverty traps where newly vulnerable households are shocked into poverty or already-poor households remain persistently poor with deteriorating incomes (Ba and Mughal 2022).

Vulnerability

The poor population is usually the most vulnerable and incurs heavy losses when faced with a disaster. Rural and urban areas feel these direct impacts disproportionately. In addition, important indirect impacts can occur. Weather shocks can result in an increase in food prices, which increases the negative impact of the shock, especially for poor rural households that depend on the local market to satisfy their food needs and are more vulnerable to food price volatility in markets and shops.

Most SSA countries depend largely on smallholder-based agriculture, rendering them more vulnerable to climate change. For example, in Mauritania, when faced with the 2008 drought, 45 percent of rural households reported loss of livestock (Ba and Mughal 2022). In Kenya, an analysis of the effects of climate shocks on household well-being shows how climate change shocks reduce the welfare of Kenyan households, particularly in rural areas, by affecting the assets households own. In contrast, in urban areas, asset ownership and access to credit can help smooth consumption, leading to no significant impact on household welfare (Manda, Oleche, et al. 2023). Another analysis of multidimensional vulnerability in Kenya has shown that rural areas are more vulnerable than urban areas, with poor nutrition and living conditions contributing more to vulnerability in rural areas (Manda, Kipruto, et al. 2023).

Poor households are also more adversely affected by climate change shocks than rich households in the short term. For example, in Ghana, drought had a significant negative effect on the consumption expenditures of rural households as opposed to no significant impact on urban households (Danso-Mensah and Oduro, forthcoming). In South Africa, a systematic review of the literature has shown that, compared to urban households, rural households are more vulnerable to climate change due to the differences in infrastructure, typical livelihoods, and income-generating activities (Zhou et al. 2022).

The impacts of climate shocks can also disproportionately affect households according to their occupation and level of education. For example, in Kenya, vulnerability decreases with the level of education (Manda, Kipruto, et al. 2023). In South Africa, shocks to mining have adverse direct consequences on workers' earnings and their households, which experience reduced remittances (World Bank 2022). Rural residents, those with lower incomes, and the Black population are disproportionately affected by multidimensional vulnerability in South Africa (Shifa, Leibbrandt, and Gordon 2023).

Inequality in vulnerability to climate shocks is also determined by gender. In Kenya and South Africa, female-headed households are generally more vulnerable to climate change shocks than male-headed households (Manda, Kipruto, et al. 2023; Zhou et al. 2022). Women are often more severely affected by climate change shocks and can face a higher burden of work. For example, water scarcity and poor sanitation can force women to walk long distances to collect water and reduce their access to education. Evidence from Nigeria has shown that adverse climate conditions have more severe impacts on women's labor market outcomes (Efobi 2022). Women who were exposed to drought when they were young had worse educational and labor market outcomes. Women who were exposed to drought were 6 percentage points less likely to have worked in the current or past year and 7 percentage points less likely to be working during the survey year, while this result does not persist for exposed men. Men who were exposed to similar circumstances as women may not have experienced similar adverse effects, given the persistent barriers to labor market participation for women, making them more vulnerable to climate shocks.

Compared to men, women also face greater health risks due to climate-related food insecurity, diseases, and extreme weather (IPCC 2022). In rural Africa, poor and female-headed households face greater livelihood risks from climate hazards. As shown in chapter 5 on gender inequality, women have less access to land ownership, which reduces their capacity to recover from income losses, as land ownership is linked to financial inclusion. A new report by the Food and Agriculture Organization shows how climate change compounds the inequalities that women face in agriculture by affecting their capacity to adapt, as discriminatory norms often reduce women's access to climate information (FAO 2023). Thus, there is little doubt about the unequal exposure and vulnerability to climate conditions within countries, usually associated with socioeconomic characteristics such as income, gender, education, or ethnicity.

Resilience

Resilience measures the ability of a population to cope with and recover from damages. The capacity to react and adapt to climate change and shocks depends on financial savings or wealth (Chancel et al. 2023). Households that can draw on financial savings or wealth tend to face smaller losses when hit by a natural disaster. However, poor households do not have savings or wealth. Indeed, some of the lowest bottom 50 percent of wealth shares are in Southern Africa, where the population is the most exposed to severe impacts from droughts and other extreme weather events (Hallegatte et al. 2017). Inequalities in asset ownership also play a significant role in households' capacity to cope with external shocks (Asmamaw, Mereta, and Ambelu 2019; Gebrehiwot et al. 2021; Janzen and Carter 2019; Zhou et al. 2022). Yet, evidence is limited on the effectiveness of assets in mitigating the effects of climate shocks in Africa.

For example, in some countries, rural households rely on crop production and livestock farming to cope with droughts and ensure home consumption. However, droughts often result in low production, which considerably reduces the purchasing power of rural households, leading to greater food insecurity. Selling livestock as a coping strategy to generate more income is often met with reticence, as poor households that sell their livestock are more likely to experience a decline in future consumption and welfare, which can lead to a poverty trap in the future (Ba and Mughal 2022).

Research has shown that, in a drought context, rural households are generally unable to restore lost livelihoods and assets. Even among farm households, the poor population is unequally affected and does not recover from shocks sufficiently to rebuild their assets. As evidence from Senegal has shown, rich households are more advantaged when coping with climate shocks due to their higher levels of savings and wealth, which allow them to diversify their crops and maintain their incomes and consumption when faced with weather shocks (Faye et al. 2019). A study of South Africa found that adaptive capacity relies on five types of capital—human, physical, financial, natural, and social—and that poverty is the greatest limitation in adapting to climate change (Zhou et al. 2022). An analysis to identify the factors determining households' resilience in Ethiopia indicated that access to assets, such as farmland and livestock holdings, along with infrastructure and social capital, is key (Asmamaw et al. 2019).

Studies have investigated the relationship among financial capability, level of education, income, and ability to cope. Evidence from Mauritania has highlighted the importance of wealth as a coping strategy (Ba and Mughal 2022). When faced with drought, household asset portfolios changed, with household wealth falling during the two periods of drought in 2008 and 2014, implying that rural households maintained consumption by liquidating their livestock assets. However, although selling livestock helped maintain consumption levels during the 2008 drought, it did not compensate the losses entirely or prevent households from reducing consumption during the 2014 drought.

Thus, assets can moderate the negative effects of climate change shocks. However, when asset depletion occurs or the magnitude of the shock exceeds the compensation by the existing assets, assets are less likely to help households cope with shocks or increase their resilience (Díaz Pabón et al. 2023). For example, in Kenya, asset ownership and access to credit only partially protected households from the negative effects of climate shocks due to asset destruction (Manda, Oleche, et al. 2023). Evidence from South Africa has confirmed that the impact of climate change shocks is lower for households that have access to assets, compared to other households (Díaz Pabón et al. 2024). A randomized controll in rural Kenya showed how wealthier households cope by selling assets, while poorer households cope primarily by cutting food consumption (Janzen and Carter 2019).

Consumption adjustment strategies were also used in rural Ethiopia, reducing the quality and quantity of food consumption, which exacerbated households' vulnerability to further shocks (Gebrehiwot et al. 2021). In Ghana, the mitigating role of asset ownership depends on the length of the shock and the type of assets, as asset portfolios remained unchanged during a short-term drought and changed only as the drought stretched beyond 24 months (Danso-Mensah and Oduro, forthcoming). Assets that are easier to liquidate, such as financial assets, were more easily used as a coping mechanism as opposed to productive assets, such as livestock and agricultural tools, which were generally maintained throughout the period of drought.

Alternatively, farmers can use their savings to smooth consumption. However, many poor households do not have savings, and those with savings risk depleting them if the shock is long, thereby falling into a poverty trap. Households can also attempt to diversify their sources of income by engaging in nonfarm activities (Ba, Anwar, and Mughal 2021). However, such activities are not always readily available in all rural areas. Therefore, due to the limited availability of efficient coping tools, rural households continue to face difficulties despite the strategies to mitigate the effects of weather shocks on income. Rural households may be stuck in poverty traps where they remain persistently poor and their incomes continue to deteriorate. Moreover, households with limited assets are unable to borrow because they do not have sufficient access to credit.

The choices of coping strategies, therefore, largely depend on the level of asset ownership and the extent of the shocks. More research is needed to support the development of ex-ante adaptation strategies and methods suitable for smallholder farmers in Africa. The next section explores policies for tackling climate change, including the adoption of safety nets, which can prove efficient for improving household well-being after a shock.

Tackling Climate Inequalities: The Way Forward

This section discusses the mechanisms of between- and within-country inequalities and solutions for reducing them.

Drivers of Unequal Impacts

Inequalities in exposure, vulnerability, and resilience are partly due to the low incomes of the poor population. These inequalities are also due to low-quality housing, which faces greater damage when struck by floods, for example. Poor households in Africa also tend to rely more on agricultural jobs and incomes, rendering them more prone to such climate shocks. In contrast, high-income households rely more on formal-sector labor incomes for their livelihoods and less on sectors directly affected by natural disasters. As households in poorer groups experience larger shocks, they are inevitably forced into adopting coping mechanisms that lead to lower productivity and consumption (World Bank 2022; Zhou et al. 2022). Multidimensional poverty remains a great limitation in adapting to climate change.

The impact of climate change on inequality largely depends on the structure of the economy and the texture of each society's inequalities. The research reviewed in this chapter makes it clear that, in almost all African contexts, agriculture is a crucial channel through which climate change exacerbates existing inequalities due to its more negative impacts on poor households. With large shares of the population in rural areas and working in agriculture, temperature increases and volatility caused by climate change have significant effects on within-country inequality (Paglialunga, Coveri, and Zanfei 2022).

Several mechanisms are involved. First, extreme weather events reduce yields and agricultural output, therefore reducing farmers' incomes. Second, disadvantaged households often live in rural areas and are more exposed to extreme weather events as their assets (livestock and land) are more affected. Finally, climate change leads to food price volatility impacting consumption patterns, especially for the poorest households, who spend a higher share of their budget on food.

Moreover, the current level of inequality exacerbates climate shocks where highly-unequal societies, in which rich households disproportionately hold economic and political power, tend to foster a more carbon-intensive future. Inequality also impedes social cohesion and the sense of social responsibility that is crucial to advance national welfare-maximizing, pro-environmental policies and holds back the development of environmental technologies (Vona and Patriarca 2011).

Analysis of resilience is useful for detailing and understanding the agency, responsiveness, and resourcefulness of vulnerable and poor populations in trying to sustain their livelihoods in the face of climate shocks and change. Nonetheless, they are severely income, asset, and wealth constrained, which impacts their capacity to respond. This chapter provides examples showing that such within-country inequalities are fundamentally consequential in allowing better-off households to withstand shocks or invest in and make longer-run adjustments.

At the same time, within-country inequalities severely limit or absolutely prevent vulnerable and poor households from such responses despite their best efforts to adapt. Therefore, delaying or avoiding key policy responses amounts to an abuse of the resilience and adaptive resourcefulness of the poor population.

The analysis in this chapter also shows that, even for better-off households in Africa, the response to systemic weather changes cannot be short-run buffering from wealth or drawing down savings. Systemic changes require systemic adaptations and adjustments to farming and livelihoods, as well as policy support.

The patterns of inequality imply differentiated responsibilities for climate change mitigation and adaptation policies. Environmental policy must consider inequalities both between and within countries.

Tackling Climate Inequality between Countries

This subsection discusses equitable energy use, as well as the roles of technology and finance, in tackling climate inequality between countries.

Equitable Energy Use

Information on the distribution of emissions must be incorporated into policy designs and climate change mitigation. Lower emissions are associated with lower levels of inequalities (Taconet et al. 2020) and can move the current patterns of growth toward more climate-friendly production and consumption patterns (Stern 2007). However, the responsibility to cut carbon emissions must be carried by the countries with the highest incomes and by the wealthiest groups within countries.

Holding the world's total carbon dioxide constant is not enough to slow global warming (Lam 2023). Low-income and low-emitting groups' essential needs, such as for domestic heating or commuting, are linked to their carbon emissions. For high-income groups, it is relatively easier to achieve a reduction in emissions and afford change. In the countries that historically have been large emitters, governments should reconsider their climate targets even beyond the new and updated targets of the 2022 United Nations Climate Change Conference in Sharm el Sheikh, Arab Republic of Egypt (Chancel et al. 2023; Lam 2023).

Recent research has suggested that restructuring current energy consumption could lift many people out of multidimensional poverty without negatively affecting climate change mitigation (Bruckner et al. 2022; Kikstra et al. 2021; Oswald et al. 2021). Kikstra et al. (2021) showed that current energy use is significantly higher than the energy needed to provide decent living standards for the entire global population. Yet, this finding masks the fact that, in areas such as SSA, the current level of energy use is insufficient to provide for basic needs, while in other, high-income regions, overall energy use is significantly above the level required to provide basic living standards. Restructuring current energy use and decreasing demand at the top of the distribution for the benefit of low-income countries would help achieve considerable progress in alleviating poverty and income inequality.

This finding suggests that poverty alleviation efforts can be combined with climate change mitigation efforts through redistribution of energy use. Oswald et al. (2021) argued that energy use and income are strongly linked and, therefore, the effects of reducing income inequality on energy consumption are significant. They suggested that reducing the share of people in energy poverty from the current 60 percent to 10 percent, through a global redistribution of income, would increase global energy consumption by only 6.7 percent. A redistribution of "carbon space" from the global top 10 percent to the rest of the global population, coupled with the development of a new model of low-carbon middle-class prosperity, is paramount to reducing multidimensional poverty while remaining within ecological limits (Bruckner et al. 2022; Lam 2023). Such redistribution will require global coordination and commitment.

Role of Technology

For technology, innovation, and investment in production and climate-smart agricultural infrastructure, low-carbon industries and infrastructures can increase resilience, boost productivity, and reduce the dependence of agricultural production on rainfall, thereby reducing inequality and adapting to climate change (Ayanlade et al. 2022; Ba and Mughal 2022). While many innovative tools and technologies have emerged in higher-income countries, differences in adaptation technology exist between higher-income countries and SSA, implying that technology transfer is required to overcome these gaps (Ayanlade et al. 2022). Higher-income countries have access to more-advanced technologies, and developing countries are more vulnerable to climate change; therefore, developing countries face greater challenges in bearing the financial costs of developing technologies on their own and without much capacity for such technological innovation. Yet, it is possible for countries in the Global South to build capacity for technological innovation. Both China and India have prioritized these policies and have succeeded (Dychtwald 2021).

The IPCC report highlighted many climate change adaptation options that SSA can adopt. However, currently, these options require technological transfers to achieve better adaptation to climate change in SSA (IPCC 2022). Ayanlade et al. (2022) argued that such transfers should entail more than the transfer of equipment and machinery and include the transfer of knowledge and skills to develop the capacity to use and adapt the technology. Although the majority of international initiatives focus on support for climate change adaptations such as solar energy, wind energy, and biofuel technology, only a few of these adaptations are used in agricultural and food systems technology in SSA. However, the agriculture sector is where technology initiatives are most needed.

For example, the Renewable Energy and Adapting to Climate Technologies Window in Africa, a project supported by the European Union, aims to address climate change burdens through climate-related technology, specifically by providing new technology to small-scale farmers. Farmers in Africa have adopted adaptation strategies that use traditional technologies for irrigation. Technologies to improve the efficiency of water management are now necessary to mitigate the impacts of drought. Farmers' preferences and needs should determine these coping strategies. Another example is the use of customized fertilizers, which has been implemented in Morocco by the OCP Group (a state-owned phosphate rock miner, phosphoric acid manufacturer, and fertilizer producer) to satisfy the needs of specific soils to help farmers in a precise and efficient way. This approach to reducing waste by reducing, reusing, recycling, and recovering consists of providing the right fertilizer at the right rate, time, and place.

Role of Finance

To tackle climate inequalities, considering the costs of adapting to climate change is essential. Most costs will be shouldered by developing countries, which are both the least well-off and the most vulnerable to the effects of climate change. These countries cannot underwrite their adaptations. Increasing the amount of funding toward climate disaster relief and losses and damages is required. At the 2023 United Nations Climate Change Conference in Dubai, United Arab Emirates, efforts were put forward to create a loss-and-damage fund, with the target beneficiaries being developing countries most vulnerable to the adverse effects of climate change.

Although adaptation finance has increased in recent years, middle-income countries have captured most of the funds, with low-income countries receiving only 8 percent of the estimated climate finance funds (Chancel et al. 2023). The majority of funds have been directed toward mitigation efforts, with adaptation remaining underfunded. To bridge this gap in financing, increasing tax revenues through progressive wealth and carbon taxes could generate important resources and reduce the burden on low-income countries and groups (Chancel et al. 2023). However, the implications of carbon taxes and reducing subsidies are complex. For example, an ex-post evaluation of a fossil fuel subsidy reform in Ghana shows ambiguous impacts of removing subsidies in developing country contexts, with the use of liquefied petroleum gas decreasing but firewood and charcoal consumption increasing (Greve and Lay 2023). The overall welfare costs were higher than the fiscal savings.

Innovative financial tools, such as contingent loans and climate-resilient debt clauses, have been suggested to build the resilience of developing countries. As vulnerable countries have fewer resources to cope with the impacts of climate change, any increasing debt burden would make them more vulnerable and less resilient in the future. Therefore, these clauses provide a pause in debt repayments for vulnerable countries in times of crisis.

Tackling Climate Inequality within Countries

Recent studies have focused on the role of inequality in limiting global warming. Wollburg, Hallegatte, and Mahler (2023) argued that growth is a driver of poverty alleviation and that the additional emissions resulting from growth and increased consumption by poor and nonpoor people in poor countries will not materially affect the global climate change challenge. They found that lowering within-country inequality would mean that less growth is needed to eliminate extreme poverty, which would reduce the emissions related to poverty alleviation even further. However, there are gaps in research on the direct impact of lowering inequality on emissions.

The existing empirical evidence is mixed on whether lowering inequality would change consumption patterns or enable climate policies that would reduce emissions. Wollburg et al. (2023) found that lowering inequality significantly reduces the carbon emissions needed for poverty alleviation.

Social Policy Interventions

Reducing inequalities requires combining economic policies with social policy interventions designed to increase the adaptive capacity of vulnerable households. Strengthening the resilience to climate risks through adaptive social protection programs would mitigate the impact of climate change and reduce its effect on inequality (Chancel et al. 2023; Manda, Oleche, et al. 2023; World Bank 2022; Zhou et al. 2022). Social protection programs must be adapted to the nature and distribution of shocks. For example, the development of policy interventions designed to enhance the adaptive capacity of food production systems, such as farmer training programs and enhanced technological advancements, would mitigate the impacts on rural income and education (Fuller et al. 2018). Social security and public transfers can play a key role in protecting low-income households from the adverse effects of climate change.

Safety net programs can take the form of cash transfers and public works programs. For example, Ethiopia's Productive Safety Net Program provides cash transfers to reduce food insecurity and poverty (Chancel et al. 2023). In Zambia, cash transfers increased the resilience of poor households when faced with a climate shock. Building up access to improved sanitation and drinking water facilities mitigates the temperature-induced risks to health and economic development.

Finally, concentrated efforts are essential to design national development policies for climate change adaptation to be implemented at the national, regional, and local levels to account for the needs of smallholder farmers in SSA. Linking traditional and local knowledge with institutional information is crucial for adaptation options in SSA to maximize optimal conditions and minimize maladaptation (Ayanlade et al. 2022).

Financial Inclusion

As climate inequalities also occur within countries, the role of financial inclusion is crucial for reducing them. Poor people disproportionately experience climate shocks and have the least access to resilience strategies that would help them adapt to these shocks. Therefore, focusing on how the poor and most-vulnerable populations can use financial services is crucial. Access to financial services such as credit, savings, and remittance products can help build resilience. Other types of products specifically designed for climate risks can help smooth consumption during periods of shocks or increase recovery after a climate shock. For example, credit products and insurance can help poor households transition into new livelihoods or diversify their sources of income. In Mozambique during the 2013 flooding, people in affected areas used their mobile wallets to receive digital money transfers from friends and family (World Bank 2022). It is also important to consider the local context, as different financial solutions are suited to different risks.

Avoiding the Risk of Maladaptation

Maladaptation can make people more vulnerable to climate change by inadvertently reinforcing or creating new sources of vulnerability, thereby reinforcing and increasing inequalities instead of reducing them (Eriksen et al. 2021; Thomas and Warner 2019; Work et al. 2019). Assessments of internationally funded interventions aimed at climate change adaptation and vulnerability reduction can help avoid the risk of maladaptation. In each country, elite capture by powerful privileged groups and the exclusion of marginalized groups from adaptation interventions can reinforce vulnerabilities.[2]

Alongside reinforcing existing inequalities and vulnerabilities, some interventions may have the risk of redistributing vulnerabilities over a larger area or among other groups, such as interventions related to water and coastal areas. Finally, in addition to reinforcing or redistributing vulnerability, some adaptation efforts can introduce new risks and sources of vulnerability, such as interventions that address short-term concerns but create long-term unsustainable paths. Climate initiatives that undermine local adaptation strategies through a top-down approach can also introduce vulnerabilities.[3]

Eriksen et al. (2021) identified four mechanisms through which such interventions can cause unintended consequences: (1) decision-makers' insufficient understanding of local contexts of vulnerability, (2) unequal participation and low representation of marginalized and vulnerable groups in planning and implementing interventions, (3) adjustment or rebranding of existing development projects as adaptation efforts, and (4) insufficient understanding of what is successful adaptation due to not understanding local contexts. To avoid maladaptive outcomes, the emerging literature has highlighted the importance of local populations participating in adaptation interventions and the need to understand the local context and drivers of vulnerability.

Adaptation should be seen as a social process addressing the underlying mechanisms of both vulnerability and climate change. Cross-sectoral and long-term planning of adaptation and mitigation responses are crucial to avoid maladaptation. This chapter shows that a precursor to such processes is understanding the prevailing inequalities in power, income, wealth, and livelihoods in every context, as well as making a commitment to confronting these. Considering inequality is central to successful responses to climate change. Recent literature has used the term *post-adaptation* to describe moving beyond past development approaches that have perpetuated historical patterns of development, toward a more-informed approach through experimentation, collaboration, and deeper learning (Eriksen et al. 2021).

Notes

1. Cool countries are typically high-income countries. China is an exception, but its income growth and small sensitivity to historical warming are explained as built on trading relationships with high-income countries. In the absence of trade, China would have grown less rapidly. Therefore, trade may serve as a buffer against climate shocks (Diffenbaugh and Burke 2019).

2. In Malawi, a study of 27 bilateral and multilateral donors found that smaller amounts of adaptation funds arrived in the marginalized areas of highest need, with the poorest areas receiving the least (Barrett 2014).

3. In Ethiopia, the Climate Resilient Green Economy Strategy has forced pastoralists in the peripheral lowlands to settle, which has led to marginalization, food insecurity, and increased vulnerability (Abbink et al. 2014; Haji and Legesse 2017).

References

Abbink, J., K. Askew, F. D. Dori, E. Fratkin, E. C. Gabbert, J. Galaty, J., Tosky, et al. 2014. "Lands of the Future: Transforming Pastoral Lands and Livelihoods in Eastern Africa." Max Planck Institute for Social Anthropology Working Paper No. 154. Leiden University. http://hdl.handle.net/1887/27586.

Ajetomobi, Joshua. 2016. "Effects of Weather Extremes on Crop Yields in Nigeria." *African Journal of Food, Agriculture, Nutrition and Development* 16 (4): 11168–84. https://doi.org/10.18697/ajfand.76.15685.

Apraku, Amos, John F. Morton, and Benjamin Apraku Gyampoh. 2021. "Climate Change and Small-Scale Agriculture in Africa: Does Indigenous Knowledge Matter? Insights from Kenya and South Africa." *Scientific African* 12: e00821. https://doi.org/10.1016/j.sciaf.2021.e00821.

Arndt, Channing, and James Thurlow. 2015. "Climate Uncertainty and Economic Development: Evaluating the Case of Mozambique to 2050." *Climatic Change* 130: 63–75. https://doi.org/10.1007/s10584-014-1294-x.

Asmamaw, Mengistu, Seid Tiku Mereta, and Argaw Ambelu. 2019. "Exploring Households' Resilience to Climate Change-Induced Shocks Using Climate Resilience Index in Dinki Watershed, Central Highlands of Ethiopia." *PLoS One* 14 (7): e0219393. https://doi.org/10.1371/journal.pone.0219393.

Ayanlade, Ayansina, Abimbola Oluwaranti, Oluwatoyin S. Ayanlade, Marion Borderon, Harald Sterly, Patrick Sakdapolrak, Margaret O. Jegede, Lemlem F. Weldemariam, and Adefunke F. O. Ayinde. 2022. "Extreme Climate Events in Sub-Saharan Africa: A Call for Improving Agricultural Technology Transfer to Enhance Adaptive Capacity." *Climate Services* 27: 100311. https://doi.org/10.1016/j.cliser.2022.100311.

Ayanlade, Ayansina, Maren Radeny, and Akintomiwa Isaac Akin-Onigbinde. 2018. "Climate Variability/Change and Attitude to Adaptation Technologies: A Pilot Study among Selected Rural Farmers' Communities in Nigeria." *GeoJournal* 83 (2): 319–31. https://doi.org/10.1007/s10708-017-9771-1.

Ba, Mamoudou, Amar Anwar, and Mazhar Mughal. 2021. "Non-farm Employment and Poverty Reduction in Mauritania." *Journal of International Development* 33 (3): 490–514. https://doi.org/10.1002/jid.3533.

Ba, Mamoudou, and Mazhar Mughal. 2022. "Weather Shocks, Coping Strategies and Household Well-Being: Evidence from Rural Mauritania." *Journal of Development Studies* 58 (3): 482–502. https://doi.org/10.1080/00220388.2021.1983168.

Barrett, Sam. 2014. "Subnational Climate Justice? Adaptation Finance Distribution and Climate Vulnerability." *World Development* 58: 130–42. https://doi.org/10.1016/j.worlddev.2014.01.014.

Bathiany, Sebastian, Vasilis Dakos, Marten Scheffer, and Timothy M. Lenton. 2018. "Climate Models Predict Increasing Temperature Variability in Poor Countries." *Science Advances* 4 (5): eaar5809. https://doi.org/10.1126/sciadv.aar5809.

Bezner Kerr, Rachel, Toshihiro Hasegawa, Rodel Lasco, Indra Bhatt, Delphine Deryng, Aidan Farrell, Helen Gurney-Smith, et al. 2022. "Food, Fibre, and Other Ecosystem Products." In *Climate Change 2022: Impacts, Adaptation and Vulnerability. Contribution of Working Group II to the Sixth Assessment Report of the Intergovernmental Panel on Climate Change*, edited by H. O. Pörtner, D. C. Roberts, M. Tignor, E. S. Poloczanska, K. Mintenbeck, A. Alegría, M. Craig, et al., 713–906. Cambridge, United Kingdom: Cambridge University Press. https://doi.org/10.1017/9781009325844.007.714.

Bourguignon, François. 2015. "Revisiting the Debate on Inequality and Economic Development." *Revue d'économie Politique* 125 (5): 633–63. https://doi.org/10.3917/redp.255.0633.

Bruckner, Benedikt, Klaus Hubacek, Yuli Shan, Honglin Zhong, and Kuishuang Feng. 2022. "Impacts of Poverty Alleviation on National and Global Carbon Emissions." *Nature Sustainability* 5 (4): 311–20. https://doi.org/10.1038/s41893-021-00842-z.

Chancel, Lucas. 2022. "Global Carbon Inequality over 1990–2019." *Nature Sustainability* 5 (11): 931–38. https://doi.org/10.1038/s41893-022-00955-z.

Chancel, Lucas, Philippe Bothe, and Tancrède Voituriez. 2023. *Climate Inequality Report 2023*. Paris: World Inequality Lab.

Cissé, Guéladio, Robert McLeman, Helen Adams, Paulina Aldunce, Kathryn Bowen, Diarmid Campbell-Lendrum, Susan Clayton, et al. 2022. "Health, Wellbeing, and the Changing Structure of Communities." In *Climate Change 2022: Impacts, Adaptation and Vulnerability. Contribution of Working Group II to the Fifth Assessment Report of the Intergovernmental Panel on Climate Change*, edited by Hans-Otto Pörtner, Debra Roberts, Andreas Fischlin, Mark Howden, Carlos Méndez, Joy Jacqueline Pereira, Roberto A. Sánchez-Rodríguez, Sergey Semenov, Pius Yanda, and Taha M. Zatari, 1041–71. Cambridge, United Kingdom: Cambridge University Press. https://www.ipcc.ch/working-group/wg2/.

Danso-Mensah, Kwadwo, and Abena D. Oduro. Forthcoming. "Climate Shocks, Assets and Welfare. Evidence from Ghana." https://tsitica.uct.ac.za/sites/default/files/media/documents/2-climate-shocks -and-household-welfare-june-2023.pdf.

Davis-Reddy, Claire L., and Katharine Vincent. 2017. *Climate Risk and Vulnerability: A Handbook for Southern Africa*. Pretoria, South Africa: Council for Scientific and Industrial Research. http://hdl.handle .net/10204/10066.

Díaz Pabón, Fabio Andrés, Muna Shifa, Vimal Ranchhod, and Takwanisa Machemedze. 2024. "Assets, Climate Change Shocks, and Wellbeing in South Africa." *Economic Society of South Africa Biennial Meeting* 92 (1): 93–104.

Díaz Pabón, Fabio Andrés, Muna Shifa, Vimal Ranchhod, Abena D. Oduro, Damiano Manda, Kwadwo Danso-Mensah, Murray Leibbrandt, and Germano Mwabu. 2023. "Climate Change-Related Shocks, Resilience, and Welfare Outcomes: Evidence from Ghana, Kenya, and South Africa." Paper presented at the Inequality, Work, and Nature Conference, November 8–9, Cape Town, South Africa.

Diffenbaugh, Noah S., and Marshall Burke. 2019. "Global Warming Has Increased Global Economic Inequality." *Proceedings of the National Academy of Sciences* 116 (20): 9808–13. https://doi.org/10.1073 /pnas.1816020116.

Dychtwald, Zak. 2021. "China's New Innovation Advantage." *Harvard Business Review*, May–June. https://hbr.org/2021/05/chinas-new-innovation-advantage.

Efobi, Uchenna. 2022. "The Long-Term Labor Market Effect of Drought Exposure: Evidence from Nigeria." *Journal of Development Studies* 58 (8): 1531–49. https://doi.org/10.1080/00220388.2022.2055464.

Emediegwu, Lotanna E., Ada Wossink, and Alastair Hall. 2022. "The Impacts of Climate Change on Agriculture in Sub-Saharan Africa: A Spatial Panel Data Approach." *World Development* 158: 105967. https://doi.org/10.1016/j.worlddev.2022.105967.

Eriksen, Siri, E. Lisa F. Schipper, Morgan Scoville-Simonds, Katharine Vincent, Hans Nicolai Adam, Nick Brooks, Brian Harding, et al. 2021. "Adaptation Interventions and Their Effect on Vulnerability in Developing Countries: Help, Hindrance or Irrelevance?" *World Development* 141: 105383. https://doi.org/10.1016/j.worlddev.2020.105383.

FAO (Food and Agriculture Organization). 2023. *The Status of Women in Agrifood Systems.* Rome: FAO. https://doi.org/10.4060/cc5343en.

Faye, Ndeye Fatou, Moussa Sall, François Affholder, and Françoise Gérard. 2019. "Inégalités de Revenu En Milieu Rural Dans Le Bassin Arachidier Du Sénégal." AFD Research Paper 115, Agence Française de Développement, Paris.

Flückiger, Matthias, and Markus Ludwig. 2022. "Temperature and Risk of Diarrhoea among Children in Sub-Saharan Africa." *World Development* 160: 106070. https://doi.org/10.1016/j.worlddev.2022.106070.

Fouquet, Roger. 2016. "Historical Energy Transitions: Speed, Prices and System Transformation." *Energy Research & Social Science* 22: 7–12. https://doi.org/10.1016/j.erss.2016.08.014.

Fuller, Trevon L., Paul R. Sesink Clee, Kevin Y. Njabo, Anthony Tróchez, Katy Morgan, Demetrio Bocuma Meñe, Nicola M. Anthony, Mary Katherine Gonder, Walter R. Allen, and Rachid Hanna. 2018. "Climate Warming Causes Declines in Crop Yields and Lowers School Attendance Rates in Central Africa." *Science of the Total Environment* 610: 503–10. https://doi.org/10.1016/j.scitotenv.2017.08.041.

Gebrehiwot, Tagel, Hailemariam Teklewold, Mintewab Bezabih, and Robel Seifemichael. 2021. "Does a Portfolio of Consumption Adjustment Coping Strategies Erode Resilience? Panel Data Evidence from Ethiopia." *World Development Perspectives* 23: 100347. https://doi.org/10.1016/j.wdp.2021.100347.

Gradín, Carlos. 2021. "Inequality by Population Groups and Income Sources: Accounting for Inequality Changes in Spain During the Recession." *Review of Income and Wealth* 67 (2): 481–508. https://doi.org/10.1111/roiw.12470.

Greve, Hannes, and Jann Lay. 2023. "'Stepping Down the Ladder': The Impacts of Fossil Fuel Subsidy Removal in a Developing Country." *Journal of the Association of Environmental and Resource Economists* 10 (1): 121–58. https://doi.org/10.1086/721375.

Haji, Jema, and Belaineh Legesse. 2017. "Impact of Sedentarization Program on the Livelihood and Food Security of Ethiopian Pastoralists." *Journal of Arid Environments* 136: 45–53. https://doi.org/10.1016/j.jaridenv.2016.10.007.

Hallegatte, Stephane, Adrien Vogt-Schilb, Mook Bangalore, and Julie Rozenberg. 2017. *Unbreakable: Building the Resilience of the Poor in the Face of Natural Disasters.* Climate Change and Development. Washington, DC: World Bank.

IPCC (Intergovernmental Panel on Climate Change). 2022. "Summary for Policymakers." In *Climate Change 2022: Impacts, Adaptation, and Vulnerability. Contribution of Working Group II to the Sixth Assessment Report of the Intergovernmental Panel on Climate Change,* edited by H. O. Pörtner, D. C. Roberts, M. Tignor, E. S. Poloczanska, K. Mintenbeck, A. Alegría, M. Craig, et al., 3–36. Cambridge, United Kingdom: Cambridge University Press.

Islam, S. Nazrul, and John Winkel. 2017. *Climate Change and Social Inequality*. New York: United Nations Department of Economics and Social Affairs.

Janzen, Sarah A., and Michael R. Carter. 2019. "After the Drought: The Impact of Microinsurance on Consumption Smoothing and Asset Protection." *American Journal of Agricultural Economics* 101 (3): 651–71. https://doi.org/10.1093/ajae/aay061.

Kikstra, Jarmo S., Alessio Mastrucci, Jihoon Min, Keywan Riahi, and Narasimha D. Rao. 2021. "Decent Living Gaps and Energy Needs around the World." *Environmental Research Letters* 16 (9): 095006. https://doi.org/10.1088/1748-9326/ac1c27.

Lam, David. 2023. "How Will Population Growth and Income Growth in the World's Poorest Countries Affect Food, Water, Energy and Climate Change?" Keynote address presented at the Inequality, Work, and Nature Conference, November 8–9, Cape Town, South Africa.

Manda, Damiano Kulundu, Samuel Kipruto, Anthony Wambugu, Martine Oleche, Paul Samoei and Germano Mwabu. 2023. "Climate Change Vulnerability in Kenya: A Spatial and Socioeconomic Analysis of Household Sensitivity". TSITICA Working Paper No. 4. June. https://tsitica.uct.ac.za/sites /default/files/media/documents/tsitica_uct_ac_za/2171/4-climate-change-vulnerability-in-kenya-june -2023.pdf.

Manda, Damiano, Martine Oleche, Samuel Kipruto, Moses Muriithi, Reuben Mutegi, and Germano Mwabu. 2023. "The Impacts of Climate Change Shocks and Asset Ownership on Household Welfare in Kenya." TSITICA Working Paper No 7. June. https://tsitica.uct.ac.za/sites/default/files/media /documents/tsitica_uct_ac_za/2171/7-impact-of-climate-change-shocks-and-asset-ownership-kenya -june-2023.pdf.

Milanovic, Branko. 2016. *Global Inequality: A New Approach for the Age of Globalization*. Cambridge, MA: Harvard University Press. https://doi.org/10.2307/j.ctvjghwk4.

Oswald, Yannick, John K. Steinberger, Daniela Ivanova, and Joel Millward-Hopkins. 2021. "Global Redistribution of Income and Household Energy Footprints: A Computational Thought Experiment." *Global Sustainability* 4: e4. https://doi.org/10.1017/sus.2021.1.

Paglialunga, Elena, Andrea Coveri, and Antonello Zanfei. 2022. "Climate Change and Within-Country Inequality: New Evidence from a Global Perspective." *World Development* 159: 106030. https://doi .org/10.1016/j.worlddev.2022.106030.

Phillips, Carly A., Astrid Caldas, Rachel Cleetus, Kristina A. Dahl, Juan Declet-Barreto, Rachel Licker, L. Delta Merner, et al. 2020. "Compound Climate Risks in the COVID-19 Pandemic." *Nature Climate Change* 10 (7): 586–88. https://doi.org/10.1038/s41558-020-0804-2.

Serdeczny, Olivia, Sophie Adams, Florent Baarsch, Dim Coumou, Alexander Robinson, William Hare, Michiel Schaeffer, Mahé Perrette, and Julia Reinhardt. 2017. "Climate Change Impacts in Sub-Saharan Africa: From Physical Changes to Their Social Repercussions." *Regional Environmental Change* 17: 1585–1600. https://doi.org/10.1007/s10113-015-0910-2.

Shifa, Muna, Murray Leibbrandt, and David Gordon. 2023. "Profiling Multidimensional Climate-Related Vulnerability in South Africa." TSITICA Working Paper No 3. June. https://tsitica.uct.ac.za/sites/default /files/media/documents/tsitica_uct_ac_za/2171/3-profiling-multidimensional-climate-change -vulnerability-june-2023.pdf.

Stern, Nicholas. 2007. *The Economics of Climate Change: The Stern Review*. Cambridge, United Kingdom: Cambridge University Press. https://doi.org/10.1017/CBO9780511817434.

Taconet, Nicolas, Aurélie Méjean, and Céline Guivarch. 2020. "Influence of Climate Change Impacts and Mitigation Costs on Inequality between Countries." *Climatic Change* 160 (1): 15–34. https://doi.org /10.1007/s10584-019-02637-w.

Thomas, Kimberley Anh, and Benjamin P. Warner. 2019. "Weaponizing Vulnerability to Climate Change." *Global Environmental Change* 57: 101928. https://doi.org/10.1016/j.gloenvcha.2019.101928.

Trisos, Christopher H., Ibidun O. Adelekan, Edmond Totin, Ayansina Ayanlade, Jackson Efitre, Adugna Gemeda, Kanungwe Kalaba, et al. 2022. "Africa." In *Climate Change 2022: Impacts, Adaptation and Vulnerability. Contribution of Working Group II to the Sixth Assessment Report of the Intergovernmental Panel on Climate Change*, edited by H. O. Pörtner, D. C. Roberts, M. Tignor, E. S. Poloczanska, K. Mintenbeck, A. Alegría, M. Craig, et al., 1285–1456. Cambridge, United Kingdom: Cambridge University Press. https://doi.org/10.1017/9781009325844.011.1286.

Vona, Francesco, and Fabrizio Patriarca. 2011. "Income Inequality and the Development of Environmental Technologies." *Ecological Economics* 70 (11): 2201–13. https://doi.org/10.1016/j.ecolecon.2011.06.027.

Winsemius, Hessel C., Brenden Jongman, Ted I. E. Veldkamp, Stephane Hallegatte, Mook Bangalore, and Philip J. Ward. 2018. "Disaster Risk, Climate Change, and Poverty: Assessing the Global Exposure of Poor People to Floods and Droughts." *Environment and Development Economics* 23 (3): 328–48. https://doi.org/10.1017/S1355770X17000444.

Wollburg, Philip, Stephane Hallegatte, and Daniel Gerszon Mahler. 2023. "The Climate Implications of Ending Global Poverty." Policy Research Working Paper 10318, World Bank, Washington, DC.

Work, Courtney, Vannrith Rong, Danik Song, and Arnim Scheidel. 2019. "Maladaptation and Development as Usual? Investigating Climate Change Mitigation and Adaptation Projects in Cambodia." *Climate Policy* 19 (Suppl. 1): S47–S62. https://doi.org/10.1080/14693062.2018.1527677.

World Bank. 2022. *Inequality in Southern Africa: An Assessment of the Southern African Customs Union.* Washington, DC: World Bank. https://doi.org/10.1596/37283.

Zhou, Leocadia, Dumisani Shoko Kori, Melusi Sibanda, and Kenneth Nhundu. 2022. "An Analysis of the Differences in Vulnerability to Climate Change: A Review of Rural and Urban Areas in South Africa." *Climate* 10 (8): 118. https://doi.org/10.3390/cli10080118.

Chapter 11

Sustainability and Patterns of Economic Growth

Rawane Yasser, Murray Leibbrandt, Anda David, Fabio Andrés Díaz Pabón, and Hélène Djoufelkit

Introduction

Promoting inclusive and sustainable economic growth as part of the United Nations 2030 Agenda places questions of sustainability and distribution at the center of the discussions. Over the past 30 years, most African countries have experienced rapid economic growth. However, economic growth has translated into poverty reduction only to a limited extent, especially for the poorest of the poor in African societies. This issue has prompted concerns about the long-term sustainability of Africa's economic expansion and its ability to translate growth success into achieving key development goals.

An extensive literature refers to the noninclusiveness of economic growth in Africa as the main reason behind its development performance (Christiaensen, Chuhan-Pole, and Sanoh 2013; Cornia 2017; Fosu 2018, 2023; Odusola 2019; Odusola et al. 2017). More pointedly, Africa's sluggish translation of economic growth into poverty reduction is seen as symptomatic of the gains from economic growth being unequally distributed and captured by those at the top of the distribution (Clementi et al. 2019), while adding to the ecological pressures that put the well-being of future generations at risk (Global Footprint Network 2023). It seems that high inequality has been one of the main culprits behind the failure of economic growth to translate into poverty reduction over the past years in Africa, as suggested by the poverty-growth-inequality (PGI) triangle (Bourguignon 2004).

This chapter benefited from valuable feedback from Harald Winkler.

Beyond these consequences for social sustainability, economic growth has not been sustainable from an environmental perspective. Carbon-intensive economic growth has had detrimental ecological effects and caused environmental destruction at an unprecedented pace (IPCC 2022). The aftermath of the COVID-19 pandemic and understanding of planetary limits have made it clear that the past patterns of growth have not been sustainable. Indeed, some authors raised this idea long before the pandemic (for instance, refer to Raworth 2022). Thus, this chapter argues that, in the post-pandemic context, going back to the old strategies of reigniting growth would at best replicate past performance, with serious consequences for climate change, poverty reduction, and the sustainability of African societies. The imperative of climate action makes business-as-usual economic growth strategies even less likely to succeed in providing an enabling environment for the whole population.

The chapter discusses the relationships among growth, poverty, and inequality, leaning on Bourguignon's (2004) PGI framework, before examining how past patterns of growth have not been sustainable from social and environmental perspectives. The PGI framework shows that inequality is key and highlights why seeking economic growth without addressing the distributive base will most likely fail to achieve the objective of reducing poverty. The chapter identifies the factors, alongside inequality, that are determinants of the unsustainability of past patterns. It then draws on alternative approaches from the sustainability literature to rethink current models of economic growth and development.

Growth, Poverty, and Inequality

The African Development Bank defines *inclusive growth* as "economic growth that results in a wider access to sustainable socio-economic opportunities for a broader number of people, regions or countries, while protecting the vulnerable, all being done in an environment of fairness, equal justice, and political plurality" (African Development Bank 2012, 1). This approach focuses on opportunities, productivity, and employment for poor and middle-class populations alike. Thus, an inclusive pattern of growth would have low levels of inequality and significant reductions in poverty. However, the rate of translation of economic growth into poverty reduction in Africa has been the lowest globally (Christiaensen et al. 2013; Cornia 2017; Odusola et al. 2017). High initial levels of inequality have been suggested as the main reason behind this performance (Bergstrom 2022; Fofana, Chitiga-Mabugu, and Mabugu 2023; Fosu 2018; Thorbecke and Ouyang 2018).

It is crucial to understand the relationships among growth, poverty, and inequality, which is the focus of this section. The chapter then turns to the broader consequences of the process of economic growth, moving beyond the impacts of growth on poverty reduction, to assess the broader socioeconomic impacts within the discussion of inclusive growth.

Growth and Poverty Reduction

Despite its fast progress in economic growth, Africa's performance in poverty reduction has fallen behind, and its rate of the translation of economic growth into poverty reduction has been less than global averages (Fosu 2018; Odusola et al. 2019). Although poverty has fallen with growth in Africa, the decline has not been as rapid as in other parts of the world, such as East Asia and South Asia (refer to figure 11.1). As a result, Africa's share of global poverty has increased. Africa is forecast to be home to 85 percent of the world's poor population by 2030 (Lakner et al. 2022). Examining the progress in poverty reduction in Sub-Saharan Africa (SSA), Fofana et al. (2023) found that 55 percent of African countries are not on track to halve the poverty rate between 2015 and 2030 under their current rates of income growth and inequality.[1]

Plotting the share of Africans in each global income group shows a concentration of the African population in the bottom of the distribution (refer to figure 11.2), making Africa's economic growth a dominant driver of income for the individuals in the lowest part of the global distribution. According to Milanovic (2016), the very poorest individuals have been locked out of growth. In 2016, 33 percent of the population of the world's poorest 10 percent (10th percentile) of the income distribution resided in SSA, compared to 21 percent in 1990, with almost no representation of Africans in the top 0.1 percent (refer to figure 11.2). Thus, the condition of the African population has worsened compared with the rest of the world, as the share of Africans in the lowest 30 percent of the income distribution has increased. The top 0.1 percent of earners globally captured 13 percent of the world's total growth.

Figure 11.1 Percentage of the Population Living on Less Than US$1.90 per Day, 1981–2019

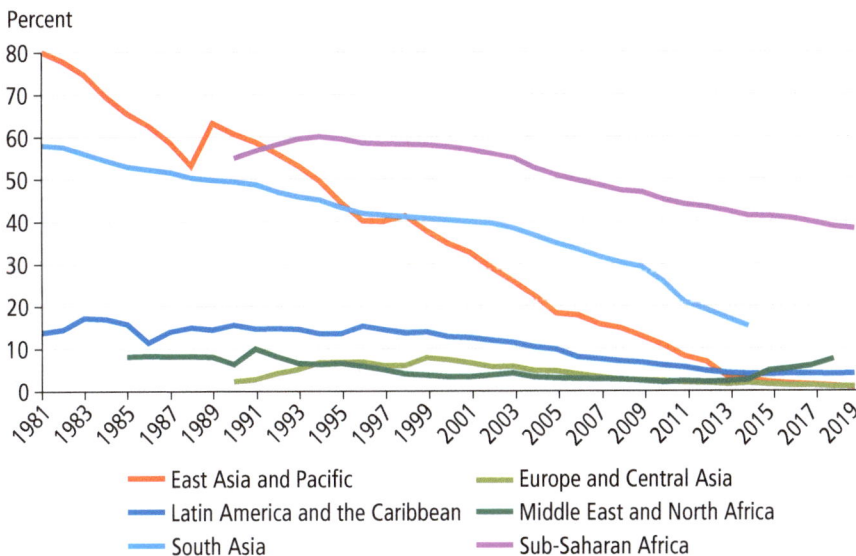

Source: Authors' elaboration using data from World Development Indicators, World Bank.

Figure 11.2 Sub-Saharan Africa's Share in Global Income Groups, 1990 and 2016

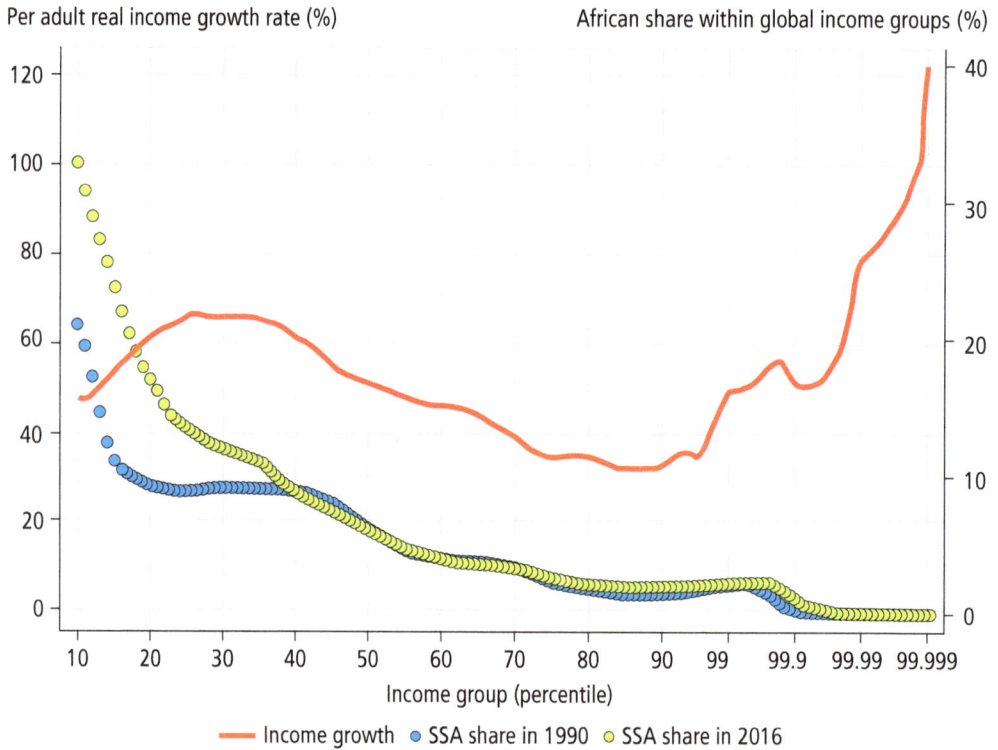

Per adult real income growth rate (%)

African share within global income groups (%)

Income group (percentile)

— Income growth   ● SSA share in 1990   ○ SSA share in 2016

Source: Authors' calculations based on replication files from WID.world.
Note: The figure shows the cumulative growth rate between 1990 and 2016 of pre-tax national income measured in 2016 purchasing power parity euros. In 2016, 33 percent of the population of the world's 10th percentile of the income distribution resided in SSA. SSA = Sub-Saharan Africa.

To understand this situation, studies have highlighted how Africa's economic growth has been unevenly distributed and has not reached many of the poor population (Chancel 2020; Christiaensen et al. 2013; Cornia 2017; Fosu 2018, 2023; Odusola et al. 2017). Research has shown that the poverty reduction effect of economic growth (the growth elasticity of poverty, or GEP) has been low in Africa, and SSA has the lowest GEP in the world. Clearly, this growth pattern is not inclusive (Cornia 2017; Odusola 2019; Thorbecke and Ouyang 2018).

When the focus shifts from income poverty to multidimensional poverty, the situation does not look better. Indeed, in Africa, the effect of growth on multidimensional poverty is estimated to be even lower than the GEP (Balasubramanian, Burchi, and Malerba 2023). Using indexes of multidimensional poverty that include education, work, and health as dimensions of poverty, Balasubramanian et al. (2023) found that a 10-percent increase in gross domestic product (GDP) decreases multidimensional poverty by only 3–4 percent.

Role of Inequality

Figure 11.3 spans Africa's positive growth era and is an African version of Milanovic's (2016) global elephant curve, which shows a noninclusive growth pattern. The African curve shares the global top-end trunk but does not have the substantial bottom-end body that makes up the rest of the global elephant. The top 1 percent of earners in Africa captured 27 percent of total growth in the continent, explaining to an extent why growth in Africa has been even less inclusive than the global situation.

Africa has demonstrated high inequality over the years (refer to chapter 1 in this book for a comprehensive view of inequality trends in Africa). Some of the most unequal countries in the world are in Africa, especially in Southern Africa (Odusola et al. 2017). Countries such as Angola, Botswana, Namibia, South Africa, and Zambia have Gini coefficients above 0.50 (UNU-WIDER 2022).

A long-standing and important tradition in development economics has examined the theoretical and empirical relationships among growth, poverty, and inequality. Kuznets articulated an inverted U-shaped development-inequality relationship in which inequality first increases and then declines as a country's GDP increases (Kuznets 1955). However, inequality patterns in Africa do not offer strong supporting evidence for Kuznets-type trajectories. Many contexts are yet to experience a decline. Batuo, Kararach, and Malki (2022) found that Kuznets curve relationships hold only for the poorest African economies. Moreover, they showed that the only factors that can tackle inequality in high-income economies are employment, the rule of law, and monetary policies. Odusola et al. (2019) found that, while inequality may have declined in Africa as a whole, this decrease was mostly driven by economies with initially lower inequality.

Figure 11.3 Growth Incidence Curve for Africa, 1980–2016

Per adult real income growth rate (%)

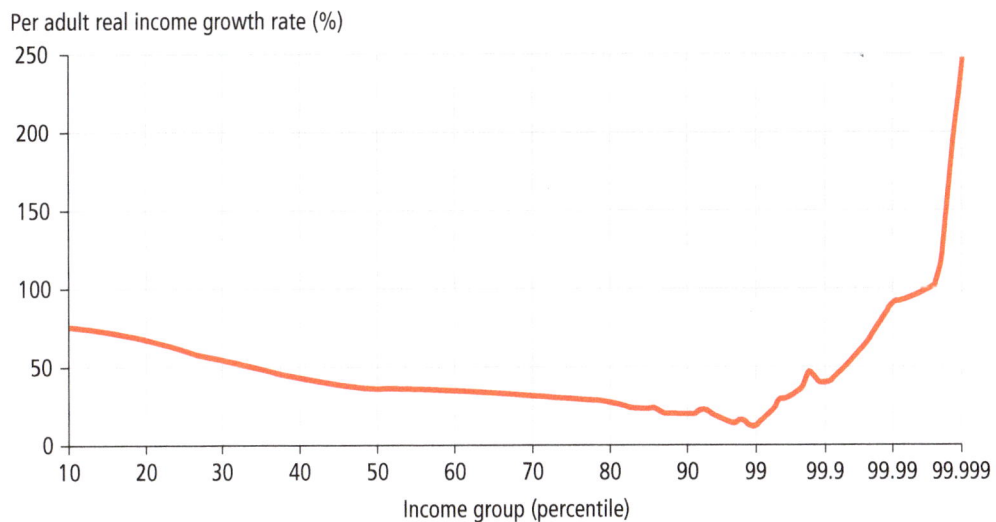

Income group (percentile)

Source: Authors' calculations based on replication files from WID.world.
Note: The figure shows the cumulative growth rate between 1980 and 2016 of pre-tax national income measured in 2016 purchasing power parity euros. Incomes of the bottom 10 percent of the top 1 percent of earners (percentile p99p99.1) grew at 13 percent between 1980 and 2016. The top 1 percent captured 27 percent of total growth.

Bourguignon (2004) and Ravallion (2005) have argued that inequality itself dampens the positive impact of growth on poverty reduction. According to Bourguignon (2004), poverty is conditioned by both the nature of inequalities and economic growth. Thorbecke (2013) found that the combination of high initial levels of poverty and inequality weakens the reducing effect of growth on poverty. Fosu (2018, 2023) extended this point, arguing that the low GEP could be a function of growing inequalities, which further reduces the impact of economic growth on the poor population.

Odusola (2019) supported the finding that inequality reduces economic growth's ability to alleviate poverty, suggesting that it also undermines social progress in domains such as education and health. This issue can trigger economic instability, thereby reducing the durability of growth. This evidence shows that efficient distribution or redistribution is key to achieving inclusive and sustained development in Africa, with economic growth only as a means, not an end.

Recent research has sought to quantify the importance of reducing inequalities to achieve the goal of reducing extreme poverty. Clementi, Fabiani, and Molini (2019) showed that poverty could have been 6–7 percentage points lower in Africa if polarization had not increased.[2] They explained that 31 African countries experienced important increases in polarization, significantly reducing the pro-poor impact of growth. To quantify the impact of reduced inequality on poverty, Lakner et al. (2022) simulated the evolution of extreme poverty until 2030 under different scenarios to forecast how inequality and economic growth evolve in each country. They found that changes in the Gini index have a larger impact on poverty than changes in economic growth. This finding is particularly relevant for SSA, where a 1-percent change in the Gini index results in a 30-percent to 40-percent change in projected poverty rates (Lakner et al. 2022). This finding also resonates with Bergstrom's (2022) identification of two important roles of income inequality in reducing poverty, namely, a direct effect and an indirect effect through the GEP.

Further research supports one or both of these channels. Through a decomposition of changes in poverty, Fosu (2023) examined heterogeneous progress in reducing poverty across African countries and its relationship with inequality. Many countries, such as Cameroon, Ghana, and Tanzania, have performed well on income growth, but their poor performance on inequality reduction has led to weak progress on poverty. In contrast, countries such as Burkina Faso, The Gambia, Guinea, Malawi, and Mauritania have had less-impressive income growth, but they transformed growth into strong poverty reduction due to improvements in their income distributions and income distribution policies.

The weak relationship between economic growth and poverty can also be explained by high initial levels of inequality, which are higher in Africa than in other regions (Bergstrom 2022; Fofana et al. 2023; Fosu 2018; Thorbecke and Ouyang 2018). While high initial poverty and inequality can reduce the economic growth rate directly, they also can reduce the poverty-reducing effect of growth (Christiaensen et al. 2013). In SSA, high levels of initial inequality and low initial income have significantly reduced the GEP (Thorbecke and Ouyang 2018).

Examining the relationships among initial inequality, change in poverty, and change in GDP shows that the higher the initial inequality is, the lower the decrease in poverty is. To describe the role of initial inequalities in poverty, annex 11A compares national Gini indexes across African countries between 1980 and 2019, using data from the World Bank's Poverty and Inequality Platform. The analysis starts by categorizing the countries by their initial Gini indexes[3] and then examines the changes in poverty in the three categories. Countries with high levels of initial inequality (Gini index higher than 50), such as Angola, Kenya, Malawi, and Zimbabwe, saw their poverty rates increase in the face of positive economic growth. These findings are consistent with recent literature, which found that, if growth is distribution neutral, then the higher the initial levels of inequality are, the lower is the share of the gains from economic growth that reaches poor people in the absence of redistribution policies (Ravallion 2022).

In addition, the inequality elasticity of poverty reduction in SSA has increased in recent years, suggesting that poverty reduction is becoming more sensitive to levels of inequality and more responsive to improvements in inequality (Thorbecke and Ouyang 2022). Socioeconomic improvements associated with reductions in inequality will benefit more poor people and, in turn, have a greater impact on poverty reduction (Thorbecke and Ouyang 2018).

In summary, the message from the development economics literature is clear: Inequality hampers the poverty-reducing impact of economic growth. Reducing inequality is key for reaching the goal of reducing poverty. Therefore, understanding and reversing the inequality dynamics in Africa are foundational for making economic growth more inclusive.

Africa, particularly SSA, has experienced a significant increase in polarization that greatly affected the lower end of the distribution (Clementi, Fabiani, and Molini 2019; Clementi et al. 2019, 2022). Analysis of this period of polarization has indicated that the growth process in SSA was accompanied by increased concentration in the upper and lower ends of the distribution, with a hollowing out of the middle (Clementi et al. 2022). The effect of polarization clearly offsets the decrease in poverty that could have taken place due to economic growth. Importantly, the studies have noted that this picture is not as starkly captured by the standard measures of inequality that are most sensitive to changes taking place around the middle or even the top end of the distribution. What emerges is a picture of noninclusive growth that increases the divide between the bottom 40 percent of the population and the rest.

For South Africa, one of the most unequal countries on the continent, Zizzamia, Schotte, and Ranchhod (2016) examined the polarized pattern of growth, revealing that the middle of the income distribution has had the lowest growth rates for most of the post-apartheid period.

Coupled with the increase in national income at the very top of the distribution and the growth of incomes at the bottom of the distribution being driven by the expansion of cash transfers, the analysis showed how past patterns of growth have not been inclusive. South Africa's polarized growth model since 1994 has resulted in inequality and few in the middle of the income distribution (Bhorat, Tseng, and Stanwix 2014).

Finally, the concept of *inequalities,* which lies at the center of social sustainability, includes not only income inequality but also inequalities in access to education and health, as well as spatial and intergenerational inequalities, as shown in the previous chapters. Inequality of opportunity, as measured by intergenerational mobility, has a detrimental impact on the effect of growth on poverty, therefore hampering the inclusive nature of growth (Ebeke 2023; refer also to chapter 8). By holding back human capital development and reducing incentives for education, inequality of opportunity makes growth less inclusive and leaves many people behind.

Why Growth Has Not Been Inclusive

This section reviews explanations for the problematic texture of economic growth, including long-run forces leading to the high dependence of many African countries on mining and natural resources, a skewed political economy, the dominance of extractive industries, the quality of employment created through growth, and the rate of employment growth lagging behind the rate of growth.

Historical, Institutional, and Structural Factors

According to Acemoglu and Robinson (2010), an important factor in sustained economic growth is *institutional formation,* which is reform of the state as it moves away from *absolutism,* in which power is absolute and unconstrained by institutions. A key legacy of the colonial period in Africa is that it constrained the possibilities for newly independent African countries to transition away from the absolutist and extractive structures embedded in colonial and institutional systems (Acemoglu and Robinson 2010). This issue has translated into sluggish growth in the long term.

In addition, an important driver of the high level of inequality in many African economies is the institutional legacy from colonial times of small European populations maintaining control of the resources along with highly extractive institutions. Some wealth was transferred to Indigenous populations on independence. However, the transfers were to small groups of African elites, thus hampering a more-equal distribution of resources and opportunities (Odusola et al. 2019). Therefore, many scholars have argued that the post-colonial growth pattern in Africa has closely maintained the form of extractive institutions from the colonial past and disproportionately benefited the political and economic elites and importer countries rather than the middle-class and poor populations (Acemoglu and Robinson 2010;

Clementi et al. 2022). The form and function of these extractive institutions have been maintained and can explain Africa's resource dependence as the main driver of its growth.

A narrower variant of this argument holds that Africa's resource dependence has been a main cause of the dampened performance of translating economic growth into poverty reduction. In countries that are more dependent on natural resources, with highly capital-intensive industries and few opportunities for local employment creation, the risk of rising inequality is higher. Growth continues to be based on the production of basic commodities and extraction of mineral resources and agriculture (Bhorat and Oosthuizen 2020). This reality helps explain why the surge in commodity prices over the past decade has driven impressive economic growth in many African countries, but it has failed to translate into improved living standards for the population (Odusola et al. 2019; Thorbecke and Ouyang 2022).

Nigeria provides an example of such a pattern of exclusive growth, mainly driven by resource extraction, in which the benefits are largely confined to the natural resource sector, with minimal impact on other segments of the economy and poverty alleviation (Thorbecke and Ouyang 2022). These processes are dynamic, and growth in resource dependence has been associated with increasing inequality as the share of mineral rents in the economy increases. This phenomenon is more prominent in Africa than in the rest of the world (Christiaensen et al. 2013; Niño-Zarazúa et al. 2023).

Institutions are one channel through which resource dependence impacts income redistribution. In the presence of natural resource rents, the strength of elite cohesion and connectedness with political regimes undermines the possibility of progressive taxation, thereby increasing inequality. Indeed, social protection and progressive taxation are used less effectively in highly resource-dependent countries. Auty (1997) showed how natural resource endowment is strongly linked to the choice of development policies. Resource-rich countries are more prone to factional political states that are mainly preoccupied with rents as opposed to resource-deficient countries that tend to have subsistence farming–dominated systems. In addition, high capital intensity in resource-dependent countries hampers employment creation.

Pattern of Economic Growth and Quality of Employment

The focus on mineral dependency has drawn attention to the need to consider the pattern of economic growth as a key determinant of low GEP. In addition to the level of economic growth, the sources and decomposition of growth matter. Growth in labor-intensive sectors, such as agriculture and light manufacturing, usually reduces poverty more than growth in capital-intensive sectors, such as mining (Christiaensen et al. 2013; Odusola et al. 2019). Sectors with higher labor productivity and labor-intensive sectors can boost wage employment and, hence, can decrease income inequality. In contrast, capital-intensive sectors can generate high economic growth but with fewer jobs, therefore increasing inequality.

Quantifying these impacts, Morsy, Shimeles, and Nabassaga (2023) found that a standard deviation increase in the movement of labor from low- to high-productivity sectors could decrease overall inequality by 0.5 percent, suggesting that positive structural transformation could lead to a sustained reduction in inequality in Africa. Winkler and Black (2021) highlighted this trade-off in South Africa, showing that post-apartheid growth has continued long-run patterns that are highly reliant on capital-intensive and low-employment-intensive industries. Thus, the country is in the difficult situation of having extremely high unemployment and inequalities and needing to restructure its industries.

According to Cornia (2017), in Africa, growth would be equalizing only if employment opportunities in rural areas and labor-intensive manufacturing improved. However, in practice, growth processes in many African countries have not followed this path (Clementi et al. 2019, 2022; Thorbecke 2013). Instead, the pattern of growth is largely driven by growth in the primary sector and a lack of development in the manufacturing sector (Djoufelkit 2008a, 2008b). That manufacturing growth has been a major driver of sustained poverty reduction and job creation in other countries is notable (Odusola et al. 2019).

Although some employment has shifted away from agriculture, it has not shifted toward manufacturing. While the share of agriculture in GDP has decreased in many African countries, most of the shift has been to the low-productivity service sector or mining. This issue does not represent a reallocation of labor to high-productivity sectors (Thorbecke 2023). Indeed, industry has grown in Africa, but it is dominated by mining activities.

The tertiary service sector has also grown, absorbing most of the shift away from agriculture. However, in many African contexts, these activities are informal and not productive. Growth has mainly taken place in mining and the informal sectors rather than in sectors in which much of the population derives livelihoods, such as agriculture and smallholder enterprises (Odusola et al. 2019). The World Bank has highlighted the transition from agriculture toward sectors characterized by low productivity as a transition from low-productivity/low-inequality sectors to low-productivity/high-inequality sectors. This issue underlies low GEP (Chuhan-Pole and Ferreira 2014).

While moving to nonagricultural employment contributes to poverty reduction according to structural transformation theories of development, in practice the quality of nonagricultural employment has been key. In many African contexts, the quality of nonagricultural jobs has not been sufficient to allow individuals to earn enough to improve their well-being significantly in the long term (World Bank 2019).

Studies have argued that enhancing agricultural production can increase the poverty-reducing impact of economic growth. The growth coming from agriculture has, on average, been more poverty-reducing than the growth coming from other sectors (Christiaensen et al. 2013).

Many African countries, especially resource-rich countries, are net importers of staple agricultural products such as rice, wheat, and sugar. This reality highlights the need to increase Africa's productivity in staple crop production. Increasing the crop productivity of smallholder farms generates the largest poverty reduction, especially with food crops (Christiaensen et al. 2013).

Countries such as Cameroon, Ethiopia, and Madagascar have followed an equalizing growth pattern as the share of labor-intensive manufacturing increased and that of mining fell. The shift to capital-intensive sectors was less marked and more equitable in a context of egalitarian land distribution. The example of these countries underscores increased agricultural productivity with egalitarian land distribution as a key determinant of inequality reduction and a sustainable growth pattern (Cornia 2017).

The cases of Ghana, Malawi, Rwanda, and Uganda also illustrate the fundamental role of agriculture as a driver of both growth and poverty reduction through strategies of agricultural development (Arndt, McKay, and Tarp 2016). In contrast, in Burkina Faso, Mozambique, Nigeria, and Tanzania, weak agricultural productivity growth has been an underlying factor in the slow rate of poverty reduction. For countries where a large share of the population works in low-productivity smallholder agriculture, increasing agricultural productivity can be a powerful tool for achieving sustained growth and poverty reduction over the long run (Roudier and Dia 2021).

Many African countries have low levels of unemployment but high levels of informality, working-poor individuals, and vulnerable employment. Therefore, Africa is better characterized as having an employment quality problem rather than an unemployment problem, with a labor market characterized by low-quality employment, high informality, low productivity, and the dominance of agriculture (Fields 2023; Fields et al. 2023). This reason is why the economic growth observed in Africa has not positively impacted working-poor individuals (Clementi et al. 2022).

According to the World Bank (2019), the growth process has not benefited the bottom 40 percent of the distribution, which is identified as those living below the poverty line and those at risk of poverty when faced with a negative shock. This segment of the population is often trapped in a labor market characterized by low productivity, high seasonality, and unstable incomes. The challenge would be not to decrease unemployment but rather to increase the productivity of the informal sector, which constitutes the largest share of employment in most African countries (refer to chapter 4).

Quantity of Employment

The earlier focus on the quality of employment is not to deny that the quantity of employment creation is also important. In Africa, economic growth has not led to

Figure 11.4 Employment and Income Growth in Africa, 1980–2017

Change in total employment (%)

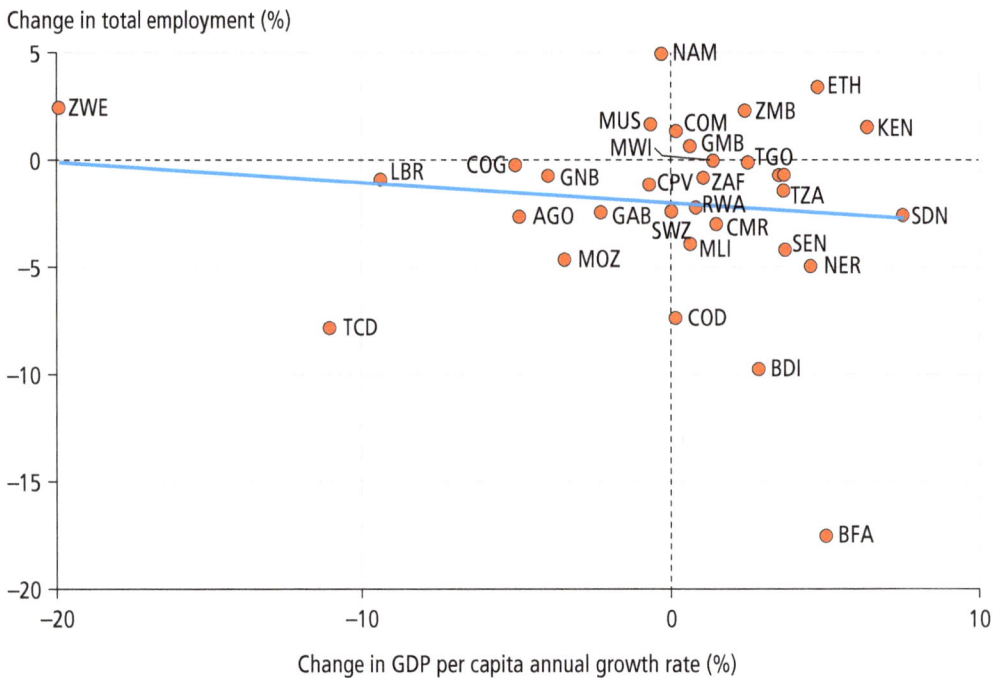

Change in GDP per capita annual growth rate (%)

Source: Authors' calculations based on World Bank data.
Note: For a list of country codes, refer to https://www.iso.org/obp/ui/#search. GDP = gross domestic product.

substantial employment creation. Crucially, employment creation has lagged behind economic growth (Odusola et al. 2019).

The correlation between employment growth and GDP growth is weak. The data analysis presented in figure 11.4 shows that economic growth has not translated into an increase in employment in Africa. Indeed, if anything, the weak trend reflects a negative relationship between growth and employment between 1980 and 2017.

As discussed in chapter 4, enabling access to labor markets is the strongest determinant of income inequality reduction. This reality is illustrated in figure 11.5, which shows that employment growth is crucial for inequality reduction, with higher employment growth being associated with lower inequality. As GDP per capita growth between 1980 and 2017 did not entail an increase in employment, it can be argued that it was also a missed opportunity to decrease inequality.

Figure 11.5 Employment and Inequality in Africa, 1980–2017

Change in Gini index

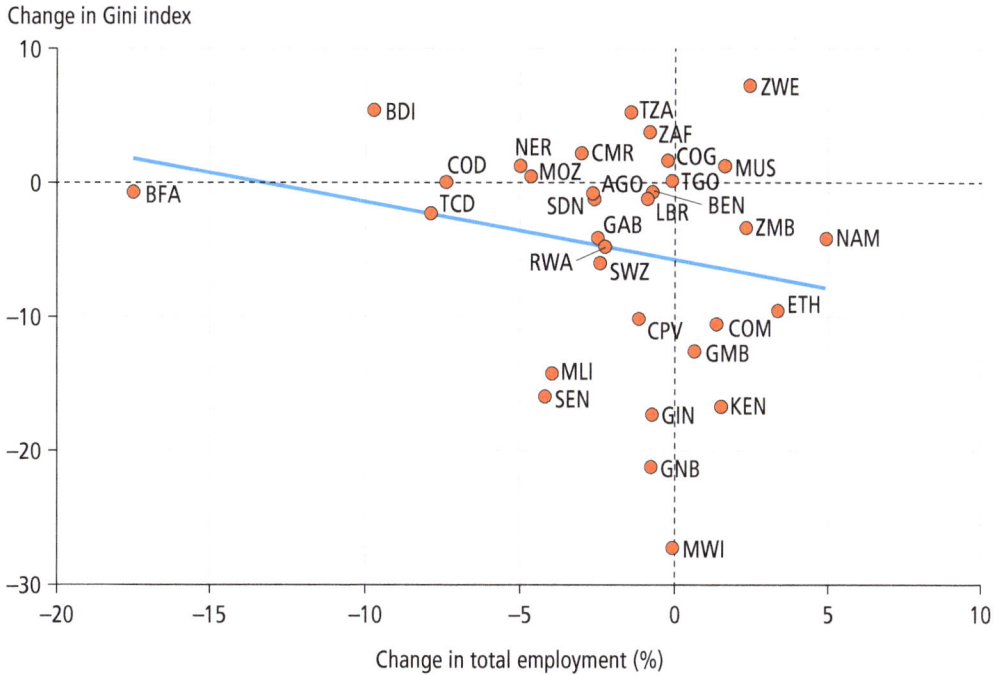

Source: Authors' calculations based on World Bank data.
Note: The x-axis shows change in the employment-to-population ratio for the population ages 15 and older. The data are for the earliest and latest available year between 1980 and 2017. For a list of country codes, refer to https://www .iso.org/obp/ui/#search.

With economic growth generating low quantities of low-quality employment, initial income inequality continues to have a strong effect on growth-poverty elasticities through initial wage inequality (Odusola et al. 2019). The contrast between high-wage incomes in the formal economy and low-wage incomes in the informal economy is persistent rather than being diluted through growth. Such a labor market is far from optimal in Africa, where the rapidly growing working-age population must be productively absorbed into the labor market. Young workers in Africa will comprise most of the world's working-age population, and they will be entering the labor market at an average annual growth rate of more than 2 percent over 2010–30. Hence, promoting job-creating growth is needed (Lam and Leibbrandt 2023; Odusola et al. 2019).

Employment is closely linked to the challenge of human capital development in Africa, whereby the poor quality of educational systems and post-primary education hinders the development of human capital and the path to more-equitable and -sustainable economic growth (Odusola et al. 2019). As discussed at length in chapter 3, Africa has achieved high primary school enrollment rates, but secondary school enrollment rates are lagging behind. This issue does not create an adequate supply of the labor skills necessary to undergird an inclusive growth path of productive employment creation that spreads the benefits of economic growth to a wider population, therefore reducing extreme inequality and poverty (Thorbecke and Ouyang 2018).

Fields (2023) summed up this situation by suggesting that, to overcome Africa's employment challenge, taking measures to achieve job-creating growth, raising the returns to self-employment, and investing in human capital formation are priority policy actions. In the current African context, increasing informal work will not be sufficient to reduce income inequality and generate growth multipliers. At the same time, the structure of African economies limits the possibility of creating quality jobs. This situation and persistent inequalities across ethnic, gender, and class lines explain the difficulties in creating equitable development (Morsy et al. 2023) and, hence, the need to think beyond economic growth.

Reducing unemployment through formal employment growth alone will not be sufficient. With the majority of young African workers moving from rural areas to cities in search of employment and ending up in urban self-employment or unemployment, addressing the informal sector is crucial (Houngbedji and Zanuso 2021). Making the informal sector a more-sustainable type of employment by creating linkages to the formal sector and providing a business environment conducive to the prosperity of the informal sector are essential for more-equitable and -sustainable growth (Odusola et al. 2019).

At the same time, agriculture plays a central role in African economies. Therefore, promoting growth in the agriculture sector and increasing its competitiveness to reduce poverty and income inequality, while decreasing its environmental footprint, are critical, too. This issue suggests retaining and even increasing policy emphasis on improving the productivity of smallholder farms through crop productivity, rural public goods, and commercial smallholder farming (Christiaensen et al. 2013).

The previous patterns of economic growth have not been inclusive due to narrow opportunities reflected by high levels of initial inequality, high dependence on mining and extractive industries, low levels of manufacturing, and employment creation lagging behind economic growth. Finally, beyond the quantum of employment opportunities, the quality of employment must remain a priority in development agendas. The narrative of the supposed trade-off implied by "any job is better than no job" is still present in policy discussions across the continent. However, the process of structural change that leads to development comes down to "people moving from bad jobs to better jobs" (Rodrik 2023). Thus, labor market institutions must be strengthened to create the conditions for employment to become a pathway to higher living standards as part of a human-centered development strategy that goes beyond traditional GDP maximization objectives.

Beyond Growth: Rethinking Models of Economic Growth

Post-COVID-19, it is imperative that economies grow again. However, stimulating economies to resume pre-COVID-19 historical growth trajectories will, at best, generate the same disappointing employment, poverty, and inequality outcomes as those detailed in this chapter. Seeking economic growth without a distributive focus to change the texture of that growth will have disappointing returns for poverty reduction. Moreover, the imperative of climate action makes such "business-as-usual" economic growth strategies even less likely to succeed in providing an enabling environment for the whole population. With few exceptions, African countries must do things differently to make economic growth more sustainable and achieve faster progress in reducing poverty.

The previous chapters explored policies to reduce inequality, which will assist in achieving more-inclusive growth. This section focuses on policies to achieve socially and environmentally sustainable growth. First, it addresses social sustainability; then, it broadens the focus on sustainable growth to include climate change. The climate change literature has contributed to framing the role of economic growth within a broader discussion of strategies for more-sustainable and -inclusive development. This framing has led to a proliferation of alternative frameworks, from minor adjustments to GDP calculations to more-radical propositions of reduced growth (Hickel 2021; Parrique 2021). The section reviews these and discusses implications for economic growth.

Social Sustainability

A first step toward social sustainability is to prioritize policies that build social and economic inclusion (UNFCCC 2023b). A prominent commonality across proponents of inclusive growth is a foundational commitment to social protection as a platform for making growth more inclusive (African Development Bank 2018; Odusola 2019; Raworth 2022).

Social protection is expanding in Africa, but coverage is too low to reduce inequality significantly. Over 1990–2010, the average social protection expenditure was 4 percent of GDP in SSA, compared to 7.1 percent globally (refer to figure 11.6, panel a). This aggregate picture is an uncomfortable average of very different expenditure patterns in countries in North Africa and SSA (refer to figure 11.6, panel b). In North Africa, social protection spending has always been substantially higher and has risen much faster as compared to SSA. Since 1990, social protection spending in SSA has been at most half the level prevailing in the world as a whole. Resource-dependent countries, which include most African countries, spend less on social protection than do non-resource-dependent countries.

Figure 11.6 Social Protection Spending, by Region

a. Regional trends, 1990–2010

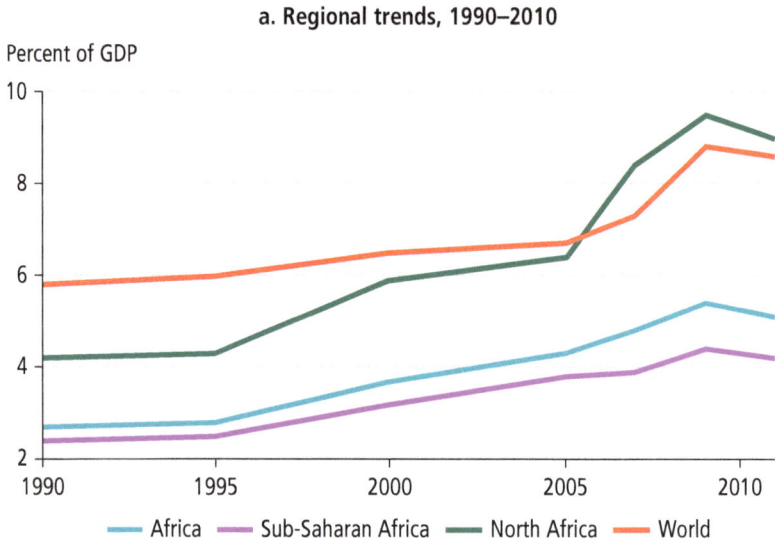

b. Africa, 2010–15 (% of GDP)

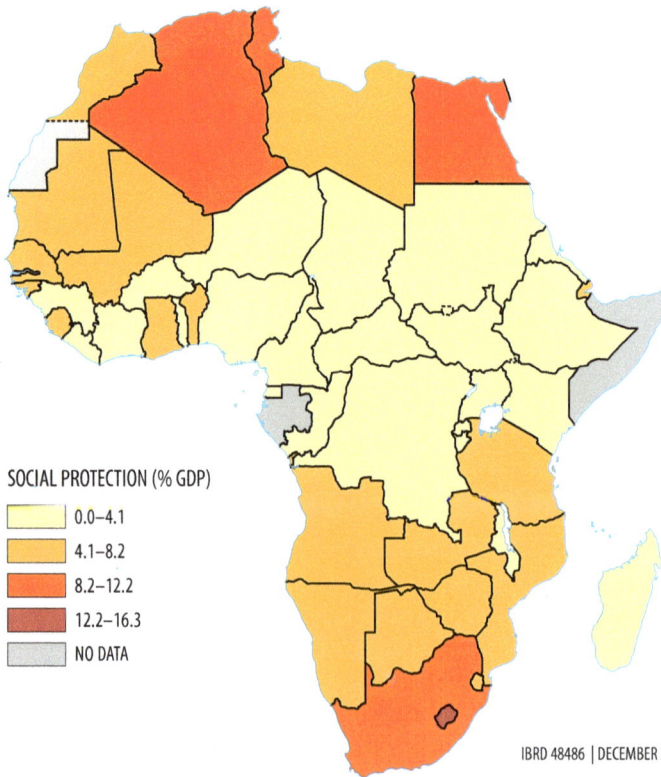

SOCIAL PROTECTION (% GDP)

- 0.0–4.1
- 4.1–8.2
- 8.2–12.2
- 12.2–16.3
- NO DATA

IBRD 48486 | DECEMBER 2024

Source: Based on David, Diallo, and Nilsson 2023.
Note: GDP = gross domestic product.

In addition to increasing the average level of spending, better targeting of social protection to the poorest quintiles would increase the inequality-reducing power of social protection in Africa (Odusola et al. 2017). Targeted social expenditures, such as means-tested cash transfers, are more effective in supporting poor and vulnerable groups and tend to have a larger impact on income growth than subsidies, such as those for energy (World Bank 2022). Chapter 9 details these expenditures.

Progressive taxation potentially can promote inclusive growth by raising revenue from the beneficiaries of noninclusive growth to fund social and labor market policies that will explicitly target the inclusion of those who were previously excluded (Odusola et al. 2019). However, many difficulties associated with raising tax revenue in Africa remain. As explored in more detail in chapter 9, much potential tax revenue is repatriated from African countries, leaving a thin Indigenous personal income tax base. This situation is compounded by personal income tax policies that are mostly indirect and regressive.

In addition, there are concerns about the commitment and capacity of African governments to implement well-targeted employment, skills, and social development policies. Lustig, Jellema, and Martinez Pabon (2023) focused on the need to identify alternative forms of taxation, revenues, and transfer schemes to achieve a more-inclusive growth pattern. Although they highlighted the importance of country-specific measures, they also targeted universal income floors, showing that, in many countries, a universal income floor requires an increase in taxes that is too significant to be fiscally viable. Progressive, targeted transfers seem to be a preferable option, at least for Botswana, Ghana, Namibia, and South Africa. They also yield better results in terms of poverty reduction.

Thinking beyond social policy to social development, the Good Life Project at the University of Leeds shows that Africa has been on an unsustainable pathway and lags in the number of social thresholds it has achieved (refer to map 11.1). Social thresholds include indicators such as life satisfaction, nutrition, sanitation, access to energy, education, social support, equality, and employment. Such indicators can constitute the center of a new approach to development that would move away from growth-centered approaches. It is worrying that few countries in Africa have achieved more than 2 of the 11 thresholds considered to be guarantees of a "good life" (O'Neill et al. 2018).

Environmental and Climate Sustainability

Global patterns of economic growth are unsustainable from an environmental perspective (Chancel et al. 2021; Godin et al. 2022; IPCC 2022; Rockström et al. 2023; Steffen et al. 2015). The Meadows report, "The Limits to Growth," was the first to discuss the limits to economic growth and resource depletion and the need to alter the current model toward a more-sustainable trend (Meadows et al. 1972). Fifty years later, the Intergovernmental Panel on Climate Change (IPCC) still warns about the consequences of the current growth realities (IPCC 2022). Despite rising pledges and targets, global warming of around 2.7 degrees Celsius (°C) above pre-industrial levels is expected by the end of (IPCC) this century, which

Map 11.1 Number of Social Thresholds Achieved

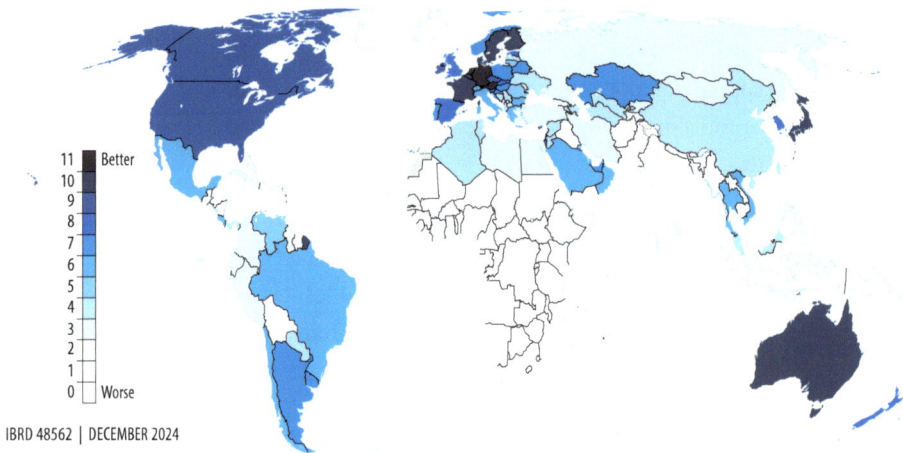

IBRD 48562 | DECEMBER 2024

Source: Based on O'Neill et al. 2018.
Note: Most indicators are for the year 2011.

is far from the aim of 1.5°C in the Paris Agreement (Lenton et al. 2023). At the 2023 United Nations Climate Change Conference in Dubai, United Arab Emirates (November 2023), the parties acknowledged that, although significant collective progress has been made, global emission trajectories are not in line with the Paris Agreement, and the window of correction is closing rapidly (UNFCCC 2023a).

Continuous highly carbon-intensive economic growth has had devastating ecological effects, with current economic activities causing environmental destruction at an unprecedented pace (IPCC 2022). These effects include increased emissions of carbon dioxide and other greenhouse gases; global warming and rising temperatures; and losses and damages due to increasing climate impacts, including loss of biodiversity. Scenarios assessed by the IPCC predict continuing global inequality in 2050, especially in energy, GDP, and emissions (Kanitkar, Mythri, and Jayaraman 2024). These environmental pressures are directly related to income growth, with the richest 10 percent generating almost half of all greenhouse gas emissions. Meanwhile, the bottom 40 percent account for 75 percent of the total income losses due to climate change and only 12 percent of greenhouse gas emissions (Chancel, Bothe, and Voituriez 2023). Chapter 10 details how the inequalities-climate change nexus manifests in different contexts across the continent.

The first limit to economic growth put forward by the literature focused on limited natural resources resulting in food shortages and starvation (Meadows et al. 1972). Later, limits in waste absorption drew attention to the damaging impact of growth in pollution causing irreparable environmental damage. Carbon emissions and global climate change are telling examples causing catastrophic damages. Rising carbon dioxide levels cause warmer temperatures,

Map 11.2 Number of Biophysical Boundaries Transgressed

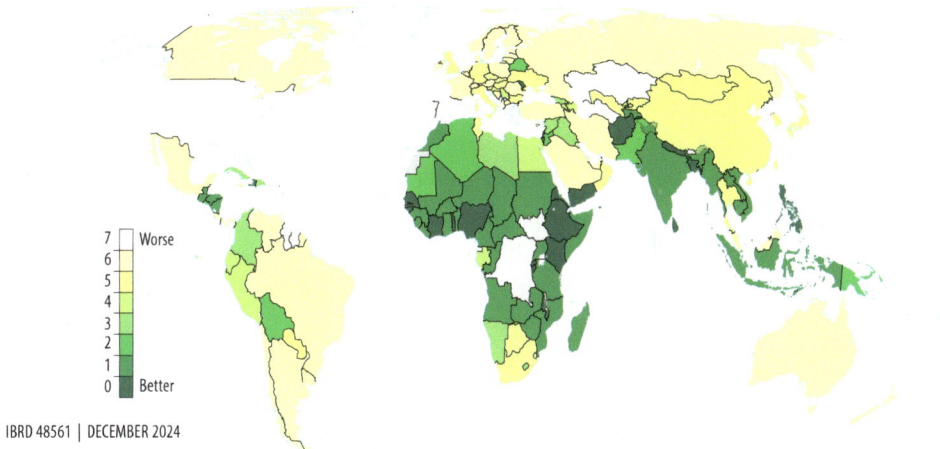

Source: Based on O'Neill et al. 2018.
Note: Most indicators are for the year 2011.

rising sea levels, extreme weather events, and many more environmental disturbances (IPCC 2022). The decline in biodiversity is another loss due to human activities.

Worldwide continued economic growth along the same path will result in continuous environmental degradation (Davidson 2000). Climate change is also a source of shocks and vulnerabilities to Africa's peoples, and adapting to and mitigating the impacts of climate change are crucial to sustainable growth in Africa. For biophysical boundaries, compared to the previous figure of social thresholds, the picture is reversed, with Africa having the highest rates of achievement of biophysical thresholds (refer to map 11.2) (O'Neill et al. 2018).

Africa has contributed the least to the greenhouse gas emissions that brought the world to this critical situation today (Chancel 2022), but the continent is the most vulnerable to its consequences (refer to chapter 10). Therefore, going forward, growth models must not only account for the errors of the past in terms of lack of economic and social inclusivity but also respect environmental boundaries. To achieve the world's poverty and climate objectives, the future and future growth must differ markedly from the past (Wollburg, Hallegatte, and Mahler 2023).

The prospect of negative environmental returns to economic growth as we know it has prompted a proliferation of alternative ways of thinking about moving beyond growth. The first group of ideas suggests adjustments to make growth more sustainable and inclusive through what is defined as *green growth*. Examples of such policies include environmental taxes, decarbonization policies, and changes in the composition of production by shifting to alternative energy supplies and alternative products such as electric vehicles. New social policies are emerging that combine social prosperity and low-carbon emissions that would allow climate change and income inequality to be tackled simultaneously (D'Alessandro et al. 2020). Lower inequality would mean that less growth is needed to eliminate extreme poverty, which, in turn, significantly reduces the emissions and ecological footprint of poverty alleviation.

However, although changes in the energy and carbon intensity of economic growth can contribute to reconciling poverty and environmental goals, in what is considered as *decoupling,* it is not sufficient to prevent global warming (IPCC 2022). Decoupling occurs when the growth rate of an environmental pressure is less than that of its economic driving force, for example, GDP. Developed countries have made efforts to reduce their environmental footprint, but this work is still not enough to be within planetary boundaries (Jensen 2023). The stark inequalities between developed and developing countries in their environmental footprints must be considered when advocating for decoupling efforts.

The second approach draws attention to the existentially threatening texture of growth in developed countries, with supporters of degrowth arguing that such growth is, in itself, a problem (Hickel 2021; Kallis 2011; Rodríguez-Labajos et al. 2019; Schmelzer, Vetter, and Vansintjan 2022). This group defines *degrowth* as a planned reduction of energy and resource use in wealthy economies in a way that frees up energy and materials for low- and middle-income countries, thus improving their well-being and reducing global inequalities (Hickel 2021). A solution to environmental and social limits would be a steady-state or shrinking economy that recognizes the planetary boundaries and seeks a sustainable economic and ecological equilibrium (Daly 1993).

Proponents of degrowth see the economic system itself as based on exploitation and inequalities and question the sustainability of green growth solutions due to the limited regenerative capacities of the ecosystem and the aggregate failure of these piecemeal approaches when benchmarked against planetary boundaries. For example, Winkler et al. (2015) argued that, to change development paths and align with sustainability constraints, redefining the social contracts in all countries is necessary, focusing on less consumption for the rich, redistribution from the rich to the poor, and changed aspirations of the middle classes.

The discourse on environmental justice in the Global South has sharpened questions on the place of the degrowth discourse in developing countries (Hickel 2021, Rodríguez-Labajos et al. 2019; Schmelzer et al. 2022). According to this literature, degrowth starts from the fact that economic growth in developed countries is unsustainable. A reorganization of these societies in a way that reduces their use of energy and resources is required.

The third approach suggests moving away from the focus on growth in what is variously called *post-growth, a-growth* (being indifferent about growth), or *beyond growth* (Jackson 2019; OECD 2020; Van den Bergh 2011). In this approach, degrowth is seen as unrealistic and ineffective for reducing environmental pressure, while green or inclusive growth is seen as acting only ex-post to remedy the problems of economic growth. Growth remains at the heart of what is hindering ecological innovation, increasing financial instability, and reinforcing inequality (Jackson 2019). Supporters call for an ex-ante design of the economy to achieve environmental and social goals through fundamental economic transformation to make employment, social security, and public services less dependent on growth.

This approach indicates a need to shift development pathways. The IPCC's sixth assessment report highlighted climate-resilient development (Working Group II) and the need to shift development pathways to increased sustainability (Working Group III). These findings from the assessment literature inform multilateral climate policy. The aim of the Paris Agreement is to "strengthen the global response to the threat of climate change, in the context of sustainable development and efforts to eradicate poverty," and one long-term goal is to make "finance flows consistent with a pathway toward low greenhouse gas emissions and climate-resilient development" (Article 2.1 c). Scaling up international public climate finance as a key measure to shift broader financial flows is an essential, although not the only, enabler of shifting development pathways.

While these approaches differ in their positions on economic growth, they all insist on rethinking and reshaping growth in line with social and environmental imperatives. However, the approaches differ in their forms of implementation. Green growth and inclusive growth focus on adjusting existing growth structures. Degrowth focuses on suspension of the Global North's growth processes to allow for a sustainable world. This change would open the sustainability space for African growth processes that serve broader African development.

The post-growth school insists that each country starts with a clearly articulated view of the sustainable, developed society it aspires to achieve. A growth and policy matrix can then be defined as a means to this end and not as an end in itself. All the perspectives see it as folly to resume business-as-usual growth processes post-COVID-19 in Africa without explicit consideration of sustainability.

Each approach puts the need for alternative indicators beyond GDP at center stage, to move the focus toward social and environmental goals. Several alternative indicators have been proposed, including the Better Life Index created by the Organisation for Economic Co-operation and Development, the United Nations' Human Development Index, and the Social Progress Index (Jensen 2023). While some of these indicators are being used to design policy strategies, none has yet reached a position comparable to GDP in political and public debates. Issues such as data availability and the lack of consensus on which indicators to use can stall and hinder the use of these indicators. Yet, a failure to benchmark a country's sustainable development goals against a set of progress metrics comes at a very high cost in terms of the policy prioritizations that will be necessary and the assessment of progress.

Conclusion

Most African countries have witnessed economic growth acceleration that began in the 1990s. This chapter has focused on an evidence-based track record of this economic growth. The evidence presented shows how economic growth in Africa has been neither sufficiently inclusive nor sustainable. Economic growth has not translated into substantial poverty reduction, evidenced by the low GEP in many African countries. Growth was largely driven by informal services and formal extractive industries, which held weak benefits for the poor population and left many marginalized from their evolving economies.

The chapter examined the poverty-growth-inequality nexus to understand both the failures of growth and the central role of inequality in impeding more-sustainable and -inclusive development. The first steps toward providing platforms for inclusion for those currently excluded from growth processes lie in well-targeted tax and revenue generation policies that fund equally well-targeted and coordinated social protection and labor market policies. Such policies are complementary to and part of the policy matrix emerging from the literature rethinking current models of economic growth to account for planetary limits. These sustainability issues require explicit attention to forge growth processes that provide an enabling environment for the whole population.

Although plenty of detailed work remains to be done on the balanced integration of these two sets of policies—tax and revenue policies and social protection and labor market policies— broader debates on growth provide an opportunity to discuss what kind of paradigm should be created to confront these multiple challenges head on. This chapter has illuminated the place of these alternative paradigms of growth in the fight against poverty and inequality in the Global South. There are pathways forward that ensure that a transition to inclusive and sustainable growth in developed countries will not hamper development in low-income countries. Sustainability will require innovation, which is costly and indicates the need for solidarity and mobilization from the richest countries to support the Global South in engaging in a sustainable development pathway. Furthermore, ending poverty and inequality within planetary boundaries will require the Global North to move away from its focus on growth as its policy objective and for the Global South, which still needs economic growth, to account for its inequalities and their reduction in policy formulation.

Annex 11A Initial Inequality, Poverty, and Growth in Income in Africa

Figure 11A.1 Change in African Poverty Levels, by Levels of Initial Inequality

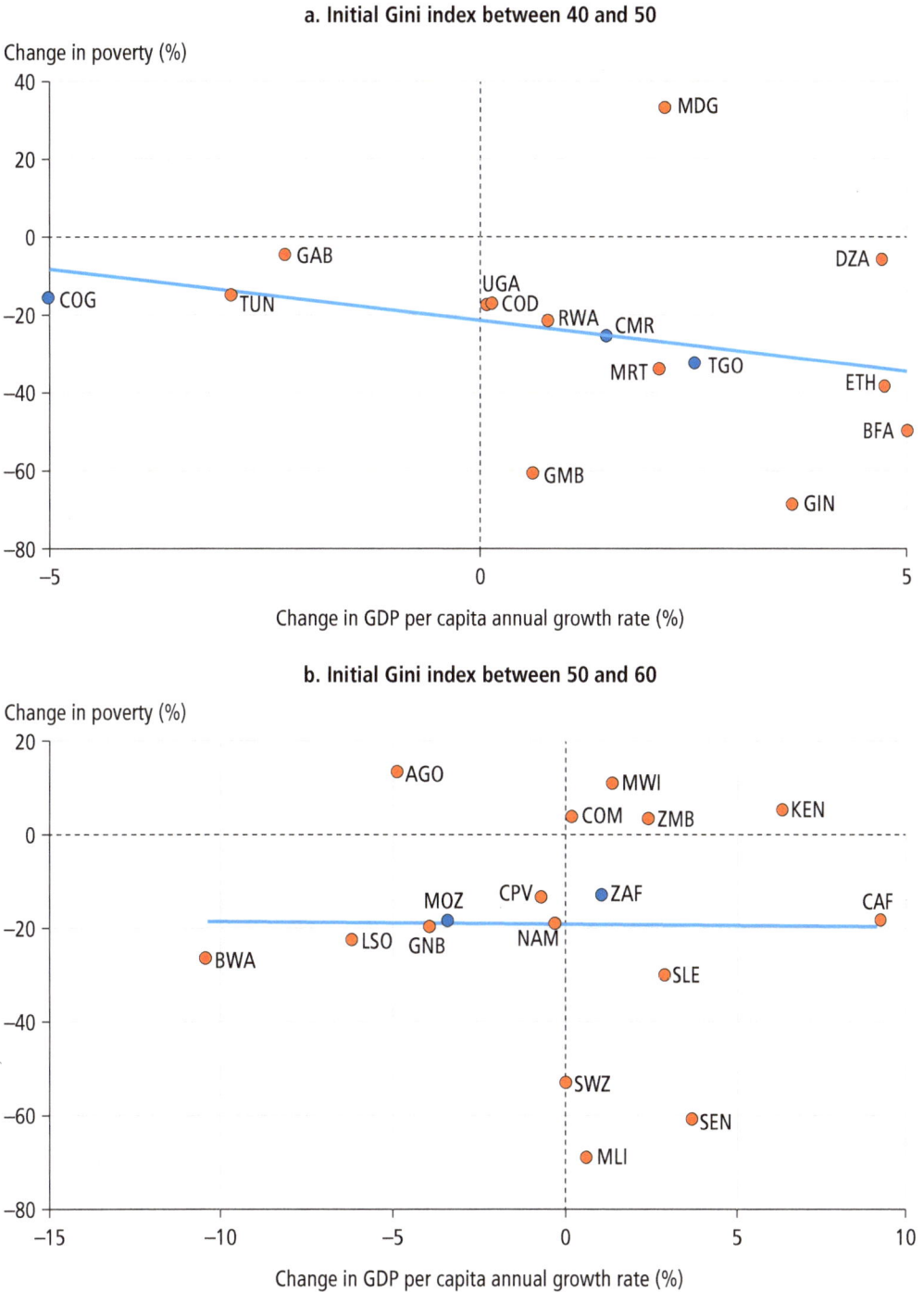

a. Initial Gini index between 40 and 50

b. Initial Gini index between 50 and 60

Source: Authors' calculations based on data from the World Inequality Database.
Note: For a list of country codes, refer to https://www.iso.org/obp/ui/#search. GDP = gross domestic product.

Notes

1. This is target 1.2 of the Sustainable Development Goal of reducing poverty by at least half in all its dimensions.
2. *Polarization* is a measure of inequality that examines the divergence of lower quintiles away from the global mean and toward a convergence at their local mean.
3. The first category includes countries with a Gini index lower than 40, the second category includes countries with a Gini index ranging from 40 to 50, and the third category includes countries with a Gini index higher than 50.

References

Acemoglu, Daron, and James Robinson. 2010. "The Role of Institutions in Growth and Development." *Review of Economics and Institutions* 1 (2). https://doi.org/10.5202/rei.v1i2.14.

African Development Bank. 2012. *Inclusive Growth Agenda*. Abidjan, Côte d'Ivoire: African Development Bank. https://www.afdb.org/fileadmin/uploads/afdb/Documents/Generic-Documents/Revised-%20 BRIEF%20-IG%20AGENDA%20-%20LTS%20FINAL%20DRAFT%20FEB20-2012%20REVISED.pdf.

African Development Bank. 2018. *African Economic Outlook 2018*. Abidjan, Côte d'Ivoire: African Development Bank. https://www.afdb.org/fileadmin/uploads/afdb/Documents/Publications /African_Economic_Outlook_2018_-_EN.pdf.

Arndt, Channing, Andy McKay, and Finn Tarp, eds. 2016. *Growth and Poverty in Sub-Saharan Africa*. Oxford, United Kingdom: Oxford University Press. https://EconPapers.repec.org/RePEc:oxp :obooks:9780198744795.

Auty, Richard M. 1997. "Natural Resource Endowment, the State and Development Strategy." *Journal of International Development* 9 (4): 651–63. https://doi.org/10.1002/(SICI)1099-1328(199706)9:4<651::AID -JID474>3.0.CO;2-4.

Balasubramanian, Pooja, Francesco Burchi, and Daniele Malerba. 2023. "Does Economic Growth Reduce Multidimensional Poverty? Evidence from Low- and Middle-Income Countries." *World Development* 161: 106119. https://doi.org/10.1016/j.worlddev.2022.106119.

Batuo, Michael E., George Kararach, and Issam Malki. 2022. "The Dynamics of Income Inequality in Africa: An Empirical Investigation on the Role of Macroeconomic and Institutional Forces." *World Development* 157: 105939. https://doi.org/10.1016/j.worlddev.2022.105939.

Bergstrom, Katy. 2022. "The Role of Income Inequality for Poverty Reduction." *World Bank Economic Review* 36 (3): 583–604. https://doi.org/10.1093/wber/lhab026.

Bhorat, Haroon, and Morné Oosthuizen. 2020. "Jobs, Economic Growth, and Capacity Development for Youth in Africa." Working Paper Series 336, African Development Bank, Abidjan, Côte d'Ivoire. https:// www.afdb.org/sites/default/files/documents/publications/wps_no_336_jobs_economic_growth_and _capacity_development_for_youth_in_africa.pdf.

Bhorat, Haroon, David Tseng, and Benjamin Stanwix. 2014. "Pro-Poor Growth and Social Protection in South Africa: Exploring the Interactions." *Development Southern Africa* 31 (2): 219–40. https://doi.org /10.1080/0376835X.2013.878242.

Bourguignon, François. 2004. "The Poverty-Growth-Inequality Triangle." Working Paper 125, Indian Council for Research on International Economic Relations, New Delhi, India.

Chancel, Lucas. 2020. *Unsustainable Inequalities*. Cambridge, MA: Harvard University Press.

Chancel, Lucas. 2022. "Global Carbon Inequality over 1990–2019." *Nature Sustainability* 5 (11): 931–38. https://doi.org/10.1038/s41893-022-00955-z.

Chancel, Lucas, Philippe Bothe, and Tancrède Voituriez. 2023. "Climate Inequality Report 2023." World Inequality Lab, Paris.

Chancel, Lucas, Thomas Piketty, Emmanuel Saez, and Gabriel Zucman. 2021. *World Inequality Report 2022*. Paris: World Inequality Lab. https://ideas.repec.org/p/hal/pseptp/halshs-03693233.html.

Christiaensen, Luc, Punam Chuhan-Pole, and Aly Sanoh. 2013. "Africa's Growth, Poverty and Inequality Nexus—Fostering Shared Prosperity." World Bank, Washington, DC.

Chuhan-Pole, Punam, and Francisco H. G. Ferreira. 2014. *Africa's Pulse*. Washington, DC: World Bank. https://documents1.worldbank.org/curated/en/179091468009576085/pdf/912070REVISED00ct20140vol100v120web.pdf.

Clementi, Fabio, Michele Fabiani, and Vasco Molini. 2019. "The Devil Is in the Detail: Growth, Inequality and Poverty Reduction in Africa in the Last Two Decades." *Journal of African Economies* 28 (4): 408–34. https://doi.org/10.1093/jae/ejz003.

Clementi, Fabio, Michele Fabiani, Vasco Molini, and Rocco Zizzamia. 2019. "Worlds Apart: What Polarisation Measures Reveal about Sub-Saharan Africa's Growth and Welfare Distribution in the Last Two Decades." ACEIR Working Paper Number 1, African Center of Excellence for Inequalities Research, University of Cape Town, South Africa.

Clementi, Fabio, Michele Fabiani, Vasco Molini, and Rocco Zizzamia. 2022. "Are We Really Painting the Devil on the Walls? Polarization and Its Drivers in Sub-Saharan Africa in the Past Two Decades." *Journal of African Economies* 31 (2): 124–46. https://doi.org/10.1093/jae/ejab006.

Cornia, Giovanni. 2017. "Inequality Levels, Trends and Determinants in Sub-Saharan Africa: An Overview of Main Changes since the Early 1990s." In *Income Inequality Trends in Sub-Saharan Africa: Divergence, Determinants and Consequences*, edited by Ayodele F. Odusola, Giovanni Cornia, Haroon Bhorat, and Pedro Conceição, 23–51. New York: Regional Bureau for Africa, United Nations Development Programme.

D'Alessandro, Simone, André Cieplinski, Tiziano Distefano, and Kristofer Dittmer. 2020. "Feasible Alternatives to Green Growth." *Nature Sustainability* 3 (4): 329–35. https://doi.org/10.1038/s41893-020-0484-y.

Daly, Herman E. 1993. "Steady-State Economics: A New Paradigm." *New Literary History* 24 (4): 811. https://doi.org/10.2307/469394.

David, Anda, Yoro Diallo, and Bjorn Nilsson. 2023. "Informality and Inequality: The African Case." *Journal of African Economies* 32 (Suppl. 2): ii273–ii295.

Davidson, Carlos. 2000. "Economic Growth and the Environment: Alternatives to the Limits Paradigm." *BioScience* 50 (5): 433–40. https://doi.org/10.1641/0006-3568(2000)050[0433:EGATEA]2.0.CO;2.

Djoufelkit, Hélène. 2008a. "L'industrie Égyptienne Depuis Le Début Des Années 1970: Histoire d'un Développement Contrarié." Document de Travail 61, Agence Française de Développement, Paris.

Djoufelkit, Hélène. 2008b. "Rente, Développement Du Secteur Productif et Croissance En Algérie." Document de Travail 64, Agence Française de Développement, Paris.

Ebeke, Christian H. 2023. "Intergenerational Mobility and the Growth–Inequality–Poverty Nexus in Africa." *Journal of African Economies* 32 (Suppl. 2): ii99–ii112. https://doi.org/10.1093/jae/ejac044.

Fields, Gary S. 2023. "The Growth–Employment–Poverty Nexus in Africa." *Journal of African Economies* 32 (Suppl._2): ii147–ii163. https://doi.org/10.1093/jae/ejac046.

Fields, Gary S., T. H. Gindling, Kunal Sen, Michael Danquah, and Simone Schotte, eds. 2023. *The Job Ladder: Transforming Informal Work and Livelihoods in Developing Countries.* Oxford, UK: Oxford University Press. https://doi.org/10.1093/oso/9780192867339.001.0001.

Fofana, Ismael, Margaret Chitiga-Mabugu, and Ramos Emmanuel Mabugu. 2023. "Is Africa on Track to Ending Poverty by 2030?" *Journal of African Economies* 32 (Suppl. 2): ii87–ii98. https://doi.org/10.1093/jae/ejac043.

Fosu, Augustin Kwasi. 2018. "Economic Structure, Growth, and Evolution of Inequality and Poverty in Africa: An Overview." *Journal of African Economies* 27: 1–9. https://doi.org/10.1093/jae/ejx036.

Fosu, Augustin Kwasi. 2023. "Progress on Poverty in Africa: The Importance of Growth and Inequality." *Journal of African Economies* 32 (Suppl._2): ii164–ii182. https://doi.org/10.1093/jae/ejac047.

Global Footprint Network. 2023. "Measure What You Treasure." https://www.footprintnetwork.org/.

Godin, Antoine, Anda David, Oskar Lecuyer, and Stéphanie Leyronas. 2022. "A Strong Sustainability Approach to Development Trajectories." *European Journal of Economics and Economic Policies* 19 (3): 381–96. https://doi.org/10.4337/ejeep.2022.0094.

Hickel, Jason. 2021. "What Does Degrowth Mean? A Few Points of Clarification." *Globalizations* 18 (7): 1105–11. https://doi.org/10.1080/14747731.2020.1812222.

Houngbedji, Kenneth, and Claire Zanuso. 2021. "Les jeunes et les enjeux du marché du travail en Afrique." In *Agence Française de Développement, L'économie africaine 2021*, 75–93. Paris: La Découverte.

IPCC (Intergovernmental Panel on Climate Change). 2022. "Climate Change 2022: Impacts, Adaptation and Vulnerability." In *Summary for Policymakers.* Cambridge, United Kingdom: Cambridge University Press.

Jackson, Tim. 2019. "The Post-Growth Challenge: Secular Stagnation, Inequality and the Limits to Growth." *Ecological Economics* 156: 236–46. https://doi.org/10.1016/j.ecolecon.2018.10.010.

Jensen, Liselotte. 2023. *Beyond Growth: Pathways towards Sustainable Prosperity in the EU.* Strasbourg, France: Directorate General for Parliamentary Research Services, European Parliament. https://doi.org/10.2861/602232.

Kallis, Giorgos. 2011. "In Defence of Degrowth." *Ecological Economics* 70 (5): 873–80. https://doi.org/10.1016/j.ecolecon.2010.12.007.

Kanitkar, Tejal, Akhil Mythri, and T. Jayaraman. 2024. "Equity Assessment of Global Mitigation Pathways in the IPCC Sixth Assessment Report." *Climate Policy* 24 (8): 1129–48. https://doi.org/10.1080/14693062.2024.2319029.

Kuznets, Simon. 1955. "Economic Growth and Income Inequality." *American Economic Review* 45 (1): 1–28.

Lakner, Christoph, Daniel Gerszon Mahler, Mario Negre, and Espen Beer Prydz. 2022. "How Much Does Reducing Inequality Matter for Global Poverty?" *Journal of Economic Inequality* 20 (3): 559–85. https://doi.org/10.1007/s10888-021-09510-w.

Lam, David, and Murray Leibbrandt. 2023. "Demographic Challenges for Global Labour Markets in the 21st Century, Africa in a Changing World." SALDRU Working Paper 303. Southern Africa Labour and Development Research Unit, University of Cape Town.

Lenton, Timothy M., Chi Xu, Jesse F. Abrams, Ashish Ghadiali, Sina Loriani, Boris Sakschewski, Caroline Zimm, et al. 2023. "Quantifying the Human Cost of Global Warming." *Nature Sustainability*. 6: 1237–47. https://doi.org/10.1038/s41893-023-01132-6.

Lustig, Nora, Jon Jellema, and Valentina Martinez Pabon. 2023. "Are Budget Neutral Income Floors Fiscally Viable in Sub-Saharan Africa?" *Journal of African Economies* 32 (Suppl. 2): ii202–ii227. https://doi.org/10.1093/jae/ejac049.

Meadows, Donella H., Dennis Meadows, Jorgen Randers, and William W. Behrens, III. 1972. *The Limits to Growth: A Report for the Club of Rome's Project on the Predicament of Mankind*. New York: Universe Books.

Milanovic, Branko. 2016. *Global Inequality: A New Approach for the Age of Globalization*. Cambridge, MA: Harvard University Press. https://doi.org/10.2307/j.ctvjghwk4.

Morsy, Hanan, Abebe Shimeles, and Tiguene Nabassaga. 2023. "Structural Change and Inequality in Africa." *Journal of African Economies* 32 (Suppl. 2): ii228–ii245. https://doi.org/10.1093/jae/ejac050.

Niño-Zarazúa, Miguel, Francesca Scaturro, Vanesa Jordá, and Finn Tarp. 2023. "Income Inequality and Redistribution in Sub-Saharan Africa." *Journal of African Economies* 32 (Suppl. 2): ii296–ii319. https://doi.org/10.1093/jae/ejac053.

Odusola, Ayodele F. 2019. "Growth-Poverty-Inequality Nexus: Toward a Mutually Inclusive Relationship in Africa." In *African Economic Development*, edited by Emmanuel Nnadozie and Afeikhena Jerome, 157–82. Bingley, UK: Emerald Publishing. https://doi.org/10.1108/978-1-78743-783-820192010.

Odusola, Ayodele F., Giovanni Andrea Cornia, Haroon Bhorat, and Pedro Conceição, eds. 2019. "Drivers of Inequality in the Context of the Growth-Poverty-Inequality Nexus in Africa: An Overview of Key Issues." In *Income Inequality Trends in Sub-Saharan Africa*, 52–73. New York: United Nations Development Programme. https://doi.org/10.18356/7b9d64b1-en.

Odusola, Ayodele F., Giovanni Andrea Cornia, Haroon Bhorat, Pedro Conceição, and United Nations Development Programme. 2017. *Income Inequality Trends in Sub-Saharan Africa: Divergence, Determinants and Consequences: Overview*. New York: Regional Bureau for Africa, United Nations Development Programme.

OECD (Organisation for Economic Co-operation and Development). 2020. *Beyond Growth*. Paris: OECD. https://doi.org/10.1787/33a25ba3-en.

O'Neill, Daniel W., Andrew L. Fanning, William F. Lamb, and Julia K. Steinberger. 2018. "A Good Life for All within Planetary Boundaries." *Nature Sustainability* 1 (2): 88–95. https://doi.org/10.1038/s41893-018-0021-4.

Parrique, Timothée. 2021. "From Green Growth to Degrowth." *Global Policy*, April 21.

Ravallion, Martin. 2005. "Inequality Is Bad for the Poor." Policy Research Working Paper 3677, World Bank, Washington, DC. https://documents1.worldbank.org/curated/ru/456501468330044447/pdf/wps3677.pdf.

Ravallion, Martin. 2022. "Growth Elasticities of Poverty Reduction." NBER Working Paper 30401, National Bureau of Economic Research, Cambridge, MA. https://ideas.repec.org/p/nbr/nberwo/30401.html.

Raworth, Kate. 2022. *Doughnut Economics: Seven Ways to Think Like a 21st-Century Economist*. London: Penguin Books.

Rockström, Johan, Joyeeta Gupta, Dahe Qin, Steven J. Lade, Jesse F. Abrams, Lauren S. Andersen, David I. Armstrong McKay, et al. 2023. "Safe and Just Earth System Boundaries." *Nature* 619 (7968): 102–11. https://doi.org/10.1038/s41586-023-06083-8.

Rodríguez-Labajos, Beatriz, Ivonne Yánez, Patrick Bond, Lucie Greyl, Serah Munguti, Godwin Uyi Ojo, and Winfridus Overbeek. 2019. "Not So Natural an Alliance? Degrowth and Environmental Justice Movements in the Global South." *Ecological Economics* 157: 175–84. https://doi.org/10.1016/j.ecolecon.2018.11.007.

Rodrik, Dani. 2023. *Better Jobs Mean Better Development*. New York: Project Syndicate.

Roudier, Philipe, and Djiby Dia. 2021. "Une Troisième Voie Pour l'agriculture Ouest-Africaine? Le Cas de l'agroécologie Au Sénégal." In *L'économie Africaine 2021*. Repères Economie. Paris: La Découverte.

Schmelzer, Matthias, Andrea Vetter, and Aaron Vansintjan. 2022. *The Future Is Degrowth: A Guide to a World beyond Capitalism*. London: Verso.

Steffen, Will, Katherine Richardson, Johan Rockström, Sarah E. Cornell, Ingo Fetzer, Elena M. Bennett, Reinette Biggs, et al. 2015. "Planetary Boundaries: Guiding Human Development on a Changing Planet." *Science* 347 (6223): 1259855. https://doi.org/10.1126/science.1259855.

Thorbecke, Erik. 2013. "The Interrelationship Linking Growth, Inequality and Poverty in Sub-Saharan Africa." *Journal of African Economies* 22: i15–i48. https://doi.org/10.1093/jae/ejs028.

Thorbecke, Erik. 2023. "The Interrelationships among Growth, Inequality and Poverty in Africa." *Journal of African Economies* 32 (Suppl. 2): ii81–ii86. https://doi.org/10.1093/jae/ejac055.

Thorbecke, Erik, and Yusi Ouyang. 2018. "Is the Structure of Growth Different in Sub-Saharan Africa?" *Journal of African Economies* 27 (1): 66–91. https://doi.org/10.1093/jae/ejw032.

Thorbecke, Erik, and Yusi Ouyang. 2022. "Towards a Virtuous Spiral between Poverty Reduction and Growth: Comparing Sub-Saharan Africa with the Developing World." *World Development* 152: 105776. https://doi.org/10.1016/j.worlddev.2021.105776.

UNFCCC (United Nations Framework Convention on Climate Change). 2023a. *Outcome of the First Global Stocktake. Decision-/CMA.5, Advance Unedited Version*. Dubai: UNFCCC.

UNFCCC (United Nations Framework Convention on Climate Change). 2023b. *Technical Dialogue of the First Global Stocktake. Synthesis Report by the Co-Facilitators on the Technical Dialogue*. FCCC/SB/2023/9. Bonn: UNFCCC. https://unfccc.int/documents/631600.

UNU-WIDER (United Nations University, World Institute for Development Economics Research). 2022. *World Income Inequality Database (WIID)—Version 30 June 2022*. Helsinki, Finland: UNU-WIDER. https://doi.org/10.35188/UNU-WIDER/WIID-300622.

Van den Bergh, Jeroen C. J. M. 2011. "Environment versus Growth—A Criticism of 'Degrowth' and a Plea for 'a-Growth.'" *Ecological Economics* 70 (5): 881–90. https://doi.org/10.1016/j.ecolecon.2010.09.035.

Winkler, Harald, and Anthony Black. 2021. "Creating Employment and Reducing Emissions: Options for South Africa." SARChI Industrial Development Working Paper Series WP 2021-06, SARChI Industrial Development, University of Johannesburg, South Africa.

Winkler, Harald, Anya Boyd, Marta Torres Gunfaus, and Stefan Raubenheimer. 2015. "Reconsidering Development by Reflecting on Climate Change." *International Environmental Agreements: Politics, Law and Economics* 15 (4): 369–85. https://doi.org/10.1007/s10784-015-9304-7.

Wollburg, Philip, Stephane Hallegatte, and Daniel Gerszon Mahler. 2023. "The Climate Implications of Ending Global Poverty." Policy Research Working Paper 10318, World Bank, Washington, DC. https://documents1.worldbank.org/curated/en/099557002242323911/pdf/IDU1bbf17510161a9145531b57a1ccaba7a1dc79.pdf?_gl=1*m6c834*_gcl_au*ODcxNDEyNjc4LjE3MTk1MDY3ODI.

World Bank. 2019. *Structural Transformation in Sub-Saharan Africa*. Washington, DC: World Bank. https://documents1.worldbank.org/curated/ar/653121569909327847/pdf/Structural-Transformation-in-Sub-Saharan-Africa.pdf.

World Bank. 2022. *Poverty and Shared Prosperity 2022: Correcting Course*. Washington, DC: World Bank. https://www.worldbank.org/en/publication/poverty-and-shared-prosperity.

Zizzamia, Rocco, Simone Schotte, and Vimal Ranchhod. 2016. "Vulnerability and the Middle Class in South Africa." SALDRU Working Paper No. 188, Southern Africa Labour and Development Research Unit, University of Cape Town, South Africa.

www.ingramcontent.com/pod-product-compliance
Lightning Source LLC
Chambersburg PA
CBHW050900210326
41597CB00002B/33